COMMUNICATION SCIENCE THEORY AND RESEARCH

This volume provides a graduate-level introduction to communication science, including theory and scholarship for master's and Ph.D. students as well as practicing scholars. The work defines communication, reviews its history, and provides a broad look at how communication research is conducted. It also includes chapters reviewing the most frequently addressed topics in communication science.

This book presents an overview of theory in general and of communication theory in particular, while offering a broad look at topics in communication that promote understanding of the key issues in communication science for students and scholars new to communication research. The book takes a predominantly "communication science" approach but also situates this approach in the broader field of communication, and addresses how communication science is related to and different from such approaches as critical and cultural studies and rhetoric.

As an overview of communication science that will serve as a reference work for scholars as well as a text for the introduction to communication graduate studies course, this volume is an essential resource for understanding and conducting scholarship in the communication discipline.

Marina Krcmar is Professor of Communication at Wake Forest University.

David R. Ewoldsen is Professor of Communication at Michigan State University.

Ascan Koerner is Associate Professor of Communication at the University of Minnesota.

COMMUNICATION SCIENCE THEORY AND RESEARCH

An Advanced Introduction

Marina Krcmar
David R. Ewoldsen
Ascan Koerner

Routledge
Taylor & Francis Group

NEW YORK AND LONDON

First published 2016
by Routledge
711 Third Avenue, New York, NY 10017

and by Routledge
2 Park Square, Milton Park, Abingdon, Oxon, OX14 4RN

Routledge is an imprint of the Taylor & Francis Group, an informa business

Library of Congress Cataloging in Publication Data
Names: Krcmar, Marina, author. | Roskos-Ewoldsen, David R., author. |
Koerner, Ascan, author.
Title: Communication science theory and research: an advanced introduction/
Marina Krcmar, David R. Ewoldsen, Ascan Koerner.
Description: New York, NY: Milton Park, Abingdon, Oxon: Routledge,
2016. |
Includes bibliographical references and index.
Identifiers: LCCN 2015040868 | ISBN 9780415533836 (hardback: alk. paper) |
ISBN 9780415533843 (pbk.: alk. paper) | ISBN 9780203113943 (ebook)
Subjects: LCSH: Communication. | Communication—Research.
Classification: LCC P90 .K675 2016 | DDC 302.2—dc23
LC record available at http://lccn.loc.gov/2015040868

ISBN: 978-0-415-53383-6 (hbk)
ISBN: 978-0-415-53384-3 (pbk)
ISBN: 978-0-203-11394-3 (ebk)

Typeset in Bembo and Stone Sans
by Florence Production Ltd, Stoodleigh, Devon, UK

Printed and bound in the United States of America by Publishers Graphics,
LLC on sustainably sourced paper.

To Mark, Maya, and Georgia for being there all along, and to Eve and Henry, because you did not arrive in time to get mentioned last time—MK

To Nancy, for all of your support—DRE

To those who matter most: Reka, Sophie, and Kira—AK

CONTENTS

Author Biographies   *ix*
Preface   *xi*
Acknowledgments   *xiii*
Introduction   *xv*

PART I
Communication Theory   1

1 An Introduction to Theory   3

2 What Is Communication?   18

3 History of Communication   37

4 Philosophical Underpinnings of the Communication
   Science Approach   58

5 Positivism/Causality/Explanation   72

6 Conducting Research in Communication Science   89

PART II
Communication Research   111

7 Mass Media Effects Models   113

8   Media Use Models   138

9   Message Processing   154

10 Interpersonal Communication   177

11 Small Group and Organizational Communication   194

12 Persuasion   212

13 Political Communication   244

14 Social Media   268

15 Health Communication   286

16 Relationships, Marriage, and Family Communication   317

17 The Future of Communication   336

Author Index   *348*
Subject Index   *352*

AUTHOR BIOGRAPHIES

Marina Krcmar (Ph.D., University of Wisconsin, Madison) is a professor in the Department of Communication at Wake Forest University. Her research focuses on the uses and effects of media, especially for adolescents and young children. Her work has appeared in numerous journals and book chapters. Her recent book, *Living Without the Screen*, was published by Routledge. She sits on the editorial boards of *Journal of Communication*, *Media Psychology*, *Journal of Children and Media*, and *Mass Communication and Society*.

David R. Ewoldsen (Ph.D., Indiana University) is a professor in the College of Communication at Michigan State University. His research focuses broadly on media psychology. Dr. Ewoldsen is founding co-editor of the journal *Media Psychology* (1998 to 2007) and he was the founding editor of the journal *Communication Methods and Measures* (2007 to 2010). He has also edited three books: *Communication and Emotion* (with Jennings Bryant and Joanne Cantor), *Communication and Social Cognition: Theories and Methods* (with Jennifer Monahan), and *The Handbook of Communication Science* (with Chuck Berger and Michael Roloff).

Ascan Koerner (Ph.D., University of Wisconsin, Madison) is an associate professor at the University of Minnesota. He studies personal relationships, especially marriage and the family.

PREFACE

The idea for this book arose in a way that is probably not at all unlike the birth of other books. One of the authors of this book was tasked with teaching a graduate-level introductory class at the University of Connecticut a dozen years ago. The class had two main goals: first, students were to develop a full research proposal, and second, they were to come away from the class with a solid understanding of communication theory. This goal is probably one shared by other graduate programs and indeed undergraduate programs that offer a more advanced introduction to communication theory courses.

That first graduate seminar was made up of a conference table full of first-year graduate students, some of whom came from communication departments, but others from English, philosophy, history, and even a mathematics department. And even among those with degrees in communication, there were students whose degrees emphasized theory and those who came from programs that taught solely marketing or PR or journalism skills. All of them needed to develop a basic understanding of the philosophy of social science, of theory construction in communication, and needed to be immersed in the field of communication. And they needed enough information about research design in order to be able to develop an overall research question, hypotheses, and a study to test them. In 15 weeks.

As many of us do when initially designing a course, the search for the perfect book began. Instead, many wonderful books were found, but all of them did only a portion of what was needed, or focused on topical issues too much or, in some cases, covered too much. So that first class, and many since then, was taught with an extensive list of chapters and articles and portions of books. When the perfect chapter or article was not available, the first author of this book developed lectures based on a fabulous class, Theory Construction, taken as a graduate student with Joe Capella at the University of Pennsylvania. However, teaching the class also pointed out a need, a gap in the literature, for an advanced introduction to communication theory and research. The idea for the book was born. Many of the chapters were crafted based on lectures from those early classes. The class was designed to introduce the philosophy of social science, issues in theory construction, seminal theories in various areas of communication, discussion of the discipline, and a solid, if brief, introduction to research design.

The book is intended to address a problem, or as many point out, one of the benefits of communication as a field: we are multidisciplinary. This multidisciplinarity allows for varied research, application of theoretical approaches that come from outside the discipline but ultimately offer an appropriate framework for the topic at hand. But this multidisciplinarity often leaves us without a common set of ideas—if not necessarily to agree on then at least to discuss. Although this book does not seek to address history and theory and findings from across the many areas of communication, including communication science, rhetoric, and critical/cultural approaches, the book does seek to recognize them. By including mention of these areas, we situate communication science in the broader field, and indeed attempt to describe the field historically in order to aid in the process. We hope to have readers walk away from the book with an understanding of the broad context of social science, the situation of the discipline of communication therein, and the context of communication science within the field. We offer an overview of current and relevant theories and research in various areas and present the basics of research design to allow students a way of thinking about exploring new research questions.

Another way of thinking about this book is that it offers a starting place for a discussion in the field of core concepts and ideas. It allows the field and the readers a way of beginning to answer the question: What is communication? Indeed, this discussion itself is a crucial one for all of us to have. This book is intended for graduate students and advanced undergraduates, but it can also be seen as a contribution to the discussion of what it is that all of us as scholars are and do. Even as this preface is written, we imagine discussions with colleagues who hopefully take a vested interest in influencing the content of subsequent editions. We hope this book fosters discussions within the field and especially in the advanced classroom where future communication scholars start their journey.

ACKNOWLEDGMENTS

Writing a book is a long process and one that is impossible to accomplish without help, both the direct kind from editors and helpful colleagues, and the indirect kind that arises from being surrounded by smart, insightful people who offer thoughtful comments even when they do not know they are doing so. We would like to thank all of them. We'd like to start by thanking Linda Bathgate, editor extraordinaire. Over the years Linda has been the ideal editor, guiding and answering questions and organizing and cheering us on, and, when necessary, applying the pressure it takes to get the work done. She has also been a great friend, meeting over meals and emails and phone conversations in a way that shows her dedication to her work, to the process, and ultimately to the project itself.

Thanks are also due to each of our universities and the colleagues who share the halls: Wake Forest University, the Ohio State University, and the University of Minnesota. Special thanks to Michael Hyde, Steve Giles, Jenn Priem, Mary Dalton, Allan Louden, Emily Moyer-Guse, Nancy Rhodes, Brandon van der Heide, Brad Bushman, Mike Slater, and Kelly Garrett for providing thoughtful conversations about communication as a discipline and what it means, or does not mean. These conversations happen in the halls, in the faculty meetings, at the end-of-year picnic, during the search committee meetings. And although the conversations were never about this book, they became about this book and the book benefitted from the insights.

With great sincerity, we would also like to thank our many graduate students over the years. You have offered us the opportunity and asked the questions that ultimately became the book. Although they are too many to mention, a few deserve special mention by name: Rory McGloin, John Velez, Morgan Ellithorpe, Courtney Anderegg, Jennifer Moreland, Ted Dickenson, Drew Cingel, Yuliya

Strizhakova, Hannah Moody, Rachel Clapp, Jordan Foley, and Theo Yakah. And finally, to Nathan Bedsole, former graduate student at Wake Forest University, who, after finishing the course, commented that the process of theory construction and the research methods it spawned was "really quite elegant." It was a wonderful assessment of the process and you deserve acknowledgment for making it.

Thanks also go out to our administrative assistants who, as we all know so well, really run the departments. To Patty Lanier, who does it all with grace, and to Gini Lentz, a wonderful administrative assistant.

Lastly, our families must be mentioned, because where would we be without them? Thank you to my children, Maya, Georgia, Eve, and Henry, for the joy and (hopefully) wisdom you have brought, to Mark Cooke for soldiering through this zoo with me and also to Nancy and Jonathan.

INTRODUCTION

The study of communication is fascinating for a number of reasons. Communication is at the core of what it means to be human. Think about those times when you are engaged in any form of communication versus those times when you are not communicating. Do you spend a larger portion of your day communicating or not communicating? Is your life more interesting when you are communicating or not communicating? Are you more likely to develop relationships by communicating or not communicating? We could go on and on, but the point is straightforward—communication is a central part of our lives. Given the centrality of communication to human existence, scholars have speculated about and studied communication since antiquity. However, the social scientific study of communication—broadly construed—began in earnest during the past century. In this book, we will cover the major theories that have emerged across the areas of study that are found within this discipline.

Communication theory is important because it hopefully allows us to understand how communication functions in our day-to-day lives as well as within the larger culture. What makes a successful campaign to get people to change their unhealthy behaviors? How does information about the newest communication technology spread through our culture? What role does disclosing something to another person play in developing a lasting relationship with her? Does watching TV change how we understand our world? These are all questions that will be addressed in this volume. But hopefully, the research that has been done to answer these questions involves more than simply saying "yes, watching a lot of television does influence how we understand our world." Instead, we want to understand *how* heavy viewing of TV influences our understanding. We want to understand what the mechanisms are by which any such influence operates. In other words, a major goal of the theories that are presented within this volume is to aid people's understanding of the various facets of what it means to communicate and what are the antecedents and consequences of communication.

Goals for This Book

This book grew out of several concerns. First, when teaching communication theory courses (typically for new graduate students), there is a lack of good textbooks. While there is a plethora of communication theory books available, most of them are written for introductory-level courses that would be taken by sophomores and juniors in college. While there is obviously a huge need for these books, they do not really address the needs of the new graduate student. For these burgeoning scholars, a common option has been to use the *Handbook of Communication Science* or related scholarly books. While the *Handbook* is an excellent resource (indeed, one of us co-edited the latest edition of it!), its intended audience was the academic community writ large and not new graduate students. Many new graduate students struggle with the *Handbook* and similar volumes because it assumes a level of familiarity with the discipline that many new students simply do not have yet. And because the audience for these scholarly books is the more advanced scholar, they leave out issues pertaining to theory construction, and to the larger field of communication. While a book the size of this one cannot provide an in-depth discussion of all of the theories of communication—or even the major theories found in the discipline, we do seek to provide a solid grounding in communication as a discipline, including some of its major areas and theories in order to provide the foundation for future incursions into the discipline. Thus, the first goal is to introduce you to theories of communication.

However, a discipline cannot be understood to be simply a list of topics and theories. Even a massive tome that listed and described every theory of communication (if such an exhaustive list could ever be derived) would not provide a true understanding of the discipline. The basis for the theories, their interconnections, how they fit into the field, indeed what communication as a discipline means, is needed to really gain an understanding of a discipline. Furthermore, as communication scholars, we also draw a lot from neighboring disciplines such as psychology and sociology. When you are done reading this textbook, we hope that you understand what the core of this discipline is. What questions do communication scholars seek to answer that are uniquely communication in nature? What theories have we developed to help us answer these questions and explain the phenomena that we are interested in exploring? But we think it is a mistake to ignore the larger context in which the discipline operates. When you are done reading this book, we also hope you understand the larger context in which this discipline resides and works. After reading this book, you should have a solid foundation for understanding the theoretical interplay between communication and disciplines such as psychology and sociology. You should also gain a sense of how communication came into being historically, what some of the major approaches are in the field of communication, and how communication science fits into that mix.

Overview of the Book

The first section of the book provides a foundation for understanding the specific domains and theories that will be discussed in the second part of the book (Chapters 7 to 16). Chapter 1 focuses on what exactly theory is and why it is so heavily stressed when doing research. Chapter 1 begins with a definition of theory drawn from Pavitt (2000, p. 111) that defines theory as a "formal system of concepts and relationships tying these concepts together, with the functions of explaining, predicting, and allowing potential control over real-world phenomena." The chapter then goes on to discuss the many aspects of a theoretical model such as concepts, phenomena, causality, models, variables, operationalizations, propositions, and linkages. In other words, Chapter 1 offers a detailed introduction to theory (singular noun) itself. Chapter 2 seeks to answer the question *what is communication?* from both a philosophical and theoretical perspective. Drawing on ideas addressed in Chapter 1, we discuss the interdisciplinary nature of communication, the philosophical roots of communication, communication as a construct and how that leads us to an understanding of the interconnections between communication variables and processes, and finally, what constitutes good communication theory and research. The third chapter continues the exploration of our discipline. As the "newest" of the social sciences, how did the study of communication emerge during the past century? A century ago, you would not find a department of communication anywhere. You might find schools of journalism, or a department of rhetoric and English. Today, most major institutions of higher learning have at least one department dedicated to the study of communication and the mass media. We explore this history of communication as a field and as an academic department.

Chapters 4 and 5 deal with more philosophical issues that are important for communication theory. In Chapter 4 we provide a synthesis of the discipline, with the focus primarily on the philosophical roots of quantitative approaches to communication science. First, we briefly introduce three broad areas of communication—communication science, critical/cultural studies, and rhetoric— echoing both the emergence of communication historically and its underlying assumptions. Second, we shift the focus to communication science and discuss its philosophical roots and underpinnings. We offer a more systematic and in-depth examination of its roots as they relate to the natural sciences, because it is the approach taken in the majority of the book. In Chapter 5 we explore what is meant by issues pertaining to positivism, causality, and explanation in the social sciences. We discuss what is meant by terms such as knowledge and how knowledge claims are made. We discuss scientific realism and how it is related to the social sciences in general and communication in particular, and we discuss the scientific method as it relates to positivism and post-positivism. By the end of Chapter 6 you should have a solid understanding of what is meant by *theory*. In the final chapter of Part I we provide a brief overview of communication research methods, including the basic mechanics of the survey, the experiment, and content analysis, three commonly used methods in the tool kit of most communication scientists.

The next section of the book begins by addressing the major theories across the various subfields within the discipline. Chapter 7 looks at what is one of the oldest traditions within the study of the media. At a basic level, theories of media effects focus on the consequences of using the media. Many of society's debates about the media—media violence, the effects of viewing pornography, or the influence of the media on how we understand our social world—are central to the study of media effects. The other side of the equation is what media people choose to consume. Violent TV programming isn't going to have any effect on people if they don't watch the programs that contain violence. So why do people consume the media that they consume? These issues broadly fall under theories of selective exposure and media use, the topics addressed in Chapter 8.

How people understand and interpret messages themselves should be central to the study of communication and is in fact the basis, though sometimes the unrecognized basis, for many other areas of communication research. However, this is an area of study that has emerged fairly recently. Chapter 9 discusses theories from psychology, communication, and cultural studies that attempt to explain how people comprehend and interpret the media that they consume. Chapter 10 introduces interpersonal communication as that which takes place between individuals and is interactive, individualized, and relational. The chapter then goes on to review areas and research in interpersonal communication by exploring communication in relationships from a functional perspective. Chapter 11 examines small group and organizational communication, again reviewing the main theories and some research findings related to communication focusing on groups and organizations.

People often communicate with the specific goal of trying to change other people's attitudes and beliefs. The study of persuasion has been central to the discipline since the ancient period, but the social scientific study of persuasion blossomed during the past century. Chapter 12 summarizes some of the major theories of attitude change and persuasion. Given the centrality of this area of study to several disciplines, there have been a large number of theories developed in this area.

Chapters 13 to 16 seek to contextualize communication. Specifically, Chapter 13 summarizes the extensive research and theorizing that focuses on the intersection of communication and politics. Certainly, given the important role of the media as a political watchdog as well as the centrality of political campaigning to our democracy, the study of political communication has been important. This chapter summarizes both research on what political stories ultimately are published as well as the impact of these published studies on the individual and the larger political system.

Chapter 14 focuses on social media. The use of social media has grown exponentially, and although research on social media, their uses, and their effects has increased remarkably, it is difficult for it to keep up with each innovation, trend, and movement. This chapter focuses on, first, evidence concerning who is using it; then, how social media are used. In both cases, research has considered social media use by both individuals and business entities. Lastly, this chapter looks at its effects by focusing on two areas that have received considerable research attention: the effect of social media on human social connectedness and social relationships, and the effect of social media on large-scale political changes.

Chapter 15 summarizes the theories that have emerged in the study of health communication since the earliest work in this area in the 1950s. Much of the work has focused on what makes a successful health campaign. More recently, scholars have begun theorizing about the role of interpersonal communication in doctor–patient interactions. Theories and research findings in this area continue to grow and gain focus in the field. This chapter introduces this compelling and important area. Finally, in terms of content areas, Chapter 16 reviews theories and research on marriage and the family. While researchers typically acknowledge the interplay between interpersonal communication more broadly and marriage and family communication, there is also consensus that relational context plays such a large role in the communication process that marriage and family communication may indeed constitute a distinct area. Indeed, since the beginning of the twentieth century, marriages and families have been investigated by social scientists of various academic disciplines, for obvious reasons. Marriages and families constitute the social building blocks of societies, and how marriages and families function affects and reflects societal functioning more generally. Furthermore, the family is also thought of as the primary socialization agent of children and adolescents. Thus, understanding marriages and families is part and parcel of understanding society and societal processes. Throughout this chapter, research on relationships and families *per se* is investigated.

The book closes with a chapter that considers the future of communication, all the while recognizing the necessity of considering the past; after all, an understanding of historical concerns aids the discipline to move forward in self-aware and productive ways. In Chapter 17, we review communication's interdisciplinary nature, consider the debate over communication's credibility, consider its external impact, and reflect on how theory and technological adaptation coalesce as distinct but interdependent ideas. We conclude with considerations for the future direction of communication scholarship.

It is our hope that in providing in these chapters an overview of theory (again, in the singular) and a review of communication theories, we provide a basis for the new scholar to approach the field with a clearer understanding of who we are, what we do, and what it means to study communication.

PART I

Communication Theory

1

AN INTRODUCTION TO THEORY

In communication, indeed in any discipline, theory is often held up as the zenith of research. Theory-driven research is not simply preferred, it is necessary to meaningful scholarship. Merely collecting data, without a theory to guide the process, is likely to lead to findings that are, at best, without meaning, and at worst, accidental, coincidental, or spurious. One could argue that along with solid research design, theory is one of the best protections against Type I error (i.e., false positives in research). In other words, with the guidance and direction of theory, one is less likely to "cry wolf" with any data-analytic findings.

But what is theory? Pavitt (2000, p. 111) defines theory as a "formal system of concepts and relationships tying these concepts together, with the functions of explaining, predicting, and allowing potential control over real-world phenomena." In other words, in order to have a theory, one must have an observed phenomenon, concepts used to label individual aspects of that observed phenomenon, and linkages between the concepts that describe and explain how they relate to one another. Ideally, that explanation would be specific, explicit, and causal. In the end, such a theory would have the benefit of allowing some degree of control over the phenomenon. For example, a solid theory of persuasion would not only explain that there were effects of, say, an anti-smoking campaign, but would describe how the effects occurred and the mechanism or processes that caused the effects; individual concepts would exist as important elements of the theoretical processes and, ultimately, that theory could provide a model for the design of future successful anti-smoking campaigns.

But such a description of theory only skims the surface. Our understanding of it is limited by our understanding of such terms as concepts, phenomenon, causality, models, and, as we continue, variables, operationalizations, propositions, and linkages. Thus, in the remainder of the chapter, we will discuss in greater detail what theory is and the terminology used to discuss it, what theory is *not*, and some steps in the development of theory.

Phenomenon as Starting Place

Often, in communication research or in research in any one of the natural or social scientific disciplines, theory begins with an observed phenomenon. In the social sciences, that phenomenon is most typically a social behavior that is enacted by a human being. The mere observation of that phenomenon, however, does not constitute a theory (Berger et al., 2010). Instead, the observation of a phenomenon should be taken as the starting place, the first step in the creation and drawing of a theory, if in fact *drawing* is the term that should be used (see below).

For example, in the mass media effects literature, several meta-analyses (Anderson & Bushman, 2001; Paik & Comstock, 1994) have been conducted that demonstrate a relationship between exposure to media violence and aggressive behavior. These meta-analyses have been taken as evidence for the link between the two variables, and in fact, some of the research has been able to test for causality through experimental design. However, simply noting a statistical relationship between the two, or even noting a causal relationship between the two by means of experimental design, does not even begin to approach theory. Rather, at this stage in the process, we have mere observation. No causal explanation, indeed, no explanation at all is offered through observation alone.

An important point to be made here is that no study, no matter how well designed, crafted, conducted, and analyzed, may be considered theoretical. Rather, research and data most often live in the service of theories. Importantly, this is not always the case, as will be discussed presently, but for the most part, data are servile to theory. Certainly data can have practical purposes in and of themselves, but a good study starts with theory. The data then are used, literally used, to test and then support or not support the theory. Data collection should be guided by theory and data analysis used to test it. A well-designed study, therefore, should be viewed as a test of a theoretical phenomenon.

Despite the data-in-service-of-theory argument, the phenomenon, or *casual* observation, often comes first. A researcher may notice, observe, or use logical analysis in identifying a phenomenon or starting place. For example, I may observe the phenomenon of aggression and wonder about its antecedents. Or, I may observe someone, a child perhaps, acting aggressively after watching a violent cartoon. Note that the co-occurrence of these two phenomena (watching the cartoon and aggression) is not a theory. It is merely an extended phenomenon. Thus, we begin with an observed phenomenon. From that starting point, we may begin to craft theoretical explanations or we may test the observation through systematic research. The process, including casual observation of the phenomenon, theoretical explanation, and systematic research, occurs in an iterative process, a process that is likely to take years. Thus, the phenomenon is often the place where theory begins. At times, theory may emerge without casual observation. For example, careful reading of many validated theories may lead a researcher to see connections between them, thus allowing for a theoretical evolution or new idea in absence of any observed phenomenon. But for the purpose of this discussion, we suggest that observing a phenomenon is a starting place.

Implicit vs. Explicit Theory

We argue above that the observation of a phenomenon is the starting place of theory. However, this is not precisely accurate because it assumes that observation is somehow without antecedent, itself. It assumes that nothing, not presuppositions, preconceptions, or biases, guided the initial observation of the phenomenon. Much recent research in perception indicates that this notion of unbiased observation is false. In fact, we might argue that a phenomenon is a type of starting place, but so is theory itself.

Berger et al. (2010) distinguish between "intuitive or implicit theories, on one hand, and formally explicated theories on the other" (p. 11). They refer to these as System 1 theories and System 2 theories, and liken them to the dual processing approach to information processing (Stanovich, 2002). In this view, cognitive processing can at times be implicit, where our perceptions, interpretations, understanding, and even memory and recall occur at the preconscious level (Gigerenzer, 2007). This, they refer to as System 1. Alternately, cognitive processing can be explicit and formal. Such is the case when we read, draw conclusions, and perhaps summarize what we have read in a systematic, consciously aware way. This, they refer to as System 2.

Theory, too, can be formulated this way. After all, we are all naïve and constant theoreticians. We observe a phenomenon; perhaps at a children's birthday party we notice the co-occurrence of wild behavior and the consumption of birthday cake. We then draw naïve conclusions about the phenomenon. We determine that sugar, found in abundance in cake, causes hyperactivity in children. We then use our theory to explain the behavior and predict future outcomes such as hyperactivity in children after any sugar consumption. We may even use our theory to guide future actions such as limiting children's sugar intake. This is an example of a System 1 theory. Interestingly, all systematic tests of this theory about sugar and hyperactivity in children have shown no support for it whatsoever (Howard-Jones, 2014).

However, there are also systematic theories, crafted, drawn, and tested by researchers. These are conscious and careful explanations of phenomena. They are guided by formal rules of logic and inference. They are mapped out and tested, either in portion or in full through the highly meticulous and methodical process of data collection and analysis. Despite the distinction drawn between these two types of theory by Berger et al. (2010), they note that there is likely an undeniable connection between System 1 and System 2 theories. In fact, it is likely that our selection of research topics, our pursuit of certain avenues of inquiry, indeed the very attention to particular phenomena over others and particular co-occurrences over others are guided by System 1 (Popper, 1959). As we continue to formalize our thinking, it is likely that we engage System 2 to a greater degree. However, it is impossible to disengage the implicit system (Kahneman & Frederick, 2002). Thus, all theory is guided by both implicit and explicit systems. However, as social scientists, we attempt to engage System 2 and in fact, we value its processes and outcomes as true theory, whereas System 1 processes and outcomes are often viewed as less important and something to be guarded against.

Therefore, we begin with observation of a phenomenon that is guided by System 1 theorizing. We continue through the process of explicit theory building, and throughout, utilize the process of systematic research to refine our theories. Once our theories are refined, we return again to systematic research in order to further test the refined theories. In the end, theory building is not a process that can be considered linear and completely systematic. Rather, it is both iterative and at times holistic. However, as we approach it in this chapter, we are forced by the linearity of writing to proceed as if it were systematic. Thus, in the next sections, we'll discuss theory building by invoking the idea of *concepts* that need to be identified and then winnowed to particular *variables*. These variables are connected to one another through theoretical linkages made up of propositions, extended propositions, proposed mechanisms, and links, thus resulting in theory. That theory can often be visually displayed by means of a *conceptual model*. Ultimately, however, it is not sufficient to craft abstract theory, or even to represent it with a model. Theory must be tested. Thus, we move to the testing phase by *operationalizing* variables for measurement's sake. These operationalized variables are also connected to one another in the prediction and testing phase through the process of *operational linkages*.

Concepts and Variables

Chaffee (1996) argues that before we can begin the process of theorizing, we need to identify a concept or concepts that will be utilized in the theory-building process. In other words, we need to identify, and label, those ideas with which we are working. For example, aggression is an idea that is frequently studied in media effects research. Scholars may investigate aggressive outcomes related to exposure to violent cartoons, or aggression as an outcome resulting from exposure to video games. In any case, aggression itself is an idea with a specific definition, and a specific label to go along with it. This clearly defined, well-articulated idea can be termed a construct, and it is one of the building blocks for a theory of social learning whereby exposure to television violence can result in increases in behavioral aggression. Through the process of theorizing, one must identify the constructs one intends to work with, explore how those constructs have been used in previous research, and subsequently decide precisely what the construct will be in the research being pursued.

However, identification of the construct is a mere starting place. Theory is typically built *on* constructs; that is, they act as a base. However, theory is not built *with* constructs. Constructs are the more abstract notion, the idea that is then more clearly demarcated by the term "variable." A variable, of course, is something that varies within a sample. Age, for example, is a ratio-level variable that does not have a more abstract construct associated with it. Often, ratio-level variables are not more clearly specified concepts; they are merely measurements of some existing, well-defined entity such as years, hours, pounds, etc. However, often in the social sciences, what we intend to measure is more abstract. But this abstract concept must be identified and measured. Once the identification takes place, and the decision is made to utilize the concept, we identify it as a variable that will be used in our theory building. In fact, we might say that a construct *becomes* a variable when we intend to measure it and when we use it in the process of theorizing.

Variables and Theoretical Linkages

Theory itself, however, is made up of more than merely variables. In order for a set of variables to be a theory, they must be connected to one another through linkages, proposed processes, and proposed mechanisms. These linkages, processes, and mechanisms are labeled in a theory as proposition statements or theoretical linkages. For example, I might state that aggression increases after exposure to television violence. This may be one propositions within a theory. However, there are different kinds of propositions, which we will briefly discuss here.

First, there are both existence statements and relational statements. The first, the existence statement, poses only that something exists: aggression was present in the television clip. These are typically assumptions within a theory and not part of the theory itself. The second, the relational statement, is the basis of good theory building. In relational statements, one or more propositions are forwarded, stating that two variables are linked in such a way that they are either associatively or causally related (Reynolds, 1971).

In the former case, a statement that includes two variables is proposed, and an association between the variables is posited. Thus, a proposition might state that "as exposure to television violence increases, aggression levels increase." In the latter case, the two variables are proposed to be causally related, with exposure to television violence *causing* increases in aggressive behavior. Note, however, that simply stating that two variables are causally linked does not provide anything in the way of explanation. Thus, ultimately, good theory not only provides causal propositions, but it breaks those propositions down to provide processes and mechanisms for the causal link. In other words, a given causal link is further dissected to propose a process that explains the causality. As mentioned earlier in the chapter, simply stating that something occurs, or that something is related, is really observation and not theory, *per se*.

Rather, in good theory building, the associative or causal link must be extended by limiting or conditional propositions. For example, when claiming that exposure to television violence is associated with increases in aggression, one might further pose the proposition that this relationship is stronger among boys, or occurs with greater frequency when the depicted violence is shown being rewarded. Thus, one proposition may claim an association between exposure to television violence and aggressive behavior. A second proposition may claim that the link is stronger for boys, that is, gender moderates the associative link between exposure and aggression. A third proposition may further claim that the link is stronger when the violent actor is shown being rewarded.

In addition to providing limiting or conditional propositions, an associative or causal link may be explained by propositions that offer mechanisms or explanations for the link. For example, various extant theorizing about the link between exposure to television violence and aggression has proposed mechanisms of increased arousal or cognitive priming. In other words, solid theory proposes not only *that* an association exists between two variables, but may offer propositions offering an explanation for the process. For example, exposure to media violence may increase physiological arousal, which may in turn increase aggressive behavior. These *process* propositions offer mediating variables between two associated variables. In any case, theory building extends "mere associations" beyond the obvious relationship between two variables and determines, by means of successive propositions, how and under what conditions the relationship occurs.

For example, sociocognitive theory (Bandura, 2002) predicts that exposure to media violence will increase aggression in viewers. This occurs because people can learn behaviors not only from direct experience but also from vicarious experience, such as media exposure. However, what makes sociocognitive theory a meaningful theory is its discussion of the mechanisms by which this imitation of violence occurs. Specifically, Bandura (2002) argues that increases in aggression resulting from exposure to media violence result from subprocesses including attention, retention, production, and motivation. These subprocesses are not proposed to be mutually exclusive, nor necessarily and solely related as a linearly progressive model. Rather, aspects of one process may influence and provide feedback to aspects of another. Thus, Bandura provides not only variables (e.g., attention) but also theoretical linkages between them. For example, the theory claims that when presented with a modeled event, an individual first attends to it based on its salience and their involvement in it. If attention is high, then individuals might also retain the information, part of which involves symbolic coding. Third, individuals respond in some way. That is, they engage in production, perhaps based on an appropriate script, and that production is guided in part by their earlier attention to and retention of the modeled behavior. Here, individuals utilize information from the environment, translate that into cognitively represented symbolic information, and ultimately generate appropriate actions. Moreover, the greater the match between the symbolic information and the planned enacted behavior, the more likely the behavior is to occur. Lastly, individuals utilize motivational processes, imagining motives for and anticipated outcomes of their actions. Actions are more likely to be imitated when rewards are anticipated. In any case, the brief discussion of sociocognitive theory here provides an example for how theoretical linkages are crafted.

Ultimately, then, theory is made up of variables, proposed linkages by means of propositional statements, and the underlying concepts and operationalizations, themselves connected through linkages, that finally explain and predict behavior. *How* the process of theorizing occurs is, however, a more complex process than can adequately be described here. Below, we will discuss the *steps* in theory building, but, as noted earlier, theory building cannot and should not be thought of as a linear process. It is only in writing about it that one is forced into linearity. Instead, it may be valuable to think of drawing as a more apt metaphor for theory building. Daly (2003) has pointed out that "drawing and theorizing are parallel processes as both are concerned with representation" (p. 771). In drawing, representation is approached as a process of duplicating what is perceived, perhaps breaking it down into smaller, more manageable parts and ultimately creating a whole that represents and offers insight into what exists. Both the details and the whole are crucial to achieving a final product. In our theorizing activity, we must also attend to the details of the connections between concepts and variables, the linkages between variables (by way of propositions), and the insight that is offered to the reader through that process. After all, if the process (of drawing, or of theorizing) does not offer insight into, and explanation of, that which is being represented, why bother? Therefore, theory is driven by the desire to explain something. But theory itself is not enough. Good theory is crafted in the mind but tested outside of it. Thus, we move from the abstract to the concrete.

Conceptual Models

Theory is, by necessity, explained through language. A good theorist can explicate his/her theory by precisely identifying and defining the concepts. In addition to deriving and explaining the concepts, and creating a solid theory that can be both explanatory and predictive, a good theorist is also able to articulate the linkages, the processes that enable concepts to be linked as observations, and precise explanations of the mechanisms that link them. But a theorist often relies on a visual depiction as well. A conceptual model allows us to clearly identify the concepts and to clearly show how they are linked. Initially, a conceptual model can provide a researcher a means for sketching out ideas. Because a conceptual model contains concepts, clearly labeled, and must identify any proposed links

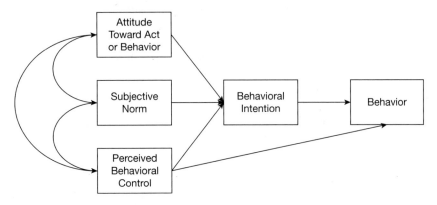

FIGURE 1.1 The theory of planned behavior.

between those concepts and might also specify the predicted direction of the proposed links, a conceptual model can help identify fuzzy thinking and force researchers, early on, to clarify and explicate and explain.

One excellent example is that of the theory of planned behavior (Ajzen & Fishbein, 2005), a well-validated theory that explains and predicts behavior. Based on literally hundreds of studies and two decades of research, the simplest conceptual model of the theory suggests that three main variables, attitude, social norms, and perceived behavioral control, work together to influence intention to engage in a particular behavior, which in turn influences our behavior. Later extensions of the theory have identified predictors of the main variables in the model and have suggested other specifications; however, a simple conceptual model (see Figure 1.1) provides the reader with a very basic understanding of the theory. It also allows the researcher to identify aspects of the model that will be tested and to articulate predictions for how various variables might be related. Conceptual models often also include positive or negative signs along the paths in order to further specify hypothesized relationships.

Operationalization and Operational Linkages

Once we have identified our concepts and variables, specified the relationship between them, perhaps presented these ideas in language, certainly, but also in a conceptual model, we must go about the task of testing the theory. However, the testing process will be addressed here only briefly and will be discussed at length in Chapter 8. In a given theory, testing includes not only identifying the variable, but measuring it as well. For example, the *concept* of aggression is one in which an offensive action or attack is used against another. As a variable, we may call this physical, or perhaps verbal, aggression. Ultimately, however, if we are to use aggression as a variable in a study, we must operationalize it. In other words, we must decide exactly how we intend to measure it. Aggression can be measured by means of a paper and pencil test, through observation of behavior, by the amount of electric shock delivered by a participant in an experiment to the confederate. Thus we have moved from the most abstract, the concept, to the most tangible, the operationalization.

However, it is not sufficient to simply state that a particular operationalization is obviously and clearly a valid measurement of a concept. The concept must be connected to the variable and ultimately to the operationalization through meaning statements, analysis, logic, and argumentation. Evidence must be provided to demonstrate the validity of the connections and linkages between them. The researcher is responsible for drawing a logical line of argument from the concept through to the operationalization. And the logic and strength of that argument ultimately provides a sense of validity. A variable can be adequately connected to a concept in a theory through the process of clear argumentation. Similarly, an operationalization can be demonstrated as a solid and valid measure of a variable in a study in part through the processes of logic. Thus, the process of moving from the abstract to the tangible, from the concept to the operation-alization, is itself a kind of theorizing.

Now, we have the concept, connected to the variable, ultimately connected to the operationalization. The predicted connection or relationship between the operationalized variables in the hypothesis, first, and in the statistical analyses, second, is referred to as the operational linkage. Operational linkages are those links that predict and test theoretical linkages. "Operational linkages may be presented in two forms, visual and statistical" (Shoemaker et. al., 2004, p. 57). That is, a connection between two variables can be shown by drawing the link, thus presenting a visual representation of the proposed relationship, or the relationship can be presented after the fact, via the statistical relationship between the variables. These are both considered operational linkages because they rely on the proposed and tested model. The links are not theoretically articulated processes, as discussed earlier. Rather they are empirical, tangible, and numeric, without meaning in and of themselves.

For example, when I predict that there will be an increase in aggressive behavior, as measured by the Buss–Perry aggression measure (1992), as exposure to media violence increases, as measured by self-reported exposure to violent television and video games, I have specified that theoretical linkage at the level of an operational linkage. Similarly, when I have measured exposure to television violence in a sample, measured aggression in that sample, and statistically examined the relationship between those variables, that statistical relationship can be thought of as an operational linkage. I have moved from the abstraction of theory to the empirical level of measurement and theory testing.

What Theory is NOT

Although much has been written about what constitutes good theory, or at least what constitutes theory at all, there remains much work in communication, and in fact in other social science disciplines, that parades as theory without actually having the qualities and characteristics of theory (Nabi & Oliver, 2010). Recall that good theory requires not only a description of a phenomenon or even a demonstration of interconnected variables, but limiting factors and conditional statements, mechanisms, and processes. Good theory requires not only a model with interconnected variables and a cursory discussion of those variables, but a careful, precise, and thorough explanation of the process at hand. Good theory, then, is not data analytic, although that may be part of the process of testing good theory. Rather, good theory is derived through logical and deductive processes, presented through rhetorical processes, and only then tested and refined through data-analytic processes. Often, researchers fall prey to calling something a theory when the conditions of theory are not met, for a rather simple reason: to craft a theory, or to say that one has crafted a theory, is exciting and important. Therefore, scholars race to label something a theory when, in fact, what they have falls quite short of actual theory.

Berger et al. (2010) describe at least two situations that result in false, or imposter, theories. First, "the term theory is sometimes misused to characterize a body of research that merely demonstrates that a particular phenomenon occurs or can be produced under a set of conditions, appending the term *theory* to the phenomenon" (pp. 9–10). Whereas the phenomenon may in fact occur, calling it a theory, or even demonstrating, experimentally, that it occurs, is just that, a demonstration of evidence for and perhaps description of the phenomenon. In order to achieve the status of theory, an observed phenomenon must be understood in terms of the processes by which it occurs, the mechanisms, cognitive or otherwise, that cause it to occur, and the means by which it can best be understood, explained, and predicted.

Second, they warn that models themselves are not theories, even if they are claimed to be so. The problem arises when sophisticated data analyses, resulting in complex and even compelling structural equation models (SEM), are sometimes claimed to be theory. In other words, a model is proposed, tested using SEM, and then the term theory is appended to the name of the model. Although this is certainly a valid way to test a theory, and perhaps even a way to explore extensions of, or contextual situations for a particular theory, it is not theory. Rather, a model, such as a regression model or a structural equation model, begins with data and, in fact, the model itself ends with data, as well. In other words, statistical analyses can be nothing more than that, ever. Certainly, data collection can and should be theory driven. Thus, the statistical model used to test that theory can be more theoretically sound. However, that still does not render the model a theory. Unless the data are gathered in a theory-driven way, the model is built to test that theory (or perhaps extend it in an *a priori* fashion), and subsequently, theory is brought back to the model and discussed, in prose, extensively, precisely, thoroughly, we do not have theory. What then makes up good theory?

Characteristics of Good Theory

In addition to having passed the test of time, good theory is also thought to have several defining characteristics. Specifically, good theory is testable, falsifiable, parsimonious, with explanatory and predictive power, and finally, of broad enough scope to be of practical use (Shoemaker et al., 2004). Theories rarely start out with this rather lofty set of characteristics. Rather, they are refined, specified, elaborated, and clarified through the process of evaluation and testing. Below, Bandura's sociocognitive theory (2002) of mass communication will be used as an example to discuss characteristics of good theory.

The earliest publication of sociocognitive theory (Bandura, 1977) occurred some 30 years ago and is still in the process of being refined through evaluation and testing. In fact, the first aspect of good theory is that it must *be* testable. In other words, the theory must be specified clearly enough, the concepts identifiable, the connections between variables clearly described. If mechanisms are thought to be at work, those mechanisms must be specified to such a degree that research can be conducted to test the proposed mechanism(s).

For example, a proposition within a larger theory might state that because middle-class children today use computers earlier and more often than ever before, the way they process information has likely changed from how children processed information in days prior to the advent of the personal computer. Although this is an interesting idea, the variables are not clearly enough specified and the mechanisms and processes are not specified. For example, notions of information processing are varied and the term itself is vague. That strategies for information processing can change is also not testable, because the very notion of change is vague, unless more precisely specified. That is not to say that the proposition is not true, only that in its current form it cannot be tested.

In addition to being testable, a second aspect of good theory is that it must be falsifiable (Popper, 1959). A theory that cannot be contradicted by any conceivable observation is not part of science. It might better be thought of as a belief, an article of faith, or an assumption. For example, the notion of creationism as an explanation for life on earth is not a falsifiable theory. Why? Not only is the evidence we have in support of it (that there is life on earth) also evidence for any number of theories that attempt to explain life on planet Earth, but there is no conceivable observation that could refute the theory. Therefore, creationism as an explanation for the existence of life on earth fails one test of good theory: that it be *potentially* falsifiable.

Third, good theory has both explanatory and predictive power. The primary purpose of theory is to explain why and how some phenomenon occurs or some behavior gets enacted. However, simply providing an explanation, *post hoc*, is not enough. A good theory can also predict future occurrences of the phenomenon or behavior, as long as one has an understanding of the particular situation and how it applies to the theory.

Fourth, good theory is parsimonious. Imagine observing a given phenomenon. In seeking an explanation for the phenomenon, further imagine deriving an explanation that does so, but in order to do so, must provide dozens of conditional statements, clauses, and limitations. For example, perhaps the sun appears to rise in the east and set in the west due to the rotation of the earth relative to the sun. However, perhaps this is only true 8 months a year, when the weather is fair, if the world's population is, on the whole, healthy that day, and if Los Angeles published its daily paper on time. Theories that have so many conditional statements, clauses, and limitations cease to be useful. Thus, good theory provides explanation and prediction that is thorough, yet is able to be thorough while being parsimonious as well.

Lastly, a good theory is broad in scope. Whereas the theory itself should be parsimonious, the *scope* of the theory, the amount of ground it covers, should be broad. If a theory can only explain and predict a behavior under very specific circumstances or only at a particular point in time, its utility as a theory is minimal. Therefore, good theory can explain and predict phenomena at various points in time, over time, and in various situations.

Processes in Theory Development

As discussed earlier, crafting a theory shares much in common with the process of drawing or sculpting. Representations are created and re-created, areas of the drawing or sculpture are revisited and revised, the entire process is three dimensional and rarely is the process undertaken in clear steps that begin at the beginning and move linearly to the end. However, because of the nature of writing, we present here the *steps* in theory development, recognizing that the term *steps* implies a linearity that we do not want to convey. However, there does not seem to be another way. Thus, we will present here the steps in the process of theory building.

First, observation or recognition of a phenomenon is typically a starting place for theory. Theory is driven by the desire to explain and predict this phenomenon; however, careful observation of it is a necessary starting point. In fact, theory often begins not only with mere examination of a behavior, but detection of regularities or irregularities in it. Reflection resulting from these early observations may provide the very first steps in progress toward more systematic theory construction.

Second, constructs must be identified and these constructs ultimately winnowed and specified as variables. This is done through the processes discussed earlier, where both theoretical and operational definitions are specified. Only after they have been specified can linkages between variables be identified and proposed in terms of relationships and direction of causality.

Third, when theory has been crafted, the process is not complete. Ultimately, systematic research must be undertaken, with the relationship between theory and research being symbiotic. Whereas good theory acts as a guide for research, suggesting potential questions and offering models for research design, research also acts as the arbiter of theory. Theory that is consistently not supported by the research is either in need of revision and respecification, or perhaps the theory is simply wrong.

Unfortunately, researchers, especially those who claim authorship of a given theory, sometimes fall prey to abusing the symbiotic relationship between theory and research. Rather than using research to potentially falsify the theory, or at least to refine it, they use research to find support for the theory. As has been quipped many times, researchers are sometimes guilty of using research as a drunk uses a lamppost: for support rather than illumination. Thus, one must be willing to truly embrace the first two characteristics of good theory: testability and falsifiability. One must be willing to search for counter-evidence in order to truly and rigorously test a theory. Only through rigorous testing do theories thrive or wither as they should.

The Role of the Social and Environmental Context in Theory

A final point that is not often addressed in discussions of theory is that theory is not crafted in a vacuum; rather, it occurs in a social and historical context that sometimes becomes evident only with the passage of time. Good theory, therefore, is derived in a particular context, but survives beyond it. Take, for example, humorism, or humoralism, a theory of the make-up and workings of the human body that thrived initially in 100–200 AD but survived long beyond that, well into the 1700s (Keirsey, 1998). Until the advent of modern medical research in the nineteenth century, humorism was the dominantly held belief concerning the workings of the human body and mind. In brief, the four humors were thought to be black bile (*melancolia*), yellow bile (*cholera*), phlegm (*phlegma*), and blood (*sanguis*), which were thought to be in balance when a person was healthy. When they were out of balance, however, disease or changes in personality occurred, with specific problems associated with specific patterns of imbalance. For our purposes, however, these humors were tellingly consistent with the then-held theory in the natural sciences of the four elements: earth, fire, water, and air. Either directly, or indirectly, the theory of the four natural elements seems to influence the theory of the four humors. Thus, the particular historical context of the four humors is better understood when we understand the parallels that existed in that time period. Eventually, neither theory was supported and they were replaced by subsequent, more detailed theories offering explanations for the respective phenomenon.

Similarly, in the 1960s, computer as metaphor for the mind was derived around the time of the popularization of the computer and its entry into the public consciousness. Terminology such as "software," "hardware," and "processing" were adopted in cognitive psychology, mirroring the terminology used in computer science (Cisek, 1999). In fact, the cognitive revolution itself followed in the footsteps of advances in computer science. None of this is intended to imply that computers are *not* an appropriate metaphor for the mind. Nor is theorizing that relies on the computer as a model for thinking necessarily incorrect. However, it is important to consider the computer and subsequent theories about the mind in the historical context in which they arose. Such awareness, with the critical eye that accompanies it, is likely to provide an environment for our theory building and theory testing that is rigorous, careful, judicious, and above all, necessary. This analytic approach will allow us to improve our theories, or, if they cannot be improved to logically and parsimoniously include the resulting data, the theory under consideration will perish, as it should, and new theories will be developed. It is in this iterative, progressive way that social science can come to a better understanding of human behavior.

References

Ajzen, I., & Fishbein, M. (2005). The influence of attitudes on behavior. In D. Albarracin, B. T. Johnson, & M. P. Zanna (Eds.), *The handbook of attitudes* (pp. 173–222). Mahwah, NJ: Lawrence Erlbaum Associates.

Anderson, C. A., & Bushman, B. J. (2001). Effects of violent video games on aggressive behavior, aggressive cognition, aggressive affect, physiological arousal, and prosocial behavior: A meta-analytic review of the scientific literature. *Psychological Science, 12*, 353–359.

Bandura, A. (1977). *Social learning theory*. Englewood Cliffs, NJ: Prentice Hall.

Bandura, A. (2002). A social cognitive theory of mass communication. In J. Bryant & D. Zillmann (Eds.), *Media effects: Advances in theory and research* (pp. 121–154). Mahwah, NJ: Lawrence Erlbaum Associates.

Berger, C. R., Roloff, M. E., & Roskos-Ewoldsen, D. R. (2010). *The handbook of communication science*. Thousand Oaks, CA: Sage.

Buss, A. H., & Perry, M. P. (1992). The aggression questionnaire. *Journal of Personality and Social Psychology, 63*, 452–459.

Chaffee, S. H. (1996). Thinking about theory. In M. Salwen & D. Stacks (Eds.), *An integrated approach to communication theory and research* (pp. 13–29). Mahwah, NJ: Lawrence Erlbaum Associates.

Cisek, P. (1999). Beyond the computer metaphor: Behaviour as interaction. *Journal of Consciousness Studies, 6*, 125–142.

Daly, K. (2003). Family theory vs. the theories families live by. *Journal of Marriage and the Family, 65*, 771–784.

Gigerenzer, G. (2007). *Gut feelings: The intelligence of the unconscious*. New York: Viking.

Howard-Jones, P. A. (2014). Neuroscience and education: Myths and messages. *Nature Reviews Neuroscience*, www.dx.doi.org/10.1038/nrn3817

Kahneman, D., & Frederick, S. (2002). Representativeness revisited: Attribute substitution in intuitive judgment. In T. Gilovich, D. Griffin, & D. Kahneman (Eds.), *Heuristics and biases: The psychology of intuitive judgment* (pp. 49–81). Cambridge: Cambridge University Press.

Keirsey, D. (1998). *Please understand me II: Temperament, character, intelligence* (p. 26). Del Mar, CA: Prometheus Nemesis.

Nabi, R., & Oliver, M. (2010). Mass media effects. In C. R. Berger, M. E. Roloff, & D. Roskos-Ewoldsen (Eds.), *The handbook of communication science* (pp. 255–272). Thousand Oaks, CA: Sage.

Paik, H., & Comstock, G. (1994). The effects of television violence on antisocial behavior: A meta-analysis. *Communication Research, 21,* 516–546.

Pavitt, C. (2000). *Philosophy of science and communication theory.* Huntington, NY: Nova Science.

Popper, K. R. (1959). *The logic of scientific discovery.* New York: Harper and Row.

Reynolds, P. D. (1971). *A primer in theory construction.* New York: Bobbs-Merrill.

Shoemaker, P. J., Tankard, Jr., J. W., & Lasorsa, D. L. (2004). *How to build social science theories.* Thousand Oaks, CA: Sage.

Stanovich, K. E. (2002). Rationality, intelligence, and levels of analysis in cognitive science: Is dysrationalia possible? In R. J. Sternberg (Ed.), *Why smart people can be so stupid* (pp. 124–158). New Haven, CT: Yale University Press.

2

WHAT IS COMMUNICATION?

Perhaps one reason that communication is so difficult to define is that it appears self-evident, obvious, and in need of no further explanation. Communication is sending and receiving messages, sharing information, interacting with others face to face or via any number of old and newly emerging technologies. To communicate is to impart thoughts, ideas, and information. However, like many concepts used in the social sciences, its simplicity is deceptive. A deeper understanding of the thing itself is needed in order to clearly understand the construct and thus study its many functioning parts. Furthermore, communication as a *discipline* is obviously connected to communication as a *construct*, but the two are distinct and an understanding of each is needed, one to inform the other.

In this chapter, we will address these two distinct aspects of communication, two aspects that are in fact relevant in any field. In the first section, we will answer the question: "what is communication?" from both a philosophical and theoretical perspective. Drawing on ideas addressed in Chapter 1, we will discuss the interdisciplinary nature of communication, the philosophical roots of communication, communication as a construct and how that leads us to an understanding of the interconnections between communication variables and processes, and finally, what constitutes good communication theory and research. As a caveat, we note that although communication as a discipline is broad, including areas as diverse as the quantitative study of message processing and performance studies, the main, although not sole, focus of this book is communication science, or the quantitative study of message production, processing, and effects. In the second section, we will consider pragmatic aspects of the field: what do communication scholars study, where is communication scholarship conducted, where is the research published, and what are the associations that make up the discipline? In short, we will answer the question from an administrative perspective. Communication is, after all, a field made up of actual individuals conducting research in real time, presenting and publishing that research, and teaching students. These are the human, physical, and organizational components of communication.

Communication and Interdisciplinarity

A quarter of a century ago, Peters (1986) asked the question: "Why has the field of communication failed to define itself, its intellectual focus and its mission in a coherent way?" (p. 527). He then went on to compare the discipline to a nation state (perhaps to a failing one, although that is a side note), because communication, he argued, suffered from an "historical anachronism in its self-image, specifically in its image of 'founding fathers,' irredentism, that is, the dream of an expanding empire regardless of its current size, philosophical poverty and even incoherence, and a limited recognition of its similarity to other nations."

These arguments, and the article that supported them, ignited a feisty debate with Gonzalez (1988), who claimed that communication has its roots in inter-disciplarity, emerging from many fields to address problems of communication. He went on to argue that with its roots and emphasis on solving practical problems, self-image was not as important as the work communication scholars were doing. Communication expanded not because of a dream of endless empire, but because of the very real applicability of a communication perspective to many problems. Finally, Gonzalez argued, rather than being an intellectual source of poverty, the interdisciplinary nature of communication, and its emphasis on practical problems, were its main strengths.

Indeed, communication as a discipline emerged from scholars in many disciplines such as rhetoric, sociology, journalism, psychology, literary criticism, education, engineering, and mathematics. Although communication research itself is still criticized for its interdisciplinarity, when some scholars claim that that factor alone means it is not yet a "real" discipline, we argue that its interdisciplinary history is inevitable and its current interdisciplinary state is just smart science. Why do we say this? Consider the history of communication (although see Chapter 3 in this volume for a detailed discussion). Scholars from various existing fields, such as Schramm and Lazarsfeld from sociology, Laswell from political science, Innis from economics, Hovland from psychology, and many others, gradually came together because they found themselves to be studying the same problem or category of problems (Herbst, 2008). Over time, some of these scholars began to define their work as communication, and communication began to emerge as a discipline. Indeed, it is logically impossible for a field to emerge as itself without input from others with other homes and other roots to help it get established. Thus, many modern fields and modern disciplines have some interdisciplinary history. As far as the current interdisciplinary nature of communication is concerned, it is good science to cross-reference, investigate, and *use* the research in other fields. In order to fully explore any phenomenon, we must know what others, communication scholars or not, have contributed to it. We maintain a communication perspective when studying these phenomena but readily absorb and apply research findings from other fields.

In fact, many areas in the social sciences are inherently, or at least in approach, interdisciplinary. While it is true that communication uses, refers to, and applies research findings, concepts, perhaps even theories from other disciplines, disciplines such as political science, psychology, and marketing utilize communication as well. In fact, it is likely that one could conceivably trace areas of research, topics of study, and cross-citations in order to understand exactly what those interrelations between disciplines look like. How might that occur? One intriguing method has been pioneered by Rosvall and Bergstrom (2007). Using citations in the social sciences, they examine the flow or pattern of citations from one social science to another in order to assess where, in the map of social science, one particular discipline is located. Although there is no emphasis on where one discipline draws theory from another, or how they are linked historically or philosophically, it does offer a snapshot of cross-pollination in terms of sheer citations. It also offers an interesting examination of the relative size of various disciplines in the social sciences (see Figure 2.1). In any case, such a map allows us to consider where communication is situated in the social sciences. It is worth emphasizing, as the authors themselves stress, that for simplicity's sake, only the most important links are shown; thus, the diagram does simplify, somewhat, the nature of cross-citations in the social sciences. Thus, although the diagram suggests that the discipline of communication cites other fields but the reverse does not occur, the diagram more aptly can be read to indicate that we cite outside of our field *more often* than we are cited. Clearly there is work to be done to amplify the value of communication research outside of the discipline. Nevertheless, it is interesting to see, from a purely citation-based approach, that communication is aligned most closely with psychology, political science, and management. It is also interesting to note that, contrary to Peters' (1986) early criticisms, a healthy discipline need not be a singular and solitary nation state. In fact, cross-referencing and cross-pollination in any discipline may well be necessary and an indication of its intellectual health.

However, moving beyond mere citation tracking, we can gain a better understanding of what communication is not only by exploring its current research trends but by looking backward and gaining an understanding of its philosophical roots.

Philosophical Roots of Communication

Thus, when we ask what communication *is*, we are forced to recognize its inherent interdisciplinarity in terms of how the research is conducted and how the findings are applied. However, really, the inherent interdisciplinarity of communication is the surface of it. Interdisciplarity, or crossing fields in order to more fully

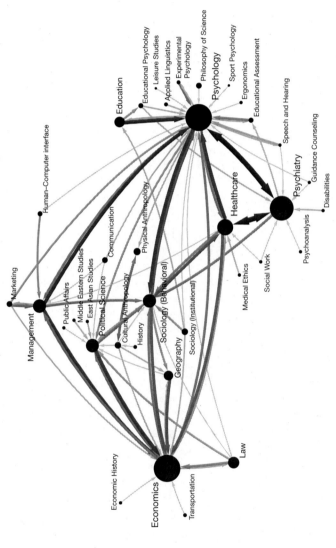

FIGURE 2.1 The social sciences, 2004. Orange circles represent fields, with larger, darker circles indicating larger field size as measured by *Eigenfactor* score™. Blue arrows represent citation flow between fields. An arrow from field A to field B indicates citation traffic from A to B, with larger, darker arrows indicating higher citation volume.

Source: The map was created using our *information flow method* for mapping large networks. Using data from Thomson Scientific's 2004 Journal Citation Reports (JCR), we partitioned 1,431 journals connected by 217,287 citations into fifty-four modules. For visual simplicity, we show only the most important links, namely those that a random surfer traverses at least once in 2,000 steps, and the modules that are connected by these links.

investigate a topic, addresses only questions of praxelogy, or knowledge practices, and not questions of ontology (what exists?), epistemology (what do we know and how do we know what we know?), or axiology (what values drive what we know?). In fact, some scholars (e.g., Herbst, 2008; Menand, 2001) have recently questioned the whole notion of interdisciplinarity, claiming, instead, that the very notion of interdisciplinarity supports the continuing existence of disciplines. In order to get our work done, we must get beyond disciplines, or be *post*-disciplinary. From that perspective, communication, unwittingly perhaps, is ahead of the curve. In any case, if interdisciplarity is relevant only praxeologically speaking (how we gather the knowledge we gain), and if we want to know what communication or communication theory *is*, we must turn to additional questions including those of ontology, epistemology, and axiology (Anderson, 1996).

Many social sciences struggle, to lesser and greater extents, with these philosophical issues. Answering these questions helps determine the kind of research one does. At the same time, the research we do helps us answer these questions, because various social science methods and theories carry with them certain assumptions that inherently point to an answer to these questions. Each of us likely has an answer to the question: what do I know to exist? This ontological question of existence is intricately linked to epistemological questions of what constitutes knowledge and how that knowledge is derived. Praxeologically, disciplines vary in terms of what practices they use to generate knowledge. Indeed, such turf wars are rife within disciplines, as well. Lastly, a careful examination of our own values may reveal to us the extent to which those values influence our research, from the topics we choose to the methods enacted. In this way, we address axiological questions. In communication, specifically, various subfields take a stand, consciously, less consciously, or self-consciously, on how they answer each of these questions.

For example, Anderson and Baym (2004) provide a template for understanding various subfields within communication as they relate to these four primary questions of ontology, epistemology, praxeology, and axiology. Basically, they suggest that within communication's many subfields (e.g., media effects, organizational communication, rhetoric), each one answers the four questions somewhat differently and thus these subfields can be understood differently at some very basic level. In fact, they go on to say that answers to these questions can be presented on a continuum, one continuum for each question, thus resulting in a typology (see Figure 2.2). For example, in the figure, the dimensions seem to fall not just on philosophical dimensions overall, but on ontological dimensions in particular. The authors argue that within the discipline of communication, we divide along these issues into two major positions, or at least into two anchors along a continuum:

> In ontology we divide over whether the objects of our analysis have an independent or socially determined existence. . . . In epistemology the

division tracks along a foundationalism that holds knowledge as the correspondence between mental impression and the true shape of the independently existent actual, and a social constructionism that holds knowledge as simultaneous enabled and constrained within social achievement. In praxelogy, most are familiar with the quantoid/qualoid disputes, but . . . the real break may be over [a split between] whether claims need to be fixed in observation or [in] ideas. Finally, in axiology, the split is across the value-free (objectivism) and value-intended (subjectivism).

(pp. 590–591)

Based on this typology, Anderson and Baym (2004) situate various approaches, scholarship communities, and research examples into quadrants, thus providing a typology for communication scholarship. For example, a recent article on

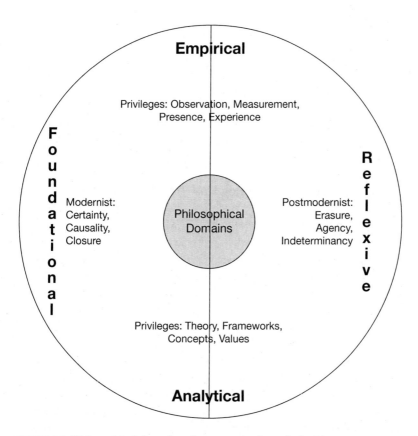

FIGURE 2.2 Philosophical domains of communication scholarship.

Source: Anderson & Baym (2004).

deception detection (Levine, 2011), a topic of interest in communication, utilized an experimental design to statistically examine the effect of sender demeanor, among other variables, on deception detection. This piece of scholarship took an ontological approach that assumed that deception detection exists independently as a construct; that epistemologically, knowledge is a true correspondence between mental impression of a thing and that thing's actual existence; that praxeologically, claims should be fixed in observation and quantitatively analyzed; and axiologically, the research could attempt to be value-free. In this way, the research was a classic piece of quantitative social science, or what is commonly referred to as communication science.

Another example of communication scholarship that we apply here to Anderson and Baym's (2004) typology is a recent study using in-depth interviews with low-income women regarding sex education (Bute & Jensen, 2011). These scholars used narrative theory and qualitative, semi-structured interviews and thematic analysis to examine how low-income women recalled their sex education and connected this to their sexual health knowledge. This piece of scholarship took an ontological approach that assumed that recall and narratives are socially determined; that epistemologically, knowledge is socially constructed; that praxeologically, claims should be qualitatively analyzed; and axiologically, the research should pursue some goal, perhaps in this case for the betterment of sexual knowledge about sexual health among low-income women. In this way, the research was a good example of qualitative, interview-based scholarship. Using this typology, we should be able to assess many (although not all) kinds of communication scholarship.

The thought-provoking exercise undertaken by Anderson and Baym (2004), which attempts to categorize communication research, allows us to understand the complexity and breadth of communication, seeing how critical studies, rhetoric, communication science, performance studies, even topical areas such as health communication can be understood in terms of their different philosophical roots. But the typology does little to provide us with a clear answer of what communication *is*, that is, the essence of communication that unites this scholarship. In fact, at the end of the article they state that "none of us can claim to be *a* communication scholar as each of us must be *some kind* of communication scholar" (p. 610). Thus, they sidestep questions about the relationship between subfields of communication and their commonalities and focus instead on divisions in the field, leaving us with no satisfying answer as to what communication is.

Perhaps this leads us to the inevitable question: is there a coherent field of communication scholarship? Have the 25 years since Peters' (1986) claim of philosophical incoherence in communication led us to believe any differently? We move now from discussing the various approaches to communication research and scholarship to attempting to see the commonality among subfields in order to get a better understanding of what communication is.

Communication: Starting with Phenomena

In Chapter 1, we argued that theory must start with a thorough exploration and explication of a particular phenomenon, and from there could move on to understanding variables, theoretical linkages between variables, and the operationalizations of those variables. If we are to begin with phenomena, in this case, communication, we have to ask, at its very root, what is communication? Certainly, there are many definitions. Introductory, undergraduate textbooks offer a good starting place to find out what communication *is*. That is, an examination of the definitions written by communication scholars offers us some insight into the epistemology of communication.

A very basic definition is offered by Trenholm (1986, p. 4): "Communication is a process by which a source transmits a message to a receiver through some channel." This basic definition specifies the need for a sender, a receiver, a message, and a channel in order for communication to be achieved. As we discuss in Chapter 3, this definition arose out of the particular pragmatic needs (e.g., to study propaganda) present in World War II, around which social scientific aspects of the discipline were built. In its simplicity, the definition may seem overly basic, but it does identify the main parts of a communicative event and, in this way, is useful in simply offering defining characteristics of the thing. In fact, colloquially, we often use the term communication in just that way: to indicate the transmission of a message or ideas from a source to a receiver. A more vague and poetic definition is provided by Barnlund (1968, p. 127), who defines communication as an "effort after meaning." Although this definition is too vague to be pragmatically useful, it does stress the importance of meaning, or as Masterson and colleagues (1983, p. 73) state, "Communication is a process through which we make sense out of the world and share that sense with others." That is, there may be more to a message than implied in the most basic definition. A message is assigned meaning, and often the very essence of effective communication is *shared* meaning. Thus, in addition to a sender, a receiver, a message, and a channel, the term *meaning* is important when defining communication. A final aspect of the definition that is often included is that of symbols. Berelson and Steiner, in an early definition (1964, p. 527), identify communication as "the transmission of information, ideas, emotions, skills, etc., by the use of symbols." Although they do not use the term *meaning* in their definition, they do imply it by extending the definition beyond the inclusion of mere information transmission.

We can see, therefore, that communication has been defined in many ways and that, at least from an epistemological perspective, we might argue that communication as a construct is defined in so many ways precisely because it existed as a colloquial term, and an oft-used one at that, long before it emerged as a potentially meaningful academic term. Unlike sociology, for example, or economics, whose academic emergence colonized sparsely populated terms, communication had to wrestle the academic term from very crowded territory and never really laid claim to it. We continue to borrow it from noncommunication scientists and continue to do so apologetically. It is in part because it is a borrowed term that there is little agreement on a single definition of communication. Instead, we can only draw some general conclusions about what communication is in terms of existing definitions. From those existing definitions, we can conclude that communication is the process of sending a message from a source to a receiver over some channel, through the use of symbols, in order to share meaning between two entities.

Given the preceding discussion, which examines several ways of thinking about what communication is, including its interdisciplinarity, its philosophical roots, and its primary definitions, it may be worthwhile to consider what constitutes communication research. Given that communication as a process is so basic to our lives, is there anything in the social sciences that *cannot* be construed as communication? And if so, we know readily that something that is everything risks being nothing in particular. In short, if communication is everything, is it nothing, really?

In short, no, everything is not communication. Rather, we address here the idea that communication is indeed a broad phenomenon, one that occurs throughout much of our days. But communication as a construct of study within the field of communication requires a communication perspective that typically has several characteristics. Earlier, we claimed that communication scholars were united by their focus on a common phenomenon. However, we can go beyond that and claim that communication as a phenomenon becomes a discipline because of the common elements in communication theory and research. Although examples from different areas of communication are relevant here (e.g., rhetoric, cultural studies, communication science), the focus will be predominantly on communication science as dictated by the primary focus of this book.

Characteristics of Communication Study

In other chapters, the specific methods and approaches of communication science will be addressed. However, here, a more broad-based approach is taken, with an attempt to identify commonalities in the study of communication, regardless of the methodological approach being taken. In fact, to some extent, the following set of elements attempts to move beyond even any specific theoretical perspectives. Not every element applies to every piece of scholarship; however, they provide a framework for understanding the commonalities across studies.

1. Communication Has, as Its Focus, a Communication Phenomenon or Incident

A speech, a persuasive public service announcement (PSA), a supportive message delivered face to face, a television program. From that starting point, these studies may diverge in terms of what *else* the researchers are exploring: the influence of the message, the cultural context in which it was produced, the use of various strategies *in* the message, the personality variables of the person who chose to consume it, for example. Furthermore, the phenomenon might be studied by means of an experiment, a textual analysis, a survey, a content analysis. But the commonality is the focus on, or inclusion of, the communication message.

2. Communication Has, as Its Focus, Communication as a Process

Many studies in communication focus on communication as a single event. However, an important, some would argue crucial, aspect of communication as a field of study is the recognition of communication as a process, wherein it is difficult to extract one message from the stream and understand it without additional elements from that stream or process. Thus, a critical analysis of a message will consider the social context in which it was produced or the individual interpretation of the message recipient. An experiment will be designed to measure a number of variables about the message recipient, or manipulate various aspects of the message reception environment. In other words, communication as a process does produce messages but communication as an area of study most often considers communication as a process and attempts to measure relevant aspects of the process.

3. Assessment of Likely or Actual Outcomes of Communication

Many studies in communication are interested in the effects or outcomes of messages. Whereas some areas, such as research on media effects, do so explicitly, exploring, for example, the effects of violent video games on players, other areas of research do so implicitly. Relational communication, for example, may explore how couples interact and the outcomes of particular messages. A rhetorical study may examine a speech and apply a given rhetorical approach to assess the persuasiveness (or likely persuasiveness) of that speech. A feminist approach to the study of teen magazines may consider how messages, in a given cultural context, function to influence girls' self-perceptions. Importantly, examination of message effects and outcomes assumes that communication is a process and, thus, is linked to characteristic #2 above, but also implies a particular way of understanding the process that sees the message itself as crucial.

4. An Understanding of the Interlocutors

Whereas messages are seen as crucial by communication scholars, the interlocutors themselves are often of primary focus in the investigation (e.g., Bodie et al., 2011;

Krcmar & Greene, 1999). The text alone is sometimes assessed by rhetoricians, critical studies scholars, and communication scientists, but usually, communication research extends the focus beyond the text to the people creating or making sense of it. In other words, and again referring back to #2 above, if communication is a process, then the individuals involved in that process are understood to bring with them social, psychological, cognitive, developmental, and other factors that may play a role in message creation and reception. Communication scholars, therefore, understand the individual as key in the process.

5. Communication Searches for Regularities, Measured or Theoretically Described

Berger et al. (2010) state that: "For communication scientists, the problem to be solved is one of identifying and then explaining regularities by constructing and testing theories" (p. 7). Whereas their focus is clearly on communication science, an area where regularities, measured and assessed statistically, are key, other areas of communication search for regularities as well. While other areas may not explore these regularities statistically, theory itself implies a generalization. A theory that applied to only one instance of an event, communicative or otherwise, would be useless. Thus, communication scientists, and communication researchers in general, seek out regularities in messages, cultural devices, speech modes, audience responses to messages, or individual responses to messages. Regularities in communication processes allow the field to exist and cohere. Without them, we could derive no generalizations whatsoever and the field would truly not exist as a field. Regularities, seeking them out, describing them, theorizing about them, and in some cases statistically measuring them, are what allows social science to progress.

6. A Consideration of the Context of a Communication

The context in which a communication occurs is relevant to the effects of that communication (Coe & Neumann, 2011). There are many ways in which communication scholars consider context, from integrating context into their understanding of a message at a theoretical level (Kosenko, 2011) to identifying and either manipulating or measuring contextual cues (Farrar et al., 2006). In most cases, communication is understood to occur in a particular context, and that context is seen as, once again, important to the process of communication. Whereas communication research does not always consider context by measuring it or mentioning it theoretically, it is typically understood to be relevant and thus part of a communication interaction. It is, therefore, a characteristic of communication as a phenomenon and often as an area of study and theorizing.

7. An Understanding of the Channels of Communication, Organizationally or Socially Defined

Communication scholars also understand that channels, be they interpersonal, face-to-face exchanges, or internet websites or television news networks, are relevant to the communication process. Indeed, when Canadian rhetorician Marshall McLuhan claimed that "the medium is the message" (Stacks & Salwen, 1996), he not only established himself as a cultural icon, he expressed a communication approach that understands that channel matters. Indeed, recent research (Lee & Shin, 2014) has found that participants showed a preference for one channel over another to deliver identical messages. Thus, communication research assumes channel to play an important role in the communicative process.

In all, what defines communication research is both its focus of study and *some* agreement among those who conduct communication research on what constitutes important areas of focus, as described above. Whereas there remains vigorous debate in the field among those who believe that mass communication and interpersonal communication are distinct fields, or those who claim that one or the other of the quantitative and qualitative approaches is irrelevant due to inherent errors in questions of ontology and epistemology (Anderson & Baym, 2004), many researchers go about their work with an acceptance of distinctions that they may or may not see as relevant. Given the inevitability of movement, if not progress, one might ask if the field of communication, coherent or not, has made progress?

Has Communication Scholarship Made a Difference?

Frey (2009) argues quite simply that the best gauge for understanding that communication scholarship has made a difference is the simple fact that it is now commonly accepted that good communication, however defined, makes for stronger relationships, better group decisions, more efficient organizations, and more seemingly electable politicians. He argues that in the 1970s, when communication as a discipline was, if not in infancy, at least in middle childhood, the notion that communication mattered to such things was radical. He claims that "there can be little doubt that the academic disciplinary study of communication . . . contributed to the explosion of 'communication consciousness' in the twentieth century" (p. 206). However, it is not clear that mere awareness of communication, as it is popularized, has anything to do with communication as a discipline. Do self-help books written to help troubled relationships cite communication scholarship?

As Timmerman (2009) argues, "media outlets fail to recognize our discipline's expertise about topics that are clearly communication-centered phenomena" (p. 202). Furthermore, Frey (2009) goes on to suggest that more use of interventions may be necessary to bridge academic research with practical application.

In either case, the mere fact that the term "communication" has made it into common use does not seem evidence itself that communication scholarship has made a difference, only that many individuals use the term. The head of household who wants to create an economical budget does not likely consult principles of microeconomics, either. So has communication made a difference?

Condit (2009) suggests that there are very few communication theories that have been developed primarily by members of the communication discipline. Rather, "our most prominent theorists are those who introduce or imitate the work of other disciplines. Most quantitative social scientists try to make themselves into psychologists and most rhetoricians make themselves into philosophers, historians and ideological critics" (p. 4). If this is the case, and it is not certain that it is, then what of interdisciplinarity? Should this be abandoned in the face of rigid adherence to communication scholarship so that the discipline itself can lay claim to any human progress resulting from a program of research? Is it necessary to have communication theory that is solely constructed by communication scholars, whose ideas themselves are based on research in communication? Logically, this endless regress would dismantle almost any social science, even older disciplines such as psychology.

Instead, the question of difference making should perhaps emphasize a different word. That is, when asked if communication scholarship has made a difference, focus can be placed on communication or on difference. With a focus on the latter, we can suggest that communication scholarship has made some difference. Certainly, more can be done, but differences have been made, several of which will be highlighted below.

First, theories have offered more than a framework on which to build additional research. If, as Kurt Lewin said, there is nothing as practical as good theory (Stacks & Salwen, 1996), then theory that is applied should indicate difference making. Seeger and colleagues (2009) make a case for diffusion of innovations, a theory that has "Profound influence in agriculture, public health, marketing and organizational studies . . . It informed development efforts in many nations in Asia, South America and Africa" (p. 15). Seeger goes on to argue that especially in areas of public health such as family planning, clean water, and AIDS prevention, the theory has been utilized and applied. From the perspective taken by Seeger, difference making can be seen when theory informs practice, either directly, as is the case with the application of diffusion of innovations, or indirectly. Kathleen Hall Jamieson and Kathleen Kendall, both communication scholars housed in communication departments, were frequent guests on NPR and the MacNeal–Lehrer news hour, utilizing their rhetorical analytical skills and rhetorical theory to assess speeches and debates during the 2008 presidential campaign (Hummert, 2009), and again in 2012.

A second way that communication scholarship has made a difference is in intervention work. By using communication theory that itself has been tested in various studies, appropriate interventions can be designed and used (e.g., Byrne

& Senehi, 2012—violence intervention studies). Subsequently, the effectiveness of a given intervention can be used as evidence that communication scholarship makes a difference. For example, several AIDS prevention campaigns have been tested utilizing a communication framework (e.g., Smith et al., 2007), campaigns encouraging the use of sunscreen have been examined (e.g., Parrott & Duggan, 1999), as have campaigns promoting a healthy diet (Parrott et al., 1996). Thus, specific campaigns are influenced by communication scholarship both in the design phase and in order to discover their ultimate effectiveness.

Third, Seeger et al. (2009) note that one of the primary ways that communication scholarship effects change is through instruction. Whereas some scholars focus their research attention on actual pedagogical practices and outcomes (e.g., McCroskey et al., 1995), many others present research in their classrooms as a means of educating future practitioners on effective persuasion techniques, for example. Communication is, after all, a practical discipline, one whose students have very clear paths from the classroom to the professional world, whether that world is one that will result in a Public Relations position, journalism profession, or, as became of one of my recent students, a political speech writer. Thus, from the theoretical to the practical, communication scholarship is difference making.

We turn our attention now to an even more pragmatic aspect of communication. When we ask: "What is communication?", an understanding of the organizational elements of communication is necessary, including attention to university departments, discipline associations, and journals. In the next section, we will explore communication not as a process with philosophical roots, theories to be explored and understood, and research to be consumed. Rather, we will examine what communication is as a discipline. In other words, we will consider the process of communication by considering the purely pragmatic part of the discipline: its academic life.

Communication in the Academy

In an academic world devoid of politics and turf wars, budgets and budget cuts, grants and ego-driven debates, researchers would go about the business of research, exploring ideas, engaging in debates purely for the excitement of knowledge building, and creating a world of research and resulting knowledge to make the world a better place. And some of that occurs. But communication as a discipline is also part of the real world of universities, where, quite simply, administrative decisions have an influence on the process of knowledge building. Whereas we will not spend too much time talking about the broad and far-reaching implications of politics and budgets across the academy, we will talk about how communication is situated in terms of its place in the academy, and its working within the discipline itself. Understanding that process can (and perhaps should) aid in an understanding of communication as a phenomenon.

As we will discuss at greater length in Chapter 3, the history of communication is one that brought together seemingly disparate areas of exploration. As a result of some combination of commonality in subject matter, administrative convenience, and historical accident, one communication department might house a scholar who explores classical Aristotelian rhetoric, a health communication researcher who conducts experiments to test the effectiveness of safe sex PSAs, a critical scholar who studies the racial implications of situation comedies, and a relational researcher who does ethnographic research on parent–child relationships in low-income families. In fact, this list is rather limited and does not quite encompass the broad scope of communication scholarship in many departments. So why, then, is it all communication?

We mentioned, first, a commonality in subject matter. At the very simplest level, communication researchers study messages. Not limited to a particular research method, communication research instead is most often boundaried based on subject matter. The universe of what is considered acceptable data, the data-gathering method, the interpretive lens by which the data are considered, the theories used, all may differ from one scholar to the next but the subject matter is somewhat constant. It is an almost embarrassing truism to say that communication scholars study communication, but we are permitted to say that, because communication is an object in and of itself. Hence, we can refer to *a* communication, whereas sociologists, anthropologists, and psychologists can make no such claim.

Second, those in communication departments exist together due to administrative convenience. Administrators in universities prefer combining departments to splitting them up. After all, one copy machine (and department secretary, and chairperson) is cheaper than two. In the post-World War II era when communication was emerging as a discipline, rather than providing communication scholars, who at the time might have had Ph.D.s from sister disciplines in any case, a separate and new department, some universities housed them in English or theater departments, or in journalism schools. These departments may have been somewhat disparate at the time but they worked, at least for the administration. Over time, as communication established itself as a distinct discipline with distinct majors and degree programs, theoretical approaches, journals, and conferences, departments may have been split into more meaningful subgroups. Or maybe not.

It is this other possibility that brings us to the third point. Communication departments may exist in their particular configuration due to historical accident, although not necessarily one with problematic outcomes. Consider the case of rhetoric. Long before mass communication scholars became interested in propaganda prior to World War II, rhetoricians, with their roots in Plato and Aristotle and Cicero, were conducting the work of rhetoric. When communication emerged as a discipline, some mass communication scholars were foisted onto their academic second cousins in rhetoric, and there they remained. Now, does this very truncated history suggest that communication does not have a coherent field, and that from a pragmatic perspective we share department space primarily through administrative action (or inaction)? Lang (2011), taking the case of mass communication and interpersonal communication, argues that the two subfields are separate disciplines, as evidenced by their institutional housing. She claims that: "they are generally located in separate departments, with the interpersonal scholars located in departments of speech communication or rhetoric, sometimes in English and at others in departments called human communication. On the other, mass communication departments are often located in schools of journalism" (p. 3). Administrative divisions, however, should be seen as just that. Indeed, we argue that communication is a single discipline because, as mentioned earlier, we share in common the focus on the phenomenon of communication. Second, new and emerging technologies have made the mass/interpersonal distinction less and less meaningful. One can already see many examples of cross-pollination where studies in traditionally mass communication areas apply traditionally interpersonal theory (e.g., Cho, 2011) in human communication research. Thus, despite a sometimes messy administrative structure, as evidenced by many variations on departments' make-ups, the administrative aspect must follow the design of the discipline and not vice versa.

Communication Associations, Conferences, and Journals

Associations and their conferences are a mainstay of academic life. Associations, whose members are often communication researchers and educators but may be professional practitioners, as well, utilize associations to keep up with news in the discipline, network with colleagues, and publicize their own work. If you browse the website of the National Communication Association (NCA), for example, you can read summaries of recent research, learn about the Association's journals, and find out about the annual conferences. The main associations in the discipline of communication are the International Communication Association and the National Communication Association. Both have thousands of members who work on issues relevant to communication by conducting research, teaching, and, in some cases, applying communication. Both are broad in scope and cover all aspects of communication, diversely defined. Other Associations as more narrow, either by focus, or by region. For example, the Association of Education in Journalism and Mass Communication focuses on mass communication alone and members typically do not study classical rhetoric, interpersonal communication, performance studies, or any of the many areas of communication that do not include a mass communication focus. Other associations, such as the Rhetoric Society of America, are also more narrowly defined. In addition to topically focused associations, smaller associations may focus on a region. For example, the United States has several smaller, regional communication associations (e.g., Central States Communication Association). Similarly, many countries in Europe and Asia also have their own communication associations (e.g., German Communication Association). Like many organizations, communication associations have hierarchies made up of elected officials, and divisions that focus on various areas of research specialty. Divisions themselves have elected officials.

Arguably the single most important aspect of association membership is participation in the annual conference, which is held in a different city each year, typically on the same week each year. Conference attendance is large (well over 5,000 participants and more than 1,200 sessions for NCA in 2014). The main goal of the conference, beyond networking and socializing, is to disseminate research conducted by the members, research that is presented in various themed panels. Acceptance of a paper and its subsequent presentation at a conference is often the first step in publishing that work.

Publication, of course, is what gets the research in the hands of other researchers, students, and practitioners. There are many communication journals and to list them would be lengthy and would risk suggesting preference for one over the other. The interested reader is directed to the database Communication and Mass Media Complete, which, as the name implies, offers a more thorough list of published communication outlets. It is through these journals that scholarship is published and disseminated. However, more importantly, what is accepted and printed in communication journals becomes the communication canon. Thus, beyond the obvious role of sharing communication scholarship, communication journals define communication. By publishing some research papers and rejecting others, journals, their editors and reviewers, subtly and sometimes not so subtly shape what we know in communication. Journals determine viable foci of inquiry, appropriate research methods, and apposite ways of presenting findings. Journals shape the discipline and its research in very meaningful ways. This is not to suggest some conspiracy theory. Simply this: research that gets published guides future research. In this way, journal editors and reviewers guide communication as a discipline to adhere to a certain way of seeing the world or, in some cases, suggest new ways. Similarly, associations exert influence on members by conference paper acceptance and presentation. Academic departments in universities, and the professors who populate them, determine what gets taught in the classroom and ultimately, then, what future practitioners deem relevant (at least in part). Thus, the very pragmatic issue of discipline structure begins to appear more important when viewed through this lens. Thus, communication is both about the philosophy and the theory that undergirds it, and the real, pragmatic aspects of the discipline. Both ultimately help answer the question: what is communication?

References

Anderson, J. (1996). *Communicative theory: Epistemological foundation.* New York: Guilford Press.

Anderson, J., & Baym, G. (2004). Philosophies and philosophic issues in communication, 1995–2004. *Journal of Communication, 4*(54), 589–615.

Barnlund, D. (1968). *Interpersonal communication: Survey and studies.* Boston, MA: Houghton Mifflin.

Berelson, B., & Steiner, G. (1964). *Human behavior: An inventory of scientific findings.* New York: Harcourt, Brace & World.

Berger, C. R., Roloff, M. E., & Roskos-Ewoldsen, D. R. (2010). *What is communication science?* Thousand Oaks, CA: Corwin Press.

Bodie, G., Burleson, B. R., & Holmstrom, A. J. (2011). Effects of cognitive complexity and emotional upset on processing support messages: Two tests of a dual-process theory of supportive communication outcomes. *Human Communication Research, 3*(37), 350–376.

Bute, J., & Jensen, R. (2011). Narrative sensemaking and time lapse: Interviews with low-income women about sex education. *Communication Monographs, 2*(78), 212–232.

Byrne, S., & Senehi, J. (2012). *Violence: Analysis, intervention, and prevention.* Athens, OH: Ohio University Press.

Cho, J. (2011). Geography of political communication: Effects of regional variations in campaign advertising on citizen communication. *Human Communication Research, 37*(3), 302–308.

Coe, K., & Neumann, R. (2011). The major addresses of modern presidents: Parameters of a data set. *Presidential Studies Quarterly, 4*(41), 727–751.

Condit, C. M. (2009). *You can't study and improve communication with a telescope.* Athens, GA: University of Georgia Press.

Eigenfactor.org. (2004). *Map of the social sciences.* Retrieved from www.eigenfactor.org/map/SocSci2004.pdf

Farrar, K., Krcmar, M., & Nowak, K. (2006). Contextual features of violent video games, mental models, and aggression. *Journal of Communication, 2*(56), 387–405.

Frey, L. R. (2009). What a difference more difference-making communication scholarship might make: Making a difference from and through communication research. *Journal of Applied Communication Research, 2*(37), 205–214.

Gonzalez, H. (1988). The evolution of communication as a field. *Communication Research, 15*(3), 302–308.

Herbst, S. (2008). Disciplines, intersections, and the future of communication research. *Journal of Communication, 58*(4), 603–614.

Hummert, M. L. (2009). Not just preaching to the choir: Communication scholarship does make a difference. *Journal of Applied Communication Research, 37*(2), 215–224.

Kosenko, K. A. (2011). The safer sex communication of transgender adults: Processes and problems. *Journal of Communication, 61,* 476–495.

Krcmar, M., & Greene, K. (1999). Predicting exposure to and uses of television violence. *Journal of Communication, 3*(49), 24–45.

Lang, A. (2013). Discipline in Crisis? The Shifting Paradigm of Mass Communication Research. *Communication Theory, 23,* 10–24. Available at http://onlinelibrary.wiley.com/doi/10.1111/comt.2013.23.issue-1/issuetoc

Lee, E., & Shin, Y. S. (2014). When the medium is the message: How transportability moderates the effects of politicians' Twitter communication. *Communication Research, 41*(8), 1088–1110.

Levine, T. (2011). Sender demeanor: Individual differences in sender believability have a powerful impact on deception detection judgments. *Human Communication Research, 3*(37), 377–403.

Masterson, J., Beebe, S., & Watson, N. (1983). *Speech communication: Theory and practice*. New York: Holt, Rinehart & Winston.

McCroskey, J. C., Richmond, V. P., Sallinen, A., Fayer, J. M., & Barraclough, R. A. (1995). A cross-cultural and multi-behavioral analysis of the relationship between nonverbal immediacy and teacher evaluation. *Communication Education, 44*, 281–291.

Menand, L. (2001). Undisciplined. *The Wilson Quarterly (1976–), 25*(4), 51–59.

Parrott, R., & Duggan, A. (1999). Using coaches as role models of sun protection for youth: Georgia's "Got Youth Covered" project. *Journal of Applied Communication Research, 27*(2), 107–119.

Parrott, R., Steiner, C., & Goldenhar, L. (1996). Georgia's harvesting healthy habits: A formative evaluation. *The Journal of Rural Health, 12*(S4), 291–300.

Peters, J. D. (1986). Institutional sources of intellectual poverty in communication research. *Communication Research, 13*(4), 527–559.

Rosvall, M., & Bergstrom, C. T. (2007). An information-theoretic framework for resolving community structure in complex networks. *Proceedings of the National Academy of Sciences, 18*(104), 7327–7331.

Seeger, M. W., Sellnow, T., & Ulmer, R. L. (2009). Crisis communication and the public health. *Journal of Communication, 59*(2), 22–24.

Smith, R. A., Downs, E., & Witte, K. (2007). Drama theory and entertainment education: Exploring the effects of a radio drama on behavioral intentions to limit HIV transmission in Ethiopia. *Communication Monographs, 74*, 133–53.

Stacks, D. W., & Salwen, M. B. (1996). *An integrated approach to communication theory and research*. New York: Routledge.

Timmerman, C. E. (2009). Introduction: Has communication research made a difference? *Journal of Applied Communication Research, 2*(37), 202–204.

Trenholm, S. (1986). *Human communication theory* (vol. 38). Englewood Cliffs, NJ: Prentice-Hall.

3
HISTORY OF COMMUNICATION

Communication is arguably the newest discipline in the social sciences. Indeed, Chaffee and Rogers (1997) maintain that communication may be the only widely accepted discipline to emerge in the United States during the past century. Further, the argument can be made that communication was the fastest-growing discipline in the social sciences during the latter part of the twentieth century. In part, the burgeoning interest in communication corresponded with the emergence of new tools of communication across the past 150 years, including movies, telephone, radio, television, and the Internet. But while research did reflect the new technologies (Anderson & Colvin, 2008), tying the emerging discipline to the emergence of new technologies oversimplifies the story. It can be argued that a distinct discipline of communication only emerged after World War II, though other scholars place the emergence of the discipline in the 1960s, and the argument has been made that the discipline is still emerging (Delia, 1987; Glander, 2009; Rogers, 1994; Sproule, 2015). But any of these dates are several decades after the widespread availability of movies and radio. So while these technologies spurred an interest in understanding communication, their invention alone cannot explain the emergence of the discipline. There were many forces that played a role in the development of this discipline including both of the world wars in the twentieth century.

Writing a history of the discipline of communication is a difficult task. To begin with, there really are a number of disciplines involved in this story (Anderson & Colvin, 2008), as was discussed very briefly in Chapter 1. Early on, there was what was historically called *speech communication*, which traces its roots to the rhetoricians of Ancient Greece.[1] During the early twentieth century, many of these departments were dominated by rhetoricians and were hostile to the emerging social sciences (Chaffee & Rogers, 1997; Sproule, 2015), though social science approaches have come to dominate the discipline in the meantime

(Anderson & Middleton, 2015). In addition, at many universities these early departments focused heavily on the teaching of communication skills rather than theoretically driven research. Second, there is a part of the discipline that reflects professional schools of journalism, which trace their roots to the early part of the twentieth century (Chaffee & Rogers, 1997). Finally, there is the part of the discipline that has emerged as the largest area within the discipline, at least in terms of publications (Anderson & Middleton, 2015), which studies communication from a social scientific approach. The use of social scientific methods to study communication started between the two world wars, but really emerged after World War II (Delia, 1987; Rogers, 1994), as will be discussed in Chapter 6. The history of this part of the discipline has received the most attention by academic writers and is often referred to as the "received view" of the discipline's history. Of course, Europe also had a history of communication research. Critical scholarship appeared in Germany at the Frankfurt School after World War I and cultural studies emerged in England starting in the late 1950s and early 1960s.

Further exacerbating an understanding of our history, the first book-length treatment of the discipline was published just over 20 years ago (Rogers, 1994). This book reflected a biographical approach to the discipline's history by focusing on the "great scholars" who played a role in the discipline's emergence. Prior to that time, the history had been retold and formalized in textbooks and debated in a few academic journal articles and book chapters. Further complicating the historical treatment of the discipline, the first few book-length treatments of the history of the discipline were written by communication scholars—not historians —and reflected the received history of the discipline (Bineham, 1988; Pooley, 2008). However, as Delia (1987) noted, the received view of the discipline is problematic for several reasons. It privileged social scientific work within the discipline, was concentrated fairly exclusively on the study of media with a focus on media effects, and ignored what was occurring in Europe (Delia, 1987; Pooley, 2008).

In the past 20 years, the received history has come under increasing attack by both historians and scholars from both the critical and cultural schools of communication (Bineham, 1988; Glander, 2009). In this chapter, we will attempt to merge these three histories—the received view, the biographical approach, and the emerging critical history—into a coherent story of how the discipline of communication came into being. We will do this by breaking the study of the emergence of communication into the period between the two world wars (1910s to 1940), World War II (1940 to 1947), and after the war (1947 to 1965). Of course, these dates are crude demarcations, but they serve a useful heuristic function.

Between the World Wars

Early academic thinking about communication arose largely out of societal concerns (Delia, 1987). These concerns included the implications of mass media and propaganda for democracy, and the impact of radio and movies on children. In addition, there was one notable example of the effect of the media on the mass public—the *War of the World* broadcast in October, 1938. Lastly, the emergence of critical scholarship in Germany arose as another important development that would influence the history of communication. In addition to these events within communication other disciplines studied communication topics and their approaches influenced the emerging discipline.

Propaganda and the Hypodermic Needle Model of Media Effects

World War I started in 1914. The United States took a strong position of neutrality in the 3 years prior to its involvement in the war in 1917. However, once the United States declared war, the government felt that public support for the war had to be quickly mobilized. Consequently, President Wilson created the Committee on Public Information (CPI) in the spring of 1917 (Starr, 2004). The CPI relied primarily on a three-pronged approach to create U.S. support for the war. First, the CPI put informal pressure on established newspapers to support the war (Glander, 2009). The Espionage Act of 1917 aided the CPI in pressuring newspapers by making it a crime to engage in communication that could undermine the military or advocate the overthrow of the government (Dewey, 1918; Glander, 2009). The Espionage Act was further strengthened by the passage of the Sedition Act a year later in 1918 (Starr, 2004). Second, the CPI created the Four-Minute Men. The Four-Minute Men consisted of approximately 75,000 volunteers who made short speeches at public gatherings across the country (Glander, 2009; Rogers, 1994).[2] These speeches were highly coordinated and their goal was to persuade the general population of the necessity of the war, to mobilize increased levels of participation in the war effort, and to respond to any exigencies that arose during the war. Finally, the CPI created and disseminated pamphlets and educational materials to schools to further garner support for the war (Glander, 2009; Rogers, 1994).

The CPI quickly changed the national attitude toward the war from one of neutrality to one of strong support for U.S. involvement in the war. However, the success of the CPI led many academics and commentators to begin questioning the use of propaganda by the government in the 1920s and onward (Glander, 2009; Rogers, 1994). For example, John Dewey—the noted education scholar and philosopher—argued in an essay in 1918 that while mobilization for the war had ended with the armistice, the use of propaganda by the government appeared to continue, and this threatened democracy. Further fueling the concern with propaganda was the rise of Fascist movements in Italy and Germany (and to a lesser extent, in the United States). But the successful use of propaganda also spurred the academic study of propaganda, such as Howard Lasswell's (1927) *Propaganda Technique in the World War* (Delia, 1987; Rogers, 1994). While this volume was primarily descriptive and atheoretical, from a methodological standpoint Lasswell's work on propaganda helped establish content analysis as a useful research tool for studying media content (Delia, 1987). Lasswell continued this work during World War II to help understand the propaganda used by both the Axis and the Allies during the war (Rogers, 1994).

Another important outgrowth of the research on propaganda was an increased interest in the study of public opinion (Delia, 1987; Glander, 2009). An important early writer on public opinion was Walter Lippmann. Lippmann was a journalist and political commentator for much of the twentieth century (Jansen, 2008; Rogers, 1994). But his book—*Public Opinion* (Lippmann, 1922)—was highly critical of the role of newspapers in democracy (Dewey, 1922). Lippmann argued that newspapers could not provide all of the information that is necessary for a functional democracy, but instead fed the stereotypes of the readers and, through this process, undermined the processes of democracy. In addition, Lippmann's writings have been credited with laying the foundation for agenda-setting theory (see Chapter 13). While some have challenged this pessimistic reading of Lippmann (Jansen, 2008), it is difficult to come away from *Public Opinion* without feeling that Lippmann is cynical about the role of newspapers in liberal democracy.[3] The starting of the journal *Public Opinion* further served to galvanize the study of public opinion as an academic area of interest. This journal served as an important catalyst for this important area of research. As a prominent outlet for research on politics and public opinion, the journal played an important role in the development of research on political communication.

Out of the research on propaganda grew one of the early theories of media effects—alternatively called the hypodermic needle or magic bullet model of media effects (Lubken, 2008). The hypodermic needle model was only vaguely specified (Bineham, 1988), but it is interpreted as maintaining that the media had powerful direct effects on its audience and operated like an injection that controlled a passive audience. One of the interesting things about this model is that while it is a widely identified early model of media effects, it is unclear where the model originated, and indeed, the hypodermic needle model may never really have been a "theory" of communication (Lubken, 2008), but rather introduced after the fact as an aspect of history. In fact, the first explicit reference to it is found in a report written by Elihu Katz in 1953 where he identified the theory, but was not an advocate for the theory (Bineham, 1988; Lubken, 2008). Lasswell's conception of propaganda likely played a role in the development of the magic bullet model of media effects (Delia, 1987; Lubken, 2008), because he clearly assumed a powerful effect of the communicator and the media on the individual listener. Likewise, Lippman's (1922) writing that newspapers were a powerful influence on people's stereotypes and knowledge of the world may have also played a role in the emergence of this model. However, it is important to note that it is unclear whether early media scholars ever actually subscribed to the hypodermic needle model or whether this is an invention of later scholars and this model was then imposed upon this earlier work (Bineham, 1988; Lubken, 2008; Pooley, 2008).

Emergence of Critical Scholarship in Germany

What has come to be known as the Frankfurt School of critical scholarship was started in the early 1920s in a loose association of scholars at the Institute for Social Research (which was founded in 1932). Notable scholars associated with the Frankfurt School include Max Horkheimer, Theodor Adorno, Herbert Marcuse, Erich Fromm, Walter Benjamin, and Jurgen Habermas (Bronner, 2011).[4] This is an eclectic set of scholars, which reflected the institute's commitment to interdisciplinary research, though critical scholars have traditionally been very critical of empirical research. The Institute for Social Research also published its own journal—*Journal for Social Research*—which served as an outlet for the scholars associated with the institute (Finlayson, 2005).

The critical scholars were a group of neo-Marxists and, to a lesser extent, Freudian scholars in Frankfurt who shared a powerful vision for media scholarship. Out of the Enlightenment period grew the modernist assumption that humans were inevitably progressing. The critical scholars challenged this assumption and they drew heavily from both Marx and Freud in leveling these challenges (Rogers, 1994). These scholars played a central role in combatting the notion of the modern and the idea that humans were inevitably making progress toward an ideal state (Bronner, 2011), though it is important to note that they were not strictly postmodernists (Best & Kellner, 1991).

While drawing from Marx, critical scholars did reject Marx's notion of economic determinism and his optimistic argument concerning the inevitability of socialism (Bronner, 2011). But they did take from Marx the idea that people are alienated from themselves through cultural apparatus that served the interests of those in power. The concept of alienation comes from Marx's manuscripts that he wrote in 1844, but which first appeared in 1932. Alienation reflects the idea that people are removed from themselves by the economic and cultural systems in which they live. For example, Erich Fromm, an early critical scholar, argued that human aggression is a consequence of an economic system that does not allow people to be creative, so that they are removed from themselves and their only way to exert control is through violence (Fromm, 1973). In other words, whereas Marx saw the powerful controlling the working class through economics, the critical scholars saw this control operating through what they called the cultural industries (Adorno, 1991). The cultural industries create desires in people for material goods that they do not need, and the pursuit of these goods serves to alienate people from their true desires (Bronner, 2011) as well as homogenizing the mass public so that the same desires are shared rather than people working toward their unique goals (Schweppenhauser, 2009). Consequently, critical scholars tend to take a very pessimistic view of culture (Lazarsfeld, 2004), and view mass culture as the creator of a passive population (Dworkin, 1997). In addition, they drew from Marx a commitment to the study of ideology. Finally, many critical scholars had a commitment to praxis—the idea that scholarship should serve to aid in the emancipation of people from power (Bronner, 2011), an idea that runs directly counter to those of the quantitative social sciences (see Chapters 4 and 5).

The Frankfurt School had to move several times due to the rise of the Nazis in Germany. Ultimately, during World War II many of the scholars associated with the Frankfurt School ended up at Columbia University in the United States. However, after the war, most of the scholars did end up back in Frankfurt as part of the institute (Bronner, 2011).

Concerns about the Influence of New Media on Children

Concerns about the damaging effects of new media on children are not a phenomenon of just that later part of the twentieth and early twenty-first centuries (Anderson & Colvin, 2008; Delia, 1987; Rogers, 1994). The introduction of new communication technologies has raised concerns about their effect on impressionable children across time (Jarvis, 1991; Wartella & Reeves, 1985). The introduction of movies for a mass audience in the early part of the twentieth century was not an exception. Parental concerns about the effects of movies on their children led to the formation of many organizations to challenge the types of movie that were being produced (Jarvis, 1991). Early attempts to regulate the movies in the late 1910s and early 1920s sprang from parental concerns for their children (Skylar, 1994).

The same concerns were raised by early media researchers. For example, the earliest book on media psychology—Hugo Munsterberg's *The Photoplay: A Psychological Study* (1916/2002)—spent a great deal of time focusing on how movies could negatively impact children by leading them into a life of delinquency. However, Munsterberg also argued that movies could be used to great educational effect if used properly. But his concern, as was the case with many social commentators and scholars at the time, was that the content of the movies that children were being exposed to modeled negative behaviors for children.

Ultimately, these concerns led to one of the largest research projects in the history of communication. The Payne Fund studies took place in the late 1920s and early 1930s (Jarvis, 1991; Rogers, 1994). The Payne Fund studies were a series of studies that used social scientific research methods to try to ascertain whether movies did have negative effects on children. A total of twelve scholarly books were produced based on these studies (Wartella & Reeves, 1985) for a grant of a little over $65,000 (Rogers, 1994).

The scholarly research generally found that the relationship between movies and various outcomes for children was complex and highly dependent on the characteristics of the children, the characteristics of the movies, and the outcome variables that were being studied (Jarvis, 1991; Wartella & Reeves, 1985). Indeed, this research involved a degree of theoretical sophistication that is not appreciated by most discussions of this research (Wartella & Reeves, 1985). However, the first volume in the series of books that resulted from the Payne Fund studies—

Our Movie Made Children—was written by a Henry James Forman (1933) for a lay audience. Unfortunately, Mr. Forman tended to exaggerate and sometimes outright misrepresent the results of the studies (Jarvis, 1991). So while the Payne Fund studies themselves highlighted the complexities of the relationship between media use and behavior, the popular media reports of the Payne Fund studies supported the hypodermic needle model of media effects (Jarvis, 1991).

Indeed, as W. W. Charters (1933) wrote in the introduction to *Our Movie Made Children*, ". . . I agree with the author [Forman] in the fundamental position that the motion picture is powerful to an unexpected degree in affecting the information, attitudes, emotional experiences and conduct patterns of children . . ." (p. viii).

Influences from Allied Disciplines

Other social scientific disciplines had developments during this time period that had important effects on the study of communication. The Chicago School of Sociology played a crucial role in the development of both the study of interpersonal communication and media effects research (Buxton, 2008; Rogers, 1994). There were a number of important early scholars at the University of Chicago including John Dewey, George Herbert Mead, and Robert Park (Rogers, 1994), some of whom played a pivotal role in the development of sociology in the first half of the twentieth century. Because the Chicago School combined a strong focus on theory with a concern for studying social problems, they were ideally suited to their work on the Payne Fund studies, which included, in addition to sociologists at the University of Chicago, scholars from several other universities including the Ohio State University and the University of Iowa (Rogers, 1994). But perhaps more importantly, theorizing at the University of Chicago focused on the symbolic nature of communication, which resulted in the development of symbolic interactionism. While symbolic interactionism has had an important influence in sociology and, to a lesser extent, psychology, it has played a pivotal role in theorizing about interpersonal communication (Rogers, 1994).

A second discipline that played an important role in shaping how the communication discipline developed was psychology. Research within social psychology had several important influences including an emphasis on the effects of communication on people. Within psychology, this primarily grew out of research by Carl Hovland, which involved a focus on the impact of persuasive messages on people's attitudes, but this will be discussed in greater detail later. A second influence evolved from Kurt Lewin's work on field theory (Rogers, 1994). Lewin's (1951) work focused on the interplay between the individual and the larger environment, and the various forces operating in the environment and how they shape human behavior. These forces encourage a person to approach or avoid elements of the larger environment. Finally, social psychology had a major impact on the methodologies used by communication scholars. Social psychology from the very beginning has relied heavily on experiments to test theories, and this emphasis on experimentation transferred to many communication scholars (Delia, 1987) (see Chapters 2 and 4 for further discussion).

A final discipline that influenced the emergence of communication that is often ignored is education (Anderson & Colvin, 2008; Delia, 1987). Education influenced the emergence and growth of communication in several ways. First, much of the early academic writings on the potential negative effects of new technologies emerged out of education. There were concerns about the influence of movies on students' intellectual development because they would spend valuable study time going to the movies instead. But it should also be noted that early scholars did see potential educational uses of these new technologies (Cressey, 1934). Education scholars also did some of the earliest research on teaching communication skills, which has played an important role in the development of departments focused on communication (Delia, 1987).

The Impact of Radio

While radio broadcasts started much earlier, network radio stations started in 1920 and were well established by the mid-1920s (Douglas, 1999; Starr, 2004). Radio is not a subject of much contemporary research by communication scholars, but the study of radio played an important role in the beginning of the discipline. The earliest work on radio included Cantril and Allport's *The Psychology of Radio* (1935), which explored some of the social impacts of radio, but included a greater emphasis on how people processed radio broadcasts. For example, the research published in this volume suggested that radio content needed to be simpler and more comprehensible than print or face-to-face communication, which is consistent with later research on how people process persuasive messages (Chaiken & Eagly, 1976, 1983).

But the major program of research on radio emerged from a grant from the Rockefeller Foundation, which got Paul Lazarsfeld involved in communication research. Paul Lazarsfeld was an Austrian-born scholar who immigrated to the United States in the mid-1930s due to the rise of fascism in Europe (Rogers, 1994). While he played a pivotal role in the development of communication scholarship, he considered himself to be a sociologist, though his Ph.D. from the University of Vienna was in mathematics (Rogers, 1994; Schramm, 1997). Lazersfeld originally went to the United States in 1933. He elected to stay there, due to political persecution of his family back in Austria. Interestingly, his ability to stay in the United States was guaranteed by his work with the Radio Research Project—a program he directed starting in 1937. The Radio Research Project was funded by the Rockefeller Foundation based on its interest in radio, which was spurred by Cantril and Allport's (1935) groundbreaking research. The research that grew out of the Radio Research Project was eclectic, but laid the foundation for a number of theories that later emerged. For example, research on listeners' motivations for listening to soap operas laid the foundation for the uses and gratifications approach to the study of media selection (Peters & Simonson, 2004). Thus, even this earliest work on radio served to shape the field of communication in ways that can still be seen today.

Perhaps one of the most important impacts of Lazarsfeld's research was his methodological innovations. His research on radio included the development of the Lazarsfeld–Stanton Program-Analyzer (also called Little Annie), which allowed researchers to record radio listeners' responses to a program or advertisements as they were listening to the program but without interrupting the program. Likewise, Lazarsfeld is credited with aiding in the development of survey methodologies and sampling procedures during his time with the Radio Research Project. For example, he conducted some of the earliest panel studies using survey methodologies. Another methodology that he helped develop during this time was focus group interviewing (Rogers, 1994). All of these are still very relevant to quantitative approaches to the study of communication (see Chapter 8).

A missed opportunity that occurred during Lazersfeld's work on the radio project was the potential melding of social scientific (or what Lazarsfeld called administrative research) and critical scholarship early in the development of the discipline (Rogers, 1994). Lazarsfeld recruited Theodor Adorno to join his team in the United States to draw on Adorno's work on music (Bronner, 2011; Lazarsfeld, 2004). Adorno was one of the critical scholars that made up the Frankfurt School, but his work there had kept him in Germany too long. With the rise of the Nazis, he needed to get out. So Lazarsfeld invited Adorno to work with him as a way to get him out of Germany, but this also filled a need for a researcher who studied music on radio and Lazarsfeld did not have anyone with this background working on the project. Adorno was a leading expert on music (Bronner, 2011; Schweppenhauser, 2009). Unfortunately, the collaboration between Lazarsfeld and Adorno did not work and Adorno soon left for California, where he aided in a now-classic collaboration on authoritarian personality (Brewer & Brown, 1998). Critically, the work of Adorno et al. (1950) not only provided an important foundation for research on intergroup relations, it also demonstrated that critical scholars could work with empirical researchers—something that the Lazarsfeld collaboration failed to demonstrate.

The Radio Research Project also made possible research on perhaps the most notorious incident in the history of the media, which occurred on October 30, 1938. The Mercury Theatre broadcast of *The War of the Worlds* suggested that people were easily misled by the media. The production was directed by, and starred, Orson Welles. After the opening credits for the Mercury Theatre, the radio play began with the announcement that the audience was listening to a big band concert from a fictional hotel in New York. During the next 45 minutes, the music was frequently interrupted, and then completely stopped, by news reports. The reports told of flashes of light from Mars, and a metallic cylinder landing at a farm at Grover Mills, New Jersey. A later news flash declared that Martians were emerging from the cylinder and using a heat ray to attack spectators. At one point, the military seemingly took over the broadcast to coordinate efforts against the Martian invaders. Civilians were advised to flee from towns in central and northern New Jersey and a list of the best escape routes was provided (Koch, 1970). Unfortunately, many people missed the opening announcement that this was a production of the Mercury Theatre. An estimated six million people heard *The War of the Worlds*' broadcast. Surveys at the time suggested that over a quarter of the six million listeners thought the news reports were real. People fled from their homes, tried desperately to seal their homes against the Martian's poison gas, or called their family and friends to warn them of the attack by the Martians and to talk with their loved ones a final time (Cantril et al., 1940). The Mercury Theatre's production of *The War of the Worlds* has gone down in history as a prime example of how powerful media can shape people's social reality. However, while Cantril et al.'s (1940) research did find a strong influence of the broadcast on people's beliefs and behavior, the picture that emerged from their research was much more complex. For example, the broadcast occurred shortly after Nazi Germany's invasion of Czechoslovakia, and Cantril et al. (1940) found that many of the people who reacted to the Martian invasion were already anxious about the possibility of another war and were convinced that the Martian invasion was actually the actions of either the Germans or the Japanese. In other words, recent events in the media may have primed people to believe that there was an invasion (see Chapters 7 and 13 for a more in-depth discussion of priming).

Rockefeller Foundation Group on Mass Communication Research

As we have already discussed, the U.S. government used propaganda to great effect after becoming involved in World War I through the efforts of the CPI (Glander, 2009). However, recall that there was a substantial backlash against these activities after the war by both educators and political commentators (Glander, 2009). With the rise of Fascist movements in both Germany and Italy, some individuals began to worry about the prospects of another war in Europe. As the 1930s drew to an end, another European war seemed certain. The question was whether and how the United States would be involved in this upcoming war against Fascist Germany and Italy. In addition, some individuals began to wonder what role propaganda would play in the United States' efforts to garner support among the population for the war (Chaffee & Rogers, 1997). Certainly, given the backlash against the CPI, the government could not afford to open another office in charge of wartime propaganda. The Rockefeller Foundation had a long-term interest in understanding the effectiveness of radio and had funded a number of projects to study the effects of radio (Pooley, 2008). Given the Foundation's background, it is not surprising that it convened a seminar to begin addressing these issues of how the government should use the media during the coming war, as well as to lay out the future of communication research (Chaffee & Rogers, 1997; Glander, 2009; Schramm, 1997). Harold Lasswell and Paul Lazarsfeld were among the scholars who participated in these meetings.

There were a number of meetings of this group in the later part of 1939 and through the summer of 1940 (Peters & Simonson, 2004; Rogers, 1994; Schramm, 1997), and these meetings had a substantial effect on both wartime media research and the future of the study of communication as well. The group appears to have firmly supported the use of propaganda as part of the war effort (Schramm, 1997). Consequently, the first meeting largely focused on laying out a plan for wartime research, because the participants felt that not enough was known about how to harness the media for the government's ends. Recall that during World War I the CPI did not rely on newspapers, radio, or movies to garner support for the war, but instead relied upon a large cohort of public speakers and educational materials that were dispersed through schools. Later meetings dealt with the direction that communication research should take, independent of the war. What were the important questions that needed to be addressed by communication scholars? The memoranda that emerged from the second meeting included a blueprint for Lasswell's (1948) infamous "who says what to whom with what effect," which arguably shaped much of the research for the next couple of decades (Rogers, 1994).

World War II

World War II was a critical event in the development of the study of media using social scientific methods (Rogers, 1994). First of all, as already discussed, numerous scholars came to the United States because of the growing Nazi threat in the years leading up to war, including Lazarsfeld and Adorno. Second, the enormity of the war meant that the United States responded to the war across a number of fronts. The lessons of World War I and the research on the media in the ensuing years meant that the government recognized the importance of the media for the war effort (Rogers, 1994). Consequently, a lot of resources were put into the study of communication during the war. While the specific results of many of the studies conducted on the war are interesting, the war was important more for who the war brought to the study of communication. Rogers (1994) argued that the war effort resulted in "an invisible college of communication scholars [that] came together in Washington, DC" (p. 10; Pooley, 2008). In other words, these scholars came together with the common goal of studying how communication could help the war effort. Out of these interactions, a vision for the future of the discipline emerged (Delia, 1987; Rogers, 1994).

The government was involved in numerous different types of communication research during the war. For example, Lasswell was brought in to head the Library of Congress's efforts to content analyze all the different types of propaganda that were being used during the war (Rogers, 1994; Sproule, 2008). Likewise, the government was involved with creating and disseminating propaganda materials to help keep civilian morale high due to the rationing that occurred during the war and the mobilization of the military industries to produce the basic materials needed to fight the war.

One of the most important research efforts during the war for the history of the discipline involved research on the effectiveness of the *Why We Fight* films. These films were created by director Frank Capra (winner of three Best Director Oscars) to try to increase the morale of soldiers who were drafted to fight in the war. There were a total of seven of these 10-minute films created (Capra, 1971). The social psychologist Carl Hovland—whom Wilbur Schramm (1997) identified as one of the "forefathers" of the communication discipline—was involved in research on the effectiveness of these films. Hovland was an experimental psychologist trained at Yale University in classic learning theory and, prior to the war, that was his primary area of research (Rogers, 1994; Schramm, 1997). Hovland came to Washington, DC in 1942 as a part of the research branch of the war department to study the effectiveness of the *Why We Fight* films (Petty & Cacioppo, 1981; Rogers, 1994). Hovland brought a systematic approach to the study of these films and focused on the impact of the films on soldiers' attitudes—thus introducing the concept of attitude to the study of media. Hovland was unique among researchers during the war period because while he was answering applied questions for the military, his work always had a strong theoretical orientation as well (Hovland et al., 1949; Rogers, 1994). Hovland's message-learning approach laid the foundation for many of the information-processing models of attitudes that are central to the study of persuasion today (Petty & Cacioppo, 1981). After the war, he brought his team to Yale and continued his systematic study of persuasion. His research at Yale resulted in approximately a book a year until 1961, when he died of cancer. Rogers (1994) also credits Hovland with helping to lay the foundation for the study of interpersonal communication, because the study of social influence has historically been an important area of study within interpersonal communication.

Another important office during the war was the Office of Facts and Figures (OFF). As already mentioned, the government deemed it important to convince the public of the need for the United States to be involved in the war. Perhaps even more important, from the government's perspective, was keeping the public's morale up during the war because of the role the public played in the military industries, recycling materials for the war effort, and in raising money to fund the war through the purchasing of war bonds. OFF was a propaganda agency created by the government to work specifically on issues of civilian morale (Rogers, 1994). Including "facts and figures" in the title was meant to hide the function that OFF was performing, but it was obvious to many that it was one of the government's propaganda organs.

Dr. Wilbur Schramm was involved with OFF early during the war effort. Schramm is often identified as the "father" of the discipline (Chaffee & Rogers, 1997; Delia, 1987; Rogers, 1994). Prior to the war, he was a faculty member in the Department of English at the University of Iowa and later the director of the prestigious Iowa Writer's Workshop. He returned to the University of Iowa as the Dean of the Journalism School when he left OFF in 1943. He was appointed as the Dean despite having limited background in journalism, but this selection was to have a profound impact on the discipline of communication. During Schramm's time in DC working on the war effort, he rubbed shoulders with many important social scientists studying issues related to communication and the media (Rogers, 1994). As a consequence of these influences on his thinking, Schramm's vision for the School included expanding its mission from a program that trained professional journalists to include courses on the social sciences to further train students and to lay the foundation for the scientific study of the media. He also proposed the creation of the first Ph.D. program in mass communication (Chaffee & Rogers, 1997).[5]

After the War

Emergence of a Paradigm

While much of the research between the two world wars had focused on the effects of communication, what emerged out of World War II and its immediate aftermath was a much stronger focus on the effects of communication. The Rockefeller Foundation meetings of 1939 and 1940 laid the foundation for the effects tradition that was to dominate the emerging discipline after the war. In particular, these meetings were the place where Lasswell began laying out the foundation for his basic model mentioned earlier—"who says what to whom with what effect," which was more formally presented in 1948 (Rogers, 1994).

At the same time, Hovland et al. (1949) laid out a similar model to guide research on persuasion and attitude change. Hovland's research program included the study of source variables (who), message variables (says what), channel variables, and receiver variables (to whom), and across all of this experimental research was a focus on attitudes (what effect). His systematic approach to studying these variables meant that Hovland's research program was extremely productive (Schramm, 1997). Essentially, Hovland would set up the critical variables such as credibility, message factors, and so forth against the various outcome variables he was interested in, such as attitude change or message retention. His systematic approach and efficiency at conducting research allowed Hovland's Yale group to be extremely productive (Rogers, 1994; Schramm, 1997).

Critically, Lasswell's question and Hovland's research program provided a model for other communication scholars to use for developing their own research programs (Rogers, 1994). They isolated the basic model and specified variables that are still recognized as relevant today. The philosopher of science Thomas

Kuhn (1970) has argued that a critical element for the emergence of an area of scientific research is an exemplar for how research should be conducted. This exemplar provides a normative example for how research should be conducted and has a powerful influence on the types of research that are conducted and the assumptions that underlie that research. So Lasswell's question and Hovland's research program provided an early exemplar for communication scholars, which shaped the direction the discipline would take in the coming decades (Sproule, 2008). They are Thomas Kuhn's (1970) exemplar.

During that same decade, Lazarsfeld et al.'s (1944) Erie county research, and Katz and Lazarsfeld's (1955) Decatur study, suggested that media messages had minimal effects on people's political choices and opinions. Instead, people were primarily influenced via interpersonal communication with trusted opinion leaders. This research resulted in the two-step model of media effects (see Chapter 13), and ultimately the emergence of the minimal effects era of media research, which arguably lasted into the late 1960s and early 1970s. This minimal effects era is surprising, though, because Hovland's work stood in stark contrast to Lazarsfeld et al.'s (1944) work: Hovland's research program found consistent effects of different variables on attitude change and persuasion. One of the paradoxes of the postwar years was the existence of a "limited effects" paradigm as well as substantial government funding for research on social influence to aid with the then heating-up Cold War, which rested on the premise that the media could be a useful weapon in the war against the Soviet Union (Pooley, 2008).

Growth of Research Institutes

In addition to the emergence of a paradigm for conducting research, the late 1940s and 1950s saw an increase in the number of research institutes in the United States (Schramm, 1997). Recall that Schramm started what is considered the first Ph.D. program in mass communication while he was Dean of the Journalism School at the University of Iowa during the war. While Lazarsfeld should arguably be credited with creating the first research institutions for the study of media (Peters & Simonson, 2004), Schramm's vision for the discipline also included the establishment of research institutions at universities for the study of communication that would attract grant money from the government and private foundations. Unfortunately, the University of Iowa did not provide Schramm with the resources to establish an institute, so in 1947 he moved to the University of Illinois where he created the Institute of Communication Research (Chaffee & Rogers, 1997). With the creation of the Institute, the University of Illinois became the model for communication programs and created a facility that allowed for the first programmatic research of communication (Chaffee & Rogers, 1997). This model was soon to move to California. In 1955, Schramm moved his operations to Stanford where he was the director of Stanford's Institute for Communication Research.

The exemplar of communication research provided by Lasswell and Hovland, along with the invisible college that was created by various scholars coming to DC to study communication-related issues, played an important role in the continued funding of communication research after the war (Glander, 2009). Indeed, as the Cold War continued, it is almost as if the government re-instituted the programs of communication research that had been operating during the war (Pooley, 2008). But this influx of resources allowed the discipline to establish itself as an important part of many universities across the United States.

In the past 20 years, critical scholars have advanced a more cynical view of the postwar growth of the discipline (Glander, 2009; Pooley, 2008). It is now known that at least part of the government funding that the newly established communication research institutes received during the Cold War came from the CIA. But it should be noted that it is not clear whether the people who received these grants actually knew they were from the CIA (Glander, 2009). However, these authors argue that the limited effects model of the media was more of a ruse than a reality and that it was used to deflect charges that the government was funding research designed at increasing the effectiveness of its continuing propaganda efforts. Specifically, by labeling this research "communication research," the government was able to avoid the backlash against "propaganda" that occurred after World War I (Glander, 2009; Sproule, 2008).

British Cultural Studies

As the social scientific approach to the study of communication gained ascendancy in the United States, an alternative approach to the study of communication was emerging in England. The opening of the Centre for Contemporary Cultural Studies (CCCS) in 1964 at the University of Birmingham is often cited as the start of British cultural studies (Redal, 2008). Of course, any history of an intellectual movement does not have a "start date" but rather reflects a long evolution of ideas, and British cultural studies is no different (Dworkin, 1997; Hall, 1996), though the founding of the CCCS certainly played a major role in legitimizing this area of study (Dworkin, 1997; Redal, 2008; Schulman, 1993).

Dworkin (1997) argues that conflicts within the British Communist Party going back to the 1930s laid the foundation for the rise of cultural studies. Specially, the disputes that arose before World War II within the British Communist Party ultimately led to the formation of the New Left in the 1950s as a reaction to these earlier disputes with hardline Marxists and the growing dominance of the Conservative Party in England. The New Left was a group of younger socialists who rejected the dominance of economics in leftist thought—thus they broke with traditional Marxist thought (Dworkin, 1997). The *New Left Review* was the journal for this group of intellectuals, which Stuart Hall edited until 1961. But there were major conflicts within the movement in the early 1960s, which ultimately led to the demise of the New Left (Dworkin, 1997).

Three people are generally credited with the beginnings of British cultural studies: Richard Hoggart, Raymond Williams, and Stuart Hall (Dworkin, 1997). Hoggart was the first director of the CCCS, but he only directed the Centre until 1970 (Webster, 2004). Both Hoggart and Williams grew up with the class segregation that characterized Britain at that time. They grew up in working-class families. Most children of working-class families stopped attending school at age 15, so Hoggart's and Williams's college attendance was unusual given their social class. Certainly holding an academic job was even more unusual. Hoggart came from a literary criticism background, but at the CCCS he rejected the elitism of literary criticism to focus on the study of mass culture (Schulman, 1993; Webster, 2004). However, despite its initial grounding in literary criticism, the CCCS was highly interdisciplinary in focus and utilized a large number of methodologies to answer the questions that arose (Hall, 1996; Roskos-Ewoldsen et al., 2007; Schulman, 1993).

Given the focus on class, and the CCCS's close ties with the New Left, a common assumption has been that this approach has strong ties with Marxism (Schulman, 1993). Certainly, British cultural studies draws from some of Marx's ideas, including a focus on class, exploitation, power, and ideology (Hall, 1996). But to argue that it takes a Marxist approach to the study of culture and the media is a mischaracterization of cultural studies (Dworkin, 1997). As Stuart Hall (1996) famously stated, they were "working within shouting distance of Marxism" (p. 265). For example, Marx did not consider the role of language and symbols within his formulations, and these have been central foci for cultural studies (Hall, 1996). However, the linkages that the CCCS did have with Marxism did result in a generally strained relationship between the Centre and the University of Birmingham (Webster, 2004).

Characteristics of British cultural studies included an obvious focus on culture. In particular, there was a clear challenge to the elitism of British culture—which makes sense given Hoggart's and Williams's background (Schulman, 1993). The influence of the mass media on culture was one particularly important area of study, in particular the role of the media in maintaining the dominant ideology in often subtle ways (Redal, 2008). While not an initial focus of cultural studies, there was a strong focus on ideology and Antonio Gramsci's notion of hegemonic ideology (Hall, 1996; Schulman, 1993). Gramsci was an Italian journalist and intellectual who wrote between the two world wars and died in prison—a political prisoner of Mussolini. While a Marxist, Gramsci broke from Marx in two important areas. First, Gramsci favored sociological explanations for human behavior over economic explanations. Second, Gramsci challenged the idea that there was a single ideology, which for Marx was tied to the economic system. Instead, Gramsci argued that there were multiple ideologies operating within a political system and these different ideologies via for dominance (Dworkin, 1997). But the hegemonic ideology was the dominant ideology within that system. The work on ideology helped spur a growth in critical gender and critical race studies that began during the 1970s (Hall, 1996; Schulman, 1993).

One characteristic of the thinking on ideology is the notion that hegemonic ideology will dictate how media messages are read. Hall's encoding/decoding model challenged this view and argued instead that messages were polysemic—that messages are open to multiple interpretations (Hall, 1996; Hall, 2001; Sproule, 2015; see Chapter 10). The encoding/decoding model assumed a more active audience than most research did at the time. Since then, work within this area has allowed for a much more active view of the audience and switched to a much greater focus on what the audience does with a text.

The CCCS was closed on July 31, 1992 with only a little over a month's warning. But while the CCCS had closed, cultural studies had spread through the world. How cultural studies has materialized is distinct across different countries (Hall, 1996), but the common concern about the relationship between culture, the media, and power remains.

Conclusion

The discipline of communication has a long and complex history—particularly during the twentieth century. The discipline has drawn from myriad different sources ranging from psychology and sociology to neo-Marxist thought. These divergent influences are reflected in the myriad of different theoretical approaches that will be found across the remaining chapters of this volume. While conscious of this bias, this chapter has privileged social scientific approaches to the study of communication. Partly this reflects the biases of earlier histories of the discipline (Bineham, 1988; Delia, 1987; Glander, 2009; Pooley, 2008). But it also reflects the dominance of the social scientific approach in terms of publications within the discipline's major journals (Anderson & Middleton, 2015) (however, see Chapters 6 and 7 for a different perspective also inherent in communication research).

Programs of research arose in response to societal problems during the early part of the discipline's history—the study of propaganda, the influence of movies on children, the role of the media in alienating the masses, the study of public opinion and elections, how to respond to the rising threat of fascism, and so forth. But as the discipline matured, research programs began to focus more on theory development and testing these theories. This was an outgrowth of a number of influences including the Chicago School, projects funded by the Rockefeller Foundation, and the collaborations that began during World War II. Importantly, this is a sign of an established discipline.

Notes

1   Sproule (2015) argues that the early history of the discipline of speech communication is really the early eighteenth century in England. Specifically, books trying to teach rhetorical skills to the larger population included teaching people how to debate, which may have played a role in the emergence of the public sphere in England.

2   With the rise of movies and radio, it may seem strange that the CPI relied on volunteers to give public speeches in support of government policy. However, the reach of radio was extremely limited at this point. Broadcast networks would not emerge until 1926, when the National Broadcasting Company (NBC) was established. Likewise, movies were still an emerging media (Starr, 2004). Although the cartel of Edison's Motion Picture Patents Company was declared illegal in 1915, its influence meant that the vast majority of films were short (limited to 10 minutes) and not suitable for propaganda efforts.

3   It is important to note that while Lippmann (1922) does appear to be very critical of the role of newspapers in democracy, he does not argue that democracy is impossible or a broken system. Rather, he argues that it will take hard work on the part of the government and citizens to be adequately informed (Dewey, 1922).

4   However, while Habermas is likely the most prolific of the early critical scholars, he has had an enduring belief in liberal democracy (O'Mahony, 2013), and some interpret him as splitting from critical scholarship because of this faith (Finlayson, 2005). Habermas left Frankfurt in 1961 (Finlayson, 2005).

5   Between the two wars, the University of Wisconsin developed a minor in journalism at the doctoral level that was aimed at students in the social sciences (Chaffee & Rogers, 1997). Schramm was certainly aware of this minor and it likely played an important role in his thinking about the Ph.D. program at Iowa.

References

Adorno, T. (1991). *The culture industry*. New York: Routledge.

Adorno, T. W., Frenkel-Brunswik, E., Levinson, D. J., & Sanford, R. N. (1950). *The authoritarian personality*. New York: Harper and Row.

Anderson, J. A., & Colvin, J. W. (2008). Media research 1900—1945: Topics and conversations. In D. W. Park & J. Pooley (Eds.), *The history of media and communication research: Contested memories* (pp. 321–344). New York: Peter Lang.

Anderson, J. A., & Middleton, M. K. (2015). Epistemological movements in communication: An analysis of empirical and rhetorical/critical scholarship. In P. J. Gehrke & W. M. Keith (Eds.), *A century of communication studies: The unfinished conversation* (pp. 82–108). New York: Routledge.

Best, S., & Kellner, D. (1991). *Postmodern theory: Critical interrogations*. New York: Guilford Press.

Bineham, J. L. (1988). A historical account of the hypodermic model of mass communication. *Communication Monographs, 55*, 230–246.

Brewer, M. B., & Brown, R. J. (1998). Intergroup relations. In D. T. Gilbert, S. T. Fiske, & G. Lindzey (Eds.), *The handbook of social psychology* (4th ed., vol. 2, pp. 554–594). New York: McGraw-Hill.

Bronner, S. E. (2011). *Critical theory: A very short introduction*. Oxford: Oxford University Press.

Buxton, W. J. (2008). From Park to Cressey: Chicago sociology's engagement with media and mass culture. In D. W. Park & J. Pooley (Eds.), *The history of media and communication research: Contested memories* (pp. 345–362). New York: Peter Lang.

Cantril, H., & Allport, G. W. (1935). *The psychology of radio*. New York: Harper & Brothers.

Cantril, H., Herzog, H., Gaudet, H., & Koch, H. (1940). *The invasion from Mars: A study in the psychology of panic*. Princeton, NJ: Princeton University Press.

Capra, F. (1971). *Frank Capra: The name above the line—an autobiography*. New York: Da Capo Press.

Chaffee, S. H., & Rogers, E. M. (1997). The establishment of communication study in America. In S. H. Chaffee & E. M. Rogers (Eds.), *The beginnings of communication study in America: A personal memoir* (pp. 125–180). Thousand Oaks, CA: Sage.

Chaiken, S., & Eagly, A. H. (1976). Communication modality as a determinant of message persuasiveness and message comprehensibility. *Journal of Personality and Social Psychology*, *34*, 605–614.

Chaiken, S., & Eagly, A. H. (1983). Communication modality as a determinant of persuasion: The role of communicator salience. *Journal of Personality and Social Psychology*, *45*, 241–256.

Charters, W. W. (1933). Introduction. In H. J. Forman, *Our movie made children*. New York: Macmillan.

Cressey, P. G. (1934). The motion picture as informal education. *Journal of Educational Sociology*, *7*, 504–515.

Delia, J. G. (1987). Communication research: A history. In C. R. Berger & S. H. Chaffee (Eds.), *Handbook of communication science* (pp. 20–98). Thousand Oaks, CA: Sage.

Dewey, J. (1918). The new paternalism. *The New Republic*, *17*, 216–217.

Dewey, J. (1922). Public opinion. *The New Republic*, *30*, 286–288.

Douglas, S. J. (1999). *Listening in: Radio and the American imagination*. Minneapolis, MN: University of Minnesota Press.

Dworkin, D. (1997). *Cultural Marxism in postwar Britain: History, the New Left, and the origins of cultural studies*. Durham, NC: Duke University Press.

Finlayson, J. G. (2005). *Habermas: A very short introduction*. Oxford: Oxford University Press.

Forman, H. J. (1933). *Our movie made children*. New York: Macmillan.

Fromm, E. (1973). *The anatomy of human destructiveness*. New York: Henry Holt.

Glander, T. (2009) *Origins of mass communications research during the American cold war*. New York: Routledge.

Hall, S. (1996). Cultural studies and its theoretical legacies. In D. Morley & K.-H. Chen (Eds.), *Stuart Hall: Critical dialogues in cultural studies* (pp. 262–275). New York: Routledge. (Reprinted from L. Grossberg et al. (Eds.), *Cultural Studies* (pp. 277–286). London: Routledge.

Hall, S. (2001). Encoding/decoding. In M. G. Durham & D. M. Kellner (Eds.), *Media and cultural studies: Keyworks* (pp. 166–176). Malden, MA: Blackwell. (Reprinted from S. Hall, D. Hobson, A. Lowe & P. Willis (Eds.) (1980), *Culture, media, language* (pp. 128–138). London: Hutchinson.

Hovland, C. I., Lumsdaine, A. A., & Sheffield, F. D. (1949). *Experiments in mass communication: Studies in social psychology in World War II: Volume III*. Princeton, NJ: Princeton University Press.

Jansen, S. C. (2008). Walter Lippmann, straw man of communication research. In D. W. Park & J. Pooley (Eds.), *The history of media and communication research: Contested memories* (pp. 71–112). New York: Peter Lang.

Jarvis, A. R., Jr. (1991). The Payne Fund reports: A discussion of their content, publication reaction, and effect on the motion picture industry, 1930–1940. *Journal of Popular Culture*, *25*, 127–140.

Katz, E., & Lazarsfeld, P. F. (1955). *Personal influence: The part played by people in the flow of mass communication*. New York: Free Press.

Koch, H. (1970). *The panic broadcast: Portrait of an event*. Boston, MA: Little, Brown.

Kuhn, T. S. (1970). *The structure of scientific revolutions* (2nd ed.). Chicago: University of Chicago Press.

Lasswell, H. D. (1927). *Propaganda technique in World War I*. London: Trench, Trubner & Co.

Lasswell, H. D. (1948). The structure and function of communication in society. In L. Bryson (Ed.), *The communication of ideas: A series of addresses*. New York: Harper.

Lazarsfeld, P. F. (2004). Administrative and critical communication research. In J. D. Peters & P. Simonson (Eds.), *Mass communication and American social thought: Key texts 1919–1968* (pp. 167–173). Lanham, MA: Rowman & Littlefield. (Reprinted from P. F. Lazarsfeld (1941), *Studies in Philosophy and Social Science* Studies, *9* (1), 2–16.)

Lazarsfeld, P. F., Berelson, B., & Gaudet, H. (1944). *The people's choice: How the voter makes up his mind in a presidential election*. New York: Duell, Sloan and Pearce.

Lewin, K. (1951). *Field theory in social science*. New York: Harper & Brothers.

Lippmann, W. (1922). *Public opinion*. New York: Free Press.

Lubken, D. (2008). Remembering the straw man: The travels and adventures of hypodermic. In D. W. Park & J. Pooley (Eds.), *The history of media and communication research: Contested memories* (pp. 19–42). New York: Peter Lang.

Munsterberg, H. (1916). *The photoplay: A psychological study*. New York: D. Appleton.

O'Mahony, P. (2013). *The contemporary theory of the public sphere*. Oxford: Peter Lang.

Peters, J. D., & Simonson, P. (Eds.) (2004). *Mass communication and American social thought: Key texts 1919–1968*. Lanham, MA: Rowman & Littlefield.

Petty, R. E., & Cacioppo, J. T. (1981). *Attitudes and persuasion: Classic and contemporary approaches*. Dubuque, IA: Wm. C. Brown.

Pooley, J. (2008). The new history of communication research. In D. W. Park & J. Pooley (Eds.), *The history of media and communication research: Contested memories* (pp. 43–70). New York: Peter Lang.

Redal, W. W. (2008). Making sense of social change: Studying media and culture in 1960s Britain. In D. W. Park & J. Pooley (Eds.), *The history of media and communication research: Contested memories* (pp. 269–290). New York: Peter Lang.

Rogers, E. M. (1994). *A history of communication study: A biographical approach*. New York: Free Press.

Roskos-Ewoldsen, B., Roskos-Ewoldsen, D. R., Yang, M., & Lee, M. (2007). Comprehension of the media. In D. R. Roskos-Ewoldsen & J. Monahan (Eds.), *Communication and social cognition: Theories and methods* (pp. 319–350). Mahwah, NJ: Lawrence Erlbaum Associates.

Schramm, W. (1997). *The beginnings of communication study in America: A personal memoir*. Thousand Oaks, CA: Sage.

Schulman, N. (1993). Conditions of their own making: An intellectual history of the Centre for Contemporary Cultural Studies at the University of Birmingham. *Canadian Journal of Communication, 18*, 51–73.

Schweppenhauser, G. (2009). *Theodor W. Adorno: An introduction* (J. Rolleston, trans.). Durham, NC: Duke University Press.

Skylar, R. (1994). *Movie-made America: A cultural history of American movies*. New York: Vintage Books.

Sproule, J. M. (2008). "Communication": From concept to field to discipline. In D. W. Park & J. Pooley (Eds.), *The history of media and communication research: Contested memories* (pp. 163–178). New York: Peter Lang.

Sproule, J. M. (2015). Discovering communication: Five turns toward discipline and association. In P. J. Gehrke & W. M. Keith (Eds.), *A century of communication studies: The unfinished conversation* (pp. 26–45). New York: Routledge.

Starr, P. (2004). *The creation of the media: Political origins of modern communications.* New York: Basic Books.

Wartella, E., & Reeves, B. (1985). Historical trends in research on children and the media: 1900–1960. *Journal of Communication, 35*(2), 118–133.

Webster, F. (2004). Cultural studies and sociology at, and after, the closure of the Birmingham school. *Cultural Studies, 18,* 847–862.

4

PHILOSOPHICAL UNDERPINNINGS OF THE COMMUNICATION SCIENCE APPROACH

Like most social sciences, communication can be sliced along any number of conceptual, theoretical, and methodological lines. Fink and Gantz (1996) conducted a content analysis of communication research in major communication disciplines and identified three major traditions: social science (referred to in this chapter as communication science), interpretive research, and critical scholarship. Anderson and Baym (2004) considered the philosophic issues in communication from 1995 to 2004 and identified *twenty-one* scholarship communities, each varying in their epistemological (i.e., ways of knowing) and methodological, and perhaps even ontological (i.e., nature of reality) approaches. Thus, these attempts to synthesize the field have resulted primarily in recognition of its breadth and diversity. The outcome of this disparate scholarship is a field that may seem chaotic even to those with a good understanding of the underpinnings of the field: what the distinctions are, why they exist, and how both philosophical assumptions and practical histories help determine the landscape of the discipline.

In this chapter, we attempt to provide our own synthesis of the discipline, with the focus primarily on the philosophical roots of quantitative approaches to communication science. First, we briefly introduce three broad areas of communication: communication science, critical/cultural studies, and rhetoric, echoing both the emergence of communication historically and its underlying assumptions. Here, it is worth noting that while we keep critical and cultural studies under the same heading, they clearly have distinct ways of knowing and distinct types of theories that are reflected in, and reflections of, their differing goals. Specifically, interpretive theory and cultural studies seek to provide contingent understanding; critical theory seeks emancipation and change (Fink & Gantz, 1996). They do, however, share a qualitative approach to research that often creates a link, however tenuous, between them. In any case, in this chapter, we do not discuss these distinctions between critical and cultural studies at length. While we provide a brief look at their differences, we fall short of examining their distinctions in depth. In fact, readers may notice that we have adopted the critical/cultural studies moniker in keeping with the title of one of the major journals in the discipline (i.e., *Communication and Critical/Cultural Studies*). Thus, critical/cultural studies share some commonalities in method and epistemology that are borne out practically in the journal's publications. In addition to critical/cultural studies, we also briefly review the ontological, epistemological, methodological, and axiological approaches of rhetoric, but do not offer great detail on these either. Instead, the discussion of these various subdisciplines serves primarily to offer a broad look at the discipline of communication rather than to provide an in-depth analysis of each area.

Second, we shift the focus to communication science and discuss its philosophical roots and underpinnings. We focus on communication science and offer a more systematic and in-depth examination of its roots as they relate to the natural sciences, because it is the approach taken in the majority of the book. Third, we discuss how communication is both a level and a topic field. We identify how these dimensions situate communication within the broader social sciences and we consider how the topics of communication bind the various areas together, while the levels of analysis are consistent with the distinctions discussed above.

A Broad-Based Look at Communication

Most communication scholars agree about what general topics constitute the field of communication. Interpersonal communication in its many contexts (e.g., family, small groups), mass media, and communication artifacts (e.g., television programs, campaign speeches) are all seen as types of communication that fall well within the parameters of the field when communication is defined broadly as anything that is concerned with messages. Admittedly, communication thus defined covers a wide range of topics, with sizeable overlaps with other social sciences. However, the issues of breadth and overlap with other disciplines are not specific to communication. Most social sciences have similarly broad definitions or have grown to include topics shared with other disciplines, albeit approached from their own perspectives and studied with various methodologies.

Within communication, however, one distinction that is often made is along epistemological lines that consider what constitutes knowledge, what the limits of knowledge are, and importantly, how we can best build a body of knowledge. Fink and Gantz (1996) conducted a large-scale content analysis that attempted to grapple with and clarify these various distinctions in the field of communication. While their analysis was limited to include only research in mass communication, the research traditions they identified exist in other areas of communication scholarship as well. In this classic work, Fink and Gantz identified three areas of research: social science, interpretive research, and critical scholarship. In the following discussion, we add rhetoric to that list, because, practically speaking, many communication departments, as well as several of the major associations of communication, not only include rhetoric in the discipline of communication, but in fact originated with departments of rhetoric and speech communication. Below, we discuss each of these, and then provide an overview to provide a broad look at the ontological, epistemological, methodological, and axiological approaches in each of the areas.

Within each of the three major communication traditions: communication science, rhetoric, and critical/cultural studies, scholars tend to share some agreement about basic ontological, epistemological, and methodological assumptions. It is *between* the various areas that disagreements arise, not simply as a point of philosophical debate but also because the areas emerged somewhat independently from different schools of thought and merged relatively late in academic history into the single discipline called communication (see Chapter 3 for a historical overview). Questions that ask what do we know, what can we know, and how can we know it are likely to be answered differently by practitioners in each of the subdisciplines. These different answers are occasionally made explicit, for example, in a philosophical debate about epistemology, but most often they are unstated and expressed implicitly in the way scholars in different areas practice their scholarship and research.

As mentioned above, the subdisciplines often draw on different philosophical traditions (also see Chapter 6), which then give rise to different bodies of theory that share a given philosophy or set of philosophies, and philosophical assumptions, by necessity, result in different *kinds* of theories. Finally, the methods used within a subdiscipline may be either obviously or simply implicitly connected to the aforementioned theories and philosophies. A method may seem to be a simple choice of how to collect data. But that choice does two things: it reveals the assumptions about the nature of reality that are held by the researcher, and it flows logically and inevitably from the school of thought to which the researcher subscribes. Therefore, acceptance of a given method reveals adherence to much more than a preference for numbers over words, or vice versa. Philosophy, theory, and method are integrally and intimately related through ontological, epistemological, and methodological beliefs. They are absolutely intricate and absolutely connected. Although it is beyond the scope of this book to thoroughly trace communication science, critical/cultural studies, and rhetoric through those ontological, epistemological, methodological, and axiological traditions, it is worth examining them in brief, summarizing them, and then considering communication science in greater depth.

Ontologically speaking, various subdisciplines in communication may have differing assumptions of what constitutes reality. To the *communication scientist*, the world is seen as real and objectively knowable. After all, communication scientists persistently seek to measure abstract entities and look for causal relations between them. This approach can be said to be rational and atomistic. Given this ontology, it follows that, epistemologically, communication scientists use a deductive approach and seek to uncover this knowable reality using methods that are themselves systematic, logical, and replicable. It is no surprise, then, to trace communication science's epistemological roots to the natural sciences, as will be discussed in the next section. In fact, surveys, experiments, and content analyses all rely on assumptions grounded in the natural sciences. The resulting axiological approach argues for a scientific practice that is unbiased and seeks to advance and build knowledge. Of course, in practice, social scientists cannot eliminate all biases. However, it is important to point out that for any bias that may exist, a specific method has been developed to minimize it. Thus, communication science takes an axiological approach that seeks to minimize bias. Any positive outcomes resulting from the research practice result from what is *done* with the findings and not from the act of research itself.

Thus, from ontology to axiology, a lineage can be traced. It would be difficult for a social scientist to engage in a piece of scholarship that utilizes a critical studies or other unscientific approach without calling into question the ontological and epistemological beliefs that brought her to the social sciences to begin with. Of course, scholars may engage in their practices without consciously considering or even being aware of their assumptions, thus allowing for the use of multiple methods and application of theories based on incompatible assumptions. In addition, not all scholars are slaves to the assumptions that underlie their main practice. Instead, they may take pragmatic stances, assuming that questions are best answered from multiple angles and disciple-like devotion to a given set of assumptions is limiting, not noble. Nevertheless, such a pragmatic approach may not stand up to philosophical scrutiny.

In sometimes stark contrast to the communication science approach, the *critical/cultural scholar* takes a phenomenological approach that perceives reality as subjective, that is, as existing within the frame of reference of the person being studied. Reality, therefore, does not exist. There is only what is experienced as reality by those who live it. Of course, there are more and less radical interpretations of this approach. From one standpoint, a cultural studies scholar might argue that no type of reality exists outside of subjective experience, which includes the physical world. From a less extreme standpoint, a critical scholar might argue that while there is an objective reality to the physical world, social reality always exists in subjective experiences. Because the relevant reality that the social sciences are about is always experienced *by* someone, any potentially existing objective reality is not relevant to social phenomena and thus communication's focus should remain on the actors in a situation and privilege should be given to their subjective perspectives.

This ontological perspective leads to an epistemology that requires a more interpretive and flexible approach to data. In other words, if the subjective experience of the actor is paramount, multiple perspectives must be considered and no single perspective privileged, particularly not that of the researcher. The researcher may offer one interpretation, but that may be only one of many important interpretations. The actor of interest and additional observers might all have interpretations that also must be considered as important points of view. This polysemic approach has resulted in the use of many methodologies: in-depth interviews, participant observation, ethnographic work, single case studies, and analysis of texts and artifacts. All of these methods may be used to address a particular research question. In addition, for both the cultural and the critical scholar, bias may not be seen as something to be minimized; rather, bias may be seen as inevitable and something to be explicitly acknowledged and included in the interpretive process. Critical scholars might additionally add to this an interest in recognizing their own biases and moving toward a particular goal, which is often emancipation and improving the lives and situations of actors. This implies a value-laden axiological approach in which some subjective realities, or perhaps more appropriately, some lived experiences, are better than others. Thus, critical scholars, in their belief in the political role of the researcher in conducting her research, stand in contrast to communication scientists, who regard their research as objective and essentially value-free.

A third area of communication, *rhetoric*, emerged from yet another philosophical school of thought. With its roots in ancient Greece and oratorical skills, it lays proper claim to being the oldest area of communication research. Its contemporary link to communication science and cultural/critical studies is due in part to shared topical focus. After all, areas such as presidential debate, advertising, and public relations can be approached by the communication scientist, the cultural/critical scholar, and certainly the rhetorician, even if their approaches differ radically and their departmental marriages are not always easy.

Contemporary rhetoric generally holds that reality is socially constructed. With its focus on language and persuasion, and an eye toward generating a reality in the audience, the ontological assumption stands at its core. In fact, in a seminal article, Scott (1967) brought ontological concerns to the forefront by claiming that "rhetoric . . . is epistemic" (p. 17). In other words, "rhetoric may be viewed not as a matter of giving effectiveness to truth but of creating truth" (p. 13). Thus, if rhetoric creates not only knowledge but truth, it stands to reason that reality is neither fixed nor finite. In this, the rhetorician shares something in common with cultural studies scholars, believing not in an objective reality to be discovered, but in a created reality—reality that the process of research actively helps create. This more contemporary approach does exist in contrast to the traditional approach, rooted in classical Greek rhetoric, in which the rhetorician's job was to reveal truth (Kennedy, 1994). Nevertheless, modern rhetorical assumption seems to have coalesced around Scott's (1967) view that truth is not immutable, but contingent. Methodologically, rhetoricians focus mainly on texts and discourse, although artifacts may also be studied using rhetorical theory and method.

The method of rhetorical study makes use of concepts rooted in traditional rhetoric (i.e., ethos, logos, kairos, mediation, etc.) to describe the social or epistemological functions of a given text or discourse. The goal of rhetorical analysis is to isolate and understand any arguments within the object of study and to identify the specific semiotic strategies employed by speakers to accomplish specific persuasive goals. Rhetorical analysis may also include an assessment of whether or not the persuasive goals were met. Thus, axiologically, rhetoric can be said to take a value-laden approach because it holds as a premise that a text can be more or less effective (Kennedy, 1994). Thus, unlike communication science, rhetorical studies tend to take a normative stance. Similar to cultural studies, and perhaps even more so critical studies, rhetorician seek to assess and improve the communicative act.

Background of Communication Science

Shifting now to a focus on the philosophical underpinnings of communication science, in order to provide a framework for the second section of the book, we turn our attention to this philosophical approach within communication science. Communication science grew out of several related disciplines such as psychology, sociology, journalism, and political science. At the time, individuals in these disciplines shared a common interest in messages and their effects on receivers. Whether those messages originated from mass media sources or interpersonal ones, by the 1990s it began to be recognized that for a unified discipline of communication to grow and flourish, commonalities, and not differences, in communication theories needed to be emphasized. With the introduction and adoption of the Internet in the 1990s, the divide between mass and interpersonal communication began to blur even further. One binding element that has lasted throughout the decades, however, is the common emphasis on the scientific method, debates notwithstanding. Although these methodological debates, and indeed the underlying philosophical debates, still occur, it is worth recognizing the common roots from which these various areas emerged.

Naturalism, Post-Positivism, and Communication Science

Naturalism, and its cousin post-positivism (see Chapter 5), is a philosophical tradition in the social sciences that grew out of the scientific method in the natural sciences. As such, those who use experimental design and surveys believe that methods from the natural sciences can and should be used to study human and social phenomena. The methods and assumptions used in the natural sciences themselves emerged from the intellectual tradition of positivism, and several of the key tenets of positivism still have substantial influence on contemporary adherents to naturalism (Bishop, 2007), although few people would identify themselves as positivists currently for reasons that will become clear presently (see Chapter 5).

The origins of positivism can be traced back to British empiricists of the seventeenth and eighteenth centuries, including John Locke and David Hume. Epistemologically, empiricism holds that an understanding of and knowledge about the world must come only from observation and experience. In the nineteenth century, Auguste Comte, arguably one of the first self-identified "positivists," argued that the goal of science is prediction, and anything that cannot be verified empirically (i.e., observed) should not be part of the scientific domain (D'Andrade, 1986), and by the middle of the twentieth century, logical positivism had emerged, with a strong influence on burgeoning social sciences. Logical positivists extended and refined positivism by arguing that meaningful statements are and should be only those that can be directly tested through observation or logically deduced from observation. However, by the latter half of the twentieth century, logical positivism had begun to fall out of favor because it became clear that it was neither philosophically nor practically tenable. For example, neither electrons (at the time) nor beliefs could be directly observed, but both could be demonstrated through theory and less direct forms of testing (Comte, 1988).

Despite the fact that positivism demonstrated itself to be more problematic than useful in the realm of philosophy, some of its main assumptions and beliefs are foundational to contemporary social sciences. First, in many areas of social science, including communication science, the pursuit of knowledge still rests on empiricism in general and empirical validation in particular. Although knowledge gained through theory is pursued and unobservable phenomena such as beliefs, motivations, and attitudes are part of the stock in trade, empirical research and measurement is an integral part of the process. Karl Popper's (1963) dictum that all theory should be falsifiable is wed to all science based on empiricism. Certainly, Popper's claims regarding falsifiability were intended as a theoretical postulate, but ultimately, it suggests empirical outcomes as necessary.

A second vestige of positivism in contemporary social science is that, like many other social scientists, communication scientists often argue that one of the main aims of research is to provide causal explanations. By identifying variables and discovering causal connections between them at a given point in time, later outcomes can be predicted as long as the input variables are recognized. For example, theory regarding marital success may identify which variables are associated with marital satisfaction and stability. These associations are then empirically tested to assess the validity of those theories. Ideally, then, an assessment of these variables in a given situation may allow researchers to predict the success of a given marriage.

Another vestige of positivism is that most communication sciences attempt to engage in value-neutral research. That is, knowledge is pursued for its own sake, and research findings are evaluated based on their truth value, not their social, political, or humanistic desirability. Social engineering is either avoided entirely or at least relegated to a secondary or tertiary position. This kind of approach, which is at odds with later philosophical movements such as the Frankfurt School and the rise of critical theory (Adorno et al., 1969), suggests that communication science should explain and predict human behavior, but should not, as a direct part of the scientific enterprise, attempt to change it. As a result, extensive efforts and methodological strategies are employed to help ensure that research questions, designs, data collections, and data analyses proceed with as little bias as possible. The results, then, are thought (or at least hoped) to be bias-free knowledge. That knowledge then might be used to help improve some situation or outcome, but the research itself strives to disconnect from that other goal. The value-neutral approach argues that social science may be able to tell us whether violent video game play increases aggressive behaviors, but social science makes no claims about the relative morality or immorality of aggression or violent video game play.

Given the connections between positivism, naturalism, and communication science, it is worth emphasizing that positivism, despite its contributions to modern social science, ultimately failed as a philosophical approach. Doctrines that disallow the study of phenomena that cannot be directly observed or that elevate observation above theory do not have the longevity needed to explore the psychological and social world of communication. Instead, adherents to naturalism, or its philosophical offspring post-positivism, embrace theory as a vital part of the knowledge-building process. They regard social and psychological phenomena that are not directly observable (e.g., attitudes, schemata) as crucial constructs in many theories and models even if, or perhaps especially because, they are challenging to measure. Finally, communication scientists see empirical pursuits as a necessary part of knowledge building, but not as its zenith.

Built on these philosophical traditions, what is it that social science in general, and communication science in particular, *does*? With reliance on theory and assistance from quantitative methods (see Chapter 8), communication science attempts to uncover facts about messages, including their content, context, causes, processes, and effects. Communication science attempts to make and test predictions regarding relationships between variables, and lastly, communication science seeks to predict and test mechanisms that help explain relationships between variables that ultimately may result in more extensive models of the communication process.

First, uncovering empirical facts may seem at first an unsophisticated goal, especially if the uncovering of a given fact does not result in the development or test of an influential theory or an understanding of causal relationships. Although social scientists often value theory and sophisticated variable analyses over simple facts, facts are a necessary aspect of the knowledge-building process and therefore integral to scientific research and methods. Without the methods used by social scientists, facts would often be determined by anecdote or folk wisdom (Bishop, 2007). Without social science and its methodological sophistication and its conceptual clarity, facts might lack in validity and reliability. Of course, what constitutes a fact is itself open to debate. The conceptualization of the ideas and the measurement used are open to assessment that may ultimately help to validate or invalidate the fact. Thus, fact finding need not be relegated to the basement of social science. If done well, it requires all the rigor of the more lauded aspects of social science: relationship testing and theory building. For example, consider a study of the influence of story format (e.g., traditional books vs. electronic books) on preschoolers' story comprehension. In order to assess if this is a worthwhile study, practically speaking, we might want to know a simple fact: what percentage of preschoolers are exposed to electronic books. A study of the influence of a particular conflict style on marital satisfaction is made stronger with an understanding of how many couples use that style of interaction. Theory regarding the role that arousal resulting from video game play plays in increases in aggression benefits from a simple understanding of how arousing video games are. Thus, facts undergird the larger social scientific endeavor and indeed do so in communication science.

A second goal in communication science is to examine relationships between variables. The statistical technique of correlation analysis was developed in the late nineteenth century by social scientists and has since been extended to more sophisticated analyses such as multiple regression and structural equation modeling, both of which are based on the same basic mathematics of the correlation. Correlation analysis and its conceptual and mathematical extensions allow researchers to examine how strongly two variables are related or how multiple variables are related to an outcome variable or variables. For example, violent video game play, aggression personality trait, and gender all correlate with aggression (Carnagey et al., 2007), and it is through techniques such as multiple regression and structural equation modeling that researchers are able to measure the magnitude of the relationship between all of these variables and aggression, and the magnitude of the relationships for each individual variable while controlling for the effects of the others.

One of the main problems with correlation, of course, is the old truism that correlation does not equal causality. A correlation between two variables is a necessary condition to demonstrate causality, but it alone is not sufficient to establish causality. Two variables may be correlated because one causes the other or because the latter causes the former. For example, observing that playing violent video games and aggression are correlated could be because violent video game play causes aggression, or because aggressive individuals play more violent video games. Another option is that a third variable is causing both variables, which are then said to have a spurious relationship. For example, growing up in a violent home could cause both the aggression and the preference for violent video games. Thus, researchers must work harder to demonstrate causality by using theory, sophisticated research designs such as experiments, and, of course, consideration of the mechanism by which two variables are related.

In fact, the testing of mechanisms is probably the third goal in communication science. Only in the past few decades, however, has the idea of a mechanism been given any serious consideration as a philosophical concept and been empirically investigated in the social sciences (Hedström & Ylikoski, 2010). Indeed, at an earlier point in the history of empirical and quantitative social sciences, explanations were seen as being most robust when they adhered to the model of the covering law. The covering law model explains events by reference to another event that is connected to the former by a necessary force, like that of a law in natural sciences. It necessarily presupposes the existence of such covering laws or general propositions and then uses correlation between the event being explained (explananda) and events argued to be its cause or set of conditions (explanantia) (Hempel, 1965). Of course, later arguments made in the philosophy of social science led us to conclude that correlation alone could not imply causality; thus, researchers began to search for causal mechanisms in a given set of relationships in order to improve explanatory power.

The basic idea of a mechanism has been described in many ways in the past decade and a half. One clear and specific definition states that a mechanism:

> (i) describes an organized or structured set of parts or components, where (ii) the behavior of each component is described by a generalization that is invariant under interventions, and where (iii) the generalizations governing each component are also independently changeable, and where (iv) the representation allows us to see how, by virtue of (i), (ii), and (iii), the overall output of the mechanism will vary under manipulation of the input to each component and changes in the components themselves.
>
> (Woodward, 2002, p. S375)

This definition argues for a set of relationships that includes systems, made up of components, generalized relationships, and resulting outcomes. A more straightforward definition simply claims that "a mechanism-based explanation is quite simple: At its core, it implies that proper explanations should detail the cogs and wheels of the causal process through which the outcome to be explained was brought about" (Hedström & Ylikoski, 2010, p. 50). Thus, mechanisms expand on the basic two-variable correlational explanation and do so by offering a conceptual explanation of the process by which the two variables are related. Ultimately, then, explanations that include mechanisms involve statistical correlations between independent variables (i.e., explanantia) and the dependent variable (i.e., explananda), but expand the conceptual model, the measurement model, and the statistical analytic model to include intervening variables that help test theory. Thus, mechanisms improve our ability to explain and predict how variables may behave in a large sample of data. Of course, due to variations within human populations on almost every phenomenon that can be measured, it is unlikely that social science will uncover law-like generalities in the way that natural sciences have done (Elster, 1999). Instead, social science typically seeks to explain and predict relationships and their mechanisms both at the psychological and sociological levels. The social sciences do so by studying large samples, employing inferential statistics with their inherent recognition of error, and ultimately attempting to explain only processes, and not individual instances of explanantia and explananda. To do that, human beings would need to demonstrate adherence to law-like behavior, which clearly does not occur.

Distinctions and Categories in the Social Sciences and in Communication

Both the early roots and the early history of communication, deriving as it did from a number of philosophical approaches, fields, and academic departments, resulted in a discipline that did not agree on its main topic(s), appropriate methods of inquiry, or even basic ontologies. Although much ink has been spilled over whether this history has resulted in a discipline that is intellectually impoverished (Peters, 1986) or practically multidisciplinary (Gonzalez, 1988), as discussed in Chapter 2, the discipline of communication can, at the very least, be referred to as broad. In attempting to understand the layout and parameters of the field, several scholars have attempted to create a kind of typology of communication, identifying various dimensions along which areas within communication might be divided.

McLeod and colleagues (2010) identified several ways that disciplines might be sliced, and other scholars in other disciplines have made similar attempts about their home disciplines or about the social sciences in general (e.g., Glass et al., 2004). For example, some disciplines identify themselves by *level of analysis*. That is, most researchers in their discipline identify variables and study phenomena at a given level, such as the broad, societal level (i.e., organizations and institutions), for example in sociology, or most of the researchers in their discipline identify variables and study phenomena at the individual level (i.e., personality, age, income), for example in psychology. Agreement tends to exist between scholars of level disciplines concerning what that level is and should be. Level of analysis suggests how close or far away we should stand from the problem in order to study it appropriately. Disciplines that identify themselves by level of analysis include sociology, psychology, and anthropology. Other disciplines identify themselves by topic or phenomenon under study. Agreement tends to exist between scholars of phenomenon disciplines concerning what should and should not be studied by those in the discipline. Political scientists, economists, geographers, and to some extant communication scholars focus on a particular *topic* or *phenomenon*.

Given that communication is generally a phenomenon, or topic, discipline, scholars within communication tend to study it at different levels. That is, communication scholars might focus on political communication, for example, but study it by examining macro-system-type phenomena (e.g., the role of financial advertising revenues in the coverage of particular political news stories) or micro-system-type phenomena (e.g., the effect of a product ad embedded in a political debate on perceptions of the debaters' performance). This tendency for scholars to study at different levels of analysis can result in two problems. The first problem is rather straightforward, although it is potentially harmful in terms of building a body of knowledge. Specifically, scholars in communication tend not only to read just in their subfield (e.g., political communication) but often also only at the same level of analysis. Thus, a given body of knowledge is built on a rather small and somewhat marooned island, leaving untapped opportunities to cross-pollinate across levels within a given topic, no matter how narrowly defined that topic might be.

A second problem is that scholars are so focused on their topic that they combine concepts from different levels in their research, potentially because they do not even recognize the importance of their system choices and system approaches. The problem with this mixing of concepts that stem from different levels of analysis is a mismatch between the phenomenon and the theory intended to explain it. Specifically, McLeod and colleagues (2010) stated that:

> Theory building requires concepts that are defined and measured at the same level as the phenomenon being explained. The history of communication is replete with examples of the mixing of "psychological" and "sociological" variables in a giant step-wise regression analysis to maximize prediction.
>
> (p. 189)

They also show concern over what they call "system jumping," where researchers may use concepts defined at one level of analysis, such as the sociological level, to explain behavior at another level, such as the psychological level.

Is this a problem? Whereas the authors themselves (McLeod et al., 2010) decry the lack of understanding that many scholars have of the levels of analysis issue, or at least the excessive pragmatism others use in willfully mixing levels of analysis, is it possible that the problem *might* be viewed as a benefit? Macro theory, which attempts to employ environmental as well as cognitive (level) variables in explaining behavior, may offer the most inclusive, and potentially most explanatory, approach to a given phenomenon. As long as theoretical rigor and measurement sensitivity are used in the process, is system jumping a problem? It is well beyond the scope of this chapter to argue for one side or the other of this argument, but it is certainly worth suggesting that a level of analysis need not be isolated theoretically and empirically in order to be a useful tool for understanding and constructing theory.

In any case, a more sensitive scheme may be most useful here, if for no other reason than it delineates more levels but also allows individual scholars to collapse across levels if it seems philosophically or theoretically warranted. For example, McLeod et al. (2010) propose a fairly logical and practical scheme that includes five levels of analysis. These include societal/global levels, industry/organizational levels, and community/neighborhood levels, all of which they specify as macro-level social systems requiring measurement of variables at the macro level. They then add to those social systems network/primary groups as a microsocial-level system and include finally the individual as a micro system (p. 189). For most topics, problems can be addressed at every system level from the societal/global all the way down to the smallest unit of analysis, the individual.

Topic fields, such as communication, draw both their strength and their weakness from focusing on a given topic, across system-level boundaries. Much can be gained when scholars with different methodological approaches research the same topics and work on the same problems. However, those very method-ological boundaries often keep scholars from reading and applying research from outside of their topic and from outside of their method. Instead, scholars may opt to read narrowly. One reason for this may be that, as discussed in this chapter, the methods, and indeed the ontology, epistemology, and axiology in various areas differ quite dramatically, making it difficult to make the much-needed connections. Thus, the subdisciplines in communication do share an interest in similar topics, but their philosophical underpinnings, combined with the issue of level distinctions, result in precisely the disparate and sometimes chaotic discipline that currently exists. That critique leveled, our breadth, and indeed practical applicability, have enabled communication to move forward in building a broad and broad-based body of knowledge.

References

Adorno, T. W., Albert, H., Dahrendorf, R., Habermas, J., Pilot, H., & Popper, K. R. (1969). *The positivist dispute in German sociology* (G. Adey and D. Frisby, trans.). London: Heinemann.

Anderson, J. A., & Baym, G. (2004). Philosophies and philosophic issues in communication, 1995–2004. *Journal of Communication, 54*(4), 589–615.

Bishop, R. C. (2007). *The philosophy of the social sciences.* New York: International Continuum.

Carnagey, N. L., Anderson, C. A., & Bushman, B. J. (2007). The effect of video game violence on physiological desensitization to real-life violence. *Journal of Experimental Social Psychology, 43*(3), 489–496.

Comte, A. (1988). *Introduction to positive philosophy* (F. Ferre, trans.). Indianapolis, IN: Hackett.

D'Andrade, R. (1986). Three scientific world views and the covering law model. In D. Fiske (Ed.), *Metatheory in social science: Pluralisms and subjectivities* (pp. 19–41). Chicago: The University of Chicago Press.

Elster, J. (1999). *Alchemies of the mind.* Cambridge: Cambridge University Press.

Fink, E. J., & Gantz, W. (1996). A content analysis of three mass communication research traditions: social science, interpretive studies, and critical analysis. *Journalism & Mass Communication Quarterly, 73*(1), 114–134.

Glass, R. L., Ramesh, V., & Vessey, I. (2004). An analysis of research in computing disciplines. *Communications of the ACM, 47*(6), 89–94.

Gonzalez, H. (1988). The evolution of communication as a field. *Communication Research*, *15*(3), 302–308.

Hedström, P., & Ylikoski, P. (2010). Causal mechanisms in the social sciences. *Annual Review of Sociology*, *36*, 49–67.

Hempel, C. (1965). *Aspects of scientific explanation*. New York: Free Press.

Kennedy, G. A. (1994). *A new history of classical rhetoric* (p. 3). Princeton, NJ: Princeton University Press.

McLeod, J. M., Kosicki, G. M., & McLeod, D. M. (2010). Levels of analysis and communication science. In C. R. Berger, M. E. Roloff, & D. Roskos-Ewoldsen (Eds.), *The handbook of communication science* (pp. 183–200). Thousand Oaks, CA: Sage.

Peters, D. H. (1986). Institutional sources of intellectual poverty in communication research. *Communication Research*, *13*, 527–559.

Popper, K. (1963). *Conjectures and refutations: The growth of scientific knowledge*. London: Routledge.

Scott, R. L. (1967). On viewing rhetoric as epistemic. *Central States Speech Journal*, *18*(1), 9–17.

Woodward, J. (2002). What is a mechanism? A counterfactual account. *Philosophy of Science*, *69*(S3), S366–S377.

5

POSITIVISM/CAUSALITY/ EXPLANATION

As we already discussed in earlier chapters, communication as an academic discipline differs from many others in that it is not grounded firmly in only one epistemological tradition, or even a family of related traditions. Rather, it is a very broad discipline with several roots, based on the humanities, the social sciences, the performing arts, and public address. As a result, not only is there a lack of consensus as to what constitutes a good or valid knowledge claim, but frequently there is intense or even vitriolic disagreement between communication scholars about even the most basic concepts of scholarship, such as the definition of knowledge or the purpose of scholarship. A lot of these disagreements run along subdisciplinary fault lines, with those more closely aligned with the humanities taking what can roughly be described as a more idealist or phenomenological view, whereas the areas more closely aligned with the social sciences take a more naturalist or realist view. It is not our intention here to enter this fray with arguments for or against either approach; this is well beyond the scope of this book. Rather, in this chapter we explain the epistemology behind the social science position on knowledge and knowledge claims, which Pavitt (1999) so aptly called "scientific realism," and others have more thoroughly discussed and fine-tuned (Bhaskar, 1987).We do this so that our readers are able to understand how knowledge claims are made and evaluated in social science. It thereby allows readers to evaluate social science research based on the standards and conventions that social scientists have created for themselves. Typically, research is evaluated from within its own philosophical and epistemological framework, because judging scholarly activity from a theoretical or methodological position that questions the underlying assumptions of that discipline makes it difficult to move forward. Although these philosophical and epistemological debates are indeed important, in order to make any knowledge claims whatsoever, we must agree on the assumptions and then move to an agreeable critique of a work itself. Thus, while we ourselves are most comfortable with knowledge claims based on scientific realism, our goal here is not necessarily to convince the reader of the superiority of this position and to encourage them to reject other viewpoints. Our goal is primarily to allow readers to distinguish good from bad *social science* (although see Chapters 6 and 7 for an alternate perspective).

Knowledge and Knowledge Claims   *The difference btwn belief & knowledge*

To discuss scientific realism, we need to start with a brief primer on knowledge and epistemology before getting into a more detailed description of social science practices in communication research. The classic definition of knowledge is the intersection of belief and truth, where the belief resides within a person perhaps as a mental representation or mental construct, and truth is an objective attribute that exists in the external world. This intersection of belief and truth is often paired with the additional condition that the belief must also be justified, a requirement that in Western tradition is attributed to Plato. This seemingly simple definition rests on a couple of important, and not entirely uncontroversial, assumptions. First and most importantly, it assumes that there exists an objectively true world that one can have beliefs about. In other words, there has to be a reality that is objective, which means that reality exists outside of, and is not dependent on, individuals' perception or experience of it to exist. This does not presume that perception is irrelevant. Instead, it suggests that a reality exists prior to perception of it, and without such an objective reality, it would be logically impossible for a belief to be either true (knowledge) or untrue (illusion). As an aside, another consequence of an objective reality is that there is utility to truthful beliefs. If there is an objective reality and humans are interacting with it, they will experience good or bad outcomes based on their actions. Truthful beliefs about the world will allow humans to predict the consequences of their behaviors and enable them to behave in a way that is advantageous rather than disadvantageous for them. By contrast, in a world without objective reality, for example, where "reality" is defined entirely by social conventions, it would be more important to have the power to shape reality in a way to bring about desired outcomes than to have truthful beliefs.

The second assumption is that human cognition allows us to hold beliefs about the world that are wrong, or untrue. Without this attribute, every belief would be true and there would be no difference between belief and knowledge. This seemingly self-evident observation is actually more complicated and surprising than it would appear on first look. Why this is so becomes clear if we consider the consequences of true and false beliefs. The adaptive value of true beliefs is immediately apparent: it allows predictions concerning the consequences of behaviors and the modification behaviors in order to achieve favorable outcomes. By contrast, in a world with objective reality, false beliefs should lead people to behave in ways that, at best, fail to maximize outcomes and, at worst, lead to undesirable outcomes. Thus, it is not clear why humans should have evolved to be able to have false beliefs. Clearly, we generally assume that animals, for example, do not have the capacity to have false beliefs. Why humans have this ability is an interesting philosophical question in its own right, but for current purposes let it suffice to postulate that humans can have false beliefs. It is this ability of humans to hold false beliefs that makes it possible to distinguish between beliefs and knowledge and also between knowledge claims that are more likely to be true and those that are more likely to be false.

A third important assumption of our definition of knowledge is that it is even possible to determine whether a belief is true or untrue, that is, whether it is justified; if not in an absolute sense, at least probabilistically. Unlike the first two assumptions, which are required by the definition of knowledge as the intersection of belief and truth and are therefore strong assumptions, this third assumption is weak in that it hinges on what is meant by "justified," recalling that in Plato's condition, a true belief needs to be justified to qualify as knowledge. Requiring beliefs to be justified before accepting them as knowledge also introduces a certain element of uncertainty into the definition of knowledge. By its very nature, a justification is an argument about the validity of a position based on evidence. While its persuasiveness often depends on the quality of the evidence, it is not just the evidence but also how it fits into a larger explanatory framework that determines how good the justification is and with it ultimately how strong the knowledge claim is. Another factor affecting the strength of knowledge claims is the fundamental assumption about humans' ability to know the truth.

If we take the extreme position that the world is basically not knowable, either because of the complexity of the world or humans' limited mental ability or both, then we must also conclude that humans will never really know what is objectively true. In this case, all knowledge is relative and, at best, an approximation of true knowledge. Furthermore, a belief might be justified and qualify as knowledge if it is consistent with any number of different criteria, for example, if it is experienced intuitively; if it follows accepted rules of common sense or rationality; or if it is revealed to the human by some sort of spiritual process or deity. In this view, knowledge and belief are not really distinct or distinguishable. If, on the other hand, we take the extreme position that humans can empirically verify observations as either true or untrue, then we can demand that a belief is only justified and qualifies as knowledge if it has withstood rigorous and quantifiable attempts at disproving it. Incidentally, this method is also called the scientific method and describes the epistemology of scientists, including social scientists (see for example, Chapters 4 and 6).

The Epistemology of Social Science

Epistemology is the branch of philosophy concerned with knowledge and ways of knowing, and is commonly used to describe the belief system underlying knowledge claims. For example, one could say that the epistemology of many religions is that of divine revelation through mediators, such as prophets; by studying sacred texts, such as the Bible, Torah, or Koran; or religious practices, such as prayer or meditation. The epistemology of social sciences, by contrast, is largely that of scientific realism. In practice, this means that knowledge claims have to be based on objective empirical observation that is consistent with predictions derived from a theoretical model.

Scientific realism refers to the specific epistemology, or theory of knowledge, that according to Pavitt (1999) underlies most, if not all, social scientific research in communication studies. According to Pavitt, social scientists are realists in the sense that they assume the existence of an objective world that exists outside and independent of the subjective experience of it. As such, any knowledge claim about the world has an objective truth value, although what that value is might not be known. They are also scientists in that they accept the scientific method as the primary method to justify knowledge claims. Practically, this means that they commit themselves to a process of scientific research to justify their knowledge claims.

The Scientific Method and Positivism

The scientific method describes a process of acquiring knowledge about the world by continually testing the predictions of a theoretical model of the real world against objective empirical observation in the real world and continually revising the theoretical model based on the results obtained from the tests. Predictions derived from theoretical models usually are called hypotheses, and the generic case that the theoretical model is false and therefore the predictions are false as well is called the null hypothesis, or H_0. In practice, because most hypotheses are about differences between groups or the association of two or more variables, the null hypothesis predicts no differences between groups or no association between variables. Thus, the scientific method is an ongoing process of proposing hypotheses, testing the hypotheses with empirical observations, retaining those parts of the theoretical model that led to supported hypotheses, and reformulating and retesting those parts of the theoretical model that led to hypotheses that were not supported. Thus, knowledge is accumulated in an ongoing, systematic way that constantly builds on itself. In the sciences, the scientific method is the only acceptable base for knowledge claims. Knowledge is constituted by those theoretical models or observations that have been supported by empirical evidence. Still untested claims about the world are propositions or, if they derive directly from a theoretical model, hypotheses to be tested.

Positivism is an approach to epistemology closely associated with natural science and the scientific method. As with so many ideas in philosophy, some of the basic ideas of positivism can arguably be traced as far back as Plato or earlier, but it emerged as a coherent theory that significantly influenced scholarship in the

Western world only during the Renaissance and Enlightenment, when it became a significant philosophical basis of natural science. At its core, positivism is based on the assumption of an observable, law-based reality. Law-based in this context means that reality is regular in structure and behavior. This regularity can be expressed in covering laws that apply to all matter regardless of observer. Examples of such absolute laws are that matter attracts matter and that isolated systems conserve their energy. That "reality" is governed by such laws thus makes possible that logic and math can be applied to observations about reality (see Chapter 6 for an alternative to the idea that math can be applied to observations), and that this application will result in necessarily true statements. In fact, positivism claims that these are the only statements that can be considered an authoritative source of knowledge. Hence the name positivism; in positivism, knowledge is limited to claims about the world that are unambiguously (positively) true, either because they are based on verifiable observations or because they must logically follow from such an observation. For example, after I weighed 1 l of water with a calibrated scale, I am positive that at 0 °C, it weighs 1 kg, as per my unbiased observation. Logic and math allow me to be equally sure that 4 l weigh 4 kg and I am also positively sure that 2 l do not weigh 6 kg, and so forth. Knowing the mass and size of other planets, I can even compute how much a liter of water weighs on Mars (0.34 kg) and Jupiter (2.36 kg) with absolute certainty.

While positivism was widely adopted by the natural sciences during and after the Enlightenment, the application of such scientific thinking to human behavior is a more recent phenomenon and often attributed to the work of nineteenth-century European scholars around Auguste Comte and Emile Durkheim. They argued that the same reasoning that restricted knowledge claims to verified observations and their logical consequences in the natural sciences also applied to human behaviors, which should therefore be studied with a scientific approach. This approach to human affairs implies that human behavior is also law governed, because only law-governed phenomena allow for generalization based on past observations of individuals. Applying positivism to human behavior also suggests that the reasons and motivations underlying human behavior are not unique to each individual and thus entirely idiosyncratic, but rather are shared among humans. How one person behaves under certain circumstances is likely similar to how any other person would behave under the same conditions; variations in individual behaviors are the result of different conditions or circumstances, not due to infinite variations in free will. The goal of social scientists, then, is to specify patterns: patterns of the causal conditions and circumstances that give rise to certain behaviors. According to social scientists, such causes can be attributes of the individual, such as personality characteristics or personal experiences, or attributers of the circumstances, such as gender roles, social relationships, or the cultural context. This position is in stark contrast to a humanist view of human behavior, which emphasizes agency and free will over regular, patterned, law-bound behavior. To be clear, social scientists would not typically argue that all human beings behave identically, but rather that patterns in personality, personal experiences, and social context give rise to notable patterns in behavior. Clearly, this discussion is ongoing and will not be resolved anytime soon, although social science has amassed significant evidence for the patterned nature of human behavior.

Ultimately, it was not the objections by humanists that led to the rejection of positivism in both natural and social sciences. Rather, the inherent problem of positivism is that it limits knowledge to that which can be unambiguously observed or deduced from these observations. The problem with this requirement is that it logically requires us to observe everything and to do so continuously, because the assumption that things or the relationships between things do not change over time is in itself in need of positive verification. Taken to its logical conclusion, this means that extreme positivism restricts knowledge claims to be valid only for past observations up to the moment the observation ends. So, an extreme positivist could accept as true the statement "when I weighed this liter of water, it weighed 1 kg," but not the statement "a liter of water weighs 1 kg," because this conclusion rests on the assumption that the weight of a liter of water remains constant, which can be verified only through repeated future observation. Obviously, this creates the problem that in positivism, real knowledge can exist only about past and present observations, never about the future. Thus, philosophically, prediction is impossible in positivism.

A second, even more serious problem with positivism is that it is logically impossible to assert the validity of a theoretical model based on *empirical observation* alone. Because theoretical models are central to science, this means that positivism cannot be the foundation of science. The problem is that in order to claim that an observation positively proves the validity of a theoretical model, one has to be able to either observe or logically exclude all other possible causes or explanations that could bring the observation about. Otherwise, it is always possible that a variable or variables that are unobserved or are not in the theoretical model are the cause or explanation of the observation. Obviously, it is impossible to observe all other possible causes or explanations. Not only is it practically difficult to measure all variables that one knows could conceivably affect the observation, but one would also have to measure variables that one does not even *know about* that could cause the observation. This problem is compounded by the fact that modern science, and social science in particular, often is concerned with and theorizes about things that are not directly observable, such as cognitive and psychological processes that take place inside the mind. While the behaviorism of the mid-twentieth century could be positivist at least in this regard because some branches of behaviorism explicitly rejected the idea that cognition or feelings mediated the connection between stimulus and behavior, the cognitive revolution in psychology made such unobservable processes central in explaining human behavior, and thus rendered direct observation difficult, if not impossible.

For example, in cognitive dissonance theory, Festinger (1957) invoked the hypothetical construct of dissonance as an unpleasant psychological state that is experienced by a person holding two incompatible beliefs, and the unpleasant arousal motivates people experiencing dissonance to change one of their beliefs so that it is compatible with the other. However, it is equally possible that human minds are structurally incapable of holding two incompatible beliefs in long-term memory and that dissonance is just a temporary byproduct, and the motivating force is cognitive rather than affective. Also possible, of course, is that God or some other force does not allow us to have incompatible beliefs, or that there is yet another, thus far undiscovered neurological mechanism responsible for both integrating beliefs and producing the feeling of dissonance. The same is fundamentally true for any observation. It is always possible that something else, so far unknown, is responsible for the observation. It is therefore simply not logically possible to claim that any given observation positively proves a theory or hypothesis. Observations can only prove themselves, and it is always possible that some other, unknown explanation is responsible for the observation and not the proposed model. The inescapable conclusion must be that positivist knowledge is provisional.

Post-Positivism

The solution to these fundamental problems of positivism is what is called post-positivism, which is closely associated with the scholarship of the Austrian-born twentieth-century philosopher Karl Popper (1959, 1963). While accepting logical negativism's conclusion that it is logically impossible to prove a positivist claim about the future validity of an observation or the validity of a theoretical model (given that *future* instances or examples could always arise to contradict a claim), he reasoned that it is possible to reject a positivist knowledge claim about an observation or theoretical model by *failing to observe* the predicted outcome, or even observing an outcome *contradicting* the prediction. He called this process *falsification*. What this boils down to essentially is that for any given prediction about what one should observe derived from a theoretical model, failing to observe the predicted outcomes requires one to reject the underlying theoretical model. For example, if I observe an apple falling from a tree a million times, this does not provide proof that gravity exists (because it may not fall the next time), but if I observe one time that it soars upward, I can reject the notion of gravity as a law.

Thus, the central idea of post-positivism is that while positivist claims about the validity of theoretical models are logically impossible, claims about the invalidity of a theoretical model that are based on empirical observations inconsistent with or even contradicting the theoretical model are not. That is, while we never can be certain that what we think is true, we can be certain about what we know not to be true. The difference is essentially in the underlying logic: Valid knowledge claims in post-positivism are therefore the reverse of the logic of positivism. Specifically, the logic of positivism states that a theoretical model is valid if the evidence supports it. However, given the logical flaws and inevitabilities discussed earlier, we arrive at post-positivism. The logic of post-positivism is that a theoretical model *could* be valid, if one fails to observe empirical evidence *in*consistent with it or even contradicting it *when trying to falsify the theoretical model*. The difference in logic may seem simple or even obvious: we either support a claim in the former case, or fail to support a counter-claim in the latter. But the difference is vital in outcome. In post-positivism, theoretical models are not supported by data that would prove them, rather they are supported by failing to discover evidence that would disprove them. In the technical language of probabilistic statistics, this failure to disprove a theoretical model is called rejecting the null hypothesis. If we reject the null hypothesis, this means our observations have not confirmed that no relationship or difference exists. Put another way: rejecting the null hypothesis means that a relationship between variables, or difference between groups, *does* exist—at least in this instance. Our observations are consistent with our theoretical model. The alternate case is the failure to reject the null hypothesis. This means that the observations are not consistent with the theoretical model, but rather support either an alternate theoretical model or no theoretical model at all.

Looking at positivism and post-positivism casually, one could conclude that the differences are largely semantic and that there is little practical difference in either proving that a theoretical model is valid or failing to prove that it is invalid, as these appear to be just the opposite sides of the same coin. As the preceding discussion has hopefully shown, however, the differences are more profound. For one, focusing on the null hypothesis does not change the fundamental fact that one cannot logically prove a positive claim to knowledge. The same way that is impossible to exclude all known or unknown other causes or variables as an explanation for an association between variables, it is equally impossible to conclude that a null hypothesis is true. The best we can do is to say that our observations are not inconsistent with it, but a failure to observe an association between variables or mean difference between groups does not prove that they do not exist. In either case, according to post-positivism, support for a hypothesis or theoretical model is always qualified. This is reflected in the language used by probabilistic statistics. Frequently used expressions include "data consistent with" or "supporting of" the theoretical model. The phrase "proof of the hypothesis or theoretical model" is never used.

What should have become apparent from the preceding discussion is another important practical implication of post-positivism: while hypotheses are positivist claims about what *is*, irrefutable knowledge is based on observation of what is *not*. For an observation of what is not to be meaningful in regard to the underlying theoretical model, however, support for the null hypothesis should be what is to be expected and rejecting the null hypothesis should only happen if the theoretical model is true. Thus, the crucial element here is that *falsification in post-positivism refers to the honest attempt to test a theoretical model in conditions that make it most likely to observe data consistent with the null hypothesis, unless and only unless the theoretical model is true.* In other words, results that fail to reject the null hypothesis must be surprising and not the expectation. In practical terms, this means that research that supports a theoretical model is research that failed in the honest attempt to show that the model is wrong. That is why, as will be discussed in Chapter 6, stringent probability rules are used. We accept a hypothesis if and only if the likelihood of our finding being chance, or a fluke, is less than 5 percent.

The philosophical–practical requirement to accumulate knowledge by rejecting null hypotheses does not lead to a theoretical focus on the null hypotheses, however. From the scientists' perspective, it is still the theoretical model that formalizes our understanding of the objective world. Consequently the theoretical model's predictions and hypotheses are still the focus of research. More importantly, though, in a practical sense, this means that testing theoretical models creates an interesting and contradicting set of challenges for researchers. On the one hand, consistent with the positive tradition, we are trying to find support for a theoretical model by observing data consistent with it. Thus, our natural inclination would be to design tests that are likely to produce data in support of the hypotheses. On the other hand, post-positivism demands that the only true knowledge claims we can make is that they failed at refuting a theoretical model. The best they can do in support of a theoretical model is to present data that did not disprove it. Ironically, the strongest test in support of a theoretical model is one with the greatest likelihood that the test would produce results that fail to support the theoretical model unless the theoretical model is true. Thus, researchers are motivated to design tests that are likely to fail to support their theoretical models, and scientific standards of research have been developed to ensure just that. This counterintuitive requirement is actually a tremendous incentive for researchers to conduct high-quality research.

Not only does falsification offer a logical means of theory building in which claims can be made, empirically tested, and, importantly, potentially shown to be incorrect, the process that Popper proposes also suggests that theory building and indeed science as a whole must become further *specified*. The role of falsification in theory building is not limited to the validation of theoretical models, but includes the specification of models as well. Popper (1963) proposed that attempts at falsification advance theoretical models and indeed science as a whole by leading to greater specification. The specification results because observations that are inconsistent with specific hypotheses rarely falsify the whole theoretical model. Rather, such results may encourage adjustments of the theoretical model and thus advance the theory. Such specification may include specific conditions under which a model operates, for whom it applies, and at what time. Thus, post-positivism (Popper, 1963) ultimately emphasizes the importance of falsifiability not only on epistemological grounds, but also for the role it plays for specificity in theory building and its guidance of empirical work.

Explanation and Causality

Regardless of epistemology, gaining knowledge rarely is an end in itself. Rather, scholars and scientists pursue knowledge to be able to understand and explain certain phenomena, usually because there is some practical utility in being able to predict specific outcomes. Thus, social scientists are concerned with understanding satisfying relationships so that we can suggest to people what to do in their relationships to make them more satisfying. Likewise, understanding well-adjusted children allows us to suggest to parents how to raise children, and understanding how media affect social behaviors allows us to design policies that regulate media content in positive ways. How one explains phenomena and what type of predictions one is able to make also depend substantially on one's epistemology. Scientific realists believe in a law-governed, objective reality, which means that explanation and causality have specific meaning for them and are closely intertwined. Causality in scientific realism describes a relationship between two or more variables that meets three criteria. First, a change in one necessarily brings about a change in the other(s); the variables are correlated. Second, the change in the causal variable precedes the change in the dependent variable(s) in terms of time ordering. Third, there is no third variable that causes the changes in both the preceding and subsequent variable(s); the relationship is not spurious. Explanation means that the causal relationships have been explicated. Thus, explanation requires that causality is established. While prediction without causation is possible, it would not qualify as explanation. To be an explanation, a prediction has to be justified by causal relationships. This also means that an explanation always also implies a prediction. In scientific realism, both explanation and causation are essentially equivalent and closely tied to governing laws in that any acceptable explanation ultimately makes reference to one or more laws, at which point it cannot be further reduced, except to other laws.

Operationalizations

Another important aspect of social science research that is associated with scientific realism is the extreme importance of operationalizations. An operationalization is how a theoretical construct will be observed in the empirical world, or how it will be measured. Thus, intelligence might be operationalized as a person's score on an intelligence test and expressed as IQ. Similarly, the love you have for a partner could be operationalized as the average score of your responses to seven semantic differentials on a questionnaire, the amount your pupils dilate when catching sight of the partner (Zuckerman, 1971), or the pattern of activation of different brain regions as observed through functional magnetic resonance imaging (fMRI) (Ortigue et al., 2010). Another way to think of operationalizations is that they are the intersection of the theoretical and the empirical. Thus, the ability of any observation to speak to the validity of a theoretical model is directly dependent on the quality of the observation. Unless the connection between a concept and its operationalization is unambiguous, the observation cannot be used to assess the validity or invalidity of a theoretical model.

In social science research, the quality of an operationalization is expressed in two attributes: reliability and validity (see Chapter 6 for a related discussion). The reliability of an operationalization refers to its tendency to produce the same quantification upon repeated measures of the same entity, or the tendency to be consistent. For example, a thermometer that would show a temperature of 90.0, 90.0, and 89.9 for three subsequent measures of your temperature would be considered to be reliable, whereas a thermometer that produces three readings of 100.3, 87.8, and 92.1 in quick succession would not. Likewise, an aggression measure that produces the same or at least very similar aggression scores for three individuals with some similar level of aggression has a high reliability, whereas an aggression measure that produces very dissimilar scores for the three individuals would have low reliability. A nice attribute of reliability from a researcher's point of view is that it can easily be assessed statistically if a concept is measured more than once. Thus, questionnaires often have several items that measure the same concept, because it allows researchers to compute some coefficient of reliability, such as Cronbach's alpha or an interclass correlation. Similar estimates of reliability exist for other types of measurement.

An astute reader may wonder how we can test for reliability when no "objective" measure of some phenomenon, such as aggression, exists. We have many measures of aggression, each of which may be reliable, but how do we know if they are measuring *aggression*? This leads us to the notion of validity, or the accuracy of a measurement. Validity refers to the correspondence between the theoretical concept and the empirical measurement, and is therefore the more crucial attribute of a measurement. In fact, validity logically necessitates reliability. If an operationalization accurately quantifies a theoretical construct, then it follows that a valid measure of the theoretical construct produces the same score in repeated measures, that is, is reliable. In that sense, validity is a sufficient condition for reliability. Unfortunately, the reverse is not true. Reliability is a necessary condition for validity because measurements of the same thing that produce dissimilar results cannot be very valid, as they clearly contain a lot of error. At the same time, however, reliability alone is not evidence for validity. For example, the reliable score of my temperature obtained by the thermometer in the above example could be because the mercury got stuck in the tube of the thermometer, and my real temperature could have been 104.0. Likewise, the similar scores on the aggression measure could be the result of bias in the observer or the very context of the measurement itself. Thus, reliability does not guarantee or even imply validity. One can imagine a very consistent measure that does not at all "get at" the thing it is trying to measure.

The reason social scientists even bother with reliability is that the validity of an operationalization cannot be easily nor conclusively established statistically or empirically. Again, we have to thank post-positivism for that. By the same logic that we can never exclude unknown alternative explanations for an association of variables or group difference, we can never exclude that an unknown variable caused the score on a measurement rather than the concept we wished to measure. Thus, the only evidence we can have for validity is circumstantial, and the reliability of an operationalization is just the first and often easiest piece of circumstantial evidence. As explained above, reliability is a necessary but not sufficient condition for validity. No or low reliability is a clear indication that the operationalization is not valid.

In addition to reliability, other observations about the operationalization provide circumstantial evidence for its validity. The first commonly used observation is *face validity*, which refers to the researchers' and readers' personal judgment that the measurement is valid "on the face of it," hence the name. Whether an answer to a questionnaire item about love validly operationalizes love depends primarily on whether the item is consistent with the theoretical definition of love as used in the study. Secondarily, it also depends on a number of assumptions we make, including about the awareness that persons have about their feelings, their ability and willingness to report such feelings on a questionnaire, and other likely factors that might have biased the results. Another type of validity based on the subjective judgments of researchers and readers is *content validity*. Content validity refers to the extent to which the entire theoretical breadth of the construct is represented in the measures. For example, if the definition of love contains emotions, behaviors, and reciprocity, then a measure has content validity to the extent that it assesses love in these three areas. A measure just assessing emotion would have no content validity in this context.

In addition to face and content validity, which depend on subjective judgment, there are also a couple of aspects of validity that are inferred based on statistical observation of the measure against some criterion. *Predictive validity* refers to the idea that a measure is valid to the extent that it is able to predict, or correlate with, measures of constructs that it should be predictive of. For example, if love is expected to predict or correlate with forgiveness and physiological arousal, then the measure of love is said to have predictive validity if it correlates with measures of forgiveness and physiological arousal, respectively. *Convergent validity* is the extent to which a measure correlates with an already established valid measure of the same or similar constructs. For example, a love questionnaire is said to have concurrent validity if it correlates with a validated measure of love, such as physiological arousal. *Discriminant validity*, in contrast, refers to the measure's lack of correlation with other measures it theoretically should not correlate with. For example, if we theorize that love is the same for both sexes, then the measure is valid to the extent that it does not correlate with biological sex.

Despite the availability of these statistical procedures to demonstrate validity of one's operationalizations, in most social science research in communication these methods are underutilized. One important reason is that there are no commonly agreed-upon effect sizes or correlations that allow one to determine the validity of a measure through statistics alone, although obviously the greater the effect size or correlation, the better (except for discriminant validity, where smaller is better). In addition to being not conclusive, strategies to establish validity statistically require additional measurements and analysis. As a result, in practical application these strategies are used almost exclusively in situations when researchers want to establish new measurements and the question about their validity looms large. In studies employing established measures, however, researchers usually are content with providing some general discussion of the instrument or examples of questionnaire items to establish face validity and reporting reliability coefficients as the only statistical indicator of validity. After all, if science (and social science) is a process of building a body of research based on previous valid work, then trusting and using existing measures is not lazy, it is good science. It also allows for comparison and compilation across studies on similar topics and constructs.

Another area where validity is an important concern is that of experimental manipulations (although see Chapter 6 for a more in-depth discussion). In social science research, the factors that are manipulated are usually those that in the theoretical model have causal relationships with the outcomes. In an experiment, research participants are randomly assigned to different conditions that result from different values on the causal factors. The random assignment to conditions causes all differences between research participants to be distributed randomly and therefore to be either unbiased or, in large groups, to cancel each other out altogether. In theory, then, the only difference between the groups is the difference in the causal factor, or the manipulation. In order to be a valid test of the theoretical model, the manipulation must be a valid operationalization of the theoretical construct. For example, if the theoretical concept is fear and the manipulation involves the fearfulness of a persuasive message, a valid manipulation must indeed create high and low levels of fear, respectively. If the message manipulation creates a different response in research participants such as anger instead of fear, the manipulation is not valid and the experiment not a valid test of the theoretical model.

Much like for the validity of measurements, most researchers rely on face validity in their manipulations. For example, a classical fear manipulation in persuasive messages is to show a person dying from smoking cigarettes. While ostensibly it is self-evident that such a message should create fear in smokers, this hunch by itself does not guarantee that the manipulation is valid. It is also possible that the emotion produced is disgust, annoyance, or even amusement or no emotion at all, depending on how exactly the message is designed or based on audience characteristics such as age and gender. Young men, for example, are almost impossible to scare with threats against their lives, because they simply perceive themselves as invincible. Thus, providing evidence for the validity of a manipulation is very important in experimental research. The established method for doing that is called a manipulation check. Essentially, this is a measure of the theoretical factor taken during or after the experiment. In the case of the fear appeal, for example, where researchers want to know if fear appeals change attitudes, they might also give research participants a questionnaire to report their emotions, or they could measure physiological arousal during the viewing of the message. This would establish, at the very least, whether or not participants felt fear as the result of the message, although it would not test whether or not the fear "worked" *per se*. Obviously, establishing the validity of these measures faces the same challenges as establishing the validity of any other measures discussed above; however, the use of manipulation checks is seen as one way of moving toward that goal.

A final threat to the validity of social science research is what is called external validity, or the ability to generalize the findings of one's research beyond the study itself. The criticism leveled frequently against research is that the findings are particular to a specific sample and cannot be generalized. The general defense against this threat is to employ a truly random sample, where random is defined not only in regard to treatment condition and manipulation, but also in terms of inclusion in the experiment (see Chapter 6 for a more thorough discussion of sampling approaches). However, as will be discussed, random sampling and its cousins (e.g., stratified random sampling) are important to, relevant to, and dependent on the question being explored.

Much of the research in communication studies and related disciplines such as psychology, however, is not intended to produce predictions of population means and similar statistics in the way public opinion polls are. Rather, they are about humans in general or about humans in special circumstances (e.g., child-hood, bereavement), relationships (e.g., marriages, friendships), or communication contexts (e.g., conflict, decision making). These studies are intended to be generalizable in the sense that they are about basic cognitive, psychological, or social processes that are assumed to be universal to all humans. In other words, these processes are assumed to operate essentially the same in all persons, regardless of their upbringing, experiences, and cultural contexts. From this perspective, who is in your sample is essentially irrelevant, because every person is like any other person in respect to the processes under investigation, and all that is needed to obtain a random and representative sample here is random assignment to treatment or control conditions, if it is an experiment. Thus, the question of external validity based on the sample rarely presents itself in this type of research and is usually resolved by random assignment from within the sample population.

This assumption of universality is seldom articulated and, on the rare occasion that it is, is usually addressed in perfunctory remarks in the discussion sections of research articles about the problem of generalization and caution not to generalize to populations other than the sample population; advice that the authors usually promptly ignore in their own discussion of results. The reasons are twofold. On the one hand, the logic is impeccable and the assumption that all humans are essentially the same represents one of the core ideologies of Western culture. If all humans are the same cognitively and function the same psychologically and socially, then it really should not matter who is in any particular study for its results to be generalizable. Any sample would produce generalizable results unless there is something obviously out of the ordinary with the sample, such as all members in the sample experiencing mental illness, for example. On the other hand, in much of social science a culture has developed that habitually uses social science students and other convenience samples in their research. By some estimates, as many of two-thirds of all research subjects in published psychological studies are Americans, of whom two-thirds are psychology undergraduates (Henrich et al., 2010). To question the external validity of studies based on these convenience samples, in other words, would seriously undermine the entire project of social science, something only few social scientists are motivated to do.

Our own take on this issue is that while we do not assume that all social science research based on convenience samples is not externally valid, social scientists in general and communication scholars in particular should pay more attention to their assumptions about universality and the representativeness of their samples. While there is considerable evidence suggesting the universality of many cognitive and social processes, this universality applies to very basic psychological and social processes only. Psychological processes that are impacted significantly by learning, experience, and culture, however, cannot be assumed to be universal, and therefore research that strives to be generalizable to humanity at large needs either to adopt better sampling strategies that result in more representative samples or to develop methods to account for and control these external influences or theorizing needs to consider the boundary conditions of the theory. In other words, what are the characteristics of the sample or the situation that may limit the generalizability of the results (McGuire, 1999). Otherwise, the external validity of this research cannot and should not be assumed. Of course, the crux here is how one determines which cognitive and social processes are basic and universal and which cognitive and social processes are sufficiently impacted by learning, experience, and culture that to test them with non-random samples threatens the external validity of the research. Clearly, there is no definite answer to this question, and our understanding of the role that learning, experience, and culture play in psychological and social processes is incomplete. However, it seems fairly obvious to us that social science as a whole is frequently erring on the side of assuming that psychological processes are universal, and as a consequence is not paying enough attention to the threat to external validity that results from the use of convenience samples. The reasons for this position are too manifold and complex to give justice to in this chapter, but they are based primarily on the egalitarian and individualistic ideology of U.S. and Western societies that dominate much of social science research and that bias researchers' fundamental assumptions about human psychology. This argument is presented in all its detail and force by Fiske et al. (1998), which we recommend to readers further interested in this topic.

In communication research in particular, most phenomena of interest are likely to be impacted by learning, experience, and cultural context. This does not mean that basic and universal processes do not play a role in communication. They most certainly do. Rather, much of what we understand to be communication, including all that involves language, employs symbolic behavior, and symbols by their very nature cannot have meaning outside of a specific cultural context. Thus, in these cases the default assumption should be that cultural context matters, and therefore the external validity of a convenience sample cannot be assumed. Therefore, researchers should be concerned about the representativeness of their samples (if not necessarily their randomness), and either employ sampling strategies that lead to greater representativeness (that is, sampling long-term couples in research on relational communication, rather than young couples available in a college sample), or provide some evidence that their sample is not biasing their results and limiting the generalizability of the results, or theorize about application of the theory.

Conclusion

In this chapter, we have discussed the philosophical underpinnings of social scientific research in communication studies. We argued that social scientists are scientific realists and believe in a law-governed, objective reality, and that their epistemology is based on post-positivism. This means that while they believe that positive knowledge is impossible, they also believe that systematic research that employs valid operationalizations and stringent tests of theoretical models designed to falsify the models but that fail to reject the null hypothesis constitutes a valid basis for knowledge claims. These knowledge claims are not limited to empirical observations only, but also to theoretical models that contain unobserved or even unobservable constructs.

References

Bhaskar, R. A. (1987). *Scientific realism and human emancipation*. London: Verso.

Festinger, L. (1957). *A theory of cognitive dissonance*. Stanford, CA: Stanford University Press.

Fiske, A. P., Kitayama, S., Markus, H. R., & Nisbett, R. E. (1998). The cultural matrix of social psychology. In D. T. Gilbert, S. T. Fiske, & G. Lindzey (Eds.), *The handbook of social psychology* (4th ed., Vol. 2, pp. 915–981). New York: McGraw-Hill.

Henrich, J., Heine, S. J., & Norenzayan, A. (2010). The weirdest people in the world? *Behavioral and Brain Sciences*, *33*(2–3), 61–83. doi:10.1017/S0140525X0999152X.

McGuire, W. J. (1999). *Constructing social psychology: Creative and critical processes*. Cambridge: Cambridge University Press.

Ortigue, S., Bianchi-Demicheli, F., Patel, N., Frum, C., & Lewis, J. W. (2010). Neuroimaging of love: fMRI meta-analysis evidence toward new perspectives in sexual medicine. *Journal of Sexual Medicine*, *7*, 3541–3552; doi:10.1111/j.1743-6109.2010. 01999.x.

Pavitt, C. (1999). The third way: Scientific realism and communication theory. *Communication Theory*, *9*, 162–188. doi:10.1111/j.1468-2885.1999.tb00356.x.

Popper, K. R. (1959). *The logic of scientific discovery*. New York: Harper Torchbooks.

Popper, K. R. (1963). *Conjectures and refutations: The growth of scientific knowledge*. New York: Harper Torchbooks.

Zuckerman, M. (1971). Physiological measures of sexual arousal in the human. *Psychological Bulletin*, *75*, 297–329. doi:10.1037/h0030923.

6

CONDUCTING RESEARCH IN COMMUNICATION SCIENCE

Communication texts are often filled with information, sometimes even things termed as *fact* about the communication process: how it operates, who does what, channels used, contexts, and outcomes. It is crucial to keep in mind as we read these facts that facts in the social sciences are derived from research; research utilizes a given methodology; methodologies can be used, misused, or mishandled. Ultimately, the quality and validity of any piece of information is based in large part on the strength of the method used to obtain that information. Thus, it is important to understand methods and, critically, to understand the research process, how it works, and ultimately, what constitutes best practice studies. In this chapter, we will first briefly review an overall approach to method in communication as it relates to the philosophical underpinnings of communication science as discussed in Chapter 4 and also issues of causality and explanation discussed in Chapter 5. Second, we will discuss how communication scientists determine a method for answering research questions and for testing hypotheses. In the final section, we will address three of the main methods utilized in communication research: survey research, experimental designs, and content analysis. We will then discuss how a given method is selected, and we will conclude with a brief discussion of new and emerging research in what is sometimes called "big data." This chapter is not intended to offer an in-depth look at research methods. Indeed, entire volumes have been written on the topic and have covered it more thoroughly. Instead, the intention is to offer a snapshot of some of the most common communication science methods and present them in the framework of communication research.

Approaching Method in Communication Science

Social science research is conducted through the use of systematic methods, based in part on those developed and utilized in the natural sciences. Social scientific methods are based on the belief that humans operate in somewhat patterned ways, and that those patterns can be detected and uncovered using systematic methods, such as experiments and surveys. When these patterns and regularities are found, theories are then developed, tested, and refined in order to help us understand and predict human behavior. Social scientists, then, believe that human behavior is patterned, not at the individual level necessarily, but at the aggregate level. That is, individuals do not necessarily operate in specifically predictable ways at all times, but across large numbers of people, patterns emerge, suggesting that as a whole, we are influenced by some variables in some ways and not by other variables. Thus, from the ontological perspective, communication scientists believe in a measureable, knowable reality. Communication scientists believe in a reality that exists, separately and objectively, outside of the knower. Although laying it all out like that makes these assumptions appear rather extreme, it is an important position to consider. At least two important points are worth noting here.

From an ontological perspective, it is both excessive and rather naïve to argue that objectivity is absolute or achievable. In fact, it is becoming harder and harder to find anyone who believes this point of view, with total positivism having fallen out of favor in the late twentieth century (Tittle, 2004). Rather, modern-day communication scientists typically avoid ontological positions that may leave the subfield appearing dogmatic and out of touch with the reality and inevitability of bias, on one hand, and of subjectivity on the other. After all, if reality can only be known through an observer, and observers are ultimately biased, does reality, writ large, matter *apart* from the observer? Of course, arguments such as these lead to a kind of solipsism that is not very useful. We may as well all go home and quit trying to discover anything. Thus, absolute positivism is likely not practical, because both the observer and the bias exist and must be dealt with. But the alternate extreme view, complete relativism, is not very practical either. Thus, modern communication scientists believe in a measureable, knowable reality, but recognize that error, both statistical and actual, exists in the research process. This provides both a challenge to precision in the conduct of research and humility in its process.

Second, although absolutism in an ontological approach is rightly out of step with contemporary research, it is impossible to deny the connection between epistemology, or how we know what we know, and our ontological position. After all, when I choose to do an experiment, for example, and carefully design a measure to test variables that exist theoretically as constructs, I am revealing my ontology whether I want to or not. The choice of a survey or experiment is inevitably and inextricably linked to a belief that we can measure things and know things and that knowledge has meaning in the world outside of the study itself. Thus, as we further refine our methods, we are wed ever more closely to an epistemology and ultimately ontology of rationalism, an important point to remember and consider with every research decision made.

Choosing a Method

Communication research remains fresh because much of it examines communication processes that change, grow, and evolve constantly. Media change at a pace with which scholars can barely keep up, organizations adopt new technologies, and interpersonal communication between couples, friends, family members, and colleagues has undergone changes, if not in substance then in the channels that people use to engage in it. It is not surprising, then, that much of communication research is topic driven. After all, change in the way things are practiced, enacted, and experienced often necessitates research. Therefore, communication research often investigates these practical questions. However, practicality as an outcome, or as a beacon to identify a topic, should not trump the importance of theory, the cautious and theory-grounded selection of variables, and the careful application of method. Therefore, in this section, we will consider how researchers select methods.

Often, the choice of a method is obviously derived from a hypothesis or a research question. Those interested in how a sample of individuals think, feel, and behave may conclude that a questionnaire design is appropriate. If they further want to look at relationships between those variables, the variables can then be selected by utilizing existing theory on the topic. Indeed, the literature on attitude, persuasion, social influence, and any number of topics has been studied for decades, offering a rich and deep body of theory that offers guidance and clear direction on which variables should be included and measured to address a given question. On the other hand, the scholar interested in causality would rightly be drawn to the experiment, because it is this design that allows her to test for precise and specific effects. Thus, the process of choosing a method can be quite top down. Although the process of linking theory and research questions is sometimes iterative, selecting the appropriate method may be obvious.

However, the choice is not always obvious and this top-down method is not always successful. Some research questions do not have a clear, well-developed method at the ready. In this case, research design can be more organic. Recently, one of us designed a research project that was based on a method that while not completely novel, was certainly not to be found in a traditional methods textbook. Interested in how individuals' moral belief systems influenced the process of decision making in video games, the study was designed to have participants play a video game and simply talk through their decisions as they made them and, importantly, explain their responses (Krcmar & Cingel, 2016). A battery of measures was used to assess their moral belief systems, a process that was derived from traditional questionnaire design, but because the study was attempting to get at the actual inner-workings of decision making, as much as possible, a think-aloud protocol was used. This method was developed by Ericsson and Simon (1980) and although not intended to assess decision making initially, the think-aloud method has been used in many contexts and could be appropriate here to assess decision-making strategies. Later, those recordings were coded. In short, utilizing a combination of traditional methods, logic, and creativity, researchers often utilize methods that do not appear in research methods textbooks. Ultimately, then, the choice of a research method can be top down, or emergent and bottom up. However, more traditional methods appear to be used more frequently. In fact, in a recent review of the methods used by media effects scholars (see Chapter 7), 71 percent of all research in the leading journals utilized quantitative methods (Potter & Riddle, 2007). Overall, approximately 30 percent were experiments and an almost-equal number were surveys. Therefore, in the following sections we will discuss several of the methods that are most often used to provide the data to test a theory.

Experimental Design

The term experiment denotes a study with several specific features. Although there are different types of experiment, from pre-experiment and quasi-experiment to the true experiment, it is only the true experiment that contains all of the features that allow for accurate claims of causality. In this section, we will briefly mention pre- and quasi-experiments but then discuss at length true experiments, because it is this design that allows for the greatest level of precision, and ultimately most valid claims for causality.

The main elements of an experiment are *manipulation*, a *control group*, *random assignment*, and environmental and observational *control*. The element most often associated with the experiment is the manipulation (sometimes also referred to as the treatment). This occurs when the experimenter deliberately introduces a change into the environment in order to see if there is some observable change in the outcome. Thus, in any study whose hypothesis includes a prediction of causality, the manipulation is the first, and necessary, part of that test. For example, in a study that aims to test the effect of violent video game play on aggressive behavior, the experimenter will have participants play a violent video game, then use some systematic and observable measure of aggression to determine if game play affected aggression. A study that uses only a manipulation is considered a pre-experiment. As the name implies, a pre-experiment has not quite achieved the level of control necessary to be termed an experiment at all. For example, if a researcher measured aggression in a group of participants, had them play a violent game and then measured aggression again, this would be considered a pre-experiment. However, the design includes many flaws. Perhaps the room became hot with the addition of more participants, making everyone annoyed and as a result more aggressive. Perhaps the experiment was timed right before lunch and the hungry participants were more aggressive because they felt uncomfortable. In any case, the pre-experimental design is thought to be just that: not quite an experiment.

In addition to the manipulation itself, however, a well-designed experiment should have a manipulation check. A manipulation check is a means of assessing whether or not the manipulation worked as intended. For example, imagine that a researcher wanted to test the effect of violent video game play on aggression. She decides to have players play a violent game; however, due to other aspects of the study, the researcher must design her own game rather than using one that is commercially available. With her limited budget, the game that is ultimately produced is not graphically sophisticated and, in fact, appears a bit comical. Even the aggression in the game is unconvincing. In this case, is the researcher really testing the effect of violent game play on aggression? If aggression remains the same after game play, could the researcher conclude that playing violent games has no effect on aggression? One way to answer this question is through a manipulation check. The researcher might allow players to play the game and then ask how aggressive the game appeared to them. She might also ask how humorous the game was. In other words, the researcher must determine if the manipulation was perceived by the participants in the way she intended. However, a manipulation (and manipulation check) alone do not create a solid experiment.

Thus, the second necessary element must be introduced. A design that is an improvement over the pre-experiment is one in which a control group is introduced. The control group goes through a set of procedures identical to the test group, but does not receive the manipulation. Thus, in our example, the researcher has participants play a violent video game; control participants play an equally exciting game that has no violence. Subsequently, everyone is tested using the same measure of aggression and average scores in the two groups are compared. Imagine that the researcher does find that those who played the violent game were more aggressive than those who played the nonviolent game. Could adequate conclusions be drawn? Perhaps not, if the researcher were somewhat hapless and had failed to include any other element than manipulation and a control group. What if people were allowed to select which group they wanted to be in? After all, it is difficult enough to drum up participants. Why not allow them the pleasure of selecting their own game type? Obviously, this would result in two groups that differed in many ways from the outset, not least of which was a preference for violent games over nonviolent ones. Thus, any differences in outcomes between the two groups cannot be said to have come from game play itself. This design, a quasi-experiment, must be improved upon still more with the introduction of random assignment.

Indeed, random assignment, as the name implies, is intended to create groups that are equal in many ways at the outset of the experiment. Each participant has a statistically equal likelihood of being assigned to each group; thus, with a large enough sample, the groups should be similar from the outset in number of males and females each group, average level of initial aggression in each group, indeed even the average height of the participants is likely to be equal for the groups. Thus, any difference *after* game play can be thought to be caused by game play itself. In sum, a true experiment requires a manipulation, a control group, and random assignment to condition; however, we have also mentioned the concept of *control* in experimental design. In fact, it is the element of control that allows researchers to make claims about the internal and external validity of their research (see Chapter 5 for a thorough discussion of measurement validity from a theoretical perspective). In fact, any number of problems can exist in an experiment that result in what are commonly termed threats to validity, and those threats can be dealt with, in part, through improved designs and, in some cases, through increased experimental control. Therefore, in the following section we will discuss threats to internal validity, external validity, and lastly, various experimental designs that may help in dealing with potential threats to validity.

Threats to Validity

Validity, in its broadest sense, simply means accuracy. A valid study is one in which the results can be said to be accurate because all of the appropriate steps were taken to insure that the study was done correctly and the results are correct. Although measurement validity, or the congruence between the operational definition and construct it is purported to measure, is crucial in any study, for the purpose of our discussion of experiments we will focus only on *internal* validity at the moment. Internal validity is evidence that any observed outcomes in the dependent variable can conclusively be attributed to the manipulation and not to some extraneous variable or source. Although that description may sound complex, really, internal validity simply answers this question: did the manipulation *really* cause that outcome or was it something else? Answering that question is vital to supporting the accuracy of the study's results. After all, in any study, elements of the design may ultimately be flawed. More than half a century ago, Campbell and Stanley (1963) wrote a slim volume enumerating various possible threats to internal validity. Although the text was never intended as a complete list of all possible ways in which an experiment's validity can be threatened, it was adopted by legions of graduate students as a kind of bible. Thus, borrowing liberally from this now-classic book, we will discuss threats to validity, recognizing that ultimately anything that happens during an experiment that can question if the manipulation *really* caused the outcome is a threat to the validity of that experiment.

Some threats to validity arise from the participants themselves. For example, the Hawthorne effect, so labeled due to the name of the company in which the effect was initially observed (Roethlisberger & Dickson, 1939), occurs when any outcomes or changes in the participants occur because they know they are being observed. Not only must they know, which they of course recognize in most experiments, but they somehow want to perform to please the experimenters. Selection bias also results from the participants themselves. When participants self-select into a study, researchers must determine if those who are in the study are similar to the population of interest and whether they behave in unusual ways simply because they are willing to participate. Yet another threat is that of statistical regression to the mean, a phenomenon that can be particularly problematic when researchers use a repeated measures design in which participants are measured on a given variable more than once. Regression to the mean is not something people do intentionally; rather, it is a mere mathematical artifact. In short, when a sample of participants is measured on a given variable, those who score very high or very low tend to move toward the sample mean on subsequent measures. This can have the effect of making it appear as if a given treatment affects only those who are in the very high or low end of the distribution to begin with. Instead, what regression to the mean results from is simple ceiling and floor effects. In short, we all vary from one measurement to the next. Absolute stability is difficult to maintain. But if a participant (or group of participants) is already scoring at the very top, or very bottom, there is really only one direction for that movement to go. This regression to the mean can masquerade as real change resulting from a treatment and therefore poses a threat to internal validity.

Other threats to validity that can be caused by the participants are mortality, maturation, and interparticipant bias. Mortality, also referred to as attrition (a term that is actually more accurate and less prone to misinterpretation), occurs when participants drop out of the study before completion due to loss of interest, moving away, or any number of reasons. Like many threats to validity, attrition poses the greatest threat when it is systematic in some meaningful way. Random attrition may not cause a big problem; however, imagine a study on marital satisfaction. Couples are tested on marital satisfaction, and then some intervention is administered to see if that intervention can help increase or maintain marital satisfaction. However, over time, some couples drop out. Although they may drop out for any number of reasons, one main reason turns out to be that they have got divorced. Clearly, any subsequent measures of marital satisfaction would be influenced by the fact that the least happy couples have systematically removed themselves from the study. The intervention might end up looking very positive indeed!

Maturation also occurs with the passage of time and can pose a threat to validity. Any study that seeks to examine children's learning over a period of time must take into account that children at the end of the school year have not only received an intervention (such as a year's worth of teaching) but have benefitted from a year of social, emotional, and cognitive development as well, things that have nothing to do with the intervention itself. Lastly, in any experiment, interparticipant bias is a concern. This occurs when changes in the outcome variable are influenced not by the manipulation itself but by the interaction between the participants during the manipulation or about the manipulation. In studying young children, it is almost impossible to run participants in groups for this reason. They invariably talk about the stimulus material, making it impossible to determine if effects were caused by the stimulus or the chatting. Overall, then, participants themselves can bias outcomes and harm validity in many ways. It is important to note that often, the most problematic threats are not merely those that occur (i.e., participants dropping out, growing older, self-selecting into the study) but those that occur systematically, in some way that correlates with the dependent measure. Recall the example of the study on marital satisfaction and the inevitable attrition of divorcing couples. Thus, validity is something that must be considered in advance of the study and attempts to eliminate threats must be worked into the design.

In addition to these threats, validity problems can arise due to the researcher. Broadly speaking, we refer to these as researcher personal attribute effects, and they occur when characteristics of the researcher, such as gender, age, race, friendliness, or other characteristics, influence the way participants respond and ultimately score on the dependent variable. Like threats from participants, researcher personal attribute effects are most problematic when they are systematic. For example, imagine a study in which male participants are randomly assigned to watch a pornographic or a neutral film. Now imagine that, in the presence of each participant, one of two assistants, one male and one female, set up the stimuli. As long as they are random about who sets up which treatment, sometimes having the male set up the pornographic clip and sometimes having the female assistant do this, no real problem should arise. However, what if the female always sets up the neutral film and the male assistant always sets up the pornography? Could this influence outcomes? Obviously, a better choice would be to have the same researcher do all of the data collection, or to randomize the jobs of the assistants. In addition to the ways in which participants may respond to characteristics of the researcher, the researcher herself may be unwittingly biased. For example, it is wise to design the study so that the researcher is unaware of (i.e., blind to) the condition the participant is randomly assigned to participate in. For example, when conducting a study on the effect of book-format (traditional vs. tablet computer format) on children's story comprehension, the researcher testing the child's comprehension should not be aware of what condition the child was in lest she subtly convey the correct answers to the child, or the incorrect ones for that matter.

The procedures themselves can cause threats to validity. Testing effects occur when scores improve when participants become more familiar with the test in a repeated design. In fact, SAT and GRE test preparation courses often tout that their course (i.e., the intervention) results in increased test scores. However, simply taking the test for the second time may have similar effects. Similarly, the Beck Depression Inventory is a measure of depression, but given the nature of the questions, research has found that simply completing the scale increases depression. Instrumentation occurs when the instrument or observation varies in a repeated measures design. For example, research assistants trained to assess young children's verbal skills may simply get better at recognizing children's instances of verbal success over time, again regardless of any treatment that may occur. Aspects of the procedures specific to the environment may also influence outcomes, and these environmental problems may occur within the environment of the study or outside of it. For example, in a study of young children's aggressive responses to a violent film, children were randomly assigned to condition. After watching the violent film, children were led to another room. In one instance, the child in front of the line bent to tie his lace, causing several children behind him to trip, and go sprawling on the floor. Obviously, aggression measures from that batch of children were discarded because aggression could no longer accurately be attributed to the violent film. In what might be considered a more truly historic influence, a study on media-induced anxiety and fear in adults and children was halted and the data considered invalid because the data collection, which began in early September of 2001, spanned September 11, 2001. Again, an external event intervened, making it very difficult to attribute any changes in outcomes to the manipulated variable.

Overall, Campbell and Stanley's (1963) initial list offered just a sample, though quite an extensive one, of possible threats to validity. In any study, any factor that may have caused changes in the dependent variable, other than the manipulation itself, is considered a threat to validity. Threats are most problematic (or maybe even solely problematic) when they influence one group more than another. Experimental design elements, such as random assignment, control groups, and controlled environments, are often able to manage potential threats.

External Validity

Studies that can readily be generalized beyond the laboratory setting are considered to be externally valid. In the traditional view, laboratory studies are high on internal validity because they maintain a high degree of control. That is, the control allows the researcher to accurately test relationships between the manipulated variable and changes in the dependent variable, ultimately allowing the researcher to draw valid conclusions. On the other hand, studies that take place outside of the lab in more natural settings have to allow for a lower degree of control but more accurately represent the real world. Thus, they maybe more externally valid. The traditional logic states that internal and external validity are inversely related: increase one and the other decreases. The more tightly controlled a lab experiment is, for example, the less it can be generalized to the "real world." A less common view, but one that is equally convincing, is the reverse argument: greater internal validity leads to greater external validity. Imagine a well-designed laboratory study on violent video games. The lab, like many game labs, is set up to look like a living room, with comfortable chairs, a coffee table, and a 42-inch screen. However, it is run like a lab, with a single player, headphones for the player to eliminate distractions to her, and a predetermined game and game play length of time. Upon conclusion of the study, the researcher has validly connected game play with increased heart rate and increased hostility. The study has high internal validity. Thus, if one can validly connect the two variables in the lab, the two should be related outside of the lab, that is, the results should have high external validity. If there are other variables that occur outside of the lab (e.g., the participant usually plays at home with an annoying roommate), this additional environmental element, the roommate, is a variable, whose presence could also be validly tested to see how the roommate influences heart rate and hostility. Thus, and contrary to the traditional argument, internal validity may well improve external validity by making findings stronger in the lab and outside of it.

Experimental Design and the Search for Validity

As discussed earlier, elements of research designs have been developed specifically to deal with threats to validity. There are six primary designs: one-shot case studies, one-group pretest–posttest design, static group comparison, pretest–posttest control group design, posttest-only control group design, and Solomon four-group design. The one-shot case study (referred to above as a pre-experiment) and the one-group pretest–posttest design both neglect to include control groups. Thus, no real statement about causality can be made. After all, history, maturation, experimenter bias, mortality, indeed many of the threats to validity occur when no control group is present. The static group comparison includes a control group, therefore is able to offer some defense against threats to validity; however, no random assignment occurs. As a result, self-selection into groups as well as systematic attrition out of the groups remain major problems. Ultimately, both a control group and random assignment are necessary for a true experiment. In fact, the remaining three designs will be the focus here, because it is these three designs that offer heightened validity because all include both control groups and random assignment.

The pretest–posttest control group design allows researchers to look at change over time or, more likely, change after the administration of some treatment. Many threats are dealt with here: history affects both groups equally, so any changes, and importantly, differences between the groups at posttest can still be attributed to the manipulation. Similarly, maturation would occur in both groups, so differences between the two groups at posttest are not likely due to maturation. However, this design introduces some threats not present in other designs: participants may learn the instrument because they complete the instrument twice, potentially resulting in testing effects. Instrumentation may also be a problem when observations occur on the same individual more than once.

In fact, one of the most common designs in communication science experiments is the posttest-only control group design. In this design, participants are randomly assigned to condition (most simply a test and control group, but more groups are possible too). However, measurement of the dependent variable occurs only once, after the treatment. Without the threats of instrumentation and testing effects, and with the benefit of random assignment, many of the major potential threats to validity are dealt with. Although some possible threats may exist, the design is both economical and efficient in its dealing with the main threats to validity.

However, the final design is really considered the gold standard. It allows the researcher to compare various groups to test for various threats. The design combines the pretest–posttest control group design, resulting in two groups, and the posttest-only control group design, resulting in an additional two groups: hence, the Solomon four-group design. This complex design allows the researcher to test for almost any threat to validity. For example, both possible testing effects can be considered, and possible Hawthorne effects as well. Ultimately, however, this is a costly design that is introduced as a *way* of considering all possible threats to validity, but it is rarely used in practice.

All of the designs above represent the manipulation of just one variable. In practice, however, study designs are often more complicated because researchers want to consider multiple effects, or the potential interaction of effects of two or more independent variables on a dependent variable. Thus, the factorial design occurs when two or more independent variables are studied at the same time. In one study that used a factorial design (Krcmar & Farrar, 2009), participants played a violent video game in either first or third person, with the blood on or off. Subsequently, various measures of aggression and hostility were taken. Interestingly, the interaction between the two elements, playing in third person with the blood on, resulted in stronger effects on the outcome measures than any of the other three conditions. This kind of finding is only possible, of course, when both independent variables are studied simultaneously. When a design has two independent variables, each with two levels, it is called a 2×2. The video game study mentioned above was a 2×2 because point of view was manipulated (first vs. third person) and blood (on vs. off) was also manipulated. When a study has three independent variables, the first with three levels and the remaining two independent variables with two levels, we call it a $3 \times 2 \times 2$. Thus, each independent variable is identified with a number, and that number identifies the number of levels in that variable. A factorial design is flexible in that it allows the researcher to examine the main effect of one variable alone (point of view, for example) or a combination of variables simultaneously (point of view, presence of blood, gender of participants). Designs can become quite complex, although the more variables that are added to the design, the more participants that are needed. This compels many researchers to keep their research designs manageable.

Surveys

Although experiments allow researchers to test for the effect of one variable on another, or more simply, for causality, surveys often allow researchers to answer different kinds of question: about the way a given sample will respond, say in an upcoming election, or more commonly, may offer the opportunity to show how variables in a given sample are related to one another. Therefore we will discuss two kinds of survey: those that require a random sample of participants and surveys that often utilize convenience samples.

Surveys utilize questions administered to samples of individuals in order to answer research questions. These questions may be open, or more often in communication science, closed-ended. The questions may be administered via paper and pencil, online, over the phone, or face to face. However, before addressing survey designs in slightly greater detail, it is important first to make a distinction between kinds of survey. It is crucial in this section to note the difference between random and non-random sampling and to discuss what each can and cannot do. It is a common mistake among those not trained in research methods to confuse sampling methods and, as a result, to be confused about what the purpose of each is. Consider, first, the researcher who wants to know how a given group of people will behave or what they think. This researcher is interested in generalizing the answer to one question to a population. The researcher may want to know how many college females have symptoms of an eating disorder, what percentage of a population is Republican, the average age at which individuals first engage in sexual intercourse, or consumers' attitude toward the new iPhone model. In order to generalize the sample's answer to the survey questions, it is vital that the sample be randomly drawn and therefore representative of the population. We refer to this kind of work as survey work, and one main purpose of this kind of survey research is to gain an understanding of the behaviors and attitudes of individuals. In fact, successfully predicting who will win a political election is based in large part on how well the sample was drawn. Only a randomly drawn, representative sample can be used to generalize an answer on a single question or single measure to a population. For example, the General Social Survey (GSS) examines attitudes, behaviors, and beliefs in American families. In 1977, for example, the GSS found that among married couples with children under the age of 18, only 32 percent disagreed with the statement "A preschooler is likely to suffer if his/her mother works" (Smith, 2009). This question, set to a randomly sampled group of Americans, offers a snapshot of attitudes in 1977. This method also allows researchers to look over time. The identical question was asked in 1985, and 46 percent disagreed with the statement, and in 2006, 59 percent disagreed. Therefore, randomly drawn samples allow researchers not only the opportunity to consider responses to a question at one point in time, but changes in the response over time can accurately be said to represent true changes in the attitude, and not variations in the sample from one time to the next, because each sample represents the population at the time.

Other kinds of sample also allow researchers to make some claims and not others. For example, a random sample means that every member of the population to which the findings are supposed to apply has an equal chance to be included in the research sample. In terms of research that is about fundamental and universal processes that apply to all humans regardless of culture, this would be theoretically the entire world population, including past and future generations. Obviously, this is not only impractical, but impossible as well. For more conscribed populations, such as all voters in a congressional district, one needs either a list with all members from that congressional district from which a random sample can be recruited, or a way to contact every member of the population to recruit them. In addition, one would need a method to compel every member randomly selected to participate, as refusal to participate is likely to bias the sample in systematic ways, making it non-random.

One solution to the problem of external validity employed by communication research that is interested in making specific predictions about specific populations is to employ sampling strategies that result in a good approximation of a truly random sample. Such strategies depend on the population one wants to make predictions about, and usually include some form of stratified random sampling. In stratified random sampling, the overall population is broken down into various sub-populations along some attributes that are suspected to influence the results for the study. Then random samples are drawn from these individual sub-populations and results aggregated across samples, often weighted to reflect the samples' relative size in the population. The basic idea behind this strategy is that the resulting sample is more representative of the actual population than a randomly selected sample of the whole population. The reason is that in practice, it is almost impossible for any researcher to devise a recruitment method that gives every population member an equal chance of being selected: address lists are incomplete, not everybody has a phone, not every voter goes to a polling place, not everyone answers questions at the door, not everyone lives in a house or apartment and has a door to answer, not everyone uses the Internet, not everyone receives letters, not everyone goes to the mall, etc. Of course, the above list is also true for sub-populations, but by selecting a recruitment method that allows for a maximal chance for representation for each sub-population, one can maximize representativeness. For example, one could recruit older people by randomly dialing landline phone numbers, younger people by sending text messages, and immigrants by going door to door in predominantly immigrant neighborhoods.

Sometimes the issue is not as much ability to recruit representatively but sample size, especially when samples are relatively small and sub-populations relatively infrequently distributed. While a sample of 400 randomly selected U.S. voters is usually sufficient to assess presidential votes with 95 percent confidence, if researchers were interested in assessing the voting behaviors of Native Americans as part of this study, the sample would be expected to contain only seven Native Americans by chance alone, based on their proportion of the overall population. This number is much too small to use in any meaningful statistical analysis. In this case, the researchers would try to oversample Native Americans, meaning they would try to collect responses from about 100 Native Americans, which would give them about a 10 percent confidence interval for them and about 6 percent for the rest of the sample, allowing for a more meaningful comparison. When reporting on the population as a whole, the results would be weighted to reflect Native Americans' relative frequency in the population. Similar strategies can be employed with any sub-population that has particular attributes, regardless of whether these attributes are demographic, psychological, or behavioral and as long as its relative frequency in the population at large is known.

Thus, stratified random sampling and related sampling strategies can be employed to obtain samples that provide a close approximation of truly random samples. These samples have known characteristics that give researchers good and unbiased estimates of population means, correlations, and effect sizes. As a result, these carefully designed samples result in studies that have much greater external validity than random samples drawn in ways that exclude members of the theoretical population in biased and/or unknown ways. Or, at least, carefully designed samples allow the researchers to draw inferences about the ways their samples are biased and the effect these biases have on the generalizability of their results.

However, a second kind of method, which also uses the survey design, or more accurately, the questionnaire design, does not require a random sample. In fact, in many well-done published studies in the social sciences, researchers use convenience samples because their goals do not involve generalizing from a sample to a population but instead may be interested in understanding the relationship between variables in a given cohort. Furthermore, if the researchers find a relationship between, say, interest in violent video games and aggression in a sample of adolescents in a mid-sized Midwestern town, it is probable that that relationship between interest in violent video games and aggression may also be present in other adolescents in other locations as well. That is, relationships between variables can be studied using convenience samples. First, we will discuss two main kinds of design: cross-sectional designs where data on a sample are gathered in as short a time frame as is feasible and collected only once; and longitudinal designs in which the same questions are asked at more than one point in time. Next we will discuss survey instrumentation and some important points about variable and measure selection in a questionnaire design.

The most commonly used design in communication science is by far the cross-sectional design. In this design, participants represent a cross-section of individuals needed to address a particular research question. As discussed above, this could be a randomly sampled cross-section from the target population, when researchers are attempting to generalize a single question or variable to a population, or it may be a non-random, convenience sample when researchers are trying to demonstrate a relationship between two or more variables overall and have no reason to believe the relationship will differ between their sample and the population to which they are generalizing. Although the data are collected at a single point in time, in actuality, the data are simply collected over a relatively short period of time that is determined to be appropriate for the design in terms of efficiency and effectiveness. As long as researchers determine that the time it took to collect the data (e.g., 2 weeks or 3 months) did not systematically influence the results (through history, for example), then it can be said to be cross-sectional, single-point-in-time data collection.

Longitudinal designs are considerably more complicated but allow researchers to answer research questions and test hypotheses that cannot be validly answered or tested using a cross-sectional design. Longitudinal designs themselves can be of two sorts: trend studies and panel studies. In trend studies, sampling is repeated more than once on the same population. That is, the items on the questionnaire remain the same, the population from which the sample is drawn remains the same, but the individuals in the sample differ across time. In actuality, this design is more like a repeated cross-sectional design. It allows researchers to examine changes in a variable over time. For example, attitudes of college students about a variety of topics may be tracked over time using this method. However, if researchers are interested in changes in the individual, the design is somewhat more complicated.

The panel study tracks specific individuals at more than one point in time, administering the same questionnaire, using the same measures that constitute the same variables. This method can be a challenge because there can be a great deal of attrition even over a short period of time. In addition, in some longitudinal designs, privacy becomes an issue, and researchers must use complicated techniques to ensure that data from a given participant at time 1 are accurately connected to the same person's data at time 2. Despite the expense of these designs, they do offer great benefits. By repeatedly surveying persons over a period of time, a panel study can examine life changes. For example, Elder (1999) conducted a panel study over a 30-year span in order to assess the influence of the Great Depression on the life course of children who had been in the fifth grade in 1932 at the height of the Depression. Initially, 167 children were sampled. They were repeatedly questioned throughout their years in school, until they graduated in 1939. Surveys were administered to these same individuals in 1941, 1943–45, 1957–58, and again in 1964. Although this extensive a longitudinal design is rare for obvious reasons, it did offer the researcher an opportunity to make compelling claims about the attitudes and behaviors of these individuals over time.

However, for many communication scientists, the value of the longitudinal design is that it allows them to make claims about causality, something cross-sectional designs are not really able to do. In a longitudinal design, researchers ask participants the same questions at two or more points in time, thus enabling them to determine if the relationship between variable A at time 1 and variable B at time 2 was stronger, or if the reverse is true: variable B at time 1 is more strongly related to variable A at time 2. For example, if a researcher wanted to better understand the effect of violent video game play on aggression, a cross-sectional design would not necessarily be able to do so. After all, violent video game play may increase aggression, but the two variables may also be related because aggressive individuals may prefer violent video games and thus play them more frequently. In a longitudinal design, the researcher can compare the effect of children's violent game play in grade 6 on their aggression in grade 10 to the effect of children's aggression in grade 6 on their violent game play in grade 10. In all likelihood, both relationships would be significant, but the researcher would be able to examine which was the stronger relationship, thus drawing logical conclusions about the direction of causality.

Content Analysis

Whereas both surveys and experiments offer researchers the opportunity to address questions concerning individuals involved in the communicative process, the goal of content analysis is to assess the content of messages. Although content analysis is a method that was designed specifically with the intent of quantifying the content of mass communication media, the method shares much in common with methods used in interpersonal communication, for example, to assess the content of messages between individuals. That is, content analysis relies on systematic coding regardless of whether media stories or interpersonal communication is being studied. In short, content analysis is used to address specific questions about messages. Coding schemes are developed to address those questions and a sample of messages is then systematically coded, counted, and quantitatively analyzed to answer a question. For example, in a recent content analysis (Yoo & Kim, 2012), researchers examined a sample of YouTube videos in order to assess how obesity is framed. They systematically coded for the topical frame and for how obese persons are portrayed. Like most content analyses, the authors began with a basic research question, developed a coding scheme using an emergent strategy in which they examined a small sample of YouTube videos to identify the main themes in the videos, then refined the coding categories with a still larger sample and lastly coded the entire sample of 417 obesity-related YouTube videos.

The process of content analysis has four main steps, although like any research, each of these main steps is comprised of many smaller sub-steps. First, and most obviously, the research question must be derived. For example, Belch and Belch (2013) were interested in the prevalence of celebrity endorsements appearing in magazine advertising and whether certain kinds of magazine featured these ad types more than other magazine types. In another recent content analysis, Morris and Nichols (2013) examined French and American fashion magazine ads in order to investigate how images of beauty differ between the two countries. They asked not only what products were advertised, but also examined how women were portrayed in terms of facial expressions, apparent roles, and attire. Padilla-Walker et al. (2013) examined a sample of Disney children's films to assess the nature of prosocial behavior. They asked how often prosocial behavior was exhibited, what kind occurred, by whom, to whom, and in what context. Obviously, content analysis is a flexible tool that can be used to assess media, from television and newspapers to YouTube and Twitter feeds.

Once the question is determined, researchers decide on a sample and a unit of analysis. Typically, the sample is drawn first. Media offer a challenge to the sampling process simply because the universe of media content is massive and ever growing. Thus, researchers typically begin with a sampling frame. For example, those interested in a sample of YouTube videos must determine if the sampling frame will be all YouTube videos uploaded in the last month or perhaps the videos with the most hits in the last year. As in all research, the decision should be based on the nature of the question. For example, in the case of the YouTube videos, if we are interested in what gets uploaded, that is, what content creators think is worthy of uploading, the frame may be all videos in the last month. However, if we are interested in what is actually being consumed, utilizing a frame that identifies the most popular videos may be more appropriate. In any case, once the frame is identified, the random sample can be drawn.

Unitization is another important step in the process. The unit of analysis is the smallest single portion of the sample that will be coded. The unit may be an entire YouTube video, or each word in the video may be separately coded. Entire characters may be coded, or each aspect of each character may be coded. In short, the unit of analysis may be any aspect of the sample, but should be small enough to be discretely identified and counted. Often, the smaller the unit the more reliable the coding. That is, an individual word may be easier to code than the entire video. On the other hand, the word may not offer enough richness to address the question being asked by the researcher. The unit of analysis must ultimately be determined with a consideration of the research question at the forefront.

Unitization is followed by a development of the coding scheme. Here, the researcher develops a scheme that will address the research question and allow coders to assess and count each unit of analysis. The development of the coding scheme is arguably the most important part of a content analysis as it helps shape the nature of the results. Excellent coding schemes offer categories that are noncomparative, mutually exclusive, and exhaustive. Once the coding scheme is developed, coders are trained. The process of training the coders relies at least in part on having developed an excellent code book. In the code book, which is essentially a set of detailed instructions to the coders, the directions should be clear and distinct enough so that, in theory, different coders could use the coding scheme and provide identical results. That is, the subjective judgment of the coder should not be part of the process. In fact, subjectivity and bias are often minimized when coders are extensively trained, offered clear directions, and given opportunity to practice on pilot data. One way to assess the success of the coding scheme and the coders themselves is to use multiple coders on the same sample. Reliability statistics (such as Krippendorf's kappa or Scott's pi) should then be calculated and reported in the resulting research report. As in any research, the "data collection," in this case, the actual coding, is followed by data analysis and interpretation of the data.

Big Data

The term "big data" is thought to have originated in Silicon Valley in the mid-1990s. Although quite a few people have laid claim to coining the term, evidence suggests that it was in fact John Mashey, a computer scientist at Silicon Graphics, a computer graphics firm that was largely in the service of Hollywood at the time. Although Mashey does not offer any printed evidence of his parent-status, he gave hundreds of talks to colleagues and potential customers in the mid-1990s, explaining the concept. Appropriately, his evidence is online in the form of presentation slides (Diebold, 2012). In any case, it is here that the term seems to have taken on the current meaning as used by computer science, statisticians, and social scientists such as communication researchers. By 1998, the *Wall Street Journal* proclaimed in a headline that "Big Data Providers Under the Internet Gun as Financial Information Gets Easier to Find" (p. B18, Zuckerman & Buckman, 1998). In the article, the authors argued that the sheer volume of data being made available by the web was undercutting the business of data providers such as Reuters. The data available online, they argued, was easy to access and of high quality, something previously provided at a premium. And, they suggested, the Internet provided so much of it. Although they called it *big data*, in the sense that there was simply a surfeit of data, there was not a sense in which the term was understood as it is now. Rather, Mashey's description of big data as a goldmine to anyone interested in questions of almost any data-analytic kind has only recently been adopted into the public lexicon.

In fact, Witten et al. (2011) presented the concept of big data almost 15 years after Mashey tried to sell Hollywood on it, in their text for the uninitiated, which seems to be most of us. They argue that:

> We are overwhelmed with data. The amount of data in the world and in our lives seems ever-increasing — and there's no end in sight. . . . Ubiquitous electronics record our decisions, our choices in the supermarket, our financial habits, our comings and goings. We swipe our way through the world, every swipe a record in a data base. The World Wide Web overwhelms us with information; meanwhile, every choice is recorded.
>
> (p. 4)

Thus, big data are those data matrices that include thousands, tens of thousands, even millions of cases and often more variables than most social scientists are able to include in a given study. After all, we are limited by the time expense and the finite patience of participants. Although some big data are in fact manually collected and therefore suffer some of the same limitations in terms of number of variables, the number of cases appears almost infinite. Alternately, both the number of cases and the number of variables may be enormous if, for example, the data are collected unobtrusively, via our online behavior. In fact, big data sets are typically completely beyond the computing power of a personal computer and, in fact, well beyond the computing power of most off-the-shelf servers.

The presence of all of this data is a goldmine to researchers, allowing for what is aptly termed "data mining." Unlike the more colloquial use of the term, as when a researcher might be accused of data mining because she or he examined a data set with no theory-driven set of hypotheses, data mining in this more contemporary sense occurs when data are stored electronically and the search is automated or augmented by a computer. Here, patterns in the data are sought automatically, identified, validated, and used for prediction. In this way, the traditional process of research is quite deductive: a given researcher utilizes a theory, designs a study based on that theory, develops and conducts a study, and ultimately collects and analyzes data. However, in the case of big data, the process is entirely inductive, as the researcher approaches an existing data set with a research question but uses rather open-ended data-analytic strategies in order to address the question. In sum, then, big data allows us to answer questions by analyzing data already present in the data stream, looking for structural patterns in the existing data and then using those to make predictions about new data—or data that have not yet occurred, in the case of machine learning.

The allure of big data is undeniable and has popularized the term data analytics. Business schools are scrambling to create data-analytics programs that offer classes that combine the best that computer science, statistics, and social science have to offer (Miller, 2013). Schools of business are doing this in large part because businesses are scrambling to hire data-analytics professionals to capitalize on all of the data out there to be had (Jain, 2013).

For social scientists, always in search of the most representative sample, this new approach offers tremendous amounts of data. At issue, of course, is how to deal with all of it. From capturing the data to issues of sampling, the problems in merely acquiring the data make traditional data collection methods appealing. Lewis et al. (2013), in an excellent methodological piece on big data, suggest using algorithmic techniques to first slice the vast amounts of data into smaller pieces for special analyses. They suggest this specifically for content analyses but the suggestion may be useful for other data as well. For example, blog posts, which are automatically time stamped, can be culled, allowing researchers to follow discussion topics during a specific time period. Next, concept mapping and textual analyses can be used to examine the most often occurring key words and visualize how they co-occur. All of these are (somewhat) automated processes that allow the researcher to examine amounts of data that would not be manageable to the human coder in a content analysis. However, as others have pointed out (Johnstone, 2002), actual pragmatic language use, as might be found in a blog, does always not lend itself well to this kind of analysis. Language use, in the end, is messy and context bound. Humans can code less of it, but can understand it with greater validity. Mahrt and Scharkow (2013) make a similar point when they argue that small-scale content analyses, when conducted on a well-drawn sample, may ultimately have greater validity than computational analyses of large amounts of data whose sampling may be called into question. Nevertheless, several studies have attempted to use predominantly computational methods with greater and less success.

For example, work being done by the Virtual Worlds Exploratorium Project (Williams et al., 2011) assesses vast quantities of data with seeming success, at least from a face validity standpoint. This consortium of twenty researchers at four universities is engaged in studying massive multiplayer online games (MMOs)—or those games that are online, always on, and in which players grow, change, and participate in long-term social groups and relationships. MMOs offer the opportunity to study the emotional, social, and even health impacts that these games may have, and do so in a way that far exceeds the generalizability of past experimental and survey research on this topic. The nature of these data allows researchers to examine the economic and social behavior, as well as the group dynamics that emerge online, finding that, in many cases, behavior online parallels behavior offline (e.g., Castronova et al., 2009). Early research in this area utilized a traditional media effects perspective in that it considered why people engage in the behaviors that they do and, ultimately, what effects they have. Using data such as the ongoing stream of social interaction data that are provided by MMOs, researchers have examined the role and effect of trust among group members (Williams et al., 2011) and how experts function in these groups (Huffaker et al., 2009). The game-based data that the consortium uses is, importantly, not a random sample of players or interactions, but rather a log of every interaction and event. The team also uses traditional survey data, linking these data to the ongoing game-based data (Castranova et al., 2009). Ultimately, the data set allows for analysis of a huge number of socially relevant questions in addition to the opportunity to test the validity and reliability of the self-report data.

Another source of communication data that moves (arguably) from the virtual world of gaming to the very real world of political communication is Twitter. From its inception in 2006, Twitter has grown to its current size: Twitter users produced 500 million discrete tweets daily (internetlivestats.com/twitter-statistics/). Twitter has been used for several research projects. Notably, Larsson and Moe (2013) utilized Twitter to follow political election campaigns in Scandinavian countries. However, as Moe and Larsson (2013) point out in a related piece, data collection of tweets can be a problem, simply given the enormous and growing data stream of tweets available. One method is to download tweets directly from the Twitter Application Programming Interface (API). However, as Boyd and Crawford (2012) point out, Twitter's public API does not provide the full sample. In fact, it is unclear exactly how the tweets are sampled to make them available, calling into question the validity of any content analytic claims that may be derived using this source. Another method is to archive the relevant messages as suggested by Moe and Larsson (2013): "The syndicated on-line service of TwapperKeeper and its self-installable, free-of-charge variety YouTwapperKeeper are two such services" (p. 119). They suggest this method as a simpler and ultimately practical data collection solution. In any case, it is clear that even accessing data becomes an issue rife with methodological pitfalls.

Nevertheless, collecting and assessing tweets via content analysis could tell us much about public attitudes to political campaigns (e.g., Larsson & Moe, 2013) as well as other social phenomena that are identified, parsed, and commented upon on social media such as Twitter, ultimately offering researchers the opportunity to assess ongoing public opinion among those who feel strongly enough to comment on it.

In the end, big data has promise, if properly handled. However, its utility, like any research method, will rest in how big data are used and applied. In fact, if there is any truth to be gained from this chapter it is that, first, research designs are only as good as the caution with which they are developed and the exactness with which they are executed. The reliability and validity of the findings ride on that very point. Second, any research question offers the opportunity to choose a traditional data collection method and well-understood design, or the opportunity to combine various methods and techniques to address a particular question. Each allows the researcher the chance to exhibit design expertise, and sometimes, a great deal of creativity. Ultimately, well-thought-out, relevant, and precise questions can only be answered by designs that exhibit those same qualities.

References

Belch, M., & Belch, G. (2013). A content analysis study of the use of celebrity endorsers in magazine advertising. *International Journal of Advertising, 32*(3), 369–389.

Boyd, D., & Crawford, K. (2012). Critical questions for big data. *Information, Communication & Society, 15*(5), 1–18. Retrieved July 17, 2014, from www.dx.doi.org/10.1080/1369118X.2012.678878

Campbell, D. T., & Stanley, J. C. (1963). *Experimental and quasi-experimental designs for research.* Chicago: R. McNally.

Castronova, E., Williams, D., Shen, C., Ratan, R., Xiong, L., Huang, Y., & Keegan, B. (2009). As real as real? Macroeconomic behavior in a large-scale virtual world. *New Media & Society, 11*(5), 685–707.

Diebold, F. (2012). A personal perspective on the origin(s) and development of "big data": The phenomenon, the term, and the discipline (2nd version). *PIER Working Paper, 13*(3), 1–8. Retrieved June 1, 2014, from www.dx.doi.org/10.2139/ssrn.2202843

Elder, G. H. (1999). *Children of the Great Depression: Social change in life experience.* Chicago: University of Chicago Press. (Original work published 1974).

Ericsson, K., & Simon, H. (1980). Verbal reports as data. *Psychological Review, 87*(3), 215–251. doi:10.1037/0033-295X.87.3.215.

Huffaker, D., Wang, J., Treem, J., Ahmad, M., Fullerton, L., Williams, D., Poole, M. S., & Contractor, N. (2009). The social behaviors of experts in massive multiplayer online role-playing games. *Computational Science and Engineering, 4*, 326–331.

Jain, P. (2013, March 27). Analytics is fast becoming a core competency for business professionals. *Forbes.* Retrieved July 17, 2014, from www.forbes.com/sites/piyankajain/2013/03/27/analytics-is-a-core-competency-for-business-professionals/

Johnstone, B. (2002). *Discourse analysis.* Oxford: Blackwell.

Krcmar, M., & Farrar, K. (2009). Retaliatory aggression and the effects of point of view and blood in violent video games. *Mass Communication & Society, 12*, 115–138.

Krcmar, M., & Cingel, D. P. (2016). Moral Foundations Theory and decision making in video game play: Using real-life morality. *Journal of Broadcasting and Electronic Media.*

Larsson, A. O., & Moe, H. (2012). Studying political microblogging: Twitter users in the 2010 Swedish election campaign. *New Media & Society, 14*(5), 729–747.

Lewis, S. C., Zamith, R., & Hermida, A. (2013). Content analysis in an era of big data: A hybrid approach to computational and manual methods. *Journal of Broadcasting & Electronic Media, 57*(1), 34–52.

Mahrt, M., & Scharkow, M. (2013). The value of big data in digital media research. *Journal of Broadcasting & Electronic Media, 57*(1), 20–33.

Miller, C. (2013, April 13). Data science: The numbers of our lives. *The New York Times.* Retrieved July 17, 2014, from www.nytimes.com/2013/04/14/education/edlife/universities-offer-courses-in-a-hot-new-field-data-science.html?pagewanted=all&_r=0

Moe, H., & Larsson, A. O. (2013). Methodological and ethical challenges associated with large-scale analyses of online political communication. *Nordicom Review, 33*(1), 117–124.

Morris, P., & Nichols, K. (2013). Conceptualizing beauty: A content analysis of U.S. and French Women's Fashion Magazine Advertisements. *Online Journal of Communication and Media Technologies, 3*(1), 49–74. Retrieved June 1, 2014, from www.ojcmt.net/

Padilla-Walker, L. M., Coyne, S. M., Fraser, A. M., & Stockdale, L. A. (2013). Is Disney the nicest place on Earth? A content analysis of prosocial behavior in animated Disney films. *Journal of Communication, 63*(2), 393–412.

Potter, W. J., & Riddle, K. (2007). A content analysis of the media effects literature. *Journalism & Mass Communication Quarterly, 84*(1), 90–104.

Roethlisberger, F. J., & Dickson, W. J. (1939). *Management and the worker: An account of a research program conducted by the Western Electric Company, Hawthorne Works, Chicago.* Cambridge, MA: Harvard University Press.

Smith, T. W. (2009). 2006–2008 General Social Survey panel validation. GSS Methodological Report No. 113. Chicago: NOR.

Tittle, C. R. (2004). The arrogance of public sociology. *Social Forces, 82*(4), 1639–1643.

Williams, D., Contractor, N., Poole, M. S., Srivastava, J., & Cai, D. (2011). The Virtual Worlds Exploratorium: Using large-scale data and computational techniques for communication research. *Communication Methods and Measures, 5*(2), 163–180.

Witten, I. H., Frank, E., & Hall, M. A. (2011). *Data mining: Practical machine learning tools and techniques* (3rd ed.). Burlington, MA: Morgan Kaufmann.

Yoo, J. H., & Kim, J. (2012). Obesity in the new media: A content analysis of obesity videos on YouTube. *Health Communication, 27*(1), 86–97.

Zuckerman, R., & Buckman, M. (1998, Nov.). Big data providers under the internet gun as financial information gets easier to find. *The Wall Street Journal,* B8, p. 18.

PART II
Communication Research

7

MASS MEDIA EFFECTS MODELS

A Brief History

Concern over the effects of media can be traced back as far as the fifth century BC (Perloff, 2009), long before what we now think of as "media" came into modern parlance. However, a more modern and perhaps scientific approach to the study of media is more commonly thought of as having its nascent beginnings in the early twentieth century (Greenberg & Salwen, 2009; see Chapter 3). Although scholars who were interested in the effects of media on audiences came from disciplines such as sociology, psychology, education, and political science, the commonality of their questions drew them together, at least topically if not always in terms of method. In fact, if we consider newspapers, radio, and, later, television to be the earliest forms of mass media, these forms were often studied by individuals who were not trained or identified as mass communication scholars for perhaps no other reason than mass communication was not yet established as its own discipline.

Overall, the decades of the 1920s and 1930s saw an emergence of what we now think of as mass communication, although, at the time, the questions were still studied in other academic disciplines. Quite simply, the emergence of mass communication as a field of study occurred due to a unique confluence of factors (see Chapter 3). First, propaganda as a concept was identified, in part due to wartime messages, and social concerns arose about it. For example, Lasswell (1927), a sociologist, claimed that media, in the form of propaganda, could encourage "millions of human beings into one amalgamated mass of hate and will and hope." This kind of concern created an environment ripe to study mass media more broadly. Second, media such as newspapers and radio expanded in terms of their reach, being adopted into homes at an ever-increasing rate, which increased concerns about the effects of these media on the impressionable minds of children

(Delia, 1987). Third, systematic methods of data collection and various measurement tools were developed. For example, starting in the 1920s, content analysis became one mode of examining the overall content of media messages (Berelson, 1952); basic survey research was used to explore various effects of mass media (Rogers, 1994); and ethnography was utilized to explore media as it related to social problems (Vidich & Lyman, 1994). Fourth, statistical techniques for analyzing large sets of data were developed, allowing for a means to deal with the large quantities of data that emerged from the former three developments. From here, early theories of strong, uniform effects emerged. Sometimes referred to as the "hypodermic needle" or the "magic bullet" models, these approaches assumed that media could influence audiences directly, and with very strong, almost invariable effect (Lasswell, 1927).

Despite the intersection of these many topics and methods of inquiry, mass communication itself did not begin to cohere as a field until the mid-1940s, when its greatest champion and administrative father, Wilbur Schramm, called attention to it. Schramm sought to establish mass communication as an independent and legitimate academic field with a firm grounding in the behavioral sciences. He brought together researchers from journalism, sociology, and psychology in a series of edited volumes from 1948 to 1972 to achieve the goal of establishing a unified field of communication, although functionally, he managed only to establish the academic field of mass communication. Interpersonal communication would go its own way for philosophical, topical, as well as merely academic reasons (Greenberg & Salwen, 2009) (see Chapter 10 for an in-depth discussion). Despite these earliest efforts, mass communication became truly recognized as an independent discipline, gaining a foothold in academia and establishing its own departments in universities by the 1960s.

What Do We Mean by Media Effects?

A careful reader would notice that in the brief history described above, the terms mass communication, mass media effects, and media effects were used to discuss an area of research without much attention to how the concepts might differ. Clearly, they do, and this issue becomes all the more relevant as we move toward a more diverse yet convergent media landscape. Mass communication was perhaps the earliest term used to describe the study of the likes of propaganda, newspapers, radio, and content such as news and advertising. Early work focused more on the former, such as propaganda and the media forms used to present it (i.e., newspapers and radio). In that era, mass communication was fairly easy to identify, even if its effects were not. In fact, early definitions linger, despite their questionable usefulness. In any case, mass communication was defined as a single, typically powerful source, delivering a message created by that source or its designees, over a particular channel with a large, heterogeneous audience, allowing for minimal feedback (Pearce, 2009). Obviously, the utility of this definition is limited given that media audiences can no longer be considered heterogeneous, nor do they need to be particularly large. Feedback is no longer difficult or delayed as it was in the time of letters to the editor. In fact, the expansion and convergence of media not only render the term "mass communication" itself obsolete, but make the study of the effects of media more variable, complex, and interesting. No longer can any one aspect of the process (e.g., lack of feedback) be considered a possible constant. Thus, it may be that the study of messages delivered over a communication channel that is *not* face to face must be studied under the rubric of media effects. Furthermore, the term *mass* media effects is equally cumbersome and ill-suited to capture current research on media. In fact, as early as 1982 some researchers (e.g., Bennett, 1982) claimed that:

> if the term "mass media" still enjoys widespread currency, this is more by force of habit than anything else; a convenient way of marking out an area of study rather than a means of stating how that area should be studied or of outlining assumptions from which research should proceed.
>
> (p. 31)

Thus, it appears that the term "mass" lost its utility long ago.

Instead, the current focus must, at a minimum, be on *media effects*, but really should focus on media *processes* and effects. Nabi and Oliver (2009) decry the state of the field as one in which researchers "chase effects rather than reflect[ing] on the processes that underlie the outcomes of media exposure" (p. 1). Perhaps an observation is that the term media "effects" has encouraged a focus on chasing effects. Had researchers chosen to study media processes from the beginning, perhaps the state of affairs would be rather different. In any case, there appears to be an emerging consensus that the term "media effects" is preferable to terms that came before, but the newer focus on processes, mechanisms, and internal states is crucial to the study of media as it currently exists in our lives. In fact, Potter and Bolls (2011) seek to explore the term media effect, stating that the term *effect* has been used rather vaguely in *all* media effects research. Although Potter and Bolls address media effects research as examining changes in perception, attitude, and behavior, they conceptualize and then categorize actual changes or *effects* as occurring in one of four ways: a gradual long-term change in magnitude; a reinforcement of a perception, attitude, or behavior; an immediate shift; or a short-term fluctuation change. They argue that whereas media effects researchers have examined all of these kinds of effects, the distinctions between them and the possible role those distinctions may have in theory building has remained relatively unexplored.

Despite problems with conceptual issues regarding the nature of effects, various models and theories of effects have emerged in the past seven decades. Thus, in the following sections we cover those theories that have focused on mere effects and outcomes, as broadly conceptualized by Potter and Bolls, as well as more recent theories that have focused on processes. The latter examines not what effect occurs, nor even the nature of the effect, but how it occurs. In terms of these processes, we can point to three distinct approaches, and they are not mutually exclusive. Several theories, such as social learning theory and the earliest approaches to cultivation theory, take a sociological approach, pointing to the culture and the external environment as the locus for any change or effect that may occur resulting from exposure to media. Other theories, such as priming, mental models, and schema theory, point to internal cognitive processes in order to explain outcomes and effects. Lastly, theories such as excitation transfer and theories related to the motivated action measure (Lang et al., 2009) explore the role of arousal in any media effect. In the following sections, each of these is explained in greater detail and the theories that fall under each of these broad umbrellas are discussed.

Sociological-Level Theories

Several theories of media effects take what might be referred to as a sociological approach in that either explicitly or implicitly, they suggest that media influences society in rather sweeping ways, at the social and cultural level. Some theories, such as cultivation theory (Gerbner et al., 1980), were, at their inception, focused on television as a cultural storyteller. Others, such as social learning theory (Bandura, 1973), focused on the role that television, as a type of social actor in our environment, could play as a model for human behavior, thus encouraging imitation. In this way, these theories argued for a media effect on perception, attitude, and behavior that occurred, with the environment as the primary conduit.

Cultivation Theory

In the late 1960s, Gerbner (1969) developed a theory of media effects that examined the influence of television exposure on perceptions of social reality. At its inception, cultivation theory was developed to help understand the consequences of living in a cultural environment dominated by television (Morgan et al., 2009). Simply put, cultivation theory argues that those who watch more television have perceptions of social reality that more closely match the main themes presented on television than those who watch less, even when important demographic variables are accounted for. Although some of the assumptions and methods of the earliest cultivation research have been heavily criticized, the main premise, that exposure to television influences our perceptions of the real world, has been studied and supported more than perhaps any other theory in the area of media effects (Nabi & Oliver, 2010).

Cultivation theory was initially tested using a two-stage approach. First, Gerbner and his team conducted content analyses, or message system analysis as it was then termed (Gerbner, 1972), to assess television's messages. The initial studies focused on the amount of violence portrayed on television. Second, cultivation analysis was conducted using survey research to examine the relationship between individuals' amount of television exposure and their perceptions of the real world regarding the message (i.e., perceptions of violence in the real world and personal fear). The earliest studies, and indeed many since then, have found a remarkably consistent relationship between exposure to television and perceptions of crime and fear, across various subgroups and populations (Morgan et al., 2009).

The theory is not without its critics, however (e.g., Hirsch, 1981; Potter et al., 1993). These tend to fall into two main categories: critiques of several of the assumptions and critiques of the methods. Initially, Gerbner argued that because the main themes of television were so consistent across programs and so persistent, actual program content did not need to be taken into consideration (Gerbner, 1972). As a result, early studies examined only how much television an individual watched and not the content or preferences of that individual. This assumption has been one of the most heavily criticized. In fact, few cultivation studies now utilize this approach and instead focus on content as well as amount of exposure, finding that content does in fact matter (e.g., Goidel et al., 2006; Holbrook & Hill, 2005). The change in this assumption comes from both the likely flaw in Gerbner's initial thinking as well as from the massive increase in the availability and variety of television content since the 1960s.

A second criticism was that cultivation theory did not emphasize the importance of individual differences and environmental effects in Gerbner's earliest research. For example, third variables such as the actual amount of crime in an individual's neighborhood and their gender are likely to influence both the amount of television viewed by that person and their perceptions of crime in the real world. As a result, many cultivation studies now measure and control for additional variables when attempting to assess the cultivation effect. Interestingly, Van den Bulck (2004) found that exposure to television, but not direct exposure to crime, predicted fear.

A third criticism of the earliest research was methodological, or more precisely, statistical. Early research reliably found significant correlations between television exposure and perceptions of crime; however, correlation does not equal causality. Critics claimed that it was equally likely that those who were predisposed to be more fearful simply sought out more television, or perhaps even more crime-related television. More recent research using longitudinal designs or experimental methods have found that although fear may predict crime viewing, there is some causal link between exposure to television violence and fear. That is, causality seems to be bidirectional or dynamic (Lang & Ewoldsen, 2010; Morgan et al., 2009).

In addition to extensive research on the effects of television exposure on perceptions of crime and fear, cultivation research has examined dozens of topics, ranging from the effect of exposure to sexual stereotyping in the media on perceptions of traditional sex roles (Ward & Friedman, 2006) to the influence of exposure to dramas featuring mentally disordered individuals and their influence on perceptions of mental health issues (Diefenbach & West, 2007). Although research on the effects of various television themes on viewers' perceptions finds quite consistent effects, considerably less research has examined the process itself or tested for specific mechanisms (see next section for notable exceptions). Nevertheless, cultivation theory itself has provided a basis for a burgeoning and theoretically rich area of research, growing from an approach whose theoretical grounding was broad, and whose assumptions and methods were sometimes imprecise, to a much more extensive yet detailed body of knowledge (Morgan et al., 2009).

Social Learning Theory

Like cultivation theory, social or observational learning theory (Bandura & Walters, 1963) was initially conceived of as an approach to understanding human learning that focused predominantly on environmental features and stimuli that might encourage imitation. In its later iteration, sociocognitive theory, the approach was grounded in cognitive processes and environmental influences (Bandura, 2008). But the earlier version, with its emphasis on observational modeling, lent itself well to media effects research. Based on basic principles of socialization that emphasized the importance of parents, teachers, peers, clergy, and other socializing agents in the environment in comprehending how learning occurs, social learning theory had its beginnings (Bandura & Walters, 1963) at almost the same time that television was becoming a staple in many homes. Thus, social learning theory was applied to television models to understand how learning might occur from mediated stimuli as well. Early research that utilized a social learning framework found that audiences, especially children, did imitate modeled behavior from television (Bandura, 1973), especially when that behavior was rewarded. Through this process of vicarious reinforcement, television could create an environment where negative behaviors such as aggression, which were readily rewarded in many television programs, could teach and encourage children's aggression in real life. As Comstock (1989) argued, television could supply not only models of specific behavioral responses but also the strategies and rules audience members could use to imitate what they saw. Decades of research have demonstrated that exposure to various media, including television (Mares & Woodard, 2012) and video games (Sherry et al., 2006), could teach everything from prosocial behavior to sexual behaviors and aggression.

The Third-Person Effect

The third-person effect is not a well-articulated theory, not even really a model. Instead, it is an extremely robust phenomenon that garners so much attention in part because it is found so reliably. At its core, the third-person effect is straightforward: we believe that media have a stronger effect on others than on ourselves and the more distant those "others" are both geographically and demographically, the more influenced we perceive them to be in comparison to ourselves (Perloff, 2009). This in itself is perhaps not all that interesting. Rather, it is the presumed extended effect of the third-person phenomenon that becomes compelling. Consider the cascading effects of the third-person phenomenon: it posits that one of the strongest influences of media is that we assume they affect others. In doing so, we then indirectly influence our perceptions of others' behaviors and attitudes. In other words, we think others are imitating or conforming to media messages. Those perceptions of others then become our social norms, or beliefs about what is normative, which in turn can influence our own behavior (e.g., Gunther, 1995; Gunther & Thorson, 1992). After all, one very strong predictor of our own behavior is our perception of how others are behaving (Ajzen & Fishbein, 1980). In a way, the third-person phenomenon implies that media may or may not influence us directly, but as long as we think it influences others, then it influences us, albeit indirectly. In sum, the third-person effect argues that media's influence on behavior and attitudes is indirect, via perceived norms.

Critics of the third-person effect have suggested that the phenomenon is an artifact of the method used to assess it. For example, Brosius and Engel (1996) suggested that the third-person effect might not emerge if the wording of the questions was changed. They suggested that allowing the respondent to feel active (i.e., "I allow myself to be influenced by advertisements") rather than passive ("I am influenced by advertisements") might attenuate the third-person effect. Surprisingly, their data did not bear out this contention. Similarly, Price and Tewksbury (1996) explored whether the phenomenon depended on the ordering of the question. That is, would the findings be attenuated if respondents were asked first about the effect of media on others and then on themselves, or vice versa? Their results suggested that in addition to being robust, the third-person effect was not influenced by the ordering of the question.

Although some research has examined the conditions of influence of the third-person effect, such as message characteristics (e.g., Meirick, 2005) and individual difference variables (Andsager & White, 2007), it remains a sociological-level theory for reasons that will be addressed presently. In terms of message characteristics, it appears that the first-person effect is strongest when participants perceive the message as undesirable (Andsager & White, 2007). Conversely, we believe we are more influenced than others when messages encourage positive behaviors such as healthy lifestyle decisions (Gunther & Thorson, 1992), especially when the arguments themselves are strong (White, 1997). In terms of individual differences, the individual difference variable that seems best able to predict a third-person effect is ego-involvement. In other words, those who feel passionately about and who are highly engaged in a particular topic are more likely than others to feel not only that the media covers the topic unfairly, but that distal others will be extremely influenced by the biased coverage (Gunther & Christen, 2002).

Although the third-person effect is presumed to influence our attitudes and behaviors via perceived norms, the data are somewhat varied in terms of actual effects. Perloff (2009) argues that third-person perceptions "exert two basic effects on opinions and behavior: defiance and compliance" (p. 263). Defiance occurs when the presumed influence of media occurs most readily for a particular topic on others whom they find objectionable. In this case, audiences are likely to take oppositional measures. For example, in cases where states have brought up amendments to state constitutions that would ban same-sex marriages, those who are against such an amendment might hear the news coverage, become concerned over the effects of the coverage on others, and then rally in opposition to the amendment. The case of compliance, on the other hand, is more closely aligned with initial descriptions of the third-person effect. That is, a given individual might change her behavior to be consistent with perceived norms of thinness, for example. This norm may emerge directly from the media, or it may emerge from her third-person assumption that others are influenced by excessively thin media depictions. In either case, defiance or compliance, the effect of the third-person phenomenon is indirect, by way of our perceptions of how others may be influenced.

Parasocial Interaction

Focus on the phenomenon of parasocial interaction dates back to Horton and Wohl (1956), who proposed that television offers a kind of parasocial relationship with viewers, allowing them to feel connected to the characters in their favorite television programs. Parasocial interaction can be defined as a kind of interaction between an audience member and a character that is "one-sided, nondialectical, controlled by the performer, and not susceptible of mutual development" (p. 215). Despite the one-sided nature of the interaction, audiences are intended to experience the interaction in a personal, immediate, and reciprocal way (Horton & Wohl, 1956). That is, audiences may experience these relationships in the same way they experience true social interactions.

Parasocial interaction had its beginnings not in research on the effects of media, but rather, its uses. Specifically, the uses and gratifications approach (see Chapter 8) identified various functions of media use. Among them was the use of media, in this case television, to provide a functional alternative to interpersonal interactions and relationships (Rosengren & Windahl, 1972). According to this approach, audiences might use television for many reasons, including to escape, to relax, to learn, or as a means of social interaction. They might supplement, complement, or even substitute television for real, human interaction. Thus, parasocial interaction can be thought of in terms of a media use. However, several studies have encouraged researchers, albeit indirectly, to think about parasocial interaction as an *effect*. Consider, for example, a classic piece of research by Perse and Rubin (1990), who found that those who sought out television for social uses sometimes ended up being more—not less—lonely after exposure to television. Thus, what may have started out as a *use* of television emerged as an effect, and not the intended one.

More recently, researchers began to consider parasocial relationships between audiences and the characters they watched, as one effect of exposure. Parasocial interaction refers to pseudosocial interactions that an audience member may have with a character that occur during the actual program. More recent research has focused on parasocial relationships, which are interactions that extend beyond the time when the character is being viewed and may in fact have an influence on future viewing, fanship, and enjoyment. Furthermore, parasocial interaction came to be understood as an important moderator of effects, across all age groups. For example, Tian and Hoffner (2010) found that children were more likely to report behavior change and imitation of characters with whom they had a parasocial relationship than one with whom they had no relationship. Among college students, Hartmann and Goldhoorn (2011) found that greater parasocial interaction with a character led to greater support of the social norms embodied by that character. Parasocial interaction seems particularly relevant to elderly viewers who may lack direct social interaction. For example, Lim and Kim (2011) found that among elderly viewers, not only did loneliness increase parasocial interaction, as might be predicted by a media use model of parasocial interaction, but that parasocial interaction then enhanced satisfaction with the viewing experience, in this case, an online shopping program. Overall, although parasocial interaction has been examined as both a predictor of uses and gratifications in media use models and as a moderator of effects, no true theory of parasocial interaction has been forwarded. However, theories of relationship have been used to try to understand the development of parasocial relationships. It is thus unclear if it will remain a mere variable, applied occasionally to broader models of media use and effects, or if it will be incorporated into a true theory that attempts to understand the precise role of parasocial interactions in the experience of media use and effects.

Agenda Setting and Framing

Agenda setting and framing are two theoretical approaches to the study of mass media that grew almost exclusively out of an interest in the role of news media in covering political issues. Therefore, these are covered extensively in Chapter 13. Here, they will be addressed briefly because at their inception, they could be classified as sociological-level theories. Although agenda setting and framing are distinct theoretical perspectives, they are often linked both topically, in their emphasis on news media, and in their approach, which for both theories started out as macro-level, sociological explanations for media effects but have emerged more recently as having clear psychological explanations. In this brief summary, we will address agenda setting and framing theory in terms of their sociological origins and describe the more recent psychological findings further on in Chapter 13.

Agenda setting focuses on the way in which news media, with its attention to particular topics (and concomitant neglect of others), can influence the perceived salience of a given topic and thus influence the public agenda (McCombs & Reynolds, 2009). In a classic and oft-repeated statement, Lippmann (1922) claimed that public opinion responds not to the environment but to the pseudo-environment created by the mass media. To test this notion, McCombs and Shaw (1972) conducted a series of studies in Chapel Hill, NC. Using content analysis of the local press, on one hand, and survey research regarding public perception of the importance of various topics on the other, they were able to establish a correspondence between the two. These studies laid the groundwork for the large body of research conducted in the area of agenda setting. The earliest research focused on issues regarding public opinion and perceived salience, without any significant attention paid to the psychological mechanisms involved in the process.

Unlike agenda setting, which focuses on the effect of mass media on what audiences think about, framing theory focuses on the way in which media presents a given story and offers a particular frame for it. This frame can then in turn influence the way audiences perceive, interpret, and make sense of a story. Framing's sociological origins can be traced back to Goffman (1974), who argued that individuals have socially shared category systems that they use to make sense of information. These shared category systems can be used by media, perhaps unintentionally, to present a story in a particular light.

One example of the potential effects of framing was recently demonstrated by Simon and Jerit (2007). Participants read one of three near-identical versions of a news story about abortion. In one version the word "baby" was used consistently, and in a second version, "fetus" was used throughout the article. In a final version, both words were used equally often. Results indicated that when the word "baby" was used, either solely or sometimes in the article, participants showed more support for regulating the procedure than participants who read the "fetus" version. In this way, the authors demonstrated an example of category framing consistent with that initially described by Goffman (1974), and showed the potentially powerful effects of framing.

Despite the breadth and reach of many of these sociological-level theories, cognitive-based theories have become increasingly important in the past three decades. Early use of computers as a metaphor for human information processing, which itself spurred on the cognitive revolution in psychology, also helped spur on theory in media research that focused on how we cognitively process media and the role that that processing plays in outcomes. Theory and research began to consider media effects as rooted in the way human beings attend to, make sense of, and are influenced by stimuli. In other words, we began to see human beings as information processors. Thus, in the following section we will review priming theory, schema, mental models, and sociocognitive theory.

Cognitive-Level Theories

Sociological theories largely dominated the study of media effects into the 1980s. At that time, scholars started to become more interested in the processes that led to media effects. Why does exposure to a television program increase a person's propensity to perceive someone's ambiguous bump as an intentional aggressive shove? Cognitive theories focus on the psychological processes that are going on within the individual that explain why the particular effect is likely to occur. For example, priming explains why the media have short-term effects on people's behavior. Conversely, schema theory attempts to explain why the media have long-term effects on people's behavior by changing people's knowledge structures.

Priming

Priming theory, broadly defined, is the "short-term impact of exposure to the media on subsequent behavior" (Roskos-Ewoldsen et al., 2009). Cognitive and social psychologists have used priming experimental methodologies since the early 1970s to study how humans process information and how that remembered information affects our behavior (Roskos-Ewoldsen et al., 2007). Priming procedures were first used to explore the representation of information in memory. Some theories of memory, such as network models of memory, assume that information is stored in memory in the form of nodes and that each node represents a unique idea (e.g., there is a "Batman" node in memory). Furthermore, these nodes are connected to related nodes in memory by associative pathways (e.g., "Batman" is linked to "Alfred" or "Catwoman" or "The Joker" but probably is not directly linked to "President Herbert Hoover"). Also, it is believed that each node has what is called an activation threshold. If the node's level of activation exceeds its threshold, the node fires, and energy flows down network pathways from the node to other related nodes. For example, if the "Batman" node fires, activation spreads from the "Batman" node to related nodes, such as "The Joker." Once a related node is activated (in this example, "The Joker"), it then requires less additional activation for it to fire. This means that the concept has been primed. As applied to the media, priming refers to the effects of the content of the media (e.g., depictions of violence, stereotypical portrayals of minorities) on people's later behavior or judgments (e.g., evaluations of the president, aggressive behavior, attention to news stories related to the teaser).

There are three important characteristics of priming. First, the effect of a prime dissipates with time. Typically, the effects of a prime on social judgments fade within 20 to 30 minutes (but may last up to an hour; Carpentier et al., 2008;

Farrar & Krcmar, 2006). Second, primes tend to have stronger effects when a situation is more ambiguous. For example, if I have just watched a violent TV show I am more likely to interpret someone accidentally bumping into me as intentional and react with hostility than if I had just watched a nonviolent show such as *Sesame Street*.

Priming has been found to be useful as an explanation for a number of the effects of the media on people's thoughts, beliefs, judgments, and behavior. For several reasons, the characteristics of the media make it a likely source of priming. First, the ubiquitous nature of the media in our lives makes it a powerful tool for priming various concepts—often outside of our awareness—that may influence how we interpret later information. In particular, situations where we have the TV on, but are not paying particular attention to it, create an ideal situation for priming to occur, because explicit awareness of a prime often mitigates the influence of the prime. Second, particular types of media, most notably the news, are well suited to act as primes. A typical newscast will cover a wide variety of topics, which may result in the priming of a correspondingly wide variety of concepts, which increases the likelihood that one of the primed items will influence how we interpret later ambiguous information. Perhaps because of its nature, few media scholars have questioned whether media priming exists, and, indeed, meta-analysis support the existence of media priming (Roskos-Ewoldsen et al., 2007).

One prominent area of research that has used priming pertains to media violence. Priming also has been used to explain the effects of rock music videos on gender stereotyping, the interpretation of ambiguous print advertisements, the impact of news teasers on attention to and memory for news stories, stereotyped judgments of blacks and women, and perceptions of rape. As will be discussed in Chapter 13, there is also an extensive literature on the impact of political news as a form of media priming.

In general, the results of the research are consistent with the priming explanation of media violence. When people are exposed to violent behavior on TV or in movies, they are more likely to think about violence, interpret ambiguous behavior in a hostile manner, and act more aggressively. For example, Josephson (1987) found that if boys had been primed with aggressive media and then played field hockey, they acted more aggressively (hit other boys with the hockey sticks or push other boys over) than did boys who had not been exposed to a violent program. Further, consistent with the time-course of priming, most of the boys were most likely to act aggressively within the first 3 minutes of play. Another interesting aspect of Josephson's study was that the men who were violent in the media clip used walkie-talkies to communicate with each other. Some of the boys in the study were interviewed prior to playing field hockey with walkie-talkies that were similar to those used in the media clip. Of interest was whether the walkie-talkies would act as a cue to remind the boys of the clip they had just watched. Consistent with a cueing hypothesis, the boys who were cued with the walkie-talkies did act more aggressively than boys who were interviewed with a standard microphone.

The newest area of research on priming is media priming and stereotypes. A growing area of research concerns the potential for the media to prime various stereotypes, including both gender (Hansen & Hansen, 1988; Hansen & Krygowski, 1994) and racial stereotypes (Oliver et al., 2007; Power et al., 1996). This area of research has grown remarkably during the past 6 years, with a focus on the impact of media primes on perceptions of both individuals in interpersonal settings and ambiguous individuals on the media, and on political judgments (Oliver et al., 2007). For example, Abraham and Appiah (2006) found that pictures of African Americans in newscasts about crime primed the racial stereotype of African Americans, which resulted in more stereotypical judgments of African Americans regarding crime and educational policies (see also Richardson, 2005). Although these studies demonstrated that depictions of African Americans in the news could prime stereotypes, which then influenced judgments of policy issues, Domke and colleagues (1999) found that how a news story about a political issue (immigration) was framed (the story focused on the economic effects versus the ethics of immigration) could influence whether racial stereotypes of Hispanics were primed, despite the fact that Hispanics were not mentioned in the story. These activated stereotypes then influenced subsequent political judgments, such as the effects of immigration on the economy (see also Domke, 2001).

Unfortunately, the research on media priming currently is disjointed and there has been little focus on understanding the cognitive mechanisms and processes underlying the media priming phenomenon.

Schema

The media can have long-term effects on people's thoughts and behaviors by creating schemas. A schema is a collection of knowledge about some concept that is stored in long-term memory (Fiske & Taylor 1991; Schank & Abelson, 1977). Unlike the network models of priming where knowledge is represented as a single concept, schema involves more complex representations of knowledge. Indeed, one of the criticisms of network models of memory is that a person's knowledge of the world involves more than just a series of hundreds and hundreds of definitions. Consequently, schemas were theorized to be an additional level of representation beyond nodes. The concept of schema was introduced in part to address this concern by hypothesizing schemas as an additional level of representation (Sun, 2002). Often, the metaphor is used that a node within a network is like a dictionary definition, whereas a schema is more like an encyclopedia entry. Schemas include information about typical elements of the concept, the relationship of the concept to other concepts, and other pertinent knowledge.

For example, a schema for action thrillers would include information about action thrillers (e.g., there is typically a male protagonist who is very tough (and perhaps is a spy); the protagonist is attractive), common elements of an action thriller (e.g., an evil person, evil henchman, an attractive woman, technological gadgets, and fast cars), the relationships between the various elements (e.g., the protagonist must stop the evil person, the evil henchman works for the evil person, the attractive woman falls in love with the protagonist), and relationships to other items stored in memory (e.g., other genres such as mysteries, romantic comedies).

Schemas are learned both through a person's own experiences with his/her real-life environment as well as by exposure to the media. For example, if a child grows up in an environment where violence constantly occurs, that child is going to develop elaborate schemas concerning violence. Likewise, watching TV will influence the types of schema that a child or adult develops. A child who watches a lot of violent media programming will develop schemas related to violence. Furthermore, watching TV violence should shape the types of knowledge that a child has about how to resolve conflict, which may be stored in schemas. As these schemas develop, it increases the likelihood that the schema will be used to interpret information (an ambiguous bump by a stranger is perceived as a shove) and guide behavior (Anderson et al., 2003).

Schemas can provide a mechanism for explaining the effects of media violence on long-term behavior, because schemas influence what people attend to in their environment, how what they see is interpreted, what they remember, how people judge behavior, and their actual behavior. For example, changes in children's schemas regarding the normative acceptability of violence predict changes in children's aggressive behavior. As children's beliefs concerning the normative acceptability of violence become more positive, the children will act more aggressively. Schemas can also explain consistency in people's level of aggression, because schemas tend to be very resilient to change (Huesmann, 1988). Another important application of schema theory for the study of the media is how schema are used to help viewers interpret and understand what they see on the media. Reconsider the action thriller schema that was discussed earlier. When viewers watch a movie that they have categorized as being an action thriller, they will use their schemas to help them interpret and understand the program (e.g., Raney, 2004). For example, viewers may expect the protagonist to fail when they first encounter the evil villain because that is a common element of action thrillers (Zacks & Magliano, 2011). Interestingly, behavior performed by the individual identified as the protagonist will be interpreted as more moral and behaviors performed by the villain will be interpreted as more reprehensible (Raney, 2004). Most action thrillers end with a fast-paced, violent clash between the protagonist and the evil villain, where the odds may appear stacked against the protagonist. But viewers anticipate that the protagonist will triumph in the end. From a media effects perspective, these expectations can moderate the impact of what is viewed. For example, if the protagonist engages in a reckless behavior that results in some harm to him- or herself, social cognitive theory would predict that the negative outcome for the protagonist should act as a vicarious punishment that decreases viewers' likelihood of engaging in the reckless behavior. But research has found that, consistent with their schemas for the genre, viewers don't expect negative effects for protagonists still to be occurring at the end of the show, with the consequence that their schema-based expectations override any potential learning that might occur based on vicarious conditions as predicted by social cognition theory (Nabi & Clark, 2008).

Despite the widespread use of schema as an explanatory device by media effects scholars, the concept of schema has been heavily criticized. First, schema theory has often been criticized for being vague. Most theorizing simply states that schemas exist as a higher-order representation, with little or no specification of the nature of this representation or the type of information that is included within a schema (Schwartz et al., 2011). Second, to the extent that predictions can be made with schema theory, the predictions concerning the influence of schemas on memory have not been supported. Third, schemas are a rather static representation of knowledge, which may be inadequate for explaining how people comprehend and interpret media stories (Roskos-Ewoldsen et al., 2007). When people process media messages, the processing can be very dynamic. For example, when watching a mystery, viewers may counterfactually "redo" something that the protagonist did in order to imagine what might have happened had the protagonist followed a different course of action, and viewers often predict likely outcomes of narratives (Raney, 2004). These types of processes require a mental representation that is more dynamic and flexible than a schema. One theory that may offer this greater flexibility is the mental models approach.

Mental Models

Mental models is a theory drawn primarily from cognitive psychology that sees cognitive processing of information to consist of abstract mental models or templates including cognitive representations of events, situations, people, concepts, settings, and interrelations involved. These models are abstract because they can include concrete representations, such as human beings, but are thought to also include abstract information such as emotions about those human beings and interrelations between representations within a given model. As such, we can think of them as the mental abstractions that we draw from things that we see and experience. Although mental models arise early in life and are built up from our individual experiences, they are also susceptible to change and can be adapted over time based on new and incoming information. Therefore, they are flexible in that they both guide and are affected by new information. Mental models have been used, therefore, to explain both our interpretations of stimuli (Roskos-Ewoldsen et al., 2002) and our responses to them (Krcmar & Curtis, 2003). Like priming and script theories, mental models are grounded in the premise of cognitive processing occurring in semantically related networks. Mental models as a framework has been used to explain media effects as diverse as the influence of media representations of ethnic stereotyping (Mastro et al., 2007); the effect of political ads on perception of a candidate (Kim et al., 2007), and the influence of violent portrayals on moral reasoning (Krcmar & Curtis, 2003).

For example, Kim and colleagues (2007) had participants read a positive or negative political ad while focusing on either the candidate or the issue. In order to examine participants' ongoing construction of a mental model as they read, they were instructed to rate each sentence as they read it in terms of how much it made them think of a particular concept. The authors found that not only did the participants' representation of the candidates differ between the positive and negative ad, but they differed between those asked to focus on the candidate or the issue. When a second group of participants were similarly prompted but were not asked to give a sentence-by-sentence assessment of the ad, their recall of the ad was predicted by the first set of landscapes. That is, the authors argued that our mental models differ based on both the stimulus and the situation, and those models then reliably predict our recall of the stimulus. The authors used these data to theoretically outline not only that mental models worked, but also how they were built and subsequently used by audiences.

Krcmar and Curtis (2003) also argued that the mental models approach can offer a theoretically meaningful way to understand why fantasy violence affects children's moral reasoning. In their study, children saw a clip in which two characters are arguing. In one condition, the characters end up in a physical fight; in the other, they are shown walking away from the conflict. Children in the physical aggression condition judged subsequent violent stories as more correct. Thus, the mental model built during the previous exposure offered the children a means of interpreting new incoming information and influenced their judgment of it.

Thus far, we have considered sociological-level theories that focus on media as a part of the social environment that influences our perceptions, attitudes, and behaviors. We have also introduced cognitive-level theories that focus more distinctly on the way we process media and how that processing then affects outcomes. Lastly, several media theories focus attention on the physiological responses that occur when media are consumed and how that arousal functions to moderate, mediate, or otherwise play an important role in effects or outcomes. We refer to these as arousal-based models.

Arousal-Based Models

Excitation Transfer

Developed by Zillmann (1983), excitation transfer (ET) focuses on the role of arousal in increasing aggression after exposure to media violence. Specifically, ET argues that separate from the extent to which depictions of violence, *per se,* may influence aggressive outcomes, the arousal that results from exposure to violent media can explain variance observed in aggressive response following exposure to different levels of media violence. Initially, when exposed to an arousing stimulus (e.g., a violent film, a ride on an exercise bicycle), a participant correctly associates the arousal with the source. However, over time, as the arousal dissipates, awareness of residual arousal becomes disassociated from the original source, making it possible for the affect-intensifying influence of this arousal to strengthen another affective experience. The transfer of arousal can thus intensify the participant's response to another source, and result in, for example, a greater aggressive response to a provocation. According to excitation transfer, then, the two conditions necessary for increased aggression are arousal from one source, and a second source that offers a provocation. Therefore, excitation transfer offers an explanation for the augmentation of provoked aggression after exposure to arousal-inducing stimuli such as media violence or pornography (Zillmann et al., 1981).

Because the theory purports that it is the arousal, and not the aggression, *per se*, that heightens outcomes, Zillmann demonstrated that other stimulating media, such as sexual content (Zillmann, 1991), could influence aggressive retaliation to a provoking source. In fact, even riding an exercise bicycle has been shown to heighten arousal and subsequently augment aggressive response to provocation (Zillmann et al., 1972).

Given that media effects theories have focused on social environment, cognitive processing, and physiological response as explanatory frameworks for various effects, recent theorizing has attempted to integrate existing theories and research findings into what might best be described as meta-theories. This integrative approach typically takes theory from each area and posits (then subsequently tests) a unified theory that considers various themes (e.g., cognition, affect, arousal) as being interrelated, interdependent, and working in concert to influence outcomes. We will refer to these as meta-theories.

Meta-Theories

The generalized aggression model (GAM; Anderson et al., 2000) is also referred to as the generalized affective aggression model (GAAM). This model argues that behavior, in this case aggression, occurs via three interrelated routes: cognitive, affective, and arousal. In a given episode, GAM considers three main foci: the person in the situation, which may be related to personological factors as well as situational inputs, their present internal states, which include the cognitive, affective, and arousal routes through which inputs into the system may have their effect on it, and the appraisal and decision-making process that results in an outcome (Anderson & Bushman, 2001). For example, a given individual may be presented with a situation. The inputs at this point may include environmental and situational cues such as the presence of an insult from an antagonist combined with an aggressive disposition (Anderson, 1997) on the part of the individual. The processing routes for that individual will then include cognitive (Anderson et al., 2000), affective (Anderson et al., 1996) and arousal. Based on that processing and the previous inputs, the situation will be appraised either automatically, or slowly and thoughtfully. This appraisal then results in some behavioral outcome.

GAM has been used to predict and explain media-induced aggression in at least two ways. First, exposure to media violence itself can be seen as a situational factor resulting in increased arousal, for example (Krcmar & Lachlan, 2009). In this case, media would act as an input that would then influence one of the processing routes. A second way the GAM may be used to explain the effects of media violence would be via the influence of media violence on long-term changes in personological traits such as aggressive disposition (Hasan et al., 2013). In this case, media violence would also act as an input, but whose effect would be primarily on an additional input variable: personality. In either case, GAM can offer a broad-based theory for understanding media's influence.

A second meta-theory that has received increasing attention in recent years is the limited-capacity model of motivated mediated message processing (LC4MP). Although it is a theory of message processing, and not of message effects, *per se*, the theory has received increasing attention in the media effects literature of late (e.g., Krcmar et al., 2014). Thus, we address the theory in this chapter, and also in greater detail in Chapter 9. In any case, LC4MP is also rooted in a networked model of memory in which information is stored in nodes that are interconnected through semantically related pathways; LC4MP focuses on the resources available and allocated to a particular processing task. As such, it is a cognitively based meta-theory that recognizes links between cognitive processing, arousal, and affect. Environmental stimuli are viewed as necessary for processing and, as such, media messages are viewed, similar to the way they are in the GAM, as an input variable in an information-processing system.

The model has several major propositions. It states that first, people are to be limited-capacity information processors (Basil, 1994). Second, it states that people have two underlying motivational systems, the appetitive (or approach) system and the aversive (or avoidance) system (Bradley et al., 1994; Cacioppo et al., 1999), both of which are automatically activated when motivationally relevant stimuli exist in the environment. The third proposition is that media are made up of multisensory stimuli in various formats (e.g., words, pictures). Last, all human behaviors are assumed to be changing and dynamic from one moment to the next. Taken together, these propositions lay the groundwork for how media are thought to be processed.

According to LC4MP, processing messages, in this case media messages, involves three major subprocesses: encoding, storage, and retrieval. Given that these subprocesses occur continuously and simultaneously, and given that individuals are limited-capacity processors, aspects of the media content, aspects of the environment, and aspects of the individual interact to determine what information is selected to be encoded, what is stored, and what is retrieved in a given moment. Furthermore, some information is automatically attended to, whereas other pieces of stimuli are attended to only with conscious effort on the part of the receiver (Lang et al., 1999). Several stimuli receive automatic attention. For example, change and novelty in the environment elicit an orienting response. In addition, motivationally relevant stimuli (Lang et al., 2004a; Lang et al., 2004b) elicit automatic attention. Motivationally relevant stimuli are those that are related to survival. Based on evolutionary theory, the appetitive motivational system evolved to help the organism get food and mates in order to ensure the survival of both the individual and the species. On the other hand, the corollary aversive motivational system evolved to protect the individual from danger. According to the theory, these basic motivational stimuli are innate, but individuals also learn that certain stimuli signal positive or negative consequences. Therefore, through the process of learning, a given individual can come to generate positive or negative responses. In terms of mediated messages, then, aspects of media elicit automatic attention, which acts as a drain on the limited processing system, whereas other aspects of media may garner controlled attention, which also acts as a drain on the limited-capacity system. These attended-to stimuli are then encoded.

Once attention is allocated and encoding occurs, the next subprocess in LC4MP is storage. Storage is conceptualized as the linking of recently encoded information to previously stored information (Baddeley, 1990; Bradley et al., 1994). This linkage occurs when new information is concurrently activated with old information. With the occurrence of concurrent old and new activations for a stimulus, the brain has an active mental representation. According to LC4MP (Lang, 2006), being active simultaneously forges the link. The more links a new piece of information has to old information, the better it is stored, resulting in greater long-term memory for it (Lang, 2006). In addition, LC4MP argues that motivational relevance leads to the automatic allocation of resources to storage. Finally, the third subprocess is retrieval. Again, this involves resource allocation that can either be automatic or rely on conscious control.

During media exposure, all three subprocesses, all of which are under the direction of both automatic and effortful resource allocation, are continuously active. However, due to the limited-capacity nature of processing, trade-offs in the encoding, storage, and retrieval processes are constantly being made. Aspects of the message, the environment, and the individual help determine the nature of these trade-offs (Lang et al., 1999). When the users' goals (e.g., responding to text messages and reading a homework assignment) and/or the demands of the messages (e.g., a surprising text message and/or a difficult reading) require more resources than the system has, overload occurs.

Various aspects of LC4MP have been tested individually, but due to the complexity of the theory, it is difficult to predict how a given individual, in a given environment, receiving a given message might respond in terms of encoding, storage, and retrieval. Of course, given that LC4MP argues for an incredibly complex, continuously active system, it stands to reason that individual predictions are not possible. Still, one might be able to imagine that overload, for example, might occur, given the known factors of the message and the environment. Ultimately, LC4MP is a meta-theory because it attempts to explain and predict multiple aspects of message processing and multiple message contents based on a single, unified yet comprehensive theory.

Conclusion

In this chapter, we examined theories of media effects or media outcomes, dividing these theories into those that take a sociological approach, those that focus on internal cognitive processes, and those that focus on arousal as a primary mechanism for effects. Lastly, meta-theories, a more recent development in media effects theorizing, are those that consider various content areas largely because they combine both levels of effects and various mechanisms in order to explain outcomes. These more complex theories attempt to integrate both the extant theorizing on media effects and the vast literature that has tested those effects. In doing so, these theories have offered perhaps a first step in bringing together a large and sometimes disparate literature.

References

Abraham, L., & Appiah, O. (2006). Framing news stories: The role of visual imagery in priming racial stereotypes. *Howard Journal of Communications, 17*, 183–203.

Ajzen, I., & Fishbein, M. (1980). *Understanding attitudes and predicting social behavior.* Englewood Cliffs, NJ: Prentice-Hall.

Anderson, C. A. (1997). Effects of violent movies and trait hostility on hostile feelings and aggressive thoughts. *Aggressive Behavior, 23*, 161–178.

Anderson, C. A., & Bushman, B. J. (2001). Effects of violent video games on aggressive behavior, aggressive cognition, aggressive affect, physiological arousal, and prosocial behavior: A meta-analytic review of the scientific literature. *Psychological Science, 12*, 353–359.

Anderson, C. A., Anderson, K. B., & Deuser, W. E. (1996). Examining an affective aggression framework: Weapon and temperature effects on aggressive thoughts, affect, and attitudes. *Personality and Social Psychology Bulletin, 22*, 366–376.

Anderson, C. A., Anderson, K. B., Dorr, N., DeNeve, K. M., & Flanagan, M. (2000). Temperature and aggression. *Advances in experimental social psychology, 32*, 63–133.

Anderson, C. A., Berkowitz, L., Donnerstein, E., Huesmann, L. R., Johnson, J. D., Linz, D., & Wartella, E. (2003). The influence of media violence on youth. *Psychological Science in the Public Interest, 4*, 81–110.

Andsager, J. L., & White, A. H. (2007). *Self versus others: Media, messages, and the third-person effect.* Mahwah, NJ: Lawrence Erlbaum Associates.

Baddeley, A. D. (1990). *Human memory: Theory and practice.* Needham Heights, MA: Allyn & Bacon.

Bandura, A. (1973). *Aggression: A social learning analysis.* Englewood Cliffs, NJ: Prentice-Hall.

Bandura, A. (2008, November). Environmental harm. *Psychology Review, 14*, 1–5.

Bandura, A., & Walters, R. H. (1963). *Social learning and personality development*. New York: Holt, Rinehart & Winston.

Basil, M. (1994). Secondary reaction-time measures. In A. Lang (Ed.), *Measuring psychological responses to media messages* (pp. 85–98). Hillsdale, NJ: Lawrence Erlbaum Associates.

Bennett, T. (1982). Theories of the media, theories of society. In M. Gurevitch, T. Bennett, J. Curran, & J. Woollacott (Eds.), *Culture, society and the media* (pp. 30–55). London: Routledge.

Berelson, B. (1952). *Content analysis in communication research*. New York: Hafner.

Bradley, M. M., Zack, J., & Lang, P. J. (1994). Cries, screams, and shouts of joy: Affective responses to environmental sounds. *Psychophysiology, 31*, S29.

Brosius, H. B., & Engel, D. (1996). The causes of third-person effects: Unrealistic optimism, impersonal impact, or generalized negative attitudes towards media influence? *International Journal of Public Opinion Research, 8*, 142–162.

Cacioppo, J. T., Gardner, W. L., & Berntson, G. G. (1999). The affect system has parallel and integrative processing components: Form follows function. *Journal of Personality and Social Psychology, 76*, 839–855.

Carpentier, F. R. D., Roskos-Ewoldsen, D. R., & Roskos-Ewoldsen, B. B. (2008). A test of network models of political priming. *Media Psychology, 11*, 186–206.

Comstock, G. (1989). *The evolution of American television*. Newbury Park, CA: Sage.

Delia, J. G. (1987). Communication research: A history. In C. R. Berger & S. H. Chaffee (Eds.), *Handbook of communication science* (pp. 20–98). Newbury Park, CA: Sage.

Diefenbach, D. L., & West, M. D. (2007). Television and attitudes toward mental health issues: Cultivation analysis and the third-person effect. *Journal of Community Psychology, 35*, 181–195.

Domke, D. (2001). Racial cues and political ideology: An examination of associative priming. *Communication Research, 28*, 772–801.

Domke, D., McCoy, K., & Torres, M. (1999). News media, racial perceptions, and political cognition. *Communication Research, 26*, 570–607.

Farrar, K., & Krcmar, M. (2006). Measuring state and trait aggression: A short, cautionary tale. *Media Psychology, 8*, 127–138.

Fiske, S. T., & Taylor, S. E. (1991). *Social cognition* (2nd ed.). New York: McGraw-Hill.

Gerbner, G. (1969). Toward "cultural indicators": The analysis of mass mediated message systems. *AV Communication Review, 17*, 137–148.

Gerbner, G. (1972). Violence in television drama: Trends and symbolic functions. In G. A. Comstock & E. A. Rubinstein (Eds.), *Television and social behavior: Vol. 1, Content and Control* (pp. 28–187). Washington, DC: U.S. Government Printing Office.

Gerbner, G., Gross, L., Morgan, M., & Signorielli, N. (1980). Some additional comments on cultivation analysis. *Public Opinion Quarterly, 44*, 408–410.

Goffman, E. (1974). *Frame analysis: An essay on the organization of experience* (vol. 4). Cambridge, MA: Harvard University Press.

Goidel, R. K., Freeman, C. M., & Procopio, S. T. (2006). The impact of television viewing on perceptions of juvenile crime. *Journal of Broadcasting & Electronic Media, 50*, 119–139.

Greenberg, B. S., & Salwen, M. B. (2009). Mass communication theory and research: Concepts and models. In D. W. Stacks & M. B. Salwen (Eds.), *An integrated approach to communication theory and research* (pp. 61–74). New York: Routledge.

Gunther, A. C. (1995). Overrating the X-rating: The third-person perception and support for censorship of pornography. *Journal of Communication, 45*: 27–38. doi:10.1111/j.1460-2466.1995.tb00712.x.

Gunther, A. C., & Thorson, E. (1992). Perceived persuasive effects of product commercials and public service announcements: Third-person effects in new domains. *Communication Research*, *19*, 574–596.

Gunther, A. C., & Christen, C. T. (2002). Projection or persuasive press? Contrary effects of personal opinion and perceived news coverage on estimates of public opinion. *Journal of Communication*, *52*, 177–195.

Hansen, C. H., & Hansen, R. D. (1988). How rock music videos can change what is seen when boy meets girl: Priming stereotypic appraisal of social interactions. *Sex Roles*, *19*, 287–316.

Hansen, C. H., & Krygowski, W. (1994). Arousal-augmented priming effects: Rock music videos and sex object schemas. *Communication Research*, *21*, 24–47.

Hartmann, T., & Goldhoorn, C. (2011). Horton and Wohl revisited: Exploring viewers' experience of parasocial interaction. *Journal of Communication*, *61*, 1104–1121.

Hasan, Y., Bègue, L., Scharkow, M., & Bushman, B. J. (2013). The more you play, the more aggressive you become: A long-term experimental study of cumulative violent video game effects on hostile expectations and aggressive behavior. *Journal of Experimental Social Psychology*, *49*, 224–227.

Hirsch, P. M. (1981). On not learning from one's own mistakes: A reanalysis of Gerbner et al.'s findings on cultivation analysis, Part II. *Communication Research*, *8*, 3–37.

Holbrook, R. A., & Hill, T. G. (2005). Agenda-setting and priming in prime time television: Crime dramas as political cues. *Political Communication*, *22*, 277–295.

Horton, D., & Wohl, R. R. (1956). Mass communication and para-social interaction: Observations on intimacy at a distance. *Psychiatry*, *19*, 215–229.

Huesmann, L. R. (1988). An information processing model for the development of aggression. *Aggressive Behavior*, *14*, 13–24. www.hdl.handle.net/2027.42/83387

Josephson, W. L. (1987). Television violence and children's aggression: Testing the priming, social script, and disinhibition predictions. *Journal of Personality and Social Psychology*, *53*, 882–890.

Kim, K. S., Roskos-Ewoldsen, B., & Roskos-Ewoldsen, D. R. (2007). *Understanding the effects of message frames in political advertisements: A lesson from text compre*hension. Paper presented at the annual meeting of the International Communication Association, San Francisco, CA. Online PDF. Retrieved December 15, 2013, from www.citation. allacademic.com/meta/p172029_index.html

Krcmar, M., & Curtis, S. (2003). Mental models: Understanding the impact of fantasy violence on children's moral reasoning. *Journal of Communication*, *53*, 460–478.

Krcmar, M., & Lachlan, K. (2009). Aggressive outcomes and videogame play: The role of length of play and the mechanisms at work. *Media Psychology*, *12*, 249–267.

Krcmar, M., Farrar, K., McGloin, R., & Jalette, G. C. (2014). Appetitive and defensive arousal in violent video games: Explaining individual differences in attraction to and effects of video games. *Media Psychology*, *18*, 527–550.

Lang, A. (2006). Motivated cognition (LC4MP): The influence of appetitive and aversive activation on the processing of video games. In P. Messaris & L. Humphries (Eds.), *Digital media: Transformation in human communication* (pp. 237–256). New York: Peter Lang.

Lang, A., & Ewoldsen, D. (2010). Beyond effects: Conceptualizing communication as dynamic, complex, nonlinear, and fundamental. In S. Allan (Ed.), *Rethinking communication: Keywords in communication research* (pp. 109–120). Cresskill, NJ: Hampton Press.

Lang, A., Bradley, S. D., & Sparks, J. V. (2004). *Processing arousing information: Psychophysiological predictors of motivated attention, sensation seeking, and substance use.* Paper presented at the annual meeting of the International Communication Association, New Orleans, LA.

Lang, A., Potter, R. F., & Bolls, P. (2009). Where psychophysiology meets the media: Taking the effects out of mass media research. In J. Bryant & M. B. Oliver (Eds.), *Media effects: Advances in theory and research* (pp. 185–206). New York: Routledge.

Lang, A., Bolls, P., Potter, R. F., & Kawahara, K. (1999). The effects of production pacing and arousing content on the information processing of television messages. *Journal of Broadcasting & Electronic Media, 43*, 451–475.

Lang, A., Sparks, J. V., Bradley, S. D., Lee, S. K., & Wang, Z. (2004). Processing arousing information: Psychophysiological predictors of motivated attention. *Psychophysiology, 41*, S61–S61.

Lasswell, H. (1927). The theory of political propaganda. *American Political Science Review, 21*, 627–631.

Lim, C. M., & Kim, Y. K. (2011). Older consumers' TV home shopping: Loneliness, parasocial interaction, and perceived convenience. *Psychology & Marketing, 28*, 763–780.

Lippmann, W. (1922). *Public opinion.* New York: Transaction.

McCombs, M., & Reynolds, A. (2009). How the news shapes our civic agenda. In J. Bryant & M. B. Oliver (Eds.), *Media effects: Advances in theory and research* (3rd ed., pp. 1–16). New York: Routledge.

McCombs, M. E., & Shaw, D. L. (1972). The agenda-setting function of mass media. *Public Opinion Quarterly, 36*, 176–187.

Mares, M.-L., & Woodard, E. H. (2012). Effects of prosocial media content on children's social interactions. In D. G. Singer & J. L. Singer (Eds.), *Handbook of children and the media* (2nd ed., pp. 197–214). Thousand Oaks, CA: Sage.

Mastro, D., Behm-Morawitz, E., & Ortiz, M. (2007). The cultivation of social perceptions of Latinos: A mental models approach. *Media Psychology, 9*, 347–365.

Meirick, P. C. (2005). Rethinking the target corollary: The effects of social distance, perceived exposure, and perceived predispositions on first-person and third-person perceptions. *Communication Research, 32*, 822–843.

Morgan, M., Shanahan, J., & Signorielli, N. (2009). Growing up with television: Cultivation processes. In J. Bryant & M. B. Oliver (Eds.), *Media effects: Advances in theory and research* (pp. 34–49). New York: Routledge.

Nabi, R. L., & Clark, S. (2008). Exploring the limits of social cognitive theory: Why negatively reinforced behaviors on TV may be modeled anyway. *Journal of Communication, 58*, 407–427.

Nabi, R. L., & Oliver, M. B. (Eds.). (2009). *The Sage handbook of media processes and effects.* Thousand Oaks, CA: Sage.

Nabi, R., & Oliver, M. B. (2010). Mass media effects. In C. R. Berger, M. E. Roloff, & D. R. Roskos-Ewoldsen (Eds.), *The handbook of communication science* (pp. 255–272). Thousand Oaks, CA: Sage.

Oliver, M. B., Ramasubramanian, S., & Kim, J. (2007). Media and racism. In D. R. Roskos-Ewoldsen & J. Monahan (Eds.), *Communication and social cognition: Theories and methods* (pp. 273–294). Mahwah, NJ: Lawrence Erlbaum Associates.

Pearce, K. J. (2009). Media and mass communication theories. In S. Littlejohn & K. Foss (Eds.), *Encyclopedia of Communication Theory* (pp. 624–628). Thousand Oaks, CA: Sage.

Perloff, R. M. (2009). Mass media, social perception, and the third-person effect. In J. Bryant & D. Zillmann (Eds.), *Media effects: Advances in theory and research* (3rd ed., pp. 252–268). New York: Taylor & Francis.

Perse, E., & Rubin, A. (1990). Chronic loneliness and television use. *Journal of Broadcasting & Electronic Media, 34*, 37–53.

Potter, R. F., & Bolls, P. (2011). *Psychophysiological measurement and meaning: Cognitive and emotional processing of media* (Routledge Communication Series). New York: Routledge.

Potter, W. J., Cooper, R., & Dupagne, M. (1993). The three paradigms of research in mainstream communication journals. *Communication Theory, 3*, 317–335.

Power, J. G., Murphy, S. T., & Coover, G. (1996). Priming prejudice: How stereotypes and counter-stereotypes influence attribution of responsibility and credibility among ingroups and outgroups. *Human Communication Research, 23*, 36–58.

Price, V., & Tewksbury, D. (1996). Measuring the third-person effect of news: The impact of question order, contrast and knowledge. *International Journal of Public Opinion Research, 8*, 120–141.

Raney, A. A. (2004). Expanding disposition theory: Reconsidering character liking, moral evaluations, and enjoyment. *Communication Theory, 14*, 348–369.

Richardson, J. D. (2005). Switching social identities: The influence of editorial framing on reader attitudes toward affirmative action and African Americans. *Communication Research, 32*, 503–528.

Rogers, E. (1994). *A history of communication study: A biographical approach.* New York: Free Press.

Rosengren, K., & Windahl, S. (1972). Mass media consumption as a functional alternative. In D. McQuail (Ed.), *Sociology of mass communications* (pp. 166–194). Middlesex, UK: Penguin.

Roskos-Ewoldsen, D. R., Klinger, M. R., & Roskos-Ewoldsen, B. (2007). Media priming: A meta-analysis. In R. W. Preuss, B. M. Gayle, M. Allen, & J. Bryan (Eds.), *Mass media effects research: Advances through meta-analysis* (pp. 53–80). New York: Routledge.

Roskos-Ewoldsen, D. R., Roskos-Ewoldsen, B., & Dillman Carpentier, F. R. (2009). Media priming: A synthesis. In *Media effects: Advances in theory and research* (3rd ed., pp. 74–93. New York: Routledge.

Schank, R. C., & Abelson, R. P. (1977). *Scripts, plans, goals, and understanding: An inquiry into human knowledge structures.* Hove, UK: Psychology Press.

Schwartz, S. J., Luyckx, K., & Vignoles, V. L. (Eds.). (2011). *Handbook of identity theory and research.* New York: Springer.

Sherry, J. L., Lucas, K., Greenberg, B. S., & Lachlan, K. (2006). Video game uses and gratifications as predictors of use and game preference. In P. Vorderer & J. Bryant (Eds.), *Playing video games: Motives, responses, and consequences* (pp. 248–262). Mahwah, NJ: Lawrence Erlbaum Associates.

Simon, A. F., & Jerit, J. (2007). Toward a theory relating political discourse, media, and public opinion. *Journal of Communication, 57*, 254–271.

Sun, R. (2002). *Duality of the mind: A bottom up approach toward cognition.* Mahwah, NJ: Lawrence Erlbaum Associates.

Tian, Q., & Hoffner, C. A. (2010). Parasocial interaction with liked, neutral, and disliked characters on a popular TV series. *Mass Communication and Society, 13*, 250–269.

Van den Bulck, J. (2004). Research Note: The relationship between television fiction and fear of crime: An empirical comparison of three causal explanations. *European Journal of Communication, 19*, 239–248.

Vidich, A. J., & Lyman, S. M. (1994). Qualitative methods: Their history in sociology and anthropology. In N. K. Denzin & Y. S. Lincoln (Eds.), *Handbook of qualitative research* (pp. 23–59). Thousand Oaks, CA: Sage.

Ward, L. M., & Friedman, K. (2006). Using TV as a guide: Associations between television viewing and adolescents' sexual attitudes and behavior. *Journal of Research on Adolescence, 16,* 133–156.

White, H. A. (1997). Considering interacting factors in the third-person effect: Argument strength and social distance. *Journalism & Mass Communication Quarterly, 74,* 557–564.

Zacks, J. M., & Magliano, J. P. (2011). Film, narrative, and cognitive neuroscience. In F. Bacci & D. Melcher (Eds.), *Art and the senses* (pp. 435–454). New York: Oxford University Press.

Zillmann, D. (1983). Transfer of excitation in emotional behavior. In J. T. Cacioppo & R. E. Petty (Eds.), *Social psychophysiology: A sourcebook* (pp. 215–240). New York: Guilford Press.

Zillmann, D. (1991). Television viewing and physiological arousal. In J. Bryant & D. Zillmann (Eds.), *Responding to the screen: Reception and reaction processes* (pp. 103–133). Hillsdale, NJ: Lawrence Erlbaum Associates.

Zillmann, D., Katcher, A. H., & Milavsky, B. (1972). Excitation transfer from physical exercise to subsequent aggressive behavior. *Journal of Experimental Social Psychology, 8,* 247–259.

Zillmann, D., Bryant, J., Comisky, P. W., & Medoff, N. J. (1981). Excitation and hedonic valence in the effect of erotica on motivated intermale aggression. *European Journal of Social Psychology, 11,* 233–252.

8

MEDIA USE MODELS

Although research dating back almost 100 years has examined the *effects* of media, when the 1920 Payne Fund studies investigated the effect of film violence on children (Lowery & DeFleur, 1995), there was a rather surprising delay in scholarly attention to the question of why we consume media in the first place. In fact, the received view of the history of the discipline is that the earliest theoretical research that focused on selective exposure to media content is the early uses and gratifications research in the late 1960s (Katz et al., 1974). Unlike other mass communication paradigms that emphasize either media content or media effects, uses and gratifications researchers were among the first to focus on media use and assume users to be active, purposeful, and selective in their media choices. Specifically, the now-classic uses and gratifications précis seeks to understand:

> the social and psychological origins of needs which generate expectations of the mass media and other sources which lead to differential patterns of media exposure (or engagement in other activities) resulting in needs gratifications and other consequences, perhaps mostly unintended ones.
>
> (Katz et al., 1974, p. 20)

However, the uses and gratifications approach is not the only, or even most theoretically compelling explanation for why individuals select media use over any other competing activity, or select one form of media over another. In this chapter, we will consider the various theories and the empirical evidence that address issues of selective exposure. In addition, the literature will be integrated into a comprehensive theoretical framework that was first introduced in a chapter on selective exposure to media violence (Krcmar, 2013).

Selective Exposure to Media

The broad-based term for research that focuses on interest in and attraction to media, either a specific medium or particular content types, falls under the designation of selective exposure. As defined by Zillmann and Bryant (1985), "selective exposure designates behavior that is deliberately performed to attain and sustain perceptual control of particular stimulus" (p. 537). In short, research into selective exposure has assumed that we voluntarily choose the stimuli that we consume, including media. Furthermore, this approach recognizes that our choices are likely guided by affective, psychological, and functional factors and seeks to uncover what those factors are and the interrelations between these factors and our ultimate media choices. There have been many approaches to considering how and why we choose the media we do (e.g., Hartmann, 2009), and many ways of grouping the resulting theories and research. However, it seems appropriate to consider our choices as deriving from several broad motivations: We choose media (and other stimuli for that matter) (1) for functional reasons such as fulfilling a need for information (e.g., uses and gratifications); (2) for affective and excitatory reasons such as fleeting moods (e.g., mood management, mood adjustment); (3) due to internal personality and dispositional factors that drive our likes and interests; (4) for sociological reasons including cultural norms that may arise from our gender or our peer group or the desires of other members in our audience group; or (5) for incidental reasons, such as what is available.

Thus, in the following sections, we will first begin by considering uses and gratifications, which takes a functional approach to questions of selective exposure. Second, we will focus on several theories that emphasize the role of *arousal and affect* in media use, including disposition theories, mood management, and mood adjustment. Third, we will focus on the areas of theory and research that emphasize the importance of *personality* in determining violent media choice. These include some uses and gratifications approaches, but also include simple variable analytic research that has examined personality variables and media choice. Fourth, we will consider the sociological factors that may influence interest in and attraction to particular media.

Uses and Gratifications

A typical study in the uses and gratifications tradition focuses on two (or sometimes more) aspects of the proposed selective exposure. For example, Katz et al. (1974), in the above-cited précis, suggest that media selection is based on social and psychological *needs* that lead to *expectations* of the mass media and other competing stimuli in the environment, which in turn result in *patterns* of media use. Those patterns of media use may *gratify* those needs, or not, and lead to some intended and *unintended consequences*.

A uses and gratifications study might examine relationships among psychological needs and patterns of media use (e.g., Krcmar & Greene, 1999). A uses and gratifications study could also look at relationships between patterns of media use and need gratification (e.g., Rubin, 1981), or motivations for use and viewing patterns (e.g., Rubin, 1983). In fact, uses and gratifications research arguably focuses on relationships between any of the main facets of needs, expectations, patterns of media use, and need gratifications. Only intense focus on unintended consequences tends to be labeled in a different category of media research, that of *media effects*. In any case, the most traditional approach utilizes a validated viewing motives questionnaire as a starting point (e.g. Rubin, 1981, 1983). By using this instrument, uses and gratifications research has documented variations in patterns of media use among different individuals (Rubin, 1983) and has demonstrated the mediating role of viewing motives in the effects of mass media (Perloff et al., 1983).

A Brief History of Uses and Gratifications

Early research in the uses and gratifications tradition was related to the identification of various motives that people bring to selective exposure and assessment of the relationship between media use *motives* and media use in general, such as exposure to various content types (e.g., news), affinity for a medium, or satisfaction with it. Because television was the dominant medium of the time, Rubin (1983) explored motives for television use, identifying nine basic motives: relaxation, companionship, habit, pass time, entertainment, social interaction, information, arousal, and escape. These earliest identified motives for television use have been applied to various media as they have emerged. As a result, additional motives have been identified, further differentiated, and collapsed (e.g., Lin, 1999); however, the initial nine serve as a basis for much of the later uses and gratifications work. Either out of tradition (more likely) or core intellectual commitment, scholars tend to look to the original television use motives typology, even in the face of new and emerging technology, often merely making minor changes to the original typology even when a technology such as cell phones is being explored.

In any case, subsequent research that attempted to replicate Rubin's (1983) original work has taken issue with both the number of motives identified and their predictive power. For example, based on Rubin's (1983) nine-factor measure, Lin (1999) identified only three motives for watching television, specifically surveillance, escape/companionship, and personal identity, and Abelman and Atkin (2000) confirmed five, specifically pass time/habit, entertainment, information, companionship, and escape. Moreover, escape was a negative predictor of television exposure in Rubin's (1983) study but a positive predictor of television exposure for children in Abelman and Atkin's (2000) study. These debates over the dimensions led Rubin (1984) to propose that the nine (or five, or three) motives could also be consolidated and collapsed into two simpler and more parsimonious dimensions: ritualistic and instrumental viewing motives. Specifically, Rubin (1984) defined ritualized media use as "a more or less habitualized use of a medium to gratify diversionary needs or motives" and instrumental media use as "a goal-directed use of media content to gratify informational needs or motives" (p. 69). Interestingly, it is this more succinct conceptualization that appears to hold up for Internet use, as well, with online users showing ritualized or instrumental use of the Internet, regardless of content.

A further refinement of the uses and gratifications typology emerged because researchers accurately noted that motives for use, or gratifications sought, were not always obtained. In fact, Perse and Rubin (1990) found that those who sought out television for social uses sometimes ended up being more—not less—lonely after exposure to television. In other words, gratifications sought and obtained are not necessarily synonymous and must be distinguished for empirical, practical, and theoretical reasons. Gratifications sought are those that we bring to a media use situation: we want to pass time, we want to feel a sense of social companionship, we want to learn something. Gratifications obtained result from a media use situation: we experienced physiological arousal, we alleviated boredom, or we exacerbated it. Nabi et al. (2006) have pointed out that the gratifications obtained from television may be neither rewarding nor enjoyable, thus underlining that not only are media *uses* and *gratifications* not always similar but that outcomes of media use are not even always gratifying. Thus, perhaps gratifications *sought* and *obtained* should be thought of as merely *needs* and *outcomes*. In fact, other conceptual and empirical criticisms have emerged over the years. Because they are reviewed thoroughly elsewhere (e.g., Rubin, 2002), we will give only a brief summary here.

Criticisms of the Uses and Gratifications Approach

Some of the criticisms leveled at the uses and gratifications approach over the years have resulted in conceptual clarification and refinement and in empirical enhancement, while other problems persist. For example, several critics have argued that researchers attach different meanings to the uses and gratifications constructs, depending on the issue they are investigating (Swanson, 1977, 1979). Similarly, some have criticized the lack of conceptual clarity in the concepts themselves (Blumler, 1979). Without conceptual clarity and agreement on the concepts that are used from study to study, the body of findings can be scattershot and lack synthesis. For example, the notion of "gratifications obtained" was initially conceived as a concept that measured whether a given media use motive was satisfied (Rubin, 2002). If a viewer sets out to learn something from the news, gratification is obtained if learning occurs. However, more recently, several researchers have argued that the construct of *gratification obtained* may be used to measure broader outcomes, such as satisfaction or enjoyment (Nabi et al., 2006; Strizhakova & Krcmar, 2003). Therefore, the notion of gratifications obtained still needs to be further clarified in order for integration across studies to occur.

A second problem exists in the media use typologies. As new media proliferate, so too do identified motives for use (e.g., Sherry et al., 2006). This has resulted in media use motives that are narrow and in some cases conceptually and theoretically uninteresting. For example, Leung and Wei (2000) found that one gratification of cell phone use was the ability to talk while mobile. Since this is an intended basic function of the cell phone, the finding may not only be obvious, but it adds nothing to our understanding of how media use motives operate. Instead, it may be more theoretically useful to investigate ways to conceptually bring together media use typologies across various media (e.g., uses of television, uses of the Internet). While it is certainly true that different media have different motivations for use, generating typologies with little attempt to integrate them at a broader level may do little to forward uses and gratifications as a meaningful theoretical approach.

Some of the assumptions of uses and gratifications have also come under fire, both in earlier research (e.g., Swanson, 1977) and more recently (Nabi et al., 2006). Specifically, Nabi and colleagues (2006) suggested that audiences may not be as active in the media selection process as the uses and gratifications approach suggests. Based on their empirical findings, they argue that "if we consider that those 'negative' gratifications were unintentionally obtained [in their study] we must then call into question how active, or in control, viewers are in the process of trying to fulfill various social and psychological needs" (p. 444). Strizhakova and Krcmar (2003) further questioned if viewers actually have access to their viewing motives. Given that some media choices are seemingly paradoxical, such as an attraction to sad media (Oliver, 1993), it is not always clear that viewers understand and are able to articulate their viewing motives. In fact, Strizhakova and Krcmar (2003) argue that a sizeable body of literature indicates that both conscious and non-conscious factors determine our behaviors, making it possible that motives for media use are not always accessible to viewers.

In addition to uses and gratifications as one way of addressing questions of selective exposure, additional methods and theoretical approaches have also considered why we watch the media or the specific media content that we do select. Importantly, several of these other approaches provide a deeper explanation for the selective exposure process, in many cases suggesting specific mechanisms that may be at work. Whereas none of these has produced the vast body of scholarship that the uses and gratifications tradition has, they are worth exploring, because some (although certainly not all) have provided explanations that are both theoretically interesting and empirically compelling.

Excitation and Affect-Based Approaches

Both affect and physiological arousal have long been considered to provide some explanation for both media effects and media choice (Zillmann, 2000). For example, in any given media choice situation, one brings a set of emotions and an arousal level. So, to say that I am "in the mood for an action/adventure film" is to imply that something about my emotional state is guiding me toward that specific type of content. In fact, a sizeable body of research supports the link between our physiological arousal, our emotions, and our media choices at a given moment (see Knobloch-Westerwick, 2006, 2014 for a review). Furthermore, several theories have emphasized the importance of arousal and affect in guiding our media choices. Specifically, the theories of mood management and mood adjustment present arousal and affect as central in the selective exposure process, whereas disposition theories rely more exclusively on affective responses and our attitudes toward characters.

Disposition-Based Approaches

One leading explanation for media enjoyment focuses on how individuals evaluate media characters, form affiliations with them, and affectively respond to them. Although this perspective is sometimes referred to as disposition theory (Raney, 2006), it is more appropriate to refer to it as an approach, because there is no one single and theoretically rich explanation of the causes, mechanisms, and outcomes. Instead, there is a compelling body of studies that suggest that we enjoy particular media in large part due to our affiliation with the characters. In fact, disposition approaches can be applied to enjoyment of a wide range of content and differ somewhat from one approach to the next, depending on the content under consideration (Raney, 2006).

Affect is at the heart of disposition theories, with enjoyment of media and attraction to it driven by our feelings about a character. For example, Raney and Bryant (2002) found that liked characters' actions were interpreted positively and disliked characters' actions were interpreted negatively for the sake of maintaining individuals' positive attitudes toward the character. Thus, viewers may accept and enjoy the actions of a liked character, even if they disapprove of the action. This would explain why audiences often cheer for the hero when s/he commits even brutal violence against the villain. Disposition theories would argue that the positive affective response to the hero would define the latitude of acceptance of the violence against the antagonist, and thus help shape the moral judgment. The moral judgment could then enhance or detract from enjoyment of the media and influence subsequent selective exposure to it.

Mood Management

Another theory that attempts to explore the selective exposure process is that of mood management. In its earliest iteration (Zillmann, 1988), this theory suggested that individuals strive to minimize negative mood states and maximize or maintain positive mood states by arranging their environment (including media) to achieve that goal. In this case, mood was conceptualized as having affective and arousal-based components. Results of research that used mood management as a framework allowed for further refinement of the theory, resulting in Zillmann's (2000) more recent thesis that offers selective exposure to media stimuli as a choice that resulted in the selection of content that was "a) excitationally opposite the prevailing states associated with noxiously experienced hypo- or hyperarousal, b) has positive hedonic value above that of prevailing states, and c) in hedonically negative states, has little or no semantic affinity with the prevailing states" (p. 104). In other words, individuals select media that produce physiological arousal that is opposite of how one is feeling *when one does not want to feel that way*, leaving them better off than they were before. If people are too aroused, they will watch calming fare, and if they are bored, they will consume arousing programming. In addition, when individuals feel bad, they do not want to consume *content* that reminds them of whatever made them feel bad in the first place. These basic principles guide media choice.

The notion that individuals will watch negatively valenced content (e.g., sad media), when it is *not* similar to our current sorrow-inducing experience, has been added to and refined in the theory over the past 30 years (notably Oliver, 2003). Thus, current research and theory in mood management no longer states that audiences will always be attracted to media offering positive hedonic valence. Instead, negatively valenced media may be appealing, but only if the storyline does not mesh too closely with negative experiences encountered recently in one's own life. In addition, some evidence suggests that bad moods, either exacerbated by or independent of media choices, may be functional. In these cases, individuals may in fact want to extend negative mood states rather than terminate them, a situation that would run directly counter to mood management theory. Thus, Knobloch (2003) has refined mood management theory to include a state referred to as mood adjustment, with focus on both the arousal-inducing and mood-influencing capabilities of mass media.

Mood Adjustment

In an extension of mood management theory, Knobloch (2003) recognizes that there are times when negative mood states such as anger, sadness, or even stress may be either functional or appropriate. In these cases we may use media, albeit unknowingly, to sustain a negative mood. Knobloch (2003) refers to this process as mood adjustment, suggesting that media selection and use may be one way we maintain or adjust our mood in anticipation of a situation requiring that mood. In one study, participants were angered by a confederate, then randomly assigned to believe that either there would, or would not, be a chance to retaliate against the confederate. For men led to believe they would have an opportunity to retaliate, they selected more hostile and bad news websites than those who did not think they'd have the opportunity to retaliate. The results of the study suggest that the participants used media to maintain their negative moods as a way of preparing for retaliation. Similarly, O'Neal and Taylor (1989) found that males are likely to choose violent, not soothing movies after being provoked by a confederate, but only when they believe they will see the confederate again, perhaps in order to maintain anger and arousal levels appropriate for any retaliation they had in mind. Interestingly, participants are typically not able to articulate their reasons for their media choice in the face of having been angered. Therefore, not only does mood adjustment theory offer some explanation for the paradox of attraction to negative media, but the theory also underlines the more complex and likely less conscious mechanisms at work in the media selection process. Unlike the uses and gratifications approach, which assumes an active and *aware* media audience, mood management and mood adjustment suggest that our motives for media choice are not always at the level of conscious awareness.

Personality Factors

Several studies have examined the relationship between personality factors and use of various media, media genres, and specific content types (e.g., Hanjun et al., 2005; Lin, 1999; Tsao & Sibley, 2004). In general, research into the relationship between personality characteristics and media exposure typically falls into one of three categories: studies relating personality characteristics to exposure to various types of media (e.g., Finn, 1997); studies relating personality characteristics to viewing motives (e.g., Conway & Rubin, 1991); and studies relating personality factors to exposure to specific content (e.g., Weaver, 1991).

One of the earliest areas of research that attempted to link personality with media use examined preference for various *media* (e.g., television vs. newspapers). For example, Finn (1997) attempted to link the five fundamental personality traits (extroversion, neuroticism, openness to experience, agreeableness, and conscientiousness) to exposure to media such as books, newspapers, television, and movies. This large-scale study demonstrated that openness to new experiences was positively related to movie attendance and pleasure reading. To a lesser extent, extroversion negatively predicted exposure to various media. The author concluded that individuals who were more open to experience overall were also more interested in media that were novel. Similarly, Weaver (1991) found that individuals who rated high on an index of psychotocism (characterized as impulsive and nonconforming individuals) were attracted to horror films, whereas those who were more neurotic showed a preference for news and informa-tion programs. Both Finn (1997) and Weaver's (1991) research suggest that, at the very least, personality can predict the type of media we use (e.g., newspapers vs. films).

Additional research has taken this approach a step further and examined the relationship between personality factors and media *content* choices and preferences. Specifically, violent television exposure is one area that has received some attention. For example, Krcmar and Greene (1999) found that sensation seeking predicted interest in and exposure to violent television and films. Slater et al. (2003) measured alienation and found that it, along with sensation seeking, could predict preferences for violent television and films. In fact, sensation seeking is arguably one of the most well-documented predictors of media preferences for specific content.

Sensation seeking, both theoretically and empirically, is related to individuals' need for stimulation (Zuckerman, 2007), testing an individual's tendency to approach, rather than avoid, novel stimuli. Although the measure is strictly self-report, the theoretical basis is biological, with higher sensation seekers having higher optimum levels of physiological arousal. Overall, high sensation seekers have lower arousal levels and require stronger, exciting, and novel messages for attracting and holding attention, while low sensation seekers have higher arousal levels and avoid exciting stimuli (Donohew et al., 1988; Donohew et al., 1980). Based on these findings, Donohew and colleagues concluded that messages that elicit sensory, affective, and arousal responses (i.e., have higher sensation value) are more effective for and attractive to high sensation seekers and also hold their attention more (Pugzles-Lorch et al., 1994).

Attraction to other forms of media is also related to sensation seeking. For example, Arnett (1991) found high-sensation-seeking teens, and especially high-sensation-seeking males, were more attracted to heavy metal music than low-sensation-seeking adolescents. Arnett attributes this to the fact that heavy metal is characterized by "heavily distorted electric guitars, pounding rhythms and raucous vocals all typically played at extremely loud volume" (p. 573). These extremes in musical quality, argues Arnett, make it attractive to high sensation seekers. Lastly, Conway and Rubin (1991) found that sensation seeking was positively related to using television for pass time and escapism motives.

Work by Nabi and colleagues (e.g., Nabi et al., 2006) utilized personality factors to examine the attraction and enjoyment of reality vs. fictional programming. The authors found that although voyeurism was related to interest in television programming, it was not in the predicted direction. Specifically, voyeurism was positively related to interest in fictional programming but negatively to reality programming. Thus, it appears that personality factors contribute to attraction to various media, genres, and content types.

Sociological Factors in Selective Exposure

In addition to personality-level variables that seem to influence how much and what kinds of media people consume, evidence suggests that people are influenced by demographic variables, or broad sociological-level factors in terms of consumption. These factors may well be related to more interesting, cognitive, or dynamic factors; however, this idea has not received much attention. Instead, scholars typically report these sociological-level variables as controls. For example, we know that boys watch more television, play more video games overall, and play more violent games than girls (Strasburger, Wilson, & Jordan, 2009). Although this well-documented finding may ultimately be related to social expectations, parenting, or even physiological differences between boys and girls, the difference is most often (although not exclusively) seen as a sociological one— arising from the mere existence of male and female children. However, according to a recent American time use survey (www.bls.gov/news.release/atus.nr0.htm) among adults, women actually consume somewhat more television than men, making it likely that physiological differences are not responsible, otherwise we might expect to see consistency between male and female differences across the life span. In fact, women also use significantly more social media than men, according to research by the Pew Foundation (www.pewinternet.org/fact-sheets/social-networking-fact-sheet).

Age also plays a role in media use. For example, young children watch approximately 24 hours of television per week. By age 11, this tapers off to 22 hours, perhaps due to increased time spent on school and social activities. People age 25–33 see an increase to 27 hours per week; then, time spent watching television climbs steadily. Those 65 and older spend more than 50 hours a week watching television, or the equivalent of a very demanding full-time job (www.bls.gov/news.release/atus.nr0.htm). According to this time use survey, television use also varies with other sociological factors. More television is consumed by those who are less educated and who have lower incomes. African Americans also watch more television than those who self-identify as white, Hispanic, or Asian American.

Social media are also influenced by these broad demographic factors. For example, women use more social media than men, spend somewhat more time on the Internet in general, and, perhaps surprising to no one, those aged 18–29 use more social media than any other age group, although importantly, the Pew study cited here did not look at those under 18 (www.pewinternet.org/fact-sheets/social-networking-fact-sheet/). Other research has suggested that adolescents use more media than any other age group (Lenhart et al., 2010), likely even more than 18–29-year-olds.

Not only is the amount of media use influenced by broad sociological factors, but the type of media consumed is obviously influenced as well. Although it is beyond the scope of this paragraph to review every demographic difference in selective exposure to content, several are noteworthy. For example, increasingly, news media exposure is influenced by political ideology. Specifically, political party identification is a strong predictor of the kind of news media people choose to consume, with those who identify as Republicans watching more Fox News, for example (Messing & Westwood, 2014). Lists of differences span genres (e.g., women consume more romantic comedies than men) and can be parsed to the level of individual shows (e.g., adolescents are more likely to watch the MTV channel than are other age groups). Such findings become tiresome given that most indicate that audience targeting is effective.

Thus far, we have explored selective exposure in terms of interest in media that may satisfy arousal needs, may be related to our attraction to specific media characters, and to our attempts, albeit unconscious attempts, to manage and adjust our moods. However, Krcmar (2013) has suggested that these disparate approaches to selective exposure might best be brought together with a meta-theoretical approach that might explain, broadly, why we enjoy and use media. Such a meta-theoretical approach could incorporate concepts associated not only with media use but also with media effects. In this way, the theory would be far-reaching and broad, which ultimately offers more explanatory power than narrow models that focus on a single phenomenon. In the next section, we will review the proposed model that is based on social cognitive theory and that helps to integrate the various theoretical and empirical approaches.

Social Cognitive Theory

Bandura's (1986) sociocognitive theory, originally developed in the area of social psychology, has been widely adopted by scholars of media (see Chapter 7). The theory itself has been summarized thoroughly elsewhere (e.g., Pajares et al., 2009); therefore, the explanation here is offered only briefly. In short, social cognitive theory, in its 40-year evolution, attempts to explain the learning and enactment of human behavior; it proposes that most behavior is the result of reciprocal determinism, or the bidirectionally linked interplay of three categories of variable. These include personal factors (such as affect and cognition, because they are individual difference variables, specific to the individual), environmental factors (both situational and environment as more broadly defined), and behavior. Because media choice obviously falls under the category of human behavior, it is clear that those factors that influence it might fall under sociocognitive theory.

Using sociocognitive theory as a starting place, we might categorize the various theories and variables we have discussed as falling under the three bidirectionally linked categories of personological factors, environmental factors, and behavioral factors.

Specifically, we have reviewed several theories that attempt to explain selective exposure, all of which can be organized under the umbrella theory of sociocognitive theory.

For example, uses and gratifications takes a functional approach to questions of selective exposure. From a sociocognitive perspective, uses and gratifications could be grouped predominantly under environmental factors, although personological factors are also relevant. For example, uses and gratifications researchers argue that many motives for media use are environmentally determined. Because individuals are bored, with nothing to do, they may want to pass time. Because they are lacking company, they may seek out the media as a social partner.

However, some research has also linked various media use motives to personality factors (e.g., Krcmar & Greene, 1999). Thus, uses and gratifications can be said to link environmental factors and personological factors to the behavior of selective exposure.

Second, several of the theories discussed in this chapter focus on *arousal and affect* in media use, including disposition theories, mood management, and mood adjustment. All of these can also be connected to both environmental factors and personological factors. For example, a boring day spent at home (an environmental factor) may be linked to low arousal levels, which in turn may encourage media use, especially more stimulating media use (e.g., Zillmann, 2000). In addition, chronically low or heightened levels of arousal may be associated with personality factors (e.g., sensation seeking), which in turn may be linked to attraction to particular media content (Krcmar & Greene, 1999). Thus, mood management, mood adjustment, and disposition theories are associated with environmental and personological factors. Third, in this chapter we focused on the areas of theory and research that emphasize the importance of *personality* in influencing media choice. Clearly, these would fall under the category of personological factors

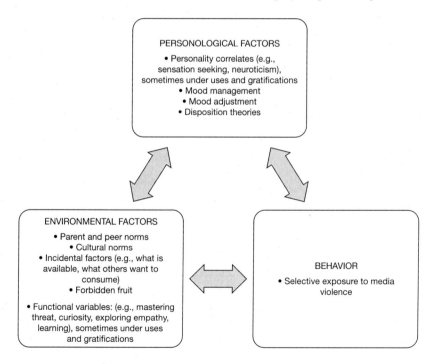

FIGURE 8.1   Bidirectionally linked factors predicting selective exposure to violent media.

★ Taken from Krcmar (2013)

Source: Adapted from social cognitive theory (Bandura, 1986).

leading to behavior. Last, we reviewed the sociological factors that influence interest in and attraction to particular media. From a sociocognitive perspective, these may fall under the category of environmental factors.

As proposed by Bandura (1986), these three categories of variable are bidirectionally linked, and thus reciprocally influence one another. For example, the environment (who I am with, what media are available) has an effect on my affect and perhaps my arousal. Affect and arousal, in turn, can influence my interactions with my environment in a given moment. Both of these factors, personological and environment, then, can influence selective exposure to media in that given moment, which, in turn, obviously influences my affect, arousal, and perhaps my interactions with that environment still further. Hence, the three categories of factor are reciprocally linked (See Figure 8.1). Thus, sociocognitive theory offers a theoretical framework for understanding media choice as a behavior that is driven by environmental and personological factors.

Thus, to the extent that social cognitive theory can be thought of as a meta-theory, or even as a meta-approach to the exploration of human behavior, it offers us at least a starting point or framework for understanding the interplay of factors that influence selective exposure. In sum, we consume media due to factors relating to us as individuals, both momentary state factors such as affect and long-term trait factors such as personality variables. We also consume media because of our environment, friends, parents, or the situation. All of these factors result in consumption of different types of media. To consider any of these alone, or even to consider one as primary, is to engage in a reductionism that is tempting, but ultimately, not explanatory.

References

Abelman, R., & Atkin, D. (2000). What children watch when they watch TV: Putting theory into practice. *Journal of Broadcasting and Electronic Media, 44*, 143–154.

Arnett, J. (1991). Heavy metal music and reckless behavior among adolescents. *Journal of Youth and Adolescence, 20*, 573–592.

Bandura, A. (1986). *Social foundations of thought and action: A social cognitive theory*. Englewood Cliffs, NJ: Prentice-Hall.

Blumler, J. G. (1979). The role of theory in uses and gratifications studies. *Communication Research, 6*, 9–36.

Colwell, J., & Payne, J. (2000) Negative correlates of computer game play among adolescents. *British Journal of Psychology, 91*, 295–310.

Conway, J. C., & Rubin, A. M. (1991). Psychological predictors of television viewing motivation. *Communication Research, 18*, 443–463.

Donohew, L., Palmgreen, P., & Duncan, J. (1980). An activation model of information exposure. *Communication Monographs, 47*, 295–303.

Donohew, L., Finn, S., & Christ, W. (1988). "The nature of news" revisited: The roles of affect, schemes, and cognition. In L. Donohew, H. E. Sypher, & T. Higgins (Eds.), *Communication, social cognition and affect* (pp. 125–218). Hillsdale, NJ: Lawrence Erlbaum Associates.

Finn, S. (1997). Origins of media exposure. *Communication Research, 24,* 507–529.

Hanjun, K., Cho, C-H., & Roberts, M. S. (2005). Internet uses and gratifications: A structural equation model of interactive advertising. *Journal of Advertising, 54,* 57–70.

Hartmann, T. (2009). *Media choice: A theoretical and empirical overview.* New York: Routledge.

Katz, E., Blumler, J. G., & Gurevitch, M. (1974). Utilization of mass communication by the individual. In J. G. Blumler & E. Katz (Eds.), *The uses of mass communication: Current perspectives on gratifications research* (pp. 19–34). Beverly Hills, CA: Sage.

Knobloch, S. (2003). Mood adjustment via mass communication. *Journal of Communication, 53,* 233–250.

Knobloch-Westerwick, S. (2006). Mood management: Theory, evidence, and advancements. In J. Bryant & P. Vorderer (Eds.), *The psychology of entertainment* (pp. 239–254). Mahwah, NJ: Lawrence Erlbaum Associates.

Knobloch-Westerwick, S. (2014). *Choice and preference in media use: Advances in selective exposure research.* New York: Routledge.

Krcmar, M. (2013). Selective exposure to violent media: A synthesis of the research and a theoretical overview. In E. Scharrer (Ed.), *Media effects/media psychology* (pp. 189–204), vol. 5 (A. Valdivia, Gen. Ed.). *The International Encyclopedia of Media Studies.* Oxford: Wiley Blackwell.

Krcmar, M., & Greene, K. (1999). Predicting exposure to and uses of violent television. *Journal of Communication, 49,* 25–45.

Lenhart, A., Purcell, K., Smith, A., & Zickuhr, K. (2010). *Social media and mobile internet use among teens and young adults.* Washington, DC: Pew Internet & American Life Project.

Leung, L. & Wei, R. (2000). More than just talk on the move: Uses and gratifications of the cellular phone. *Journalism & Mass Communication Quarterly, 77,* 308–320.

Lin, C. A. (1999). Online-service adoption likelihood. *Journal of Advertising Research, 3,* 79–89.

Lowery, S., & DeFleur, M. (1995). *Milestones in mass communication research: Media effects* (3rd ed.). New York: Longman.

Marvin, C. (2002). On violence in media. *Journal of Communication, 4,* 142–149.

Messing, S., & Westwood, S. J. (2014). Selective exposure in the age of social media: Endorsements trump partisan source affiliation when selecting news online. *Communication Research, 41*(8), 1042–1063.

Nabi, R. L., Stitt, C. R., Halford, J., & Finnerty, K. L. (2006). Emotional and cognitive predictors of the enjoyment of reality-based and fictional television programming: An elaboration of the uses and gratifications perspective. *Media Psychology, 8,* 421–447.

Oliver, M. B. (1993). Exploring the paradox of the enjoyment of sad films. *Human Communication Research, 19,* 315–342.

Oliver, M. B. (2003). Mood management and selective exposure. In J. Bryant, D. Roskos-Ewoldsen, & J. Cantor (Eds.), *Communication and emotion: Essays in honor of Dolf Zillmann* (pp. 85–106). Mahwah, NJ: Lawrence Erlbaum Associates.

O'Neal, E. C., & Taylor, S. L. (1989). Status of the provoker, opportunity to retaliate, and interest in video violence. *Aggressive Behavior, 15,* 171–180.

Pajares, F., Prestin, A., Chen, J., & Nabi, R. L. (2009). Social cognitive theory and media effects. In R. L. Nabi & M. Oliver (Eds.), *Media processes and effects* (pp. 283–297). Thousand Oaks, CA: Sage.

Perloff, R. M., Quarles, R. C., & Drutz, M. (1983). Loneliness, depression, and the uses of television. *Journalism Quarterly, 60,* 352–356.

Perse, E. M., & Rubin, A. M. (1990). Chronic loneliness and television use. *Journal of Broadcasting and Electronic Media, 34*, 37–53.

Pugzles-Lorch, E., Palmgreen, P., Donohew, L., Helm, D. M., Baer, S. A., & Dsilva, M. U. (1994). Program content, sensation seeking, and attention to televised anti-drug public service announcements. *Human Communication Research, 20*, 390–412.

Raney, A. A. (2006). Why we watch and enjoy mediated sports. In A. A. Raney & J. Bryant (Eds.), *Handbook of sports and media* (pp. 313–329). Mahwah, NJ: Lawrence Erlbaum Associates.

Raney, A. A., & Bryant, J. (2002). Moral judgment and crime drama: An integrated theory of enjoyment. *Journal of Communication, 52*, 402–415.

Riddle, K., Eyal, K., Mahood, C., & Potter, W. J. (2005). Judging the degree of violence in media portrayals. *Journal of Broadcasting & Electronic Media, 50*, 270–286.

Rubin, A. M. (1981). An examination of television viewing motivations. *Communication Research, 8*, 141–165.

Rubin, A. M. (1983). Television uses and gratifications: The interactions of viewing patterns and motivations. *Journal of Broadcasting, 27*, 37–51.

Rubin, A. M. (1984). Ritualized and instrumental television viewing. *Journal of Communication, 34*(3), 67–77.

Rubin, A. M. (2002). The uses and gratifications perspective of media effects. In J. Bryant & D. Zillmann (Eds.), *Media effects: Advances in theory and research* (pp. 525–548). New York: Routledge.

Sherry, J. L., Lucas, K., Greenberg, B., & Lachlan, K. (2006). Video game uses and gratifications as predictors of use and game preference. In P. Vorderer & J. Bryant (Eds.), *Playing computer games: Motives, responses, and consequences* (pp. 213–224). Mahwah, NJ: Lawrence Erlbaum Associates.

Slater, M. D. (2003). Alienation, aggression, and sensation-seeking as predictors of adolescent use of violent film, computer and website content. *Journal of Communication, 53*, 105–121.

Slater, M. D., Henry, K. L., Swain, R. C., & Anderson, L. L. (2003). Violent media content and aggressiveness in adolescents. *Communication Research, 30*, 713–736.

Strasburger, V. C., Wilson, B. J., & Jordan, A. B. (2009). *Children, adolescents, and the media*, 3rd ed. Thousand Oaks, CA: Sage.

Strizhakova, Y. & Krcmar, M. (2003, May). *Do we have access to our viewing motives? Assumptions in and extensions of uses and gratifications.* Paper presented at the annual conference of the International Communication Association, San Diego, CA.

Swanson, D. L. (1977). The uses and misuses of uses and gratifications. *Human Communication Research, 3*, 214–221.

Swanson, D. L. (1979). Political communication research and the uses and gratifications model: A critique. *Communication Research, 6*, 37–53.

Tsao, J. C., & Sibley, S. D. (2004). Displacement and reinforcement effects of the internet and other media as sources of advertising information. *Journal of Advertising Research, 44*, 126–134.

Weaver, J. B., III. (1991). Exploring the links between personality and media preferences. *Personality and Individual Differences, 12*, 1293–1299.

Zillmann, D. (1988). Mood management: Using entertainment media to full advantage. In L. Donohew, H. E. Sypher, & E. T. Higgins (Eds.), *Communication, social cognition and affect* (pp. 147–171). Hillsdale, NJ: Lawrence Erlbaum Associates.

Zillmann, D. (2000). Mood management in the context of selective exposure theory. In M. E. Roloff (Ed.), *Communication yearbook 23* (pp. 103–123). Thousand Oaks, CA: Sage.

Zillmann, D., & Bryant, J. (Eds.) (1985). *Selective exposure to communication* (pp. 533–567). Hillsdale, NJ: Lawrence Erlbaum Associates.

Zuckerman, M. (2007). The sensation seeking scale V (SSS-V): Still reliable and valid. *Personality and Individual Differences, 43*(5), 1303–1305.

9

MESSAGE PROCESSING

Communication scholars have a longstanding interest in the consequences of communication. Going all the way back to the early part of the twentieth century, the focus of most research and theorizing has been on what effects occur because of interpersonal communication or media use. However, little research has focused on what people are doing while they are actually processing communicative exchanges or messages. While there is little research on media in this domain, there is even less research on attention in other communicative domains such as interpersonal communication, organizational communication, or social influence (Roskos-Ewoldsen & Roskos-Ewoldsen, 2010). This chapter will focus on the limited theorizing that has occurred about what people do when they are processing media messages, including issues of attention, comprehension, engagement, and retention.

Attention involves processes that result in some information being made available for analysis by the cognitive system (Anderson & Kirkorian, 2006). In other words, attention involves selecting some information in the environment to process while other information is excluded. This is referred to as *selective attention* (Lang, 2000). However, research on attention differentiates between automatic and controlled processes. Within this context, automatic processing refers to processes that are outside of an individual's conscious control. For example, people automatically comprehend words that are spoken in a language they understand. Likewise, people automatically orient their attention to sudden movement. Controlled processes, on the other hand, are under an individual's control. For example, when a person is first learning to read, determining what word a string of letters stands for requires deliberation and takes cognitive effort. Likewise, if people actively search for videos on YouTube of their favorite band playing a recent song, they formed the intention to engage in this activity. Typically, controlled processes require substantially more cognitive resources than automatic processes.

There are two major lines of research involving attention to the media. One line focuses on whether children's attention to TV is passive, whereby their attention is "captured" by TV, or active, whereby they select what to attend to in their environment. The second line of research focuses more on people's attentional processing of media messages and the impact of limited attentional cognitive resources.

Children's Attention to Television

Media scholars and developmental psychologists began studying which factors influenced children's allocation of attention to TV in response to fears about the impact of television on children's development. An early question in this area of research involved whether children passively receive messages or are more active in their processing of TV messages. The question of passive versus active processing has formed the basis for much of the research in this tradition. However, while this research focuses primarily on visual attention, the auditory channel of TV is also important. It ends up that children can often understand much of what is occurring in a TV program simply by listening to that program.

Part of the research on children's attention has focused on the formal features of TV. Formal features are the features or codes of TV that are independent of content and result from the editing and production process, but formal features do inform the content of a program (Anderson & Kirkorian, 2006; Huston & Wright, 1983). Formal features of TV include such things as edits, pacing, special effects, zooms, dissolves, fades, music, pans, voice-overs, and sound effects. Formal features often operate as a syntax for TV and movies by offering a structure for the programming (Huston & Wright, 1983). For example, fades indicate a change in location and time.

Generally, the research in this area has been atheoretical, which is surprising given its 30-plus years of research history (Anderson & Kirkorian, 2006). Nevertheless, Anderson and Field (1983) argue that principles of how children attend to TV have been established. While it is unclear whether all of the phenomena they discussed have achieved the status of principles, the list provides a summary of what has been learned about children's attention to TV over the past 40 years of research. Below is a summary of several of the principles most relevant to the theories discussed in this chapter.

First, how long children look at a TV increases from infancy through about age 12, where it generally peaks (Anderson et al., 1986). For example, Alwitt et al. (1980) observed children in three 1-hour sessions. The percentage of eyes-on-screen time increased from 38.5 percent for 3-year-olds to 48 percent for 5-year-olds. This suggests that children are learning how to watch TV as they develop.

Second, attentional looks are brief. Typically, children engage in a large number of looks at a TV program, and no single look is particularly long. Preschool children will look at and away from TV more than two times a minute, averaging over 150 looks in an hour (Anderson et al., 1981), and over 60 percent of the time a child looks at the TV less than 5 seconds before looking away again. Likewise, close to 50 percent of the looks at the screen for undergraduates watching TV lasted less than 1.5 seconds (Hawkins et al., 2005). Further, the looks of both adults and children are strategic and the looks aid in comprehension.

Third, attention has inertia. Although children tend to have many short looks at TV, the longer they look at TV, the less likely they are to stop looking at TV. This phenomenon is known as attentional inertia (Anderson & Field, 1983; Krull & Husson, 1979). In other words, as attention to TV is sustained, it becomes more resistant to distractions (Anderson et al., 1987). Attentional inertia may play an important role in children's learning of the syntax of formal features (discussed below). Attentional inertia probably results in the child paying attention to TV when he or she normally would not because the content of the program is becoming more difficult to comprehend. In turn, this means that the child may be exposed to new formal features that he or she will slowly become familiar with and implicitly learn how these features function within TV programming (Anderson & Lorch, 1983; Roskos-Ewoldsen & Roskos-Ewoldsen, 2010).

Fourth, children learn how to use the formal features of TV to guide their attention to and comprehension of TV programs, and they begin to learn how to use these codes by the time they are 4 years old, but perhaps even at an earlier age (Calvert et al., 1982; Kirkorian et al., 2012; Krull & Husson, 1979; Pittorf et al., 2014; Rice et al., 1983). Children begin paying greater attention to structured rather than random programming as early as 18 months (Anderson & Kirkorian, 2006). Research also suggests that children transfer what they learn about formal features of a particular program to other programs that are similar (Crawley et al., 2002). Furthermore, children as young as 3 years old use the behavior of other people who are viewing the TV to guide their attention to TV (Anderson et al., 1981).

Some formal features of TV are more likely to automatically attract children's attention than others (Anderson & Field, 1983; Anderson & Kirkorian, 2006), even when the content of the show is not comprehensible or the child has not been looking at the screen. For example, movement, major transitions (e.g., from the show to a commercial), applause, laughter, other sound effects, animation, women's voices, children's voices, and the presence of puppets all attract children's attention independent of content and previous attention (Alwitt et al., 1980).

Interestingly, children also seem to strategically use some formal features to aid in their comprehension of, and to decrease their attention to, television (Campbell et al., 1987). These features include still pictures and male voices. Alwitt et al. (1980) hypothesized that this is learned behavior; through past television exposure, children have learned that these formal features typically signal content that is less comprehensible to them and, as a result, they use these features to avoid what is likely to be incomprehensible anyway. Finally, children also monitor the auditory track of a TV program to determine when they need to pay more attention to the program (Anderson & Kirkorian, 2006). Clearly, if children are using the formal features of TV to guide when they need to look to the screen to comprehend the program, then auditory features must play an important role in signaling to the child that important things are about to occur in the story (Bickham et al., 2001).

Models of Children's Attention to TV

One model that has been discussed in the literature is the passive model. But the passive model has tended to be a ruse against which other models are compared. Indeed, the passive model seems to reflect cultural truisms instead of being a serious scientific theory. According to the passive model, TV captures our attention and then controls what we attend to in our environment. The model assumes, first, that TV is a highly salient visual stimulus that easily captures children's attention through the formal features of television, and that TV maintains people's attention by offering programming that is novel or in some way reinforces the viewer (Anderson & Field, 1983; Bickham et al., 2001). The role of the viewer's intentions and goals is minimal (Anderson & Lorch, 1983). The passive model also assumes that attention to TV leads to comprehension. Consequently, according to the passive model, educational TV can be made more effective by simply making it more attention grabbing. As Bickham et al. (2001) note, this model is captured by the phrases we use to describe children's viewing, such as, "They vegged out in front of the TV." It is worth noting that the passive model has received little support and few researchers recognize it as viable.

The alternative model is the *active model*. The active model argues that children work dynamically to comprehend what is going on when watching television and that when children look at TV, the look has functional reasons such as aiding comprehension (Anderson & Field, 1983; Bickham et al., 2001). More recent research with adults exploring the neurological processing involved with watching narrative is consistent with the idea that processing narrative film is an active and dynamic process (Anderson et al., 2006). The formal features of TV are used to guide the allocation of attention. Research does suggest that children use the formal features of a program to guide their attention to the screen, so that they are looking at the screen during critical points in the show (Lorch et al., 1979), and additional evidence supports this finding in adults, as well. According to the active model, ease of comprehension drives the allocation of attention (Anderson & Field, 1983). If a show is easy to understand, the child does not need to pay much attention to the program and will look away and engage in other activities. Similarly, if a program is too complex for the child to understand, the child will stop looking at the TV and will engage in other activities, unless TV is the only option. Children pay the most attention to programs that they can comprehend but are not too easy to comprehend (Anderson & Field, 1983; Bickham et al., 2001).

Traveling Lens Model

One model that is predictive of children's TV viewing behavior is the traveling lens model (Rice et al., 1983). According to the model, attention to television is a function of familiarity with how television operates and of habituation. At high levels of familiarization with TV, children are less likely to pay attention because they have learned how to use the formal cues of a TV show to increase the efficiency with which they process the show. Alternately, they are so habituated to the programming that it is no longer of interest. At the other extreme are programs that use techniques that are unfamiliar to children, or programs where the topic is so novel it is beyond the children's ability to understand. In either case, attention to the program is very low. Between these two extremes, attention to the TV follows a curvilinear function such that, as familiarity increases to an optimal level, attention to the program will also increase, but attention will start to decrease when there is too much novelty or lack of understanding of the content of the show and/or the formal features used in the show. In other words, programming that is moderately comprehensible to the child will result in the highest levels of attention (Valkenburg & Vroone, 2004).

As children develop and gain more experience with TV, the entire distribution of the television content that children will attend to shifts toward programming that is more complex (Huston et al., 1990). What were once programs that were attended to with great detail are now programs that have become habitualized, and programs that were once novel and too complex for the child to understand are now moderately comprehensible because the child is better able to process the material (Crawley et al., 2002).

Attentional Sampling Model

Another model of children's attention to television is the sampling model of attention (Huston & Wright, 1983). It is designed to explain how children strategically use formal features and random samples of looks at TV to guide their viewing of TV. This model argues that children take small samples of TV programming by looking quickly at the TV to determine if it is interesting and comprehendible. When a sampling gaze captures programming that is important to the show, children become more engaged in their viewing. This pattern may explain, at least in part, why viewing times become progressively longer and attentional inertia sets in (Hawkins et al., 2005). This visual sampling by the child is almost certainly not systematic or random. Rather, children's sampling may be driven, at least partly, by the formal features of the program, as well as what is occurring in the auditory track of the program. How systematically children sample is predicted by the overall comprehensibility of the TV program (Hawkins et al., 1991). Consistent with this idea, more recent research suggests that attentional inertia is tied to children's and adults' strategic viewing of TV (Hawkins et al., 2005).

Capacity Models of Message Processing

Several broader models of attention and message processing have developed, which draw upon limited-capacity models of human cognition (Fisch, 2000; Lang, 2000; Lang et al., 2008). There are limits to what the cognitive system can do. People can attend to a limited amount of information in the environment at any particular moment, and the capacity of short-term memory limits people's ability to process information (Baddeley, 2007). For example, a lot of resources may be required if a person is trying to understand a complex lecture in a required class. Conversely, if a person is watching a highly familiar TV show, then very few resources may be necessary in order to process the show. Many models of cognition assume that there is a resource pool with a limited amount of resources that can be used to process information across encoding, storage, and retrieval (Basil, 1994; Kahneman, 1973; Lang, 2000). Two models have been developed which focus on the implications of the limited capacity of the cognitive system on the processing of media messages. Fisch (2000) developed his capacity model to explain when children learn from educational television. Lang's limited-capacity model of motivated message processing focuses on the role of motivation within a limited-capacity framework.

The Capacity Model

The capacity model focuses primarily on the limitations of short-term memory on children's processing of narrative educational television (Fisch, 2000). However, a critical element in the model is children's motivation to process the story content, because motivation is tied to the amount of effort that a child will expend to process the narrative story. Higher levels of motivation correspond to more cognitive resources available in working memory for processing the story. The model makes several assumptions about how children process narratives. First, the model posits that children will give priority to the narrative content over the educational content when processing educational programming. While narrative processing is assumed to be the default, children can choose to focus more on the educational content. For example, if the child knows that mastery of the educational content is important, then the child may choose to prioritize that content over the narrative content. Second, the cognitive resources that are available for processing the educational content is a function of the resources allocated to processing the narrative content. As more resources are necessary for processing the narrative content, fewer resources are available for processing the educational content.

The resources that are necessary to process a story and to learn the educational content include those necessary for processing the story itself, the resources necessary for processing the educational content, and the degree to which the educational content and story content overlap (Fisch, 2000). As the overlap between the two goes up, the resources necessary to process and learn the educational content decrease. Anything that increases the efficiency of processing of the educational and narrative content will ease processing and free up resources for other tasks such as storage of the educational content (Campbell et al., 1987; Fisch et al., 2001; Fisch et al., 1999; Piotrowski, 2014). For example, prior knowledge of the story or education content, repetition of information, the comprehensibility of the story (both clarity and explicitness), and the viewer's motivation for watching the narrative all influence the ease of processing of the story and of the educational content.

Children learn more from educational television the more resources they have available for processing the educational component of the story. An easy-to-process narrative that children are highly motivated to process and where there is a lot of overlap between the narrative story and the educational content should maximize learning of the educational content. Higher motivation to process the story should result in the children allocating more resources to watching the narrative, while the overlap between the narrative and educational content, as well as the ease of processing the narrative, should both result in more resources being available for processing the educational content. Importantly, not only are there more resources for processing the educational content, but there are also more resources available to aid in the storage of the educational content in long-term memory. This final component of the limited-capacity model of motivated message processing, then, states that factors such as high motivation, overlap between narrative and educational content, and ease of narrative should all result in easier processing but also more efficient memory storage.

Limited-Capacity Model of Motivated Mediated Message Processing

Lang's limited-capacity model of motivated mediated message processing (LC4MP; Lang, 2000, 2006; Lang et al., 2006) focuses on the dynamics of attention within a limited-capacity information-processing model of cognition (see Chapter 7 for an additional discussion). Lang (2000) notes two basic assumptions of this approach. First, people actively process information within the cognitive system and, second, their ability to process information is limited by that same cognitive system, consistent with Fisch's (2000) capacity model.

The information-processing framework that Lang (2000) uses maintains that there are three basic cognitive processes: encoding, storage, and retrieval (Basil, 1994; Lang, 2000, 2006). Encoding includes those processes (e.g., attention, perception, comprehension) involved with bringing information into the cognitive system from the external environment. Storage involves incorporating the attended-to information in a mental representation and storing it in memory. The final process is retrieval, which involves activating information that has been previously stored in memory. Activation from memory allows the activated information to aid in the comprehension of incoming information (see later in this chapter). Although it is easy to think of these three stages as discrete and following a linear progression, the three processes interact dynamically, and all three operate simultaneously. Also, it is important to note that all three of these processes require resources to operate. If people do not have any cognitive resources available to encode information, then either the information will not be stored in long-term memory or an impoverished representation of the information will result.

To understand how media stimuli are processed requires an understanding of what resources are available and how they are allocated. This is accomplished within the LC4MP by considering the following: total resources, resources allocated, resources required, resources remaining, and resources available. Total resources refer to the total cognitive resources in the resource pool. Resources allocated refer to the resources that are actually available for a processing task. The resource allocated to a task may be equivalent to the total resources, but probably is not. Resources required are the resources that are necessary to complete a task. If the resources that are allocated are greater than the resources that are required, then the stimuli should be successfully processed. Resources remaining refer to the difference between total resources and resources required. Again, resources remaining and resources allocated may be the same if total resources are equivalent to allocated resources, but this is unlikely the case. Resources available is the difference between the resources allocated and the resources required.

The reasons for these fine-tuned distinctions are several (Lang, 2000; Lang et al., 2008). First, people may not allocate all of the available resources to a task at hand because they are cognitive misers. Unless highly motivated, people tend to use as few resources as necessary. Thus, a distinction is made between total resources and allocated resources. Second, people will allocate resources only as required by the task. If people are watching a program they have seen before, fewer resources may be required because of the familiarity of the program. Conversely, if the production is such that the visual elements of the programming are important (e.g., many of Hitchcock's movies; Bordwell, 2005), then more resources may be required. In both cases, the same amount of resources may have been allocated to the TV program, but different amounts were actually used, leaving some allocated resources available in one case but not in another. Third, some elements in the environment will automatically draw resources. For example, as already discussed, some formal features automatically attract attention (e.g., unrelated cuts), drawing resources from the total pool of resources without conscious allocation of resources.

The LC4MP maintains that motivation is fundamentally tied to the approach or appetitive system on one hand and the avoidance or aversive system on the other (Bradley & Lang, 2007; Cacioppo & Berntson, 1994). Information that is coming into the cognitive system may activate one or both of these systems. When either or both the appetitive and the aversive systems are activated, then more resources will be allocated to the cognitive system, and the more these systems are activated, the more resources are allocated (Lang, 2006; Lang et al., 2008).

Within this model, media messages may receive insufficient or limited processing for two basic reasons. First, there may not be enough resources available to process the message fully (i.e., the required resources exceed the total resources). For example, a message on a topic that a person does not understand may require so many resources that, even though all of that person's resources may have been allocated to the task, the required resources will exceed what is available and the system is overloaded. Second, there may be enough resources available to process the message, but those resources are not allocated to the task for reasons such as insufficient motivation or because the person is multitasking (e.g., resources required exceed resources allocated). For example, when a person is cooking and watching TV at the same time, there may not be enough resources available to process the TV program entirely.

Watching TV involves a number of simultaneous cognitive processes. TV viewing often requires people to engage in processing auditory and visual information and integrating these two channels of information (Lang et al., 1999) in order to gain understanding. In addition, viewers are storing new information in memory and activating existing knowledge to aid in comprehending the program. Research under the rubric of the LC4MP model focuses on how resources are allocated to the various processes that are occurring and the effects of differential resource allocation on attention, encoding, and retrieval.

If messages are simple, increasing people's attention to a message through the inclusion of formal features that orient attention, such as edits, results in improvements in memory for the message. This finding suggests that there were available resources (i.e., more resources allocated than required) that could be diverted to encoding processes. Conversely, with a complex message, the addition of formal features that increase orienting responses tends to lead to decrements in memory. This finding suggests that when people orient to some cue in the environment, they automatically draw resources away from encoding processes. The result is that there are insufficient resources available for encoding and memory for the information will be worse. The decreased performance on memory tests is one indication that the resources required have exceeded the resources allocated to the task.

Although the LC4MP is a theoretically oriented model of message processing, it provides important practical insights for message production. For example, if a message is primarily intended to convey information, then the message should be constructed to maximize the resources that are available for encoding information. In this instance, the number of structural features of the message that will result in orienting responses should be tied to the informational complexity of the message. As information complexity increases, the message should minimize the number of orienting responses, because they may interfere with encoding processes by requiring more resources than allocated, or even more resources than in the total pool (Fox et al., 2007; Lang, 2006). A final point concerns the applicability of the model. While the name of the model suggests it is limited to attention to mediated messages, the model should apply across contexts. Obviously, in interpersonal settings, the focus would not be on cuts and edits, but the same underlying dynamics would be in operation.

Comprehension

When people watch a movie, one of their basic goals, however implicit, is to have a coherent understanding of what they are watching. To accomplish this, viewers construct mental representations of the movie as the movie unfolds. This representation includes information about the characters and situations within the movie, and prior expectations based on knowledge about the movie genre, as well as the director and/or the actors and actresses starring in the movie. This combination of information provides the basis for understanding the movie as it unfolds and for predicting future events in the movie. Unfortunately, little research has focused on how people create a coherent understanding of what they are watching (but see Lee et al., 2013; Livingstone, 1987, 1989, 1990a, 1990b; Morley, 1992, 1999). This section of the chapter will focus on two research traditions that have sought to understand how we comprehend the media. One tradition can be traced back to Stuart Hall's (2001/1980) essay on the encoding/decoding model, which arose within British cultural studies. This research tradition focuses on the global comprehension and representation of media stories. A second tradition focuses on the role of situation models in the comprehension of visual and text stories (e.g., Busselle & Bilandzic, 2008; Roskos-Ewoldsen & Roskos-Ewoldsen, 2010; Roskos-Ewoldsen et al., 2007).[1]

The Encoding/Decoding Model

Stuart Hall's (2001) essay, "Encoding/Decoding", asked two fundamental questions: How do audiences comprehend or *read* a media text and what techniques do the media use to constrain how the text is read? This was to become a major area of research within British cultural studies. The paper was originally a lecture that Hall presented at the Centre for Mass Communications Research at the University of Leicester.[2] In this essay, Hall questioned the idea of a dominant media system presenting an ideology that the masses unwittingly are compelled to accept (Condit, 1989; Hall, 1994). Hall's point was that an audience can decode a message at odds with the formulation intended by the individuals who created the message. The variability in how a message is read is driven by divergences in the codes that are used at encoding and decoding. The basic point that Hall made in this essay is that the audience is not just a passive recipient of a message; rather, it is the audience that is active and its reading of the message influences the impact of that message on that audience (Hall, 1994; Morley, 1992).

Any message is polysemic in that it can be read in different ways. Hall (2001) is careful to note that the people involved in the production of the message will use different techniques to attempt to secure a preferred or dominant reading of the text (Hall, 2001; Morley, 1992) by constraining how the text can be read, so that the reading favors the preferred or dominant reading. Drawing on Parkin's (1971) work on the influence of class on meaning-systems, Hall's original formulation of the encoding/decoding model held that there were three categories of reading of a message. First, there is the *dominant reading* of the message, which is consistent with the reading intended by the message producers. Parkin argued that the primary meaning-system that arises within a culture reflects that dominant worldview, and that people will interpret messages within that worldview. Second, there is a *negotiated reading*, which is in large part consistent with the preferred reading, but is situated in that it acknowledges the interests of the individual decoding the message, so that the interpretation of the message does not entirely reflect the dominant reading. Third, there is an *oppositional reading* of a message, which acknowledges the preferred reading of a message, but rejects that reading. Parkin characterized this as a radical meaning-system.

Clearly, understanding factors that influence how a message is read by an audience is central to understanding how people comprehend and interpret media stories. Within Hall's original encoding/decoding model (Hall, 2001), how a message is read is closely tied to issues of class, drawing upon Parkin's (1971) writings. However, it is important to note that Hall did not intend to argue that class deterministically shapes how a message will be read (Morley, 1992). Rather, social class will influence how a message is read through the various codes that different social classes acquire due to their economic standing. In other words, while Hall clearly acknowledges the role of cognition in the decoding process, his primary interest is in how sociological factors influence how the message is comprehended.

Later research clearly demonstrated that while class did influence how texts were read, other factors played a much larger role (Morley, 1999). Rather, how audiences read a message was more complex than the encoding/decoding model's original formula (Fiske, 1987; Storey, 2003; Turner, 1990). For example, the same audience had different, often contradictory, readings of what they watch. This suggests that people inhabit many different cultures (e.g., professor, parent, soccer fan, agnostic, and so on) and that the cultural set of meanings that influences how a text is read can vary within the same individual (Radway, 1991; Storey, 2003). A critical question that arose out of early research on the model concerns the *preferred* reading of a text. As Morley (1992) put the question, is the preferred reading of a text inherent in the text, or does the audience bring it to the text, with the consequence that the preferred reading could change across time? Research suggests the answer is both. The early research on dominant or preferred readings was done in the context of news stories, where the ideological implications of one reading of a story over another are fairly clear. However, determining the preferred reading is usually more complicated than this. For example, what is the preferred reading of a soap opera, a tearjerker, or a situation comedy? The notion of a preferred reading seems better suited to documentary-style shows and does not work particularly well with entertainment shows (Brooker, 2000; Fiske, 1987; Morley, 1992).

Several issues with the encoding/decoding model have emerged. One issue is how free an audience is to *read* a media message. Clearly, Hall (2001) emphasized the polysemic nature of media messages, but we can consider just *how* polysemic media messages are. It is conceivable that alternate readings are possible, but not infinite and not likely. For example, Both Hall (2001) and Morley (1992) point to the dynamic interplay between the producers of a media message and the audience. Indeed, when reading Hall's discussion of the dominant, oppositional, and resistance readings of a text, it is clear that each of these audiences "understands" the text to be about the same thing. That is, they share an understanding of the denotative meaning of the text. As Condit (1989) argues, what differs across these audiences is the interpretation of the text—not its comprehension. Condit refers to this as a *polyvalence* reading of a text, rather than a polysemic reading, because the text is understood to be about the same thing, but the valuation of the story differs across audiences.

Conversely, Fiske (1987; Fiske & Hartley, 1978) emphasized the overwhelming power of the audience to find distinct meanings within a text. For example, Ang (1985), in her study of *Dallas*, argued that people read *Dallas* in relation to their lives and, given the multifaceted nature of people's lives, different readings of *Dallas* should emerge. Likewise, people are motivated, at least in part, to write fan fiction because it allows them to interact with the story and to insert their interpretations into the story (Jenkins, 2006; Okdie et al., 2014). Consequently, Fiske argues that the reading of a TV show is the result of a negotiation between an ambiguous media text and a culturally situated audience. A study by Hodge and Tripp (1986) involved the attraction of young school children to *The Prisoner*. *The Prisoner* was a soap opera set in a women's prison. The show was immensely popular with school-aged children because the prison life portrayed in the show was decoded by the children as representing their life in school.

Later research built on the encoding/decoding model by providing psychological support for the arguments that Stuart Hall advanced by determining whether people formed a unified mental representation of a movie or TV series (Livingstone, 1989, 1990b). The focus on the mental representation of the show is important, because that mental representation should directly reflect how people understand the show. Research using the mental representation approach has focused on people's perceptions of the characters within a story, rather than the story itself, because stories typically reflect the dynamic interplay between the various characters involved in the story (Livingstone, 1987, 1989, 1990a, 1990b; Rowell & Moss, 1986). The most extensive line of research in this area was conducted by Livingstone (1987, 1989, 1990a, 1990b) and focused on the mental representations that resulted from watching soap operas such as *Dallas* and the ITV's *Coronation Street*. Across a series of studies, Livingstone found that not only did people create coherent representations of TV series, but there was a high degree of consensus regarding these representations (Livingstone, 1987). Furthermore, the representations that emerged in these studies closely matched those that emerged from studies that relied on more traditional techniques used to test the encoding/decoding model. For example, gender was a clear dimension for both *Dallas* and *Coronation Street*, but the representation of gender for *Dallas* followed traditional gender themes (i.e., the dominant reading where masculine was associated with potency or power), whereas the representation of gender for *Coronation Street* involved nontraditional gender roles (i.e., an oppositional reading where feminine was associated with potency or power). Notably, there was consensus for these representations for each show.

There are many issues that have arisen in response to Hall's (2001) encoding/decoding model that are beyond the limits of this chapter (see Morley, 1992). However, it is important to remember that when he presented the encoding/decoding paper at the University of Leicester, Hall did not think the paper was presenting a model of how messages are comprehended or read (Hall, 1994). Rather, he hoped that a more detailed model would develop out of his preliminary framework. In fact, other models have been developed to try to understand how individuals process media messages.

Mental Models

Mental models are cognitive representations of events, objects, or situations, including the people, concepts, settings, and interrelations involved. As such, we can think of them as the mental abstractions that we draw from things that we see and experience. For example, many of us have a mental representation for mother, a first birthday, or vacation—each of these might be both general (e.g., vacations) and specific (e.g., a vacation we took). Although mental models arise early in life and are built up from our individual experiences, they are also susceptible to change and can be adapted over time based on new and incoming information. Therefore, they are flexible in that they both guide and are affected by new information. Mental models have been used, therefore, to explain both our interpretations of stimuli (Roskos-Ewoldsen et al., 2002) and our responses to them (Krcmar & Curtis, 2003). Importantly in this context, mental models are thought to be a framework for understanding how we take in and encode messages. The mental abstractions, or mental models, are activated as we process information. Although the mental models approach has been used to understand how we interpret stimuli, one lingering issue is that mental models are conceptualized as stagnant models, and therefore not effective in understanding how we make sense of ongoing streams of information such as those found in media narratives.

Situation Models and Comprehension

Thus, situation models are seen partly as an extension of the mental models approach; however, a situation model is a dynamic mental representation of a situation (Busselle & Bilandzic, 2008; Roskos-Ewoldsen & Roskos-Ewoldsen, 2010; van Dijk & Kintsch, 1983). According to van Dijk (1995), these situation models are constructs in memory that represent what a situation or event described in a text is *about*, rather than a literal representation of the text itself, and rather than an abstraction of a situation. They are used in the comprehension of text discourse and movies. That is, they are ongoing, dynamic abstractions of an event that unfold in conjunction with a story, but also, given our general understanding of a given situation, help guide incoming information.

In addition to being a mental representation of a specific story or episode, situation models have specific temporal and spatial constraints (Busselle & Bilandzic, 2008; Radvansky, 2008; Roskos-Ewoldsen et al., 2004; Roskos-Ewoldsen & Roskos-Ewoldsen, 2010). Recall that a mental model is a more abstract representation; like a situation model, a mental model has temporal and spatial constraints, but these constraints will typically be looser and not based on a specific story as it unfolds. Importantly, situation and mental models represent knowledge *about* some event or events. These representations are spatially and temporally contextualized.

This is somewhat similar to a schema, but a schema is a more abstract representation that is knowledge *of* something (D'Andrade, 1995; Shore, 1996). For example, a schema for "zombie shows" would include little or no temporal or spatial information and that information would related to items *within* the schema (e.g., time passes between being bitten by a zombie and becoming a zombie), but it does not contextualize the representation. Rather, the schema would include information about what the important elements of a typical zombie show are, but the schema itself is not contextualized within a specific time or place.

The Landscape Model

The landscape model is a model of comprehension that is concerned with how people generate a coherent understanding of a story by looking at the relationship between the online processing of a story and the memorial representation of that story (van den Broek et al., 1996; van den Broek et al., 2005; van den Broek et al., 1999); thus the model tries to account for the connection between online, ongoing processing and mental abstractions that are stored in memory, a connection that is necessary for comprehension to occur. Therefore, the landscape model incorporates both the level of activation of individual concepts in memory as well as their co-activation. When concepts within a story are co-active, they form linkages in memory with each other. It is the latter process of linking co-activated concepts that provides the basis for coherence of a story and affords predictions about which concepts are more likely to be recalled, including those involving inferences drawn while reading the story.

There are four general sources of activation of concepts while attending to a story (van den Broek et al., 1996; van den Broek et al., 1999). First, concepts within the current sentence (for a book) or scene (for a movie) will be activated. Second, concepts from the immediately preceding sentence or scene should still be activated, albeit at a lower level of activation, unless they were the focal point of the previous scene, they were related to active goals of the protagonists or antagonists in the previous scene, or they involved events that were antecedents to some subsequent event that is occurring in the current scene. Third, concepts from earlier in the story may be reactivated because they are necessary for maintaining the coherence of the story. Fourth, world knowledge that is necessary for understanding the story will be activated.

The landscape model has been tested with text-based stories (van den Broek et al., 1996; van den Broek et al., 1999) and it does an excellent job of accounting for participants' memory for a text-based story (van den Broek et al., 1996; van den Broek et al., 1999). The original landscape model assumed a single representation of a text. But many media stimuli involve both visual and verbal information (Lee et al., 2008). Consequently, Lee et al. (2008) modified the landscape model by incorporating the dual code theory of memory into the model (Paivio, 1986, 1991). Dual code theory posits that verbal and visual information is represented separately in memory. Further, concepts are better remembered when they are represented in two codes than when they are represented in only one code. While the dual code landscape model has not been extensively tested, research has provided strong support for the model (Lee et al., 2008). The landscape model has also been used to predict people's memory for product placements within a film (Yang & Roskos-Ewoldsen, 2007).

The Event-Indexing Model

Another approach for investigating story comprehension is based on the event-indexing model (Zwaan et al., 1995). The event-indexing model focuses on events and the creation of situation models. When people process a narrative, they create multiple situation models, with each model corresponding to a unique event within the story (Wyer, 2004; Zwaan et al., 1995). The event-indexing model assumes that people monitor the events within a story using five indices (Magliano et al., 2001; Zwaan & Radvansky, 1998; Zwaan et al., 1995): changes in time, changes in space, establishment of a causal relationship between antecedents and conse-quences, focus on the protagonist's goal, and focus on different agents or objects. The event-indexing model further assumes that as more of the indices change simultaneously (i.e., a change from night to day concurrently with a change in location), people are more likely to update their situation model of the story or create a new situation model that corresponds to a new event (Magliano et al., 2001). Research has found that people do monitor movies using these dimensions (Magliano et al., 2001; Magliano et al., 2005; Magliano & Zacks, 2011).

In order to maintain the global coherence of a story, linkages need to be created between the various situation models that are created while comprehending the narrative. The event-indexing model assumes that these linkages are formed in several ways. If there is overlap in the dimensions, then the scenes will be linked (Wyer, 2004). For example, if a new scene occurs in the same spatial location and with the same protagonists as an earlier scene, then linkages with that earlier scene will be formed. In addition, people will create linkages between the situa-tion models within a story by drawing backward inferences. A backward inference *foreshadowing* involves people drawing linkages between an earlier scene and the current scene in order to understand what is occurring in the current scene. Cataphora occurs when something earlier in a narrative refers or foregrounds something that will occur later. When the later event occurs, people draw a backward inference to the earlier information in order to better comprehend what is occurring in the narrative at that point. In this way, two situation models (the earlier event and the current event) are linked, which helps with creating a structure for the narrative. Research has found that people do engage in backward inferences while watching movies, and this helps to organize the mental representation of the story (Lee et al., 2013).

Model of Narrative Comprehension and Engagement

When processing a narrative message, viewers are often transported into the story. Transportation involves the feeling of being a part of or absorbed into the narrative's story world (Cohen, 2006; Oliver, 2009). Research suggests that transportation is an important part of the experience of narrative and plays a role in enjoyment (Bilandzic & Busselle, 2011; Oliver, 2009). Busselle and Bilandzic's (2008) model of narrative comprehension and engagement approaches trans-portation into a narrative from the perspective of narrative comprehension. They note that the perceived realism of a narrative story plays an important role in how the story is processed and enjoyed. Realism can reflect external realism—does the story match the world as the viewer understands it?—or narrative realism. Narrative realism focuses on the story world and consistencies within that story world. When there are inconsistencies between the story and either external or narrative realism, the story will be more difficult to comprehend and transportation in and enjoyment of the story will both suffer (Bilandzic & Busselle, 2011).

Operating within a mental models framework, the model of narrative comprehension and engagement provides the most complete model of narrative processing and comprehension to date. The model assumes that people construct a story world when processing a narrative story (Busselle & Bilandzic, 2008). The story world is a mental model of the world operating within the narrative. Often these worlds can be specific places within the real world (e.g., New York), or fictional places set within the real world (e.g., Gotham City). These models draw heavily upon viewers' pre-existing knowledge of the world. But many narratives have fictional worlds that do not match our external reality (e.g., the Lord of the Rings (LoR)). These story models include the logic of the world within the narrative. One would not expect to find orcs at a New York Yankees game, but finding them at the gates of Mordor makes perfect sense within the LoR. When there are internal inconsistencies within the story world, processing of the narrative will become more difficult to the extent that the inconsistencies are salient and important (e.g., while an orc using an iPad outside the gates of Mordor is an interesting mental image, such a scene would probably disrupt processing of the LoR story). In addition to story models, the model also posits that people create character models for the characters within the narrative. Like the story model, the character models will rely on people's prior knowledge—particularly early in a narrative. But as individuating information is presented, the character model should reflect that new information.

The model of narrative comprehension and engagement also maintains that there are situation models that correspond to the events within the narrative. Recall that situation models are highly malleable and are constantly being updated throughout a narrative. However, the story world and character models are much more static. Obviously, they can be updated as the narrative progresses and new information is introduced within the story, but compared to the situation models for the story, they change much less.

According to Busselle and Bilandzic's (2008) model, transportation occurs when people can place themselves within the story model while processing the narrative (also referred to as engaging in a deictic shift). Transportation into the story world can be disrupted, however, if the narrative is low in realism. For example, Busselle and Bilandzic (2008) argue that if there are inconsistencies between the situation models for the narrative, the story model, and the character models, or within the story model itself, then viewers should be less likely to make the deictic shift and experience less transportation.

Conclusion

How messages are processed is a critical part of the communication process. However, communication scholars have largely ignored these processes. Instead, attention to and comprehension of messages is typically taken as a given. Consequently, we have a limited understanding of factors that influence attention to and comprehension of mediated messages or how these processes dynamically interact. The recent research in both of these domains highlights how communication scholars can study attention and comprehension in mediated messages. Critically, the theories that have been outlined in this chapter can also be used to understand attention and comprehension in contexts outside of the media, such as interpersonal and group settings.

Notes

1   Communication scholars make the distinction between comprehending a text or film and interpreting it. Comprehension involves understanding the story as it is written or seen, whereas interpretation involves explaining the potential deeper meanings of the story. Semiotics offers yet a third level to understanding. According to Eco (1990; see also Eco, 1979), understanding a text is a complex interplay between the creator of the text and the reader of the text, and this interplay includes shared cultural knowledge. The critical point from this perspective is that the reader's understanding of the text is biased in part by his or her own experiences. As a result, two people with different experiences may understand the text differently. On the flip side, the more shared experiences and cultural knowledge, the more similar the understanding.
2   Hall (1994) characterized this essay as a polemic against the traditional effects research because that research tradition assumed perfect communication. In other words, media effects researchers of the time assumed that all members of the audience understood a media message in perfect accord with each other. This assumption permitted the experimental testing of the effect of some message characteristic, such as violence, on some outcome variable, such as aggression, but it lacked a way to identify underlying individual differences in media effects.

References

Alwitt, L. F., Anderson, D. R., Lorch, E. P., & Levin, S. R. (1980). Preschool children's visual attention to attributions of television. *Human Communication Research, 7*, 52–67.

Anderson, D. R., & Field, D. E. (1983). Children's attention to television: Implications for production. In M. Meyer (Ed.), *Children and the formal features of television: Approaches and findings of experimental and formative research* (pp. 56–96). Munich, Germany: K. G. Saur.

Anderson, D. R., & Lorch, E. P. (1983). Looking at television: Action or reaction? In J. Bryant & D. R. Anderson (Eds.), *Children's understanding of television: Research on attention and comprehension* (pp. 1–33). New York: Academic Press.

Anderson, D. R., & Kirkorian, H. L. (2006). Attention and television. In J. Bryant & P. Vorderer (Eds.), *Psychology of entertainment* (pp. 35–56). Mahwah, NJ: Lawrence Erlbaum Associations.

Anderson, D. R., Choi, H. P., & Lorch, E. P. (1987). Attentional inertia reduces distractability during children's TV viewing. *Child Development, 58*, 798–806.

Anderson, D. R., Fite, K. V., Petrovich, N., & Hirsch, J. (2006). Cortical activation while watching video montage: An fMRI study. *Media Psychology, 8*, 7–24.

Anderson, D. R., Lorch, E. P., Smith, R., Bradford, R., & Levin, S. R. (1981). Effects of peer presence on preschool children's television-viewing behavior. *Developmental Psychology, 17*, 446–453.

Anderson, D. R., Lorch, E. P., Field, D. E., Collins, P. A., & Nathan, J. G. (1986). Television viewing at home: Age trends in visual attention and time with TV. *Child Development, 57*, 1024–1033.

Ang, I. (1985). *Watching Dallas: Soap opera and the melodramatic imagination* (D. Couling, trans.). London: Methuen. (Original work published in 1982).

Baddeley, A. (2007). *Working memory, thought, and action.* Oxford: Oxford University Press.

Basil, M. D. (1994). Multiple resource theory I: Application to television viewing. *Communication Research, 21*, 177–207.

Bickham, D. S., Wright, J. C., & Huston, A. C. (2001). Attention, comprehension, and the educational influences of television. In D. G. Singer & J. L. Singer (Eds.), *Handbook of children and the media* (pp. 101–119). Thousand Oaks, CA: Sage.

Bilandzic, H., & Busselle, R. W. (2011). Enjoyment of films as a function of narrative experience, perceived realism and transportability. *Communications, 36*, 29–50.

Bordwell, D. (2005). *Figures traced in light: On cinematic staging.* Berkeley: University of California Press.

Bradley, M. M., & Lang, P. J. (2007). Emotion and motivation. In J. T. Cacioppo, L. G. Tassinary, & G. Berntson (Eds.), *Handbook of psychophysiology* (3rd ed., pp. 581–607). Cambridge: Cambridge University Press.

Brooker, W. (2000). *Batman unmasked: Analyzing a cultural icon.* New York: Continuum.

Busselle, R., & Bilandzic, H. (2008). Fictionality and perceived realism in experiencing stories: A model of narrative comprehension and engagement. *Communication Theory, 18*, 255–280.

Cacioppo, J. T., & Berntson, G. G. (1994). Relationship between attitudes and evaluative space: A critical review, with emphasis on the separability of positive and negative substrates. *Psychological Bulletin, 115*, 401–423.

Calvert, S. L., Huston, A. C., Watkins, B. A., & Wright, J. C. (1982). The relation between selective attention to television forms and children's comprehension of content. *Child Development, 53*, 601–610.

Campbell, T. A., Wright, J. C., & Huston, A. C. (1987). Form cues and content difficulty as determinants of children's cognitive processing of televised educational messages. *Journal of Experimental Children Psychology, 43*, 311–327.

Cohen, J. (2006). Audience identification with media characters. In J. Bryant & P. Vorderer (Eds.), *Psychology of entertainment* (pp. 183–198). Mahwah, NJ: Lawrence Erlbaum Associates.

Condit, C. M. (1989). The rhetorical limits of polysemy. *Critical Studies in Mass Communication, 6*, 103–122.

Crawley, A. M., Anderson, D. R., Santomero, A., Wilder, A., Williams, M., Evans, M. K., & Bryant, J. (2002). Do children learn how to watch television? The impact of extensive experience with Blue's Clues on preschool children's television viewing behavior. *Journal of Communication, 52*, 264–280.

D'Andrade, R. G. (1995). *The development of cognitive anthropology.* Cambridge: Cambridge University Press.

Eco, U. (1979). *The role of the reader.* Bloomington, IN: Indiana University Press.

Eco, U. (1990). *The limits of interpretation.* Bloomington, IN: Indiana University Press.

Fisch, S. M. (2000). A capacity model of children's comprehension of educational content on television. *Media Psychology, 2*, 63–91.

Fisch, S. M., Truglio, R. T., & Cole, C. F. (1999). The impact of Sesame Street on preschool children: A review and synthesis of 30 years' research. *Media Psychology, 1*, 165–190.

Fisch, S. M., McCann Brown, S. K., & Cohen, D. I. (2001). Young children's comprehension of educational television: The role of visual information and intonation. *Media
Psychology, 3,* 365–378.

Fiske, J. (1987). *Television culture.* London: Methuen.

Fiske, J., & Hartley, J. (1978). *Reading television.* London: Routledge.

Fox, J., Park, B., & Lang, A. (2007). When available resources become negative resources:
The effects of cognitive overload on memory sensitivity and criterion bias.
Communication Research, 34, 277–296.

Hall, S. (1994). Reflections upon the encoding/decoding model: An interview with Stuart
Hall. In J. Cruz & J. Lewis (Eds.), *Viewing, reading, listening: Audiences and cultural reception*
(pp. 253–274). Boulder, CO: Westview Press.

Hall, S. (2001). Encoding/decoding. In M. G. Durham & D. M. Kellner (Eds.), *Media
and cultural studies: Keyworks* (pp. 166–176). Malden, MA: Blackwell. (Reprinted from
S. Hall, D. Hobson, A. Lowe, & P. Willis (Eds.) (1980), *Culture, media, language*
(pp. 128–138). London: Hutchinson.)

Hawkins, R. P., Yong-Ho, K., & Pingree, S. (1991). The ups and downs of attention to
television. *Communication Research, 18,* 53–76.

Hawkins, R. P., Pingree, S., Hitchon, J., Radler, B., Gorham, B. W., Kahlor, L., Gilligan,
E., Serlin, R. C., Schmidt, T., Kannaovakun, P., & Kolbein, G. H. (2005). What
produces television attention and attention style? Genre, situation, and individual
differences as predictors. *Human Communication Research, 31,* 162–187.

Hodge, R., & Tripp, D. (1986). *Children and television: A semiotic approach.* Cambridge: Polity
Press.

Huston, A. C., & Wright, J. C. (1983). Children's processing of television: The informative functions of formal features. In J. Bryant & D. R. Anderson (Eds.), *Children's
understanding of television: Research on attention and comprehension* (pp. 39–68). New York:
Academic Press.

Huston, A. C., Wright, J. C., Rice, M. L., Kerkman, D., & St. Peters, M. (1990).
Development of television viewing patterns in early childhood: A longitudinal
investigation. *Developmental Psychology, 26,* 409–420.

Jenkins, H. (2006). *Fans, bloggers, and gamers: Media consumers in a digital age.* New York:
New York University Press.

Kahneman, D. (1973). *Attention and effort.* Englewood Cliffs, NJ: Prentice-Hall.

Kirkorian, H. L., Anderson, D. R., & Keen, R. (2012). Age differences in online
processing of video: An eye movement study. *Child Development, 83,* 497–507.

Krcmar, M., & Curtis, S. (2003). Mental models: Understanding the impact of fantasy
violence on children's moral reasoning. *Journal of Communication, 53,* 460–478.

Krull, R., & Husson, W. (1979). Children's attention: The case of TV viewing. In
E. Wartella (Ed.), *Children communicating: Media and development of thought, speech,
understanding* (pp. 83–114). Beverly Hills, CA: Sage.

Lang, A. (2000). The limited capacity model of mediated message processing. *Journal of
Communication, 50,* 46–70.

Lang, A. (2006). Using the limited capacity model of motivated mediated message
processing to design effective cancer communication messages. *Journal of Communication,
56,* S57–S80.

Lang, A., Potter, R. F., & Bolls, P. D. (1999). Something for nothing: Is visual encoding
automatic? *Media Psychology, 1,* 145–163.

Lang, A., Potter, R. F., & Bolls, P. D. (2008). Where psychophysiology meets the media: Taking the effects out of mass media research. In J. Bryant & M. B. Oliver (Eds.), *Media effects: Advances in theory and research* (3rd ed., pp. 185–206). Mahwah, NJ: Lawrence Erlbaum Associates.

Lang, A., Bradley, S. D., Park, B., Shin, M., & Chung, Y. (2006). Parsing the resource pie: Using STRTs to measure attention to mediated messages. *Media Psychology, 8,* 369–394.

Lee, M., Roskos-Ewoldsen, B., & Roskos-Ewoldsen, D. R. (2008). Applying the landscape model to comprehending discourse from TV news stories. *Discourse Processes, 45,* 519–544.

Lee, M., Roskos, B., & Ewoldsen, D. R. (2013). The impact of subtitles on comprehension of narrative film. *Media Psychology, 16,* 414–440.

Livingstone, S. M. (1987). The implicit representation of characters in *Dallas*: A multidimensional scaling approach. *Human Communication Research, 13,* 399–420.

Livingstone, S. M. (1989). Interpretive viewers and structured programs: The implicit representations of soap opera characters. *Communication Research, 16,* 25–57.

Livingstone, S. M. (1990a). Interpreting a television narrative: How different viewers see a story. *Journal of Communication, 40*(1), 72–85.

Livingstone, S. M. (1990b). *Making sense of television: The psychology of audience interpretation.* Oxford: Pergamon.

Lorch, E. P., Anderson, D. R., & Levin, S. R. (1979). The relationship of visual attention to children's comprehension of television. *Child Development, 50,* 722–727.

Magliano, J. P., & Zacks, J. M. (2011). The impact of continuity editing in narrative film on event segmentation. *Cognitive Science, 35,* 1489–1517.

Magliano, J. P., Miller, J., & Zwaan, R. A. (2001). Indexing space and time in film understanding. *Applied Cognitive Psychology, 15,* 533–545.

Magliano, J. P., Taylor, H. A., & Kim, H. J. J. (2005). When goals collide: Monitoring the goals of multiple characters. *Memory & Cognition, 33,* 1357–1367.

Morley, D. (1992). *Television, audiences & cultural studies.* London: Routledge.

Morley, D. (1999). The Nationwide audience: Structure and decoding. In D. Morley & C. Brunsdon (Eds.), *The Nationwide television studies* (pp. 111–228). London: Routledge. (Reprinted from D. Morley (1980), *The Nationwide audience: Structure and decoding.* London: British Film Institute.)

Okdie, B. M., Ewoldsen, D. R., Muscanell, N. L., Guadagno, R. E., Eno, C. A., Velez, J. A., Dunn, R. A., O'Mally, J., & Smith, L. R. (2014). Missed programs (you can't TiVo this one): Why psychologists should study media. *Perspectives on Psychological Science, 9,* 180–195.

Oliver, M. B. (2009). Entertainment. In R. L. Nabi & M. B. Oliver (Eds.), *Sage handbook of media processes and effects* (pp. 161–176). Thousand Oaks, CA: Sage.

Paivio, A. (1986). *Mental representations.* New York: Oxford University Press.

Paivio, A. (1991). Dual coding theory: Retrospect and current status. *Canadian Journal of Psychology, 45,* 255–287.

Parkin, F. (1971). *Class inequality and political order.* New York: Praeger.

Piotrowski, J. T. (2014). The relationship between narrative processing demands and young American children's comprehension of educational television. *Journal of Children & Media, 8,* 267–285.

Pittorf, M. I., Lehmann, W., & Huckauf, A. (2014). The understanding of pans in 3- to 6-year-old children. *Media Psychology, 17,* 332–355.

Radvansky, G. A. (2008). Situation models in memory: Texts and stories. In G. Cohen & M. A. Conway (Eds.), *Memory in the real world* (pp. 229–247). New York: Psychology Press.

Radway, J. A. (1991). *Reading the romance*. Chapel Hill, NC: University of North Carolina Press.

Rice, M. L., Huston, C. A., & Wright, J. C. (1983). The forms of television: Effects on children's attention, comprehension, and social behavior. In M. Meyer (Ed.), *Children and the formal features of television: Approaches and findings of experimental and formative research* (pp. 21–55). Munich, Germany: K. G. Saur.

Roskos-Ewoldsen, B., Davies, J., & Roskos-Ewoldsen, D. R. (2004). Implications of the mental models approach for cultivation theory. *Communications, 29*, 345–363.

Roskos-Ewoldsen, B., Roskos-Ewoldsen, D. R., Yang, M., & Lee, M. (2007). Comprehension of the media. In D. R. Roskos-Ewoldsen & J. Monahan (Eds.), *Communication and social cognition: Theories and methods* (pp. 319–350). Mahwah, NJ: Lawrence Erlbaum Associates.

Roskos-Ewoldsen, D. R., & Roskos-Ewoldsen, B. (2010). Message processing. In C. Berger, M. Roloff, & D. R. Roskos-Ewoldsen (Eds.), *Handbook for communication science* (2nd ed., pp. 129–144). Thousand Oaks, CA: Sage.

Roskos-Ewoldsen, D. R., Roskos-Ewoldsen, B., & Dillman Carpenter, F. R. (2002). Media priming: A synthesis. In J. Bryant & M. B. Oliver (Eds.), *Media effects: Advances in theory and research* (2nd ed., pp. 97–120). New York: Routledge.

Rowell, J. A., & Moss, P. D. (1986). Mental models of text and film: A multidimensional scaling analysis. *Educational Psychology, 6*, 321–333.

Shore, B. (1996). *Culture in mind: Cognition, culture, and the problem of meaning*. New York: Oxford University Press.

Storey, J. (2003). *Cultural studies and the study of popular culture* (2nd ed.). Athens, GA: University of Georgia Press.

Turner, G. (1990). *British cultural studies: An introduction*. Boston, MA: Unwin Hyman.

Valkenburg, P. M., & Vroone, M. (2004). Developmental changes in infants' and toddlers' attention to television entertainment. *Communication Research, 31*, 288–311.

van den Broek, P., Rapp, D. N., & Kendeou, P. (2005). Integrating memory-based and constructionist processes in accounts of reading comprehension. *Discourse Processes, 39*, 299–316.

van den Broek, P., Risden, K., Fletcher, C., & Thurlow, R. (1996). A "landscape" view of reading: Fluctuating patterns of activation and the construction of a stable memory representation. In B. Britton & A. Graesser (Eds.), *Models of understanding text* (pp. 165–188). Mahwah, NJ: Lawrence Erlbaum Associates.

van den Broek, P., Young, M., Tzeng, Y., & Linderholm, T. (1999). The landscape model of reading: Inferences and the online construction of a memory representation. In H. van Oostendorp & S. R. Goldman (Eds.), *The construction of mental representations during reading* (pp. 71–98). Mahwah, NJ: Lawrence Erlbaum Associates.

van Dijk, T. A. (1995). On macrostructures, mental models, and other inventions: A brief personal history of the van Dijk–Kintsch theory. In C. A. Weaver, S. Mannes, & C. R. Fletcher (Eds.), *Discourse comprehension: Essays in honor of Walter Kintsch* (pp. 383–410). Hillsdale, NJ: Lawrence Erlbaum Associates.

van Dijk, T. A., & Kintsch, W. (1983). *Strategies of discourse comprehension*. New York: Academic Press.

Wyer, R. S. (2004). *Social comprehension and judgment: The role of situation models, narratives, and implicit theories.* Mahwah, NJ: Lawrence Erlbaum Associates.

Yang, M., & Roskos-Ewoldsen, D. R. (2007). The effectiveness of brand placements in the movies: Levels of placements, explicit and implicit memory, and brand choice behavior. *Journal of Communication, 57,* 469–489.

Zwaan, R. A., & Radvansky, G. A. (1998). Situation models in language comprehension and memory. *Psychological Bulletin, 123,* 162–185.

Zwaan, R. A., Langston, M. C., & Graesser, A. C. (1995). The construction of situation models in narrative comprehension: An event-indexing model. *Psychological Science, 6,* 292–297.

10

INTERPERSONAL COMMUNICATION

Defining Interpersonal Communication

All communication is ultimately communication between people, but not all communication is interpersonal, at least not in the sense in which the term is used in the discipline of communication. When used to designate intra-disciplinary boundaries, interpersonal communication refers to communication that takes place between individuals that at a minimum is (a) *interactive*, such that all parties are able to address each other and respond to one another; (b) *individualized*, such that communicators are aware of each other as unique individuals, rather than solely as occupants of social roles, such as sales clerk, teacher, police officer, or audience, for example; and (c) *relational*, such that communicators are in ongoing interpersonal relationships with one another that assume future interactions, such as dating, marriage, family, or work group relationship.

This broad definition of interpersonal communication combines aspects of communication that are observable behaviors with aspects of communication that are located in the minds of communicators and therefore are not directly observable. Consequently, interpersonal communication is a phenomenon that exists simultaneously in the empirical-material world in the form of, for example, words and nonverbal behaviors, and in the world of individual cognition in the form of, for example, perceptions and emotions, and also in the social world in the form of, for example, symbols, shared meaning, and social rules and norms. To say then that interpersonal communication is complex and multifaceted is, if anything, an understatement. However, it is a mistake to interpret this to mean that because interpersonal communication is complex and simultaneously exists in such diverse spheres, the only way to truly understand and to study interpersonal communication is through research that is equally complex and that takes all these spheres into account simultaneously. This is simply not feasible. As explained by

Bonini's paradox (Bonini, 1963), theoretical models of complex systems tend to become less understandable the more complete they become. Thus, any truly useful theoretical model of interpersonal communication must be much less complex than the phenomena it attempts to explain. This requires the working definitions of interpersonal communication that scholars use to be much narrower than the very broad definition of interpersonal communication that we have just used to define the *discipline* of interpersonal communication.

Before we come to these narrower definitions, however, it makes sense to briefly get a sense of the relevance of interpersonal communication to the discipline. It should be obvious from the just-provided definition of interpersonal communication that interpersonal communication scholars deal with a very wide range of phenomena. Also indicating that studying interpersonal communication is a huge undertaking is the fact that humans spend almost the entirety of their waking hours communicating, the majority of it interpersonally (Barker et al., 1980). As early as 1929, researchers observed that college students spent about 75 percent of their waking hours either listening (42 percent) or talking (32 percent) to others (Rankin, 1929). These percentages did not change significantly in research reported in the 1950s (Bird, 1954). More recently, there are some changes in communication behaviors as persons in technologically advanced societies tend to engage more frequently with mass media and the Internet, which has reduced the percentage of communication that is interpersonal to about 50 percent, with about two-thirds of that time spent listening and one-third talking (Emanuel et al., 2008). Furthermore, the technology gap between countries is rapidly closing with the spread of smart phones across the globe. Still, at least in terms of time spent, interpersonal communication constitutes about half of all human activity and is arguably the activity that most clearly differentiates us from other living things and most distinctively makes us human beings.

While the broad definition of interpersonal communication is useful in that it delineates the discipline of interpersonal communication, it is too broad to be very useful in telling us how interpersonal communication works. To investigate how interpersonal communication works, we need more fine-tuned approaches and definitions of interpersonal communication that are narrow enough to allow us to focus on specific phenomena and processes that we can fruitfully investigate in more manageable theoretical models. Of course, the trade-off is that each more narrow definition excludes potentially important aspects of interpersonal communication and creates an incomplete picture of how interpersonal communication works in the real world. This trade-off can only be resolved, in the end, when combining the knowledge gained by the various narrow approaches into a whole that results in a deeper and a more complete understanding of interpersonal communication.

In this chapter, then, we will show how interpersonal communication has been investigated using a number of different approaches that employ fairly narrow definitions of interpersonal communication based on different functions of interpersonal communication. We also use these different approaches and narrowly focused definitions of interpersonal communication to impose an order to the interpersonal communication discipline, so that we can more easily review it for our readers. It does not mean that all scholars in the field of interpersonal communication necessarily agree that this is an exhaustive list of possible functions or definitions of interpersonal communication, nor would individual scholars whose work we present under one definition necessarily agree with our classification of their work. In short, this order is neither the natural order nor even necessarily how the discipline sees itself, but rather imposed by us on the discipline for the purpose of presenting it to our readers.

A Functional Approach to Interpersonal Communication

When confronting how to study a vast field such as interpersonal communication, researchers have a number of choices concerning how to approach their subject of study. Some researchers, for example, focus on the means of communication, and analyze how language is used and how grammar, syntax, and phonetics contribute to the meaning communicators assign to their behaviors. Others focus on the impact of social institutions on behaviors and study how cultural norms and values affect interpersonal behaviors. Yet another group of scholars take a psychological approach and investigate how individuals' internal needs and wants motivate different kinds of communicative behavior. None of these approaches is inherently superior to any other. Rather, each one attempts to answer different questions and to provide different types of explanation for behaviors. If there is a bias in the field of interpersonal communication to favor psychologically based theory and explanations, it is because of the widely held and shared belief that brain activity (in the broadest sense, cognition and the mind) precedes and determines communicative behavior. Still, there are many interpersonal communication scholars who favor socio-cultural or sociological approaches, based on the assumption that meaning and meaning making are primarily social processes that are best understood on a sociological level. Similarly, interpersonal communication scholars have a wide range of methods at their disposal, which they can use to investigate the phenomena that they are interested in, from critical to interpretive to qualitative to quantitative social science.

Thus, for those who research interpersonal scholarship, and in the present case, provide an overview of that scholarship, there are many choices of how the field might be delineated and divided. One could divide the discipline based on the social or psychological processes thought to underlie behaviors, or based on the methods one uses to study interpersonal communication. Furthermore, one could also divide the field based on the means persons use to communicate, or based on the types of relationship that persons are engaged in. Another useful way, and the way we have chosen to approach interpersonal communication scholarship in this chapter, is to employ a functional approach that asks: "what functions does interpersonal communication serve?" and to group research of interpersonal communication based on the basic functions it serves. This allows for a categorization that focuses discussion of the scholarship in useful ways, which, in our opinion, makes it both easier to present and more accessible to our readers.

Functions of Interpersonal Communication

In our reading of interpersonal communication (IPC) scholarship, there are at least five basic functions that interpersonal communication serves and that can be used to delineate different types of interpersonal communication research. First, interpersonal communication functions to *create, develop, and maintain interpersonal relationships*. The second function of IPC is to *exchange information*. The third function is to *define and give meaning* to persons' experiences. The fourth function is to *create a shared social reality for self and other*. Finally, the fifth function is to *influence others*. Clearly, these five functions are not mutually exclusive. Interpersonal communication behaviors can, and frequently do, serve multiple functions simultaneously. For example, interpersonal communication that informs can also give meaning to events, create a shared social reality, influence one another, and maintain a relationship. Nonetheless, for both theoretical and pragmatic reasons, it seems that many scholars seem to focus their research on primarily one of these five functions, which makes it possible to describe interpersonal communication research along these narrowly defined functions first, before trying to broaden the discussion and ultimately, understanding interpersonal communication in its full complexity.

Function One: Relationship Development and Maintenance

Maybe the most obvious function of interpersonal communication is that it allows people to develop, maintain, and end relationships with others. Humans are an extremely social species and being in close interpersonal relationships is a basic need for a vast majority of people. In fact, the right to communicate and associate with others is regarded a basic human right, and involuntary isolation from others is universally regarded as torture (Mendez, 2011). Communication is the primary means by which humans relate to one another, and interpersonal communication and relationships are so intertwined that for a number of interpersonal communication scholars, interpersonal communication is basically equivalent to interpersonal relationships. In fact, Knapp (1984) published an early and widely adopted textbook in interpersonal communication that conceptualized and organized interpersonal communication research around stages of relationship development, and which was, and continues to be, very influential in the discipline.

Identifying interpersonal communication as a basic human need and motivation leads to an interest in the psychological processes underlying communication behaviors, and this interest has been a defining characteristic of interpersonal communication scholarships from its very beginning. Many of the early interpersonal communication scholars' interest in psychology impacted both their methodology and theoretical thinking. In terms of methodology, interpersonal communication scholars relied heavily on quantitative social science, with a premium placed on knowledge derived from experimentation. Theoretically, interpersonal communication behavior was thought of as originating from motivation and learning, and later, in responses to the cognitive revolution in psychology, also as originating from other mental processes as well.

Among the earliest motivations implicated as underlying interpersonal communication were those stemming from what were presumed to be universal human needs, such as Maslow's needs of love and belonging, esteem, and self-actualization, respectively, and Schutz's (1958) basic interpersonal needs of inclusion, control, and affection. Communication scholars employing these theories argued that these needs can only be fulfilled in interpersonal relationships and that therefore interpersonal communication can be explained by individuals' pursuit of these needs. Essentially, these early scholars adopted a functional approach by asking what function interpersonal communication served for individuals. Thus, they regarded interpersonal communication as a means that can be best understood through an appreciation of the ends it serves. Because these ends (e.g., love, affection, inclusion, esteem, control, and self-actualization) seem in particular to depend on closeness and intimacy in relationships, the study of interpersonal communication from a relationship development perspective privileged closeness and intimacy as concepts of main concern over other properties of relationships.

Because of the overwhelming focus on closeness and intimacy, early theories that dominated the field and still are a mainstay of introductory texts are those that focus on intimacy and relationship development. A typical example is social penetration theory (Altman & Taylor, 1973). According to this theory, the function and purpose of interpersonal communication is primarily to reveal oneself to the other in order to achieve intimacy and self-actualization. The level of self-disclosure determines the intimacy achieved in a relationship, such that the greater the depth and breadth of self-disclosure, the greater the intimacy. Motivation to self-disclose is thought to be determined by social exchange principles. Social exchange principles largely view the process of self-disclosure (for example) as negotiated exchanges between parties. More specifically, social exchange theory suggests that decisions to disclose are based on a subjective cost–benefit analysis and a comparison of alternatives, and as such, takes a fairly economic approach to ideas of social exchange in general and decisions to disclose in particular (Altman & Taylor, 1973).

A consequence of this social exchange approach is that the theory of social penetration asserts that self-disclosure that increases in both breadth and depth is ultimately self-reinforcing (because the more self-disclosure, the more rewarding the interactions, and the more one party discloses, the more the other will as a means of exchange). In normal circumstances, this exchange process should lead any interpersonal relationships to ever-greater levels of intimacy. Ultimately, this not only makes intimacy the paramount goal of any interpersonal relationship and interaction, it also makes intimacy and the movement toward ever-increasing intimacy normative in interpersonal relationships and implicitly defines interpersonal relationships that do not achieve great levels of intimacy as lacking. While this might be appropriate for relationships that aim to become enduring romantic unions, this view is clearly too limiting for most interpersonal relationships people actually have, which are characterized by more moderate levels of intimacy, such as friendships, relationships with members of the extended family, and coworkers, to name but a few.

A second theory that was extremely influential in the beginning of interpersonal communication as a discipline and that was based on assumptions similar to those of social penetration theory is the stage model of relationship development (Knapp, 1984). In this model, interpersonal relationships develop in a predictable pattern, from initiating, experimenting, intensifying, and integrating to bonding. These states are characterized not only by ever-increasing degrees of intimacy and self-disclosure, but also by increasing interdependence and social integration. However, unlike social penetration theory, this model is not strictly linear in the sense that it also ascribes specific communication behaviors that are unique to each stage. For example, small talk that superficially addresses a wide range of topics and functions to identify areas of common interest and values is limited to the initiating stage. Likewise, expressing attitudes to draw boundaries around the couple is behavior associated with the intensifying stage.

A third influential theory also heavily influenced by the relationship development framework and social penetration theory was uncertainty reduction theory (URT; Berger & Calabrese, 1975). This theory also proposed that someone is motivated to get to know the other person through behaviors such as self-disclosure, but differs from them in important ways. First, URT presumes that the reason persons are motivated to reduce their uncertainty is not so much a desire for intimacy, but rather a need for predictability. Second, following from the first presumption, the theory limits this motivation to primarily the early stages of relationships.

More recently, uncertainty has been reconceptualized as relational uncertainty (Solomon & Knobloch, 2004) regarding the role of self, other, and the relationship itself that emerges in response to relational turbulence. Relational turbulences are events usually external to the relationship that disrupt the routine of day-to-day interactions because they raise questions about the assumptions underlying the relationship or lead to perceptions of partner interference with the relationship.

Relational turbulence can occur at any stage of the relationship, making uncertainty reduction and uncertainty management important processes of relationship maintenance and not just relationship initiation (Afifi & Weiner, 2004).

In addition to uncertainty management, a number of other communication behaviors have been associated with relationship maintenance. Positive maintenance behaviors such as positivity, assurances, openness, sharing tasks and social networks, identified by Stafford and Canary (1992), and negative behaviors, particularly enacted during conflict, also have received considerable attention. In particular, Gottman's (1994) research on the conflict behavior of couples and the negative effects of conflict strategies, which he labeled "the four horsemen of the apocalypse" (criticism, defensiveness, contempt, and stonewalling), as well as Sillars's (Sillars et al., 2000) work on attributions during relationship conflict and Caughlin's (2002) work on demand–withdrawal patterns in marital interactions, illuminated the role that negative interactions play in relationship satisfaction, stability, and maintenance.

There can be no doubt that interpersonal communication is closely related to interpersonal relationships, but that does not mean that relationship concerns are the only motivating force behind interpersonal communication. Individuals in close relationships communicate with their partners for a number of other reasons as well, and relationship concerns may very well be in the background during most interpersonal interactions while other reasons more directly influence how the individuals communicate.

Function Two: Information Exchange

One of the most influential and probably the most easily recognizable model of communication is Shannon and Weaver's (1949) information exchange model: Sender → Message → Receiver. Although developed originally by and for telecommunication engineers, it has informed interpersonal communication from its earliest beginnings. Applied to interpersonal interaction, this model suggests that senders use messages to transmit information to receivers. Thus, this model makes the message central to interpersonal communication, as it contains the information that is exchanged between communicators. Also very important are the processes of encoding and decoding, which for information to be exchanged with high fidelity have to be mirror images of one another. Finally, this model also contains the concepts of channel, noise, and interference, suggesting that noise and interference are the main threats to successful interpersonal communication.

The sender → message → receiver model makes intuitive sense to most scholars of interpersonal communication, and it has been clearly influential in the field. For example, much of early interpersonal influence and persuasion research has focused on message design and message features. Early interpersonal influence research that investigated whether arguments phrased in passive or active voice are more persuasive, for example, was clearly informed by this model. Likewise, early scholarship in interpersonal conflict communication also focused on message features, and much of what these researchers found has become widely accepted as best practices in interpersonal communication. Advice such as: sandwich criticism in between two statements of praise or appreciation, or grammatically take ownership of one's own emotions as in: "when you do X, I feel Y," stem from research focused on message content. Other notable findings by research inspired by the information-processing model include research investigating redundancy in oral communication as a means of overcoming noise (Hsia, 1968) and Kraut's research on the important role that feedback plays in dyadic communication (Kraut et al., 1982). Finally, research that focuses on consistency between verbal and nonverbal communication, such as paralinguistic cues and facial expressions, also are fundamentally based on the sender–message–receiver model of interpersonal communication.

A significant shortcoming of this approach, however, is that there is too much reliance on the idea that meaning is essentially fixed in a message and that therefore the main problem of communication is to maintain message fidelity. Thus, the model seems to suggest that at least theoretically, a perfectly encoded and decoded message has the same meaning for senders, receivers, and observers and therefore can be entirely unambiguous. All attention is directed at message content and the message attributes that increase fidelity, and on mechanisms that reduce channel noise or other, similar interferences. More importantly, this at least implicitly reduces all interpersonal problems to mere message transmission problems and implies that better messages can solve them. Clearly, this model of communication is too message focused and ignores the important contribution that context makes to meaning. It also ignores the fluidity of meaning and that the meaning individuals assign to communication may change during interactions as well as in retrospection.

Function Three: Define and Give Meaning to Individual Experiences

Another function that guided early research in interpersonal communication and that became prominent partly because it constituted a response to the shortcoming of the sender–message–receiver model is that of meaning making. One of its more significant representatives is symbolic interactionism, a view of interpersonal interaction first formalized by Mead and put in print by Blumer (1969). In this view, the meaning of utterances and other types of communicative behavior is not fixed either in the code or symbols used in messages, nor is it only situated in the cognition of individual communicators. Rather, meaning originates from the very interaction between two or more individuals, and while the meaning of an utterance can be remembered and used in future interactions, it also is temporally bound. Meaning is constantly in flux, constantly created and re-created, and originates within the interaction. Defining interpersonal communication as primarily a means to create meaning highlights the symbolic nature of interactions. By definition, symbols are used to represent something else (the referent) and are arbitrary in the sense that the connection between symbol and referent is tenuous and depends to a large extent on uses and conventions within a speech community. In addition, the connections between symbols and meaning are made in individuals' thoughts and cognitions. Thus, any interaction using symbols requires communicators to reestablish the connection between symbol and referent, and creates the opportunity to affirm, reject, and change the meaning associated with the symbols they use in their interactions.

Interpersonal communication research that is informed by symbolic interactionism is primarily concerned with the processes by which meaning emerges *from* interaction. Such research can focus on linguistic devices that communicators employ, or social mechanisms that define meaning. Of particular relevance is meta-communication, or communication about the interaction and the relationship. Such meta-communication often represents overt attempts to determine the meaning of messages, as well as that of other behaviors that can give meaning to interactions, such as nonverbal behaviors.

One important interpersonal communication theory that deals with negotiation of meaning is Baxter's (1988) dialectical theory. Adapting classical Hegelian theory to interpersonal communication, she argues that relationships are driven by a constant need to resolve dialectical tensions. Dialectical tensions are simultaneous but contradictory needs that are pursued in relationships, such as the need for autonomy and connectedness. Other important dialectical tensions often relevant to close relationships include openness and closedness, novelty and predictability, and equality and inequality. Other dialectics may exist, but these are the primary ones that seem to exist in ongoing relationships. Unlike Hegelian theory, which argues that history is advancing through the process of tensions between theses and antitheses that ultimately lead to temporary resolutions in the form of synthesis, in Baxter's theory dialectical tensions are concurrent rather than sequential. Different dialectical tensions might appear sequential as they become more or less relevant at a given time for a relationship, but at any given time there is more than one tension at play in a relationship. Also, unlike Hegelian theory, in Baxter's model dialectical tensions are never fully resolved in the form of syntheses. Rather, a couple might achieve a temporary equilibrium for specific dialectical tensions, but these tensions always have the potential to emerge or reemerge to play a dominant role in the relationship. While dialectical tensions are primarily used to explain the dynamics within dyadic relationships, they also can be applied to analyze the tensions within individuals or in the relationships that dyads have with other persons or social structures, such as families, communities, or even societies.

Dialectical theory is a good example of an interpersonal theory that focuses on defining and giving meaning to persons' relationships. The idea that close relationships are ongoing negotiations about what partners and their behaviors mean for one another is a powerful one, and has stimulated a tremendous amount of research in the interpersonal field, much of it qualitative rather than quantitative, perhaps because qualitative work is more suited to this kind of inquiry. It is also appealing because it highlights the inherent open-endedness of interpersonal relationships and their equally inherent dynamic nature. In dialectical theory, there are no solutions to interpersonal relationships, and every new interaction and every encounter has the potential to radically change the relationship.

Probably the most serious shortcoming of the theory is that it is essentially not falsifiable, and therefore the quality of knowledge claims resulting from research employing it is often difficult to assess. Because there are a theoretically infinite number of dialectical tensions that are also by fiat not resolvable, there are no testable hypotheses that can be derived from the theory, other than the most general prediction that there will be dialectical tensions present in the relationship. As a result, researchers who rely on this approach too frequently end up concluding that there are the same three or four dialectical tensions that are present in most relationships (e.g., autonomy–connectedness, openness–closedness, and novelty–predictability), without really advancing our understanding of interpersonal relationships. We might add that this is not a weakness of the theory as much as of the research conducted by those using it and their relative lack of imagination and creativity in designing the research. Research on dialectics might be more beneficial, for example, if more research were conducted on how dialectical tensions are best balanced.

A weakness that is probably more directly attributable to how the theory was formulated originally is the relative underconceptualization of the role that power plays in interpersonal relationships. If relational dialectics are indeed primarily *between* individuals, then interpersonal power should play an outsized role in determining whose thesis will prevail. That is, one partner will likely be more successful in defining the meaning that communication and ultimately relationships have. This is particularly true in situations where there is no inherent or natural solution (i.e., synthesis) for the tension. In absence of such a synthesis, there must be other means by which one thesis will win over the other, interpersonal power being the most intuitively obvious one.

Addressing this lacuna, more recently Baxter (2011) has made a move to a more "critical" stance. She now positions relational dialectics more empathetically, whereas originally they were taken as "intertextual." In other words, dialectics are seen as not "merely" intertextual but as a situation in which power (over, of) is crucial. This means that any utterance has to be understood as occurring in the context of multiple simultaneous dialogues, some more proximate and some more distal to the actual relationship. More importantly, however, some discourses are more privileged in terms of meaning making, whereas others are more marginalized in the social and cultural context. Thus, in dialectical tensions, the discourse in line with the culturally more powerful is more likely to prevail than the discourse that is more in line with the marginalized position. With this move, Baxter localizes interpersonal power as originating from social structures and institutions. This not only clarifies the role of interpersonal power in relational dialectics, but it also has injected new energy into an important area of interpersonal communication research and scholarship.

Function Four: Create Social Reality for Self and Other

A fourth important function of interpersonal communication is that it creates social reality for the self and other. Social reality can be defined as the social equivalent to the physical environment; that is, social structures that are perceived with similar concreteness and inevitability as the physical, material world, and that are similarly perceived to be outside of one's own control. Even though we intellectually understand that social reality is somewhat arbitrary and one can act contrary to social laws (which is not the case with physical laws such as gravity), one also recognizes that fundamentally social reality is based on the agreement of the people that constitute one's social environment. Thus, the power to determine and change social reality ultimately rests within the dynamic interactions of the group rather than the individual, as does the power to sanction violations of the rules of that constructed social reality. As such, social reality has an almost physical quality and force that constrains individual communication behaviors not unlike the physical world does, making the reality part of social reality an apt description rather than a metaphorical one. At the same time, social reality is a social phenomenon that emerges out of interaction and is constantly re-created, changed, and reified in social interactions. That is, for its very existence it depends on the active participation of social actors. The absence of social interactions and communication would also signify the end of the social reality.

This view is particularly relevant to macro or sociological approaches to human communication, and arguably is one of the fundamental assumptions that make social science possible in the first place. In the realm of interpersonal communication, social reality is particularly relevant for, and frequently related to, self and other and how self and other are perceived and actualized in close relationships. Although humans are obviously material beings and cognitions originate in brains and therefore also have a material base, perceptions of self and other are only partially based on physical manifestations of self and other. Rather, self and other are largely perceived in social terms. This means for self that rather than being based primarily on introspection, self is perceived and deduced from others' approaches and reactions to self. This is the conception of "the looking glass" self famously articulated by James (1890) and Cooley (1902) and more recently understood as consisting of various self-related schemata (e.g., Baldwin, 1992). Likewise, others are also primarily conceived of in social terms, particularly in relation to self. Fiske and colleagues have established an impressive series of studies demonstrating that our social cognition and memory of others is organized largely around the type of relationships we have with other people rather than their personal attributes (Fiske, 1993; Fiske & Haslam, 1997; Fiske et al., 1991). In these studies, *relationship types* were better predictors of social substitutions (e.g., calling someone by the wrong name) or erroneously directing actions at others (e.g., driving to the wrong person's house) than any demographic or personal attribute, such as ethnicity or age. The only exception was gender, which while clearly a personal attribute still has tremendous relational relevance.

For interpersonal communication, this means that communication behaviors of individuals are often motivated by self-presentational concerns, which in more superficial settings can be conceptualized as impression management, but for most people in close interpersonal relationships come closer to self-actualization or self-completion (Wicklund & Gollwitzer, 1982). In other words, in interpersonal relationships and through interpersonal communication, people experience what is in terms of cognition and information processing their most central and most important cognitive structure: the self. Even more than experiencing, however, in interpersonal relationships and through interpersonal communication individuals have the opportunity to actively create a version of themselves that, if accepted by others, gains social reality. Consequently, above and beyond any instrumental or relational outcomes, interpersonal communication is the main mechanism by which a self is actualized, and gaining social reality for self should be a central concern in any interaction. At the same time, in our interactions with others, we also give or deny social reality to their versions and representations of themselves. Thus, the process of creating social reality for self is mutual, and demands from individuals not only that they present a version of self that others can give reality to, but that others should be sensitive to their attempts at establishing a self and give reality to it.

There is a significant amount of research in interpersonal communication that fundamentally addresses the function of creating social reality for self and other. For example, research on self-monitoring (Snyder, 1974) has made the awareness of how self is perceived central to explaining individual communication behaviors, such as deception in job interviews (Hogue et al., 2013), or self-presentation strategies on Facebook (Rosenberg & Egbert, 2011). Similarly, research by Jung and Hecht (2004) has demonstrated that perceived gaps between communicated and desired identity negatively affect self-reports of relationship satisfaction, feeling understood, and reports of communicative appropriateness and effectiveness in close relationships. This and similar research suggests that creating social reality is an important function of interpersonal communication and has significant effects on how persons communicate interpersonally.

Function Five: Influencing Others

A fifth fundamental function of interpersonal communication is to influence others. Influence is most often defined as having occurred when a person behaves differently than they would have done in the absence of the influence attempt, with behavior broadly understood to include psychological responses such as a change in belief, attitude, or affect. As a social species, humans survived and thrived throughout history because of their extraordinary ability to cooperate and coordinate their activities with one another, allowing them to live under almost any conditions and to dominate nature unlike any species before them (Koerner & Floyd, 2009). Such coordination obviously requires that humans are able to influence one another, but also that they are able to resist influence attempts that would not benefit them.

In interpersonal communication, influence is usually called compliance gaining, to emphasize the interactional, interdependent, and often spontaneous nature of these interactions. In contrast, persuasion is influence in a more formal and often mediated communication environment, in which messages are designed and delivered deliberately to have specific effects on audiences. In persuasion, there is often a deliberate attempt to change beliefs and attitudes, ideally through well-reasoned arguments presented in purposefully designed and delivered messages. In interpersonal compliance gaining, by contrast, the focus is more often on behavior change, and the methods and messages are often less deliberate, less well planned, and the arguments less well reasoned. Instead, compliance-gaining messages are typically seen as subtle, and not necessarily recognizable influence attempts. In the worst cases they are ripe with inarticulate messages that beg and plead, or use coercion and even threats.

Research in interpersonal compliance-gaining has mostly been concerned with identifying different types of messages or influence strategies used in interpersonal influence attempts, as well as those factors that affect which strategies are used and how effective they ultimately are in achieving the desired outcomes and responses from others. Influence strategies have been conceptualized typologically, that is, messages are assigned to a specific category of appeal type. For example, Marwell and Schmitt (1967) identified sixteen different influence message types, including promise, threat, liking, pre-giving, aversion, debt, altruism, as well as positive and negative expertise, moral appeal, self-feeling, esteem, and altercasting. Recognizing that the effectiveness of interpersonal influence attempts is not solely a function of the message design but rather of the interaction of the message with relational and other contextual factors, other researchers have attempted to identify underlying dimensions that characterize and distinguish different influence messages and situations. For example, Burgoon et al. (1987) assessed the dimensions of composure, formality, immediacy, similarity, receptiveness, and dominance of dyadic relationships and correlated those to perceptions of message effectiveness for different message types. For doctor–patient communication, they found that receptivity, or openness, interest in, and the willingness to listen to the patient was the best predictor of patient satisfaction, although not of compliance *per se*. The effects of the other dimensions were weaker still.

In another example of such research, Hample and Dallinger (2002) investigated the impact of situational factors including: personal benefit, situation apprehension, resistance to persuasion, right to persuade, intimacy, dominance, relational consequences, and evaluation of the influence messages. They found three underlying dimensions or roots that predicted influencers' message choices. The first root, mainly comprised of the expected resistance and the anticipated relational consequences of the compliance attempt, had the greatest effect on message selection, such that in situations in which little resistance was anticipated or potentially negative relational consequences were anticipated, influencers were most likely to avoid strong influence messages. The second root, which primarily loaded on the dominance of the target and harm to self, suggested that message senders are concerned about their own face. Lastly, the third root, which loaded primarily on message effectiveness and harm to other, suggested that sources consider these two factors concurrently and weigh them against each other. These findings are generally buttressed by a substantial body of research that used politeness theory (Brown & Levinson, 1978) to conceptualize the idea that influence messages are created and used based on concerns about the positive (to be liked) and negative (to be autonomous) faces of both senders and receivers. Often, these concerns do not result from the behavior being advocated by the influence attempt, but rather from the relational implication of yielding or resisting the request itself.

Overall, compliance-gaining research has done a good job of locating influence and persuasion in the relationship context and articulating how concerns for self, other, and the relationship affect yielding and resisting to influence based on factors not primarily related to the influence messages or the behaviors they advocate. In that respect, compliance-gaining research makes those relationship factors a central concern in more traditional persuasion research (Petty & Cacioppo, 1986).

Conclusion

In this chapter, we used a functional approach as a meta-theoretical framework to discuss interpersonal communication, thus allowing for a view of interpersonal communication that is both somewhat novel and informative and that suggests ways in which one can bring cohesion to this varied field. Clearly, the functional approach is not universally accepted as the best way to organize the field. In fact, currently there is no dominant meta-theory in the field, even though many of the approaches discussed here and several others are often treated as if they were by their proponents. This general lack of agreement about a meta-theoretical approach has not hindered individual research, which is often conducted at high levels of quality in terms of the phenomena investigated, the quality of data amassed, and insight gained into human communication. What the lack of agreement currently prevents, however, is a concentrated effort to combine the knowledge gained about interpersonal communication into a coherent body of knowledge. Currently, most of the gained knowledge stands by itself, with no clear relevance to other knowledge about interpersonal communication. We would expect that sooner rather than later, such meta-theories will emerge or be applied. Strong contenders in our estimation are evolutionary theory, which has made significant inroads in the social sciences as diverse as psychology and economics, and the relational model theory (Fiske, 1991), which is one of the few truly grand theories of relationships that exist in relationship research. Of course, it is also possible that the field will follow Baxter into critical theory, in part as a way to overcome challenges to the synthesis of more social-science-based research. In any case, it is clear that in the area of interpersonal communication, there are many compelling and robust findings and several solid and well-supported theories. However, synthesis of these findings and theories is needed in order to arrive at an overarching and persuasive understanding of the interpersonal communication process.

References

Afifi, W. A., & Weiner, J. L. (2004). Toward a theory of motivated information management. *Communication Theory, 14*, 167–190.

Altman, I., & Taylor, D. A. (1973). *Social penetration: The development of interpersonal relationships*. Oxford: Holt, Rinehart & Winston.

Baldwin, M. W. (1992). Relational schemas and the processing of social information. *Psychological Bulletin, 112*, 461–484.

Barker, L., Gladney, K., Edwards, R., Holley, F., & Gaines, C. (1980). An investigation of proportional time spent in various communication activities by college students. *Journal of Applied Communication Research, 8*, 101–109.

Baxter, L. A. (1988). A dialectical perspective on communication strategies in relationship development. In S. Duck (Ed.), *Handbook of personal relationships* (pp. 257–274). London: Wiley.

Baxter, L. A. (Ed.). (2011). *Voicing relationships: A dialogic perspective*. Thousand Oaks, CA: Sage.

Berger, C. R., & Calabrese, R. J. (1975). Some exploration in initial interaction and beyond: Toward a developmental theory of communication. *Human Communication Research, 1*, 99–112.

Bird, D. E. (1954). Have you tried listening? *Journal of the American Dietetic Association, 30*(3), 225–228.

Blumer, H. (1969). *Symbolic interactionism: Perspective and method*. Englewood Cliffs, NJ: Prentice-Hall.

Bonini, C. P. (1963). *Simulation of information and decision systems in the firm*. Englewood Cliffs, NJ: Prentice-Hall.

Brown. P., & Levinson, S. (1978). Universals in language usage: Politeness phenomena. In E. N. Goody (Ed.), *Questions and politeness: Strategies in social interaction* (pp. 56–289). Cambridge: Cambridge University Press.

Burgoon, J. K., Pfau, M., Parrott, R., Birk, T., Coker, R., & Burgoon, M. (1987). Relational communication, satisfaction, compliance-gaining strategies, and compliance in communication between physicians and patients. *Communications Monographs, 54*(3), 307–324.

Caughlin, J. P. (2002). The demand/withdraw pattern of communication as a predictor of marital satisfaction over time. *Human Communication Research, 28*, 49–85.

Cooley, C. H. (1902). *Human nature and the social order.* New York: Scribner's.

Emanuel, R., Adams, J., Baker, K., Daufin, E. K., Ellington, C., Fitts, E., Himsel, J., Holladay, L., & Okeowo, D. (2008). How college students spend their time communicating. *The International Journal of Listening, 22*, 13–28.

Fiske, A. P. (1991). *Structures of social life: The four elementary forms of human relations.* New York: Free Press.

Fiske, A. P. (1993). Social errors in four cultures: Evidence about universal forms of social relations. *Journal of Cross-Cultural Psychology, 24*, 463–494.

Fiske, A. P., & Haslam, N. (1997). The structure of social substitutions: A test of relational models theory. *European Journal of Social Psychology, 27*, 725–729.

Fiske, A. P., Haslam, N., & Fiske, S. T. (1991). Confusing one person with another: What errors reveal about the elementary forms of social relations. *Journal of Personality & Social Psychology, 60*, 656–674.

Gottman, J. M. (1994). *What predicts divorce? The relationship between marital processes and marital outcomes.* New York: Lawrence Erlbaum Associates.

Hample, D., & Dallinger, J. M. (2002). The effects of situation on the use or suppression of possible compliance-gaining appeals. In M. Allen, R. W. Preiss, I. M. Gayle, & N. Burell (Eds.), *Interpersonal communication research: Advances through meta-analysis* (pp. 187–209). Mahwah, NJ: Lawrence Erlbaum Associates.

Hogue, M., Levashina, J., & Hang, H. (2013). Will I fake it? The interplay of gender, Machiavellianism, and self-monitoring on strategies for honesty in job interviews. *Journal of Business Ethics, 117*, 399–411.

Hsia, H. J. (1968). Output, error, equivocation, and recalled information in auditory, visual, and audiovisual information processing with constraint and noise. *Journal of Communication, 18*, 325–345.

James, W. (1890). *The principles of psychology.* Cambridge, MA: Harvard University Press.

Jung, E., & Hecht, M. L. (2004). Elaborating the communication theory of identity: Identity gaps and communication outcomes. *Communication Quarterly, 52*, 265–283.

Knapp, M. L. (1984). *Interpersonal communication and human relationships.* Boston, MA: Allyn & Bacon.

Koerner, A. F., & Floyd, K. (2009). Evolutionary perspectives on interpersonal relationships. In S. W. Smith & S. R. Wilson (Eds.), *New directions in interpersonal communication research* (pp. 27–47). Thousand Oaks, CA: Sage.

Kraut, R. E., Lewis, S. H., & Swezey, L. W. (1982). Listener responsiveness and the coordination of conversation. *Journal of Personality and Social Psychology, 43*, 718–731.

Marwell, G., & Schmitt, D. R. (1967). Dimensions of compliance-gaining behavior: An empirical analysis. *Sociometry, 30*, 350–364.

Maslow, A. H. (1943). A theory of human motivation. *Psychological Review, 50*, 370–396.

Mendez, J. (2011). Interim report of the special rapporteur on torture and other cruel, inhuman or degrading treatment or punishment. UN Doc. A/66/268. Retrieved from www.solitaryconfinement.org/uploads/SpecRapTortureAug2011.pdf

Petty, R., & Cacioppo, J. T. (1986). *Communication and persuasion: Central and peripheral routes to attitude change.* New York: Springer.

Rankin, P. T. (1929). Listening ability. *Chicago Schools Journal, 12*, 177–179.

Rosenberg, J., & Egbert, N. (2011). Online impression management: personality traits and concerns for secondary goals as predictors of self-presentation tactics on Facebook. *Journal of Computer-Mediated Communication, 17*, 1–18.

Schutz, W. (1958). *The interpersonal underworld*. Palo Alto, CA: Science & Behavior Books.

Shannon, C. E., & Weaver, W. (1949). *The mathematical theory of communication*. Urbana, IL: University of Illinois Press.

Sillars, A., Roberts, L. J., Leonard, K. E., & Dun, T. (2000). Cognition during marital conflict: The relationship of thought and talk. *Journal of Social and Personal Relationships*, 17, 479–502.

Snyder, M. (1974). Self-monitoring of expressive behavior. *Journal of Personality and Social Psychology*, 30, 526–537.

Solomon, D. H., & Knobloch, L. K. (2004). A model of relational turbulence: The role of intimacy, relational uncertainty, and interference from partners in appraisals of irritations. *Journal of Social and Personal Relationships*, 21, 795–816.

Stafford, L., & Canary, D. J. (1992). Relational maintenance strategies and equity in marriage. *Communications Monographs*, 59, 243–267.

Wicklund, R. A., & Gollwitzer, P. M. (1982). *Symbolic self completion*. Mahwah, NJ: Lawrence Erlbaum Associates.

11

SMALL GROUP AND ORGANIZATIONAL COMMUNICATION

Small groups and organizations are social institutions that have been constituted with specific goals and purposes in mind. Individuals participate in these groups with the explicit knowledge and under the assumption that their purpose is to coordinate their behaviors and achieve, or at least attempt to achieve, these goals and purposes. Because groups and organizations coordinate behaviors of members, articulate goals, monitor performance, and take corrective actions by means of communication, it seems reasonable to assume that communication in groups and organizations is primarily strategic (Conrad & Poole, 2012). Strategic in this context is defined as intentional, planned, and directed at long-term goals, both on the level of individual communication behaviors as well as on the level of group and organizational structures. Structures of groups and organizations reflect strategic choices about the goals that are pursued as well as the processes used to achieve the goals. For example, juries in criminal cases are organized flatly and their communication is prescribed to be participatory and deliberate, with secret ballots and a foreperson as a facilitator rather than as a decision maker because their purpose is to arrive at a correct and unanimous determination of a defendant's guilt or innocence. In contrast, a fire company is organized hierarchically, with well-defined roles for firefighters, driver engineer, and lieutenant and equally rehearsed procedures that maximize speed and efficiency.

At the same time, however, groups and organizations are also spaces in which persons conduct their daily lives and indeed are the social beings that we humans are. Consequently, not all communication in groups and organizations is strategic from the group's or organization's perspective. Rather, persons in groups and organizations are also motivated by the same needs and wants that motivate them in their everyday private lives and interpersonal relationships. In Chapter 10 we described five functions of interpersonal communication in close relationships.

While not all are equally relevant in group and organizational settings, they do exist as meta-goals in all interpersonal relationships and affect individual communicative behaviors in group and organizational settings as well. Arguably, it is the tension between communication engaged in for strategic group and organizational purposes and communication engaged in for personal purposes that defines much of the research in small group and organizational communication. In other words, groups and organizations are made up of human beings, and human beings are not apt to leave their interpersonal needs by the door when they enter an organization. In any event, in this chapter we will consider the strategic aspects of communication originating from group or organizational needs and how they interact, are constrained by, or enhanced by interpersonal needs and wants of group and organization members. We begin by considering how persons communicate in organizations and how organizational requirements and structure inform their behaviors. Then, we consider communication in small groups.

Similarities between Group and Organizational Communication

Small group and organizational communication historically are two different areas of concentration within communication studies, and generally for good reasons. Small group communication is conceptually aligned more with interpersonal communication, because one of the defining characteristics of small groups is that all members can and usually do engage with one another and group members perceive one another as individuals rather than actors in specific social roles. That is, they perceive them as being motivated by psychological processes as much as being socially motivated. Organizational communication, on the other hand, is more influenced by macro processes and concerns with communication practices that originate with organizational structures and cultures. One can also think of the former as a bottom-up and the latter as a top-down approach to communication. Despite these differences, they have a number of important commonalities. In addition to the shared strategic nature of the communication, relationships in groups and organizations usually have clearly defined power hierarchies, with leaders and supervisors exerting significant control over the behaviors of lower-ranked group members. Furthermore, both groups and organizations establish rules and norms that are unique to their communication. Finally, groups most frequently are formed within organizations, suggesting that small groups communicate in the context of, and therefore are part of, organizational communication.

Organizational Communication

Probably the most common meta-theoretical framework underlying investigations of organizational communication is system theory (Katz & Kahn, 1966). The basic tenets of systems theory that are relevant to organizational communication are wholeness, non-summativity, hierarchy, self-regulation, and openness. *Wholeness* refers to the property of systems that to understand them and their functioning, the whole system has to be considered, as all parts are dependent on each other. This means that parts of a system cannot be understood or investigated in isolation, but the system and all its interactions and complexity have to be investigated in order to understand how the parts perform. For example, to understand how the sales department of an organization works and why it fails to achieve its goals, it is necessary to also investigate other parts of the organization, such as manufacturing or human resources. *Non-summativity* refers to the notion that the whole is greater than, or different from, the sum of its constituent parts (or what is often referred to as a gestalt). The interaction between the parts and the properties of the group that emerge out of these interactions is a crucial aspect of the system. Thus, even assessing all parts of an organization and their individual performances does not enable one to assess the performance of an organization as a whole. *Self-regulation* refers to the property of systems that they have goals, an awareness of whether they are achieving these goals, and the ability to change processes (or the rules of the group) and behavior to pursue their goals. *Hierarchy* refers to the property of systems that they themselves are constituted of smaller systems and simultaneously also constitute larger systems. From a theoretical perspective, this suggests that there is always uncertainty about whether investigators have drawn the appropriate boundaries around the systems or subsystems they are investigating. Finally, *openness* refers to the property of systems that they interact with their environments in that they receive input from them and send output to them. This input and output can be in the form of information, money, material goods, services, or really anything socially meaningful that can be exchanged with others. This interaction with the larger environment is what allows the system to grow and develop rather than devolve, according to systems theory. Although it is perfectly sensible to regard organizations as systems, system theory has enough ambiguities that it becomes difficult to generate many testable hypotheses based on it, or singular predictions for any given phenomenon. Simply put, in system theory, it is always possible that one has focused on the wrong (sub)system or the wrong emerging property of the system in one's explanations. As a consequence, while systems theory is relevant in organizational communication research, it is rarely used as a proximate explanation of communication in organizations.

Organizations as Cultures

One very useful way of thinking about organizations and the influence they have on how members communicate is to employ the concept of organizational culture. This perspective is also likely to result in proximal explanations. In this view, organizations establish their own set of norms and rules that govern the relationships between members, between members and the organization, and between members and outsiders, such as customers, regulators, and the public at large. While the comparison to social culture is the most direct in regard to the reach and pervasiveness of organizational rules and norms, there are fewer similarities in how organizational and social culture originate. Social cultures and their rules for communication emerge more or less spontaneously based on the beliefs, values, and practices of their members. While social hierarchies and status do play a role in whose views and values are most represented in a social culture and what behaviors are rewarded and which ones are sanctioned, culture is ultimately participatory and all members must reify it through constant participation. This also means that cultural change can be brought about bottom up as well as top down. In addition, only a small fraction of social cultural practices are codified in the form or laws and regulations. The vast majority of rules and norms are implicit and rarely even verbalized.

By contrast, organizational culture, or at least parts of it, often is the result of purposeful planning and design. While organizational cultures also require shared values and beliefs of members, their origin is less accidental than in social cultures. In addition, large organizations spend significant time and resources on codifying their culture into written policies, guidelines, and best practices, and even small organizations often have similar explicit manifestations of at least parts of their desired culture in the form of employee handbooks and written office policies. Of course, not all such written rules are necessarily adopted and enacted by all members, but at the very least these explicit rules represent an outward expression of the leadership of organizations in regard to the organizational culture they desire.

To understand organizations as cultures, and communication within them as expressions of organizational cultures, does not deny the relevance and impact of social culture on organizations and their communication. Clearly, many of a social culture's values and practices are reflected in organizational cultures, and often society at large will impose its values and norms on organizations. For example, various laws govern the employer–employee relationship and workplace safety, forbid sexual harassment and discrimination, and regulate various other aspects of organizational life. Still, most organizations manage to create unique organizational cultures that differ from those of society at large and from the cultures of other organizations. This suggests that the processes of how members are acculturated and learn to participate in and reify their organization's culture are relevant to how members communicate.

One good example of a theory that takes the organization-as-culture approach and directly investigates these acculturation and socialization processes in organizations is Myers's (2009; Myers & Oetzel, 2003; Scott & Myers, 2010) theory of membership negotiation. They use the term negotiation rather than socialization or acculturation to emphasize the mutual influence that organizations and new members have on one another. Not only are new members familiarized with the rules and norms of the organization and socialized into an existing organizational culture, but they also have their own set of beliefs and values that they bring into the organization and that have the potential to affect its culture. As such, there truly is a negotiation, albeit an implicit one, between organizations and new members as to the rules and norms that will govern the new members' communication.

Member negotiating is a broad concept that incorporates many communication behaviors and that even has been used as an organizing framework to discuss research in organizational communication (see Myers et al., 2011). Rather than being a sequential process with a defined end, member negotiation consists of a number of simultaneously ongoing and essentially open-ended processes, all of which involve communication. Probably the most important process of these is becoming familiar with supervisors. The supervisory role is one that is typically explicitly charged with representing the organization toward new members and socializing them so that they can become functional members of the organization. Supervisors are also explicitly acting on behalf of the organization, and in many cases are the only ones who do. Furthermore, supervisors not only articulate the explicit rules and norms of an organization and the expectations for a new member, they are also in a position to reward and punish new members for their performance explicitly in regard to organizational goals and compliance with organizational culture. As such, they are the most immediate and often the only official representative of the organization to verbalize the values, norms, and ultimately the culture of the organization. Of course, there are also implicit or "unwritten" rules and norms in every organization, and supervisors may not be aware of and certainly cannot explicitly communicate these implicit rules to other employees.

Becoming acquainted with coworkers is another important process of member negotiation. Unlike supervisors, who often are compelled by their own roles to represent the official version of organizational culture, coworkers inform new members of how organizational culture is actually practiced and realized in everyday interaction (e.g., the more implicit rules of the organization), that is, the informal culture of the organization. Especially in situations where there is a great divergence from official and actual organizational culture, coworkers can be invaluable sources of information for new members. Even in cases where official and actual culture largely overlap, there are always areas not covered by official policies or directions by supervisors, and coworkers are the only available source of information for new members. Often, behaviors are not addressed by supervisors or covered by explicit policies because they are considered of no relevance to the goals of the organization. For example, from an organization's perspective, it might be irrelevant whether coworkers sign birthday cards for one another or bring cake to the office or do not acknowledge their birthdays at all. Other behaviors not covered by policy arise in response to novel or unique circumstances that the organization has no prior experience with and has not planned for. For example, only relatively recently have organizations faced members posting work-related information on social media, and, as a result, only a few organizations have devised official policies about it.

Negotiating roles and developing job competencies are two other important processes of member negotiation (Myers et al., 2011). Roles refer to the official tasks that members have to perform in their organizations and the manner in which these tasks are accomplished. Job competencies refers to the appropriate and necessary skills to fulfill the duties associated with roles. These two processes are relevant to organizational communication, not only because they involve communication between old and new members, including supervisors, but also because they represent an area in which new members can innovate by accomplishing their goals in novel ways and thereby affect organizational culture. Likewise, new members have the opportunities to bring new skills and new competencies to their organizations that have the potential to change or expand role descriptions and work processes and ultimately affect change in organizational culture. Thus, how organizations and members define roles and the behaviors associated with them both depends upon and has the ability to change organizational culture.

The other processes of member negotiation (Myers et al., 2011) include acculturating, being recognized, and becoming involved. Acculturating refers to the process by which new members learn about and accept existing organizational culture. Acculturation occurs without much active innovation on the part of new members and consists largely of conforming to existing cultural norms. The main way in which new members may affect organizational culture in this process is by rejecting organizational culture and failing to acculturate, which usually has negative consequences for both parties without much positive change. Being recognized refers to the process of being noticed and rewarded for their performance, either as it relates to organizational goals or to organizational culture. Much of this recognition is earned by conforming to existing expectations and therefore tends to reinforce existing culture rather than being innovative. Only when new members are recognized for unexpected or novel behavior does member recognition introduce the chance for new cultural values or norms. Importantly, however, these innovations are then more the result of supervisor conduct than the conduct of the new member. Finally, becoming involved refers to the process of identifying with the organization and deriving personal satisfaction and validation through membership in the organization. It also refers to new members going above and beyond their job description in contributing to the organization and its goals. To the extent that they are successful and the new behaviors have a positive impact, they can contribute to new cultural norms and expectations for other members of the organization.

Thus, the theoretical model of member negotiation (Myers et al., 2011) articulates a well-reasoned and comprehensive approach to organizational communication. It is based on the organization-as-culture approach and emphasizes the interdependencies between organizations and their members. While focusing ostensibly on how new members that enter an organization are acculturated while simultaneously affecting change in organizational culture, most of the processes they describe in reality are open-ended and ongoing. Thus, they apply not only to new members, but really to all members of an organization, especially those organizations that face a lot of internal and external changes due to developing technologies and manufacturing processes. Even industries that have not changed in decades nonetheless face a changing social environment or aging workforce that requires them to adapt and change and renegotiate their cultural rules and norms. In regard to the tension between organizational requirements and individual needs, this approach favors organizational requirements as explanations for organizational communication. While individual members have some autonomy to act and to affect organizational culture, their goals are largely similar to those of the organization, or at least are not contrary to it.

Organizations as Designed Machines

Another fruitful approach to organizational communication that is among the oldest but still useful perspectives is that of organizations as machines (Conrad & Poole, 2012). This approach is based on the assumption that organizations, and with them organizational communication, are primarily defined by their structures and predetermined processes, which are designed to complement each other. In this view, organizational interests are paramount, and individual needs are recognized as potentially interfering with those of the organization. However, the approach goes on to suggest that well-designed structures and processes can prevent these interferences or at least mitigate their negative effects. Essentially, this requires that structures and processes are designed not only to create optimal outcomes for the organization, but also to minimize the opportunities for members to make choices about their behaviors, as these choices are the ones that can create unanticipated problems for the organization. As a consequence, organizations that adopt such organizational structures are also those that are perceived as most limiting to the desire for autonomy of their members. Ironically, this approach to organizations emerged at least partially in response to the dehumanizing working conditions during the Industrial Revolution, which were attributed to capricious and ineffective management. Clear roles and lines of communication were intended to create fair and equitable treatment for workers and to encourage collaboration between workers and management (Sewell & Barker, 2006).

Even though the machine metaphor has been criticized for seemingly reducing the role of human beings to "mere cogs in the machine" that fulfill their assigned duties mindlessly and automatically, leadership and how it is communicated is nonetheless of paramount concern in this approach to organizational communication. Accordingly, because process is central to the organization and members have to be aware of their precise roles and expectations for their behaviors, these roles and expectations have to be communicated explicitly, monitored, and enforced by supervisors and other leaders within the organization. This requires leaders to be knowledgeable about the processes, the roles each member plays in them, and their actual performance. It also requires of them to be motivated and able to train their subordinates, inform them of what is expected of them, and to intervene with corrective action if performance falls short of expectations. To be able to reinforce desired and inhibit undesired behaviors by their subordinates, supervisors also are required to use rewards and punishments and administer them in a way that is perceived to be fair and equitable. Although money in the form of salary, bonuses, or spending accounts is the most obvious reward system in most organizations, the ability to schedule work hours or vacations, select projects to work on, or bestow awards such as employee of the month are other means by which supervisors can reinforce behaviors.

In addition to being responsible for communicating organizational goals down the chain of command and monitoring their implementation, leaders also fulfill critical functions in communicating information back up the chain of command, such as the problems encountered on the production floor or feedback from customers. Decision making is usually centralized at the top of organizations and critically dependent on accurate and timely information coming from within the organization. Thus, leaders and supervisors are conduits for communication in both directions, but this can be challenging for both structural and psychological reasons. Structurally, each level of an organization represents a bottleneck, as it is impossible to pass along all information unfiltered from below. Consequently, supervisors at each level have to decide what information to pass along and what to filter out, which can be difficult, especially if they are not fully aware of what information is needed by decision makers. Psychologically, there is also a tendency for members to minimize problems. Reasons may include the fear of being held responsible for the problems they report (shoot the messenger), the perception that their supervisors are not interested in problematic information, or because reporting bad news could be perceived as implicit criticism of the structure or processes and ultimately their superiors. As a consequence, supervisors in tightly organized and regulated organizations are often not able to provide accurate and pertinent information to those above them in the organizational structure.

It is difficult if not impossible to design structures and processes that deal well with unanticipated situations. Therefore, organizations with tight structures and processes can perform well only in situations that are foreseeable and predictable. Usually, this requires a thorough understanding of what the organization does and a stable environment to operate in. The more unpredictable the environment, the more organizations need to encourage structures and processes that allow for more decentralized decision making and direct communication channels to decision makers. These ideas have found expression in advice to managers and organizations to "think outside the box," or more recently to focus on "disruptive innovation" (Christensen, 1997).

Organizations as Networks of Relationships

A third useful view of organizations is that of organizations as relationship networks. This view highlights the interpersonal nature of relationships in organizations and emphasizes the interpersonal motivations of members and how that affects their communication. In evolutionary history, humans did all their activities in just one group, their extended family or tribe, and there was no distinction between public and private lives *per se*. Cooperation and organizing with non-family members around a common goal or activity probably started when our hunter-gatherer ancestors organized in temporary groups to hunt, engage in warfare, or harvest fruits, for example. As life and social structures grew more complex and non-related humans began to live together in settlements, organizing around common goals became more permanent and humans now spend much of their time in temporally stable organizations with non-family members. This means that they need to fulfill their interpersonal and social needs, which have not fundamentally changed over time, in the context of organizations rather than exclusively within families. These needs are basic human motivations that often are pursued even outside individuals' awareness (see Chapter 10 on interpersonal communication), and these needs become particularly relevant for behavior in cases where individual needs are not met in other contexts.

There are various theories of personal needs, including Maslow's (1954) hierarchy of needs, which includes love and belonging and esteem, and Schutz's (1958) interpersonal needs for inclusion, affection, and control. They, and others like them, assert that fulfilling these needs is a fundamental human drive that governs much human behavior, even those that ostensibly are about something else altogether. Thus, individuals want to be affiliated with other members of their organizations, feel included and liked by them, and also be able to reciprocate those feelings to other members. At the same time, they want to experience themselves as competent in discharging their duties and also receive esteem, status, and respect from their coworkers. Need for control refers to both the need to exert control and to be controlled in relationships, but for most individuals it also refers to a desire for a certain amount of autonomy and agency.

Modern organizations, of course, exist primarily to achieve instrumental goals and have structures and processes in place primarily designed to achieve these goals. Thus, in organizations in which structures and processes make it difficult or even impossible for members to fulfill their interpersonal and psychological needs, there often is a tension that members experience between organizational demands, on the one hand, and their own interpersonal and psychological needs on the other. Frequently, such tensions lead to frustration and similar negative experiences for members, which may lead them to be less involved and less committed to the organization and organizational goals. In turn, these feelings lead to low morale, sub-par performance, absenteeism, and other problem behaviors from the perspective of the organization.

Organizational and personal needs, however, need not be at odds with one another. In fact, they often go hand in hand, and many organizations have recognized that interpersonal need fulfillment is a tremendous motivator that can be employed strategically for the benefit of both the member and the organization. An obvious example is the need for esteem and recognition. As long as the organization serves as a positive reference group for its members' identity (Tajfel & Turner, 1979), members who are advancing the goals of the organization should also experience an increase in their social status and esteem with other members of the organization. Thus, organizations that have mechanisms to identify and publicly recognize members can take advantage of members' personal drive for status and esteem in order to motivate them to advance organizational goals. Another good example is the need to be liked and included. Members want to feel liked and to be included in the activities of an organization. Thus, organizations that find ways to include members in activities above and beyond their job descriptions, for example, through volunteer work or membership on committees, respond to members' needs for inclusion. This, in turn, increases members' identification, commitment, and satisfaction with the organization and increases their overall productivity.

There are theories of management that suggest that organizations organize their work processes in ways to take full advantage of organizations' ability to fulfill the interpersonal needs of their members. Management strategies such as participatory decision making (Miller & Monge, 1986) or structuring organizations as interconnected teams (Likert, 1961) are attempts to align organizational goals with personal and interpersonal goals such that they reinforce each other rather than becoming barriers. Organizations employing these strategies often lose efficiencies because part of "work time" is spent on social tasks, but they gain organizations that are more flexible than traditionally structured organizations in responding to changing environments, they can benefit from more localized and therefore often better decision making, and also save on resources otherwise spent on monitoring and reinforcing behaviors, as teams often manage themselves.

Not surprisingly, leadership and how it is communicated play critical roles in these strategies as well. The concept of leadership itself, however, differs across organizations. For example, Northouse (2010) defined leadership as transactional, by which he meant leadership that is not only open to and supportive of subordinates, but represents a true dialogue between supervisors and subordinates in which supervisors must negotiate and legitimatize their leadership, position, and rank. At the same time, transactional leadership does not just involve organizational goals. Leaders must be sensitive and responsive to the personal and interpersonal needs of members, and because they are representatives of their organizations, their feedback, be it praise or rebuke, is particularly meaningful for members.

An even broader concept of leadership sees leadership in organizations as any behavior that advances organizational goals and that is distributed among all members of an organization. It becomes even broader when organizational goals are expanded to include being responsive to the personal needs of members. For example, anti-harassment policies are grounded in the belief that members have a need to be free from harassment. Given this need, organizations should make that their own goal as well, because in doing so they are responsive to employees' interpersonal goals, which itself helps forward organizational goals. Likewise, many employers now recognize that health and well-being are important needs for employees and make it part of their mission to encourage healthy habits in their employees. In these instances, the line between organizational and personal becomes blurred. Cynics will point out that organizations will only incorporate those personal goals that ultimately benefit the organization's bottom line, such as health because it increases productivity and decreases sick days, but even if true, the benefits for members are real.

Not all organizations, however, strategically or accidentally take advantage of the personal and interpersonal needs of their members by aligning them with those of the organization. In such cases, members nonetheless pursue their personal and interpersonal needs within organizations, but through informal rather than formal communication networks. Such informal networks may exist in parallel to official organizational networks, without much contact or interaction between the two. More likely, however, there is significant overlap between the two, if for no other reason than that key members are part of both networks. In these cases, informal networks can be used to accomplish organizational tasks and goals, such as bestowing rewards or punishment, socializing new members, or enforcing implicit rules. Alternatively, informal networks can also interfere with organizational functions, such as when social relationships make organizations unwelcoming to minorities, for example. Because these networks are not officially part of the organization, they are more difficult to control and police by organizational leadership or outside regulatory bodies. Sometimes, entrenched interests within organizations take advantage of informal networks to further their own interests, such as "old boys' networks" that hire and promote members of their in-group. At other times, they provide a resource for the less powerful within the organization to resist management or the public, for example, when rank-and-file police officers refuse to testify against one another.

None of the three views of organizational communication discussed here is necessarily more accurate or valid than the others. They all highlight and emphasize different aspects of organizational communication, but they all describe phenomena that are probably present in every organization. How useful they are in analyzing and improving the communication in organizations will depend on the different organizations and the different environments in which they operate. What they have in common, however, is highlighting that organizational communication, while strategic in servicing organizational goals, is nonetheless multifaceted and impacted by and responsive to the personal and interpersonal goals of members. Smart managers and leaders recognize this tension and attempt to align organizational and personal goals.

Small Group Communication

Small group communication has many similarities to organizational communication. Most notably, small group communication is also strategic and goal directed and most frequently occurs in an organizational setting. Also, like members of organizations, members of small groups also pursue personal and interpersonal goals in addition to group goals, and this goal pursuit can enhance or interfere with achieving group goals. But there are also important differences between organizations and small groups. Unlike organizations, most small groups are temporary and they are organized around achieving a specific goal or set of goals, and terminate once the goal is reached (or the group failed to reach it). They are also usually flatter hierarchically than an organization, although there may be an acknowledged or assigned leader with final decision-making power. More frequently, however, the leader is more a facilitator in charge of process than a final decision maker, and group members are brought together because they are of similar rank or ability, if often with different expertise. Finally, they are small enough that it is likely that each member has a personal relationship with each of the other members, something that is not usually possible in organizations. By personal relationship we mean that others are perceived and communicated with as individuals motivated by individual psychology, rather than as representatives of social roles.

Small Groups as Cultures

Like organizational communication, there are a number of different approaches to small group communication that in many aspects mirror those of organizational communication. We examined various approaches to studying organizations (e.g., organizations as culture, organizations as networks of relationships), and can map similar demarcations onto small group communication. For example, an approximation to the cultural approach is the idea that small groups go through a sequential process of establishing communication rules and norms, or, as might otherwise be considered, establishing culture. Among the most memorable of those is Tuckman's (1965) forming, storming, norming, and performing sequence. The *forming* stage is characterized by small talk, impression-formation, and the development of initial interpersonal liking and trust, which allow the group to enter the *storming* stage. In this stage, group members voice disagreements about goals, processes, and roles, but eventually are able to resolve these conflicts and to come to agreement about their goals and processes. In the *norming* stage, they solidify their agreements to normative expectations for group communication, which then enables them to reach peak efficiency and quality in the *performing* stage.

The comparison to culture is appropriate here, because while the ultimate outcome goals might be predetermined and given to the group from the outside, groups establish their own set of norms and procedures as well as their own structure through a process not unlike that of how new members are acculturated to organizations. Of course, small groups have more freedom to establish their own norms, and therefore members of small groups are more involved in creating the unique cultures of their groups and have greater individual influence on norms compared to new members that enter existing organizations, but the communication involved is quite similar. However, one should not overlook that groups do usually operate within established (organizational) cultures that bias members toward existing rules and norms and constrain their choices to some extent. For example, it is unlikely that a small group in an American organization would delegate final decision-making authority to one member who is free to disregard majority opinion, or create a process that explicitly excludes minorities or women. Thus, small group cultures are created but influenced by the larger culture group, be that the organization or, in this case, national cultural norms.

Small Groups as Machines

There are many approaches to small group communication that share similarities with the organization-as-machine approach to organizational communication. In fact, because of their smaller number of members and their resulting relative simplicity, it is much easier to devise processes that achieve particular outcomes for small groups than it is to devise such processes for organizations. We already mentioned how different structures and communication processes distinguish juries from fire companies and allow both to obtain their goals and objectives in very different ways. Likewise, there is a plethora of prescriptions and recommendations for how groups should operate and communicate to achieve specific outcomes. These prescriptions and recommendations address a wide range of tasks and outcomes, including but not limited to creativity (Hare, 1982), decision making (Fisher & Ellis, 1980), project management (Keller, 1986), mediation, conflict resolution (Jehn & Mannix, 2001), and crisis management (King, 2002).

These prescriptions share the assumption that similar processes lead to similar outcomes even in different groups, suggesting that process is more important than personal ability or psychological tendencies of individual group members. They also assume that group members, in their interactions, are primarily motivated by group goals and are willing and able to suppress their own behavioral tendencies and to enact the recommended behaviors more or less faithfully. Finally, they also assume that group members are not subject to outside pressure, or are able to resist it. While there is plenty of evidence in the management and organizational communication literature that suggests that most of the recommendations are at least reasonably effective in bringing the desired outcomes about, in some circumstances these assumptions might be overly optimistic, if not outright naïve. In one famous case study, the Kennedy administration had specific group decision-making processes in place (e.g., the President does not express any preferences at the outset of discussion), and had clear roles (e.g., Bobby Kennedy being devil's advocate) that should have prevented poor decision making due to the phenomenon later known as groupthink (Janis, 1972, 1982). Despite these efforts, it succumbed to groupthink when making the decision to enter the Vietnam War (Janis, 1972). Thus, protocols *can* help improve organizational communication and decision making, but they cannot guarantee it.

Small Groups as Relationship Networks

A final set of approaches to small group communication shares similarities with the organizations as networks of relationships approach to organizational communication. Like their counterparts in organizational communication, these approaches are based on the assumption that small groups are another social context in which individuals pursue important personal and interpersonal goals. In fact, small groups might be a more attractive context for pursuing these goals than organizations, because small groups do not usually have preassigned roles and leadership positions with their associated social benefits and thus these social benefits are more easily obtainable in small groups than organizations. At the same time, a small group may lack relationship histories that constrain choices or bias how group members are perceived. Finally, because small groups often negotiate their processes and outcomes, it is easier for small group members to align their personal and interpersonal goals with those of the small group. For example, if the goal of the group is to determine a vendor for a particular product, then convincing the group that my favored vendor is the best choice accomplishes both the group's goal as well as my goals of being a leader and gaining status with group members.

One important interpersonal goal and relationship variable that is of particular relevance in small group communication is interpersonal power. In organizations, power is usually tied to organizational titles and roles, and while certainly in the long run associated with how individuals communicate, it is not the immediate outcome of communication behaviors. In small groups, by contrast, power is usually much more obtainable and immediately tied to communication behaviors. Also, because small groups engage overwhelmingly in decision making of some sort, power and influence are relevant to group goals and group communication in ways that they seldom are in other organizational contexts. It is no surprise, then, that the ways in which power is asserted, resisted, and communicated is of particular relevance to small group communication researchers.

Power is usually defined as the ability to influence, which in turn is defined as being exerted to the extent that a person does something that they otherwise would not have done in terms of thoughts, feelings, or behaviors (French & Raven, 1959). When investigating influence in groups, French and Raven (1959; Raven, 1965) determined that interpersonal power stems from six different sources. *Reward* and *coercive* power refer to the ability to give rewards or hand out punishment, usually because the person controls desirable resources. *Legitimate* power refers to power that comes with a social role, such as supervisor, or from social convention, such as the need to reciprocate a supportive behavior. *Expert* power, as the name suggests, stems from the perceived expertise of the source, and *informational* power stems from the perceived strength of an argument and evidence and is based in the perceived external validity and truthfulness of the argument. Finally, *referent* power stems from the perceived social desirability of the source and the social status that affiliating with the source bestows. In this model, humans are overwhelmingly rational and give social power either out of obvious self-interest (i.e., reward, coercive, legitimate, and referent power), or because it leads to the objectively best decisions for the group (i.e., expert and informational power).

Not all theories of interpersonal power in small groups see power as based on rationality, however. Early experimentation by Sherif (1935) and Asch (1955), for example, showed that individuals conformed to majority opinions even while firmly believing that they were wrong. Clearly, social processes related to acceptance and inclusion motivate members to accept, or at least conform to, group decisions that they believe to be faulty. Other research in group dynamics has discovered numerous other instances in which individual group members have acted against their own better judgment in order to gain social acceptance or status with group members. One such process is the risky shift (Stoner, 1968) or choice shift (Wallach et al., 1962) phenomenon, which describes groups as taking much greater risks or being much more cautious with their decisions than the average of the individuals in the group would suggest, based primarily on their perceptions of what majority opinion was and their desire to gain social favors by being more extreme than the average.

Another way to conceptualize the competing influences on small groups is the notion of informational versus normative influence (Boster & Cruz, 2002). Originally used to describe conformity with and without private acceptance, respectively (Deutsch & Gerard, 1955), informational influence refers to influence that is based on the strength, or sometimes on the mere existence, of the arguments and evidence, whereas normative influence is based only on the desire to conform with the group, without believing in the validity of the arguments. It is interesting to note that in these conceptualizations, internal acceptance depends on the validity of arguments, and social pressures can only lead to surface acceptance that will not persist beyond the group interactions. This strikes us as an overly rational position that might be observed in experiments with university students, who for their own reasons are interested in projecting rational and evidence-based decision making. We are not convinced that the same processes would be observed in more natural (i.e., not university lab) settings. As Caldini (2008) has demonstrated in many experiments, people comply and are persuaded (i.e., internally accept a position) by a number of social processes that do not rely on the elaboration of rational arguments but that consider social variables, such as majority opinion, the observable behaviors of others, or how others react to behaviors and expressed opinions, *prima facie* as evidence of the correctness of a position or behavior. It is unlikely that this does not apply to small group decision making.

Conclusion

As this discussion of communication in organizations and small groups has shown, these contexts are prime examples of the richness of communication phenomena and the importance of context for communication behaviors. Organizational and small group communication can be approached from a number of different views (we chose three among many more that have been employed by researchers) that each illuminate and emphasize different aspects of communication. None is inherently superior to or closer to the truth than any other; how useful they prove depends on the organization and what one wants to know about communication. What this discussion also showed, however, is that there are limits to the extent that communication can be controlled and preplanned in small groups and organizations. Even though organizations and small groups provide communicators with clear goals to achieve and structures and processes strategically designed to achieve these goals, ultimately members' communication behavior is only partially motivated by these goals. Equally forceful motivators of communication behaviors are the personal and interpersonal goals that individuals pursue in their relationships with group members and organizations: goals that arise out of their own needs and the fact that humans are inherently social creatures. Consequently, groups and organizations that manage to align their goals with the personal and interpersonal goals of their members have much greater likelihood of achieving their own instrumental goals. Groups and organizations, however, that fail to align their own and their members' goals will experience interference, if not outright counteraction, from members trying to achieve their personal goals.

This necessity to align members' personal and interpersonal goals with organizational goals raises a number of important ethical questions, which thus far we have avoided. Most importantly: Is it ethical for organizations and small groups to set up processes and structures strategically that achieve organizational goals because they also provide social benefits and need fulfillment for members? Some have argued that such action is inherently manipulative and exploitive of the group or organizational members. Others have taken a more utilitarian approach and made that determination dependent on how ethical the organizational goals are in the first place. In the latter view, rewarding a supervisor with status for increasing the productivity of her department might be ethical in principle, but not if the workers in her department are children, for example.

Another important ethical question is that given the fact that members rely on organizations and small groups for need fulfillment, does that obligate organizations to provide these opportunities or even to make meeting the personal and interpersonal needs of members part of the organizations' missions and goals? We are inclined to answer this second question in the affirmative, but are keenly aware that in the field of communication as well as in society at large, we are just beginning to consider these questions.

References

Asch, S. E. (1955). Opinions and social pressure. *Scientific American*, *193*, 31–35. doi:10. 1038/scientificamerican1155-31.

Boster, F., & Cruz, M. (2002). Persuading in the small group context. In J. Dillard & M. Pfau (Eds.), *The persuasion handbook: Developments in theory and practice* (pp. 477–495). Thousand Oaks, CA: Sage. doi:10.4135/9781412976046.n24.

Caldini, R. (2008). *Influence: Science and practice* (5th ed.). Boston, MA: Allyn & Bacon.

Christensen, C. M. (1997). *The innovator's dilemma: When new technologies cause great firms to fail*. Boston, MA: Harvard Business School Press.

Conrad, C., & Poole, M. S. (2012). *Strategic organizational communication: In a global economy* (7th ed.). Oxford: Wiley Blackwell.

Deutsch, M., & Gerard, H. B. (1955). A study of normative and informational social influence upon judgment. *Journal of Abnormal and Social Psychology*, *51*, 629–636.

Fisher, B. A., & Ellis, D. G. (1980). *Small group decision making: Communication and the group process*. New York: McGraw-Hill.

French, J., & Raven, B. (1959). The bases of social power. In D. Cartwright (Ed.), *Studies in social power* (pp. 150–167). Ann Arbor, MI: Institute for Social Research.

Hare, A. P. (1982). *Creativity in small groups*. Thousand Oaks, CA: Sage.

Janis, I. L. (1972). *Victims of groupthink: A psychological study of foreign-policy decisions and fiascoes*. Boston, MA: Houghton Mifflin.

Janis, I. L. (1982). *Groupthink: Psychological studies of policy decisions and fiascoes*. Boston, MA: Houghton Mifflin.

Jehn, K. A., & Mannix, E. A. (2001). The dynamic nature of conflict: A longitudinal study of intragroup conflict and group performance. *Academy of Management Journal*, *44*(2), 238–251.

Katz, D., & Kahn, R. L. (1966). *The social psychology of organizations*. New York: Wiley.

Keller, R. T. (1986). Predictors of the performance of project groups in R & D organizations. *Academy of management journal*, *29*, 715–726.

King III, G. (2002). Crisis management and team effectiveness: A closer examination. *Journal of Business Ethics*, *41*, 235–249.

Likert, R. (1961). *New patterns of management*. New York: McGraw-Hill.

Maslow, A. (1954). *Motivation and personality*. New York: Harper.

Miller, K. I., & Monge, P. R. (1986). Participation, satisfaction, and productivity: A meta-analytic review. *Academy of Management Journal*, *29*, 727–753.

Myers, K. K. (2009). Workplace relationships. In S. Smith & S. R. Wilson (Eds.), *New directions in interpersonal communication* (pp. 135–156). Thousand Oaks, CA: Sage.

Myers, K. K., & Oetzel, J. G. (2003). Exploring the dimensions of organizational assimilation: Creating and validating a measure. *Communication Quarterly*, *51*, 438–457.

Myers, K. S., Seibold, D. R., & Park, H. S. (2011). Interpersonal communication in the work place. In M. L. Knap & J. A. Daly (Eds.), *The Sage handbook of interpersonal communication* (pp. 527–562). Thousand Oaks, CA: Sage.

Northouse, P. (2010). *Leadership: Theory and practice* (5th ed.). Thousand Oaks, CA: Sage.

Raven, B. H. (1965). Social influence and power. In I. D. Steiner & M. Fishbein (Eds.), *Current studies in social psychology* (pp. 371–382). New York: Holt, Rinehart & Winston.

Schutz, W. C. (1958). *FIRO: A three dimensional theory of interpersonal behavior*. New York: Holt, Rinehart, & Winston.

Scott, C. W., & Myers, K. K. (2010). Toward an integrative theoretical perspective of membership negotiations: Socialization, assimilation, and the duality of structure. *Communication Theory, 20,* 79–105.

Sewell, G., & Barker, J. (2006). Max Weber and the irony of bureaucracy. In M. Korczynski, R. Hodson, & P. K. Edwards (Eds.), *Social theory at work* (pp. 56–87). Oxford: Oxford University Press.

Sherif, M. (1935). A study of some social factors in perception. *Archives of Psychology, 27* (187), 1–60.

Stoner, J. A. (1968). Risky and cautious shifts in group decisions: The influence of widely held values. *Journal of Experimental Social Psychology, 4,* 442–459.

Tajfel, H., & Turner, J. C. (1979). An integrative theory of intergroup conflict. In J. A. Williams & S. Worchel (Eds.), *The social psychology of intergroup relations* (pp. 33–47). Belmont, CA: Wadsworth.

Tuckman, B. (1965). Developmental sequence in small groups. *Psychological Bulletin, 63,* 384–399. doi:10.1037/h0022100.

Wallach, M. A., Kogan, N., & Bem, D. J. (1962). Diffusion of responsibility and level of risk taking in groups. *Journal of Abnormal and Social Psychology, 68,* 263–274.

12

PERSUASION

The study of attitudes and persuasion can be traced back to the earliest years of the twentieth century (Allport, 1935). This early research focused on issues such as discrimination, the attitude–behavior relationship, and persuasion (McGuire, 1985). However, the emergence of the social scientific study of persuasion can be traced to the middle of the twentieth century. In particular, World War II played a critical role in bringing together scholars from several different disciplines to focus on the war effort, including scholars from social psychology, sociology, and communication within the United States (Rogers, 1994). But research on persuasion emerged as a major area of study in the social sciences in the mid-1950s (McGuire, 1985).

The study of persuasion has gone hand in hand with the study of attitudes. The goal of many persuasive messages and campaigns is to change a target audience's behavior. The assumption within this area of research during the early part of the twentieth century was that attitudes predicted behavior (Fazio & Roskos-Ewoldsen, 2005). In other words, if you wanted to study the outcomes of persuasion, it was easier to study attitudes instead of behavior. Consequently, attitudes became the focus of much of the research on persuasion (Rhodes & Ewoldsen, 2013).

What Exactly Is Persuasion?

While there are disagreements over the scope of persuasion, the classic definition of persuasion is that it focuses on the use of symbols in order to reinforce existing attitudes and behavior or to bring about a voluntary change in another person's attitudes or behaviors (Dillard, 2010). Important characteristics of this definition include the fact that persuasion involves the use of symbols to intentionally create an attitude or to bring about attitude change. As Miller (1980/2013) notes, persuasion can be used to engage in what he termed response-shaping, response-reinforcement, and response-changing. Response-shaping refers to the use of persuasion to *create* attitudes or to aid in the learning of new behaviors. For example, much of the research using principles of classical conditioning involves response-shaping or attitude formation (Burgoon et al., 1981). As the name implies, response-reinforcement involves *strengthening* existing attitudes so that they are more resistant to change. Work on inoculation, with its focus on making attitudes more resistant to change, is a classic example of research on response-reinforcement persuasion (Compton, 2013). Finally, response-changing is what is typically conceived of as involving persuasion: the changing of a person's attitude or behavior.

These distinctions are important because different strategies are likely more effective for response-shaping than response-changing. For example, the mere exposure effect almost certainly is limited to response-shaping or attitude formation (see section on attitude formation). Conversely, research on attitude accessibility typically involves strengthening an existing attitude or response-reinforcement (Roskos-Ewoldsen, 1997; Roskos-Ewoldsen et al., 2004). Unfortunately, research and theorizing on persuasion rarely keep these distinctions in mind. For example, one of the criticisms of the elaboration likelihood model is that while the theory is a theory of response-shaping, response-reinforcement, and response-changing, the theory has predominantly been tested within the context of response-shaping or attitude formation (Hamilton et al., 1993).

Definition of Attitude

Attitudes are generally defined as a hypothetical construct that involves an evaluative response to an attitude object (Eagly & Chaiken, 1993). Attitudes are hypothetical because an attitude cannot be seen. Instead, people's attitudes are inferred based on observations of their behavior. An evaluative response involves a judgment of how good or bad something is or how much a person likes or dislikes that object. Attitude object is defined very broadly to include things (pencils, spiders, Diet Coke), people (your next-door neighbor, President Lincoln, Erasmus), and even abstract concepts (democracy, racism). Some definitions suggest that attitudes are learned (Kiesler et al., 1969), while other research suggests that there might be a genetic component involved in the transmission of certain types of attitudes (Tesser, 1993).

One of the early models of attitudes is the tripartite model (Breckler, 1984; Rosenberg & Hovland, 1960), which assumes that attitudes are composed of three elements: affect, behavior, and cognition (hence, the model is also called the ABC model of attitudes). Affect refers to the visceral feelings that a person has toward an attitude object. Behavior involves how a person acts toward the attitude object. Cognition involves a person's beliefs about the attributes of the attitude object. Later versions of the tripartite model assume that affect, behavior, and cognitions both influence what a person's attitude is as well as being influenced by the attitude in a dynamic relationship (Eagly & Chaiken, 1993). One implication of the tripartite model is that attitudes that are primarily affective in nature are changed by different persuasive appeals compared to attitudes that are primarily cognitive in nature (Edwards, 1990; Fabrigar & Petty, 1999). Consequently, research on persuasion should consider whether the primary basis for the attitude is affective or cognitive, or a mix of affective and cognitive components.

Theories of Attitude Formation

The next section will focus on theories of how attitudes are either formed or changed. There are myriad ways in which attitudes are formed (Eagly & Chaiken, 1993). Given the almost exclusive focus on persuasion by communication scholars, it may seem strange to discuss attitude formation independent of messages, because these are not related to theories of persuasion, *per se*. But this section will focus on two theories of attitude formation that have particular relevance to the study of persuasion—the mere exposure effect and conditioning—because both have implications for persuasion.

Mere Exposure Effect

As the name implies, the mere exposure effect involves attitude formation through a process of simple exposure to an unfamiliar attitude object.[1] The basic finding is that the more times people are exposed to novel stimuli, the more they will like that stimuli. For example, in the classic demonstration of the mere exposure effect, Zajonc (1968) found a positive relationship between exposure and positive attitudes, such that as the number of exposures increased, so did participants' liking for the items. A meta-analysis of over 200 mere exposure studies demonstrated that the effect is highly reliable (Bornstein, 1989). Monahan et al. (2000) further demonstrated that the mere exposure effect not only influences liking toward the novel items, but also results in increases in people's moods when they are later exposed to those items. Perhaps more importantly, the mere exposure effect has been demonstrated in real-world settings including political campaigns (Grush et al., 1978; Schaffner et al., 1981), advertising (Hekkert et al., 2013; Morgenstern et al., 2012; Zajonc & Rajecki, 1969), product placements (Matthes et al., 2007), and brand choice (Baker, 1999; Janiszewski, 1993).[2]

Most theoretical explanations of the mere exposure effect have focused on perceptual fluency (Bornstein & D'Agostino, 1994; Schimmack & Crites, 2005; Winkielman et al., 2003). These explanations maintain that the more times people are exposed to an object, the easier it is for them to process that item. The ease in perceptual processing is hypothesized to translate into more positive liking for the item (Jones et al., 2010). The perceptual fluency explanation seems far removed from anything that communication scholars might find interesting. However, think about web-based persuasion. While little research on web-based persuasion has focused on the ease of processing messages online, it is not difficult to think of web-based presentations that, at a basic level, are easier or more difficult to process. The perceptual fluency explanation would predict that those presentations that are easier to process should evoke, at least initially, positive affective responses due to the ease of processing. Indeed, research has demonstrated that perceptual fluency—operationalized as the quality of images on an online shopping website—did influence customers' aesthetic reactions to merchandise and their purchase intentions (Im & Ha, 2011; Im et al., 2010).

Conditioning

Conditioning involves the transfer of an attitude from one object to another object. For example, if an object toward which people have no prior attitude (the conditioned stimuli or CS) is repeatedly paired with an object that people have a prior attitude toward (the unconditioned stimuli or UCS), research has found that people will develop an attitude toward the first object (CS) that is consistent with the attitude toward the second object (UCS). This type of attitude formation has traditionally been discussed as an example of classical conditioning (Burgoon et al., 1981; Kiesler et al., 1969). However, more recent research suggests that there are at least two different processes by which attitudes can become conditioned: classical conditioning and evaluative conditioning (Walther & Langer, 2010).

Classical conditioning involves pairing of the CS (people do not have an existing attitude toward this object) with the UCS (people do have an existing attitude toward this object) across a large number of trials, and the CS appears either simultaneously with or prior to the UCS in the pairings. The classic demonstration of this effect is Pavlov's dog, where the CS was a bell tone and the UCS was meat powder. While the bell tone does not naturally produce salivation by the dog (so it is the conditioned stimulus), the meat powder does naturally produce a salivation response in a dog (so it is the unconditioned stimulus). However, if the bell tone is paired on enough trials *and* on a consistent basis with the meat powder, the bell tone will begin to elicit the salivation response independent of the meat powder Research starting in the 1950s demonstrated that people's attitudes could be classically conditioned in the same way (Burgoon et al., 1981; Staats & Staats, 1958; Staats et al., 1962; Zanna et al., 1970). For example, Zanna et al. (1970) found that after enough pairings, people developed negative attitudes toward words that were paired with the start of a shock and positive attitudes toward words that were paired with the stopping of a shock.

The standard interpretation of these results is *signal learning*, based on the idea that the CS (the word paired with the start of a shock) operates as a signal that something bad will happen (being shocked). It is generally accepted that classical conditioning occurs because the occurrence of the CS predicts that either a positive or negative outcome is going to occur (Rescorla, 1988). This is similar to the notion of utilitarian attitudes that will be discussed in the section on attitude functions. Also consistent with the signal learning interpretation of classical conditioning is the process of extinction. Extinction occurs when the UCS stops occurring after the CS. When this happens and the initial attitude was developed via classical conditioning, the attitude will weaken and eventually go away, because the CS no longer operates as a signal that the UCS is going to occur. Thus, classical conditioning is held to operate primarily through cognitive processes.

There has been a lot of controversy concerning whether classical conditioning actually occurs or not (Eagly & Chaiken, 1993). Today, it seems clear that classical conditioning of attitudes is a real phenomenon. However, the research on classical conditioning produced a second phenomenon by which conditioning can occur—evaluative conditioning (Kruglanski & Stroebe, 2005). While classical conditioning and evaluative conditioning are similar, there are several important distinctions. First, going back to the tripartite model, evaluative conditioning involves affective processes, whereas classical conditioning is more cognitive in nature. Second, while it may take many trials for the attitude toward the CS to develop with classical conditioning, attitudes develop much more quickly with evaluative conditioning (Baeyens et al., 1993). Finally, attitudes developed through classical conditioning will go extinct if the pairing between the CS and UCS no longer occurs. However, attitudes based on evaluative conditioning do not seem to go extinct when the pairing between the CS and UCS is stopped (De Houwer et al., 2001).

There are numerous theoretical explanations for evaluative conditioning. For example, Jones et al. (2010) propose that evaluative conditioning occurs due to people's misattributing the attitudinal response to the UCS as being an attitudinal response to the CS. Attitudinal misattribution occurs when people think they have developed an attitude toward some object because of the properties of that object, when in fact their attitudinal response is a reaction to something else that is paired with that object. Consider the pairing of an attractive location with a soft drink. If it is clear that the positive evaluative response is to the attractive location, then there will be no misattribution effect. However, if the viewer is not clear what is causing the positive evaluative response, then the evaluative response may be attributed as resulting from the soft drink and the viewer will begin developing a positive attitude toward the soft drink. In other words, because the source of the positive evaluative response is unclear, the evaluative response may transfer from the attractive location to the soft drink.

While classical and evaluative conditioning may seem far removed from persuasion, in fact they both have important implications for attitude change and persuasion. First, while understudied, research has found that advertisements and product placements can create attitudes through conditioning (Baker, 1999; Groenland & Schoormans, 1994; McCarty, 2004). Second, there is an extensive literature on the effects of message sources on persuasion (Miller, 1987; O'Keefe, 2002). Messages that are attributed to liked or attractive sources are typically more persuasive than messages that are attributed to disliked or unattractive sources. Conditioning provides an explanation for source effects in persuasion. The liking of the source can be conditioned—either through classical or evaluative conditioning—to the topic of the message (Eagly & Chaiken, 1993; Till et al., 2008).

Theories of Persuasion

Dissonance Theory

Dissonance theory is one example of the general category of consistency theories. As the name suggests, consistency theories maintain that one of our primary motivations is to be consistent.[3] The basic premise of consistency theories is that a person's beliefs or attitudes should follow from one another and behavior should follow from the person's beliefs. Dissonance theory is by far the most influential of the consistency theories and is still extensively used over a half a century after its introduction by Leon Festinger in 1957 (Cooper, 2007).

Dissonance theory focuses on the relationship between any two beliefs or between a belief and behavior related to that belief.[4] However, belief is defined rather broadly. The relevant beliefs can be people's opinions, the beliefs people have about their behavior, or beliefs about the world (Festinger, 1957). The basic idea of dissonance theory is that inconsistencies between people's various beliefs or between their beliefs and behavior result in an aversive arousal state. This aversive arousal state creates a drive that the individual is motivated to decrease. Festinger (1957) used the example of hunger and thirst as similar drive-like states. While it is certainly desirable to get rid of thirst by drinking something that tastes good, there are situations where it doesn't matter what a person drinks as long as it quenches that person's thirst. Dissonance arousal operates in the same manner: it is intrinsically rewarding to rid the self of dissonance arousal. Typically, people will change their attitude to be consistent with their behavior in order to decrease dissonance, because once the attitude is changed, there is no longer an inconsistency between the behavior and the new attitude.

Relations between Beliefs and the Magnitude of Dissonance

According to dissonance theory, there are two important relations between any two beliefs or between a belief and people's behavior. A consonant relationship exists when the two beliefs are congruent with each other. One way to think about consonant relationships is that one belief could be used as support for another belief when explaining why the other belief is accepted. However, dissonance theory is most concerned with dissonant relationships between two beliefs.

A dissonant relationship exists when either the two beliefs are incongruent with each other or they do not flow from one another. In other words, using one of the beliefs to explain why the other belief is accepted would not make sense.[5] Dissonance theory predicts that when two beliefs or a belief and a behavior are in a dissonant relationship with each other, then dissonance arousal should occur.

Obviously, not all dissonant experiences are the same. Sometimes the experience of dissonance can be very minor, whereas other times, the experience of dissonance can be strong and can result in substantial changes in people's attitudes or belief system (Festinger, 1957). Several factors have been hypothesized to influence the magnitude of dissonance arousal, including the importance of the beliefs and the ratio of dissonant to consonant beliefs.

First, as the importance of beliefs to people increases, the more they will experience dissonance if they act in a manner that is inconsistent with the beliefs. Generally, importance is tied to how central the belief is to the self-concept. Second, as the ratio of dissonant to consonant beliefs increases, the greater the dissonance people will experience (assuming the beliefs are equally central to the self-concept). If people engage in behavior that is dissonant with a large number of beliefs and consonant with only a few beliefs, then they will experience more dissonance than if the behavior has equal numbers of dissonance and consonant beliefs associated with the behavior. Of course, importance to the self-concept can influence this ratio, so that if there are equal numbers of dissonance and consonant beliefs, but the dissonant beliefs are central to the self-concept, then more dissonance will be experienced than if the consonant beliefs were central to the self-concept.

How Dissonance Is Decreased

Based on the factors that influence the magnitude of dissonance that people experience, there are several ways dissonance can be reduced. First, people can change a dissonant attitude, belief, or behavior to make the relationship consonant. The majority of research on dissonance theory has tested whether people will change their attitudes when they engage in behavior that is dissonant with the previous attitude (Cooper, 2007; Festinger & Carlsmith, 1959). If the discrepant attitude is changed, then the relationship is consonant and the dissonance goes away.

However, if an attitude is tied to the self-concept or too resistant to change, then there needs to be ways to decrease dissonance without actually changing the attitude. One way to do this is to add beliefs that are consonant with the discrepant behavior and thereby change the ratio of dissonant to consonant beliefs (Beasley & Joslyn, 2001; Brehm, 1956). By adding more consonant beliefs, the ratio of consonant beliefs to dissonant beliefs is changed and the result will be a decrease in dissonance. Research suggests that voters may engage in processes such as these after voting in an election (Beasley & Joslyn, 2001). On the other hand, people will also undo the dissonance-invoking behavior if they can (Powers & Jack, 2013). Similarly, a person can decrease dissonance by altering the importance of either the original beliefs or the discrepant behaviors. Instead of adding new consonant or dissonant beliefs, people will increase the importance of consonant beliefs and decrease the importance of dissonant beliefs. A final way to decrease dissonance is called attitude bolstering (Sherman & Gorkin, 1980). Attitude bolstering involves the situation where a person engages in a behavior that is dissonant with an attitude that is central to a person's self-concept. In this situation, people will engage in additional behaviors that are consistent with the original attitude in an attempt to change the ratio of dissonant behaviors to consonant behaviors.

There has been extensive research testing dissonance theory since its inception in the 1950s (Cooper, 2007; Eagly & Chaiken, 1993). This research has largely supported the predictions made by dissonance theory. However, dissonance theory does have its detractors, in the form of alternative theories that have been proposed to explain the same phenomenon that dissonance theory explains (Bem, 1967, 1972; Cooper & Fazio, 1984).

Limiting Conditions on Dissonance Theory

Given the advanced age of dissonance theory, it is not surprising that research has found that dissonance does not always occur when the theory predicts it should occur. Indeed, several limiting conditions for dissonance effects have been identified. First, research has found that if people feel they do not have any choice in engaging in the dissonant behavior, they will not experience dissonance arousal because the behavior can be rationalized as not inconsistent with the person's attitudes or beliefs. Thus, having an authority figure to point to as the cause of behavior may minimize or eliminate dissonance.

Second, whether the behavior has aversive consequences or not has been found to be a critical factor in whether dissonance occurs or not. Dissonance is particularly likely to occur if people believe their behavior could possibly have aversive consequences for themselves or important others. However, if people do not believe there will be aversive consequences to their behavior, they will not experience dissonance. Indeed, research suggests that parents who emphasize personal responsibility in their communication with their children increase the magnitude of dissonance that their children will later experience if children's beliefs do not match their behavior (Ellithorpe et al., 2014).

A third limiting condition involves the foreseeability of the aversive consequences. If a person learns of possible aversive consequences of behavior only after they have engaged in the behavior, then they are less likely to experience dissonance because they can rationalize that they did not know that any potentially bad outcomes could happen as a consequence of their behavior.

Relevance of Cognitive Dissonance for the Study of Communication

As mentioned earlier, it seems strange to include dissonance theory in a chapter on persuasion. As O'Keefe (2002) notes, the theory never was designed to be a theory of persuasion. However, dissonance theory does a good job of explaining some forms of persuasion, such as the self-prophecy effect (Sherman, 1980). The self-prophecy effect involves having people predict what they will do in the future. Research has found that if people predict their own behavior, they will engage in socially desirable behaviors that they would not likely engage in without the prediction. Research also supports the dissonance explanation for this phenomenon. People do engage in their predicted behaviors, even when they likely would not have engaged in the behaviors without the prediction, in order to avoid the dissonance that would occur from acting inconsistently with their prophecy (Spangenberg et al., 2003). Likewise, recent research on vicarious dissonance and hypocrisy-induced dissonance provide fruitful avenues for exploring the use of dissonance within persuasion contexts. Vicarious dissonance occurs when a member of an in-group engages in a behavior that has aversive consequences and the group may be perceived as responsible for the behavior (Cooper, 2010). For example, if a member of an in-group engaged in a racist act that received a lot of public attention, other members of the in-group might experience vicarious dissonance. As a result, other in-group members may engage in attitude bolstering, a process by which they might engage in behaviors that support nonracist attitudes and thus regain consonance (Hamilton et al., 2002). Likewise, hypocrisy-induced dissonance involves reminding people of times when they have engaged in behaviors that are discrepant with their current attitudes (Dickerson et al., 1992; Stone et al., 1994). Again, research suggests that people do experience dissonance because they are reminded that they have acted hypocritically and they will engage in attitude bolstering as a way to decrease dissonance arousal.

Furthermore, dissonance theory has greatly informed our understanding of many social influence processes, and the theory has been remarkably influential across a number of domains of interest to communication scholars (Cooper, 2007; Miller, 1987; O'Keefe, 2002). For example, dissonance theory has played a major role in research and theorizing about selective exposure (Knobloch-Westerwick, 2015), finding that people choose to consume media consistent with their attitudes and behaviors. And indeed, dissonance theory continues to be used to theorize about varied communication phenomena (Donsbach & Mothes, 2012). Thus, although dissonance theory may seem unimportant to communication research at first glance, because it is a theory of attitude *formation*, further examination demonstrates that the theory is useful in understanding attitude change and therefore, by extension, persuasion processes.

Self-Perception Theory

Bem (1967, 1972) proposed self-perception theory as an alternative to dissonance theory. Self-perception theory maintains that people explain their own behavior in the same way that they try to explain other people's behaviors. Specifically, people consider two things: their behavior and the situation in which the behavior occurs. Using these two pieces of information, people make attributions about the causes of their own behavior or other people's behavior. If people engage in a behavior because of elements in the situation, then they will attribute the cause of the behavior to the situation. However, if people engage in a behavior of their own volition and there are no obvious situational causes of the behavior, then they will attribute the cause of the behavior as reflecting their attitude. Finally, Bem theorized that self-perception processes were most likely to occur when a person's attitude was ambiguous or weak.

Self-perception theory was proposed as an alternative to dissonance theory because Bem hypothesized that if people engaged in behavior that is inconsistent with their beliefs or attitudes, then they either infer that the behavior reflects their attitude and change the attitude to be consistent with the behavior, or they infer that their behavior reflects some type of situational constraint on that behavior and there is no attitude change. Thus, Bem argued that inconsistencies between people's beliefs and their behavior resulted in attitude change, not because of dissonance arousal but because of normal attributional processes. Importantly, when the behavior is perceived as freely chosen, people will change their attitude without experiencing any dissonance arousal, according to self-perception theory.

Obviously, these competing theories beg the question whether dissonance or self-perception theory is the correct theory. However, research suggests that the answer is not as simple as that. Instead, research suggests that both theories are correct, but that they operate in different situations (Fazio et al., 1977). Specifically, if people's behavior is severely at odds with their attitudes or beliefs, then they will experience dissonance arousal and dissonance processes will operate. Conversely, if a person's behavior is close to their original attitude or beliefs, then they may change their attitude, but through the processes outlined by self-perception theory.

Self-perception theory has been used by communication scholars across a broad array of areas, including studying the effects of video game play on self-perceptions (Klimmt et al., 2009), the influence of avatars in video games (Yee & Bailenson, 2007), compliance gaining in various contexts (Burger & Caldwell, 2003; DeJong, 1979), and media effects on body image (Wilcox & Laird, 2000). The Proteus effect provides an interesting example of self-perception theory. The Proteus effect is the finding that people take on the characteristics of the avatars they use in the virtual world (Yee & Bailenson, 2007; Yee et al., 2009). To explain this seemingly unusual finding, researchers have looked to research on attractiveness and interpersonal interactions. While past research has found that attractive people self-disclose more than less attractive people, subsequent research has found that research participants with a more attractive avatar self-disclosed more than did research participants with a less attractive avatar, even though only the research participant was aware of the relative attractiveness of the avatar. The fact that only the research participants knew of the avatar's attractiveness strongly suggests that self-perception processes were operating in the context, because the only difference between the two conditions is how the research participants could perceive their avatar and, hence, themselves (Yee & Bailenson, 2007).

Discrepancy-Based Models of Persuasion

One factor that should influence persuasion is the discrepancy between people's attitudes or beliefs and the position advocated in a message. Obviously, if a message advocates what people already believe, then there is no discrepancy and they will not change their attitude. However, as the message becomes more discrepant, attitude change also increases, up to a point (Fink & Cai, 2013; Fink et al., 1983). If a message is widely discrepant from what people believe, then attitude change is not as likely to occur. Thus, the straightforward hypothesis that the more discrepant the message is, the more attitude change occurs, has not been supported (Fink & Cai, 2013).

An early model that focused on the relationship between message discrepancy and persuasion is social judgment theory (Sherif & Hovland, 1961; Sherif et al., 1965). To address the complexity of the relationship between discrepancy and persuasion, social judgment theory advanced the idea of attitudinal latitudes (Sherif & Hovland, 1961; Sherif et al., 1965). Within social judgment theory, people's initial attitude or position on an issue serves as the attitudinal anchor. Around the anchor are positions that are not completely acceptable, but are satisfactory. These positions are referred to as positions that fall within the latitude of acceptance. Conversely, there are other positions that presumably are quite discrepant from the anchor and these are unacceptable. These positions fall within the latitude of rejection. Those positions that do not fall within the latitude of acceptance or rejection fall within the latitude of noncommitment and represent positions toward which people are either indifferent or ambivalent.

Social judgment theory assumed that if a message falls within the latitude of acceptance, the attitude (or anchor) would move toward the advocated position, and the more discrepant the advocated position was from the anchor, the more attitude change would result from the persuasive message (Sherif & Hovland, 1961). Note that the attitude would not move all the way to the advocated position, but the attitude would change in the *direction* of the advocated position. Conversely, if a message advocated a position that fell within the latitude of rejection, there would be little or no attitude change. Social judgment theory also hypothesized that people showed biases in how they perceive persuasive messages by positing that both assimilation and contrast effects can occur when people are presented with persuasive messages (Sherif & Hovland, 1961). Assimilation effects occur when a message is perceived as closer to the attitudinal anchor than it is in reality. If a message falls within the latitude of acceptance, the message is likely to be assimilated toward the attitudinal anchor. Contrast effects occur when a message is perceived as farther from the attitudinal anchor than it is in reality. If a message falls within the latitude of rejection, the message is more likely to be perceived as being in greater contrast to the attitudinal anchor.

Another important concept that social judgment theory incorporated was ego-involvement (Hovland et al., 1957). Ego-involvement involves the degree to which a topic is related to how people define themselves or how central the topic is to the self-concept. People who have high ego-involvement in an issue are harder to persuade than people who have low ego-involvement in the issue. Social judgment theory explained this by positing that people who are ego-involved in a topic have smaller latitudes of acceptance and larger latitudes of rejection than do people who are not ego-involved with a topic. This translates into more pronounced assimilation and contrast effects (e.g., more biased processing) for people who are highly ego-involved when they process a message (Johnson & Eagly, 1989).

Attitude change is a slow process according to social judgment theory (Eagly & Chaiken, 1993). First, people's attitudes will move toward the advocated position, but rarely all the way to that position. Second, given that attitude change is a function of how discrepant a message is from a person's anchor, if people assimilate a message toward the attitudinal anchor because it falls within the latitude of acceptance, then the message is perceived as less discrepant and there will be less attitude change. Furthermore, people who are ego-involved show more pronounced assimilation and contrast effects, which means they will be harder to persuade.

Unfortunately, social judgment theory is not a particularly influential theory today, because the empirical work on message discrepancy has generally not supported the theory (Eagly & Chaiken, 1993). That said, it is important to understand social judgment theory, because many of the ideas from it, including assimilation and contrast effects, ego-involvement, and latitudes of acceptance and rejection, are still important in recent theorizing on persuasion and attitude change.

It is also important to note that despite the lack of support for social judgment theory, work on message discrepancy has continued (Fink & Cai, 2013). This research has demonstrated that message discrepancy does influence persuasion, but that the relationship is fairly complex, reflecting such issues as the relative importance of actual message discrepancy vs. psychological or perceived message discrepancy (Fink et al., 1983). Perhaps more importantly, this research has resulted in a much-needed focus on attitude consolidation. When people are persuaded, the resulting new attitude is not likely formed during or immediately following the persuasive message. Instead, a person may vacillate between various positions before settling on a final (or consolidated) attitude. This line of research has suggested that indeed this is the case, though substantially more research and theorizing is necessary to more fully understand this process (Fink & Cai, 2013; Roskos-Ewoldsen, 1997).

Motivational Approaches: Attitude Functions

Why do people have attitudes? Do different attitudes exist for different reasons? Do people's reasons for having attitudes influence what types of messages will be persuasive? These are the types of questions addressed by research within the attitude functions tradition. The attitude functions approach started with the assumption that different attitudes may indeed serve different functions. In discussing the functional approach, we will use Carpenter et al.'s (2013) three generations of theorizing about attitude functions as a framework.

The first generation of theorizing involved identifying what functions attitudes serve. The original work on attitude functions was independently conducted by Smith et al. (1956) and Katz (1960). Because they were working independently, they came up with different lists of attitude functions, though there is a remarkable level of overlap between the two sets of posited attitude functions (Carpenter et al., 2013; Hamilton, 2007; Kiesler et al., 1969). A consensus emerged that the following five functions best capture the early work: utilitarian, value-expressive, social-adjustive (or identification), ego-defensive, and knowledge. Attitudes that serve the utilitarian function develop because the attitude object has helped people obtain positive outcomes and/or avoid negative outcomes. Attitudes that serve the value-expressive function develop because the attitude object is in some way relevant to people's values or ideals. Attitudes that serve the social-adjustive (or identification) function develop because the attitude object helps people identify with important other people or referent groups. Attitudes that serve an ego-defensive function are unique because they reflect more of the individual's internal conflicts or anxiety and this anxiety is projected onto an attitude object that is in some way associated with the conflict. For example, people who are feeling a great deal of anxiety because of a bad economy may scapegoat affirmative action because they associate affirmative action with their anxiety about losing their job. The knowledge function is the least studied and understood of the attitude functions (Carpenter et al., 2013). The basic idea is that attitudes that serve the knowledge function help people to create a cohesive and under-standable social world. Some scholars have argued that all attitudes serve the knowledge function (Fazio, 1986; Roskos-Ewoldsen, 1997). More recently, Herek (1986) proposed a typology based on how attitudes serving different functions would be formed. The typology includes three categories of attitude functions. The first category includes attitudes serving an instrumental function (the original utilitarian function). The second category includes attitudes serving a symbolic function (the original value-expressive, social-adjustive, and ego-defensive functions). The third category includes attitudes serving the knowledge function.

The second generation of research on the function of attitudes focused on the implications of those functions for understanding persuasion. The matching hypothesis specifies that if there is consistency between the function addressed in the appeal and the function the attitude serves for an individual, the persuasive appeal will be more persuasive. For example, if an attitude serves the utilitarian function, a persuasive appeal focusing on the utilitarian nature of the attitude object will be more persuasive than a persuasive message focusing on the values that the attitude object reflects (Carpenter et al., 2013; DeBono, 2000; Maio & Olson, 2000; Rhodes et al., 2009). Previous work has found that various personality traits relate to the matching hypothesis. For example, high self-monitors (people who monitor the situation to determine how to act) are more likely to have attitudes that serve a social-identity function and are more persuaded by appeals to the social-identity function. Conversely, low self-monitors (people who are influenced more by their own attitudes and values to determine how to act) are more likely to have attitudes that serve a value-expressive function and are more persuaded by appeals that address that value-expressive function (DeBono, 2000; however, see Wang, 2012). Likewise, certain types of objects are more likely to serve certain types of functions (Shavitt, 1990). For example, a refrigerator is likely to serve a utilitarian function, whereas perfume is more likely to serve a social-identity function. Again, consistent with the matching hypothesis, research has repeatedly shown that appeals to the matching function are more persuasive than mismatched appeals (DeBono, 1987; Maio & Olson, 2000; Shavitt, 1990).

The third generation of research has moved beyond the matching hypothesis to focus on how people process persuasive messages (see next section). Generally, this research has found that the matching hypothesis translates into this: arguments that are perceived as stronger by the audience are going to be more persuasive. Specifically, if an attitude serves a utilitarian function, arguments within the message that focus on *utilitarian* costs or benefits of the attitude object will be judged as stronger than arguments that focus on the value-expressive function or social-identity function (Hullett, 2002, 2004; Hullett & Boster, 2001). These findings suggest that although these three categories of functions may in fact exist, utilitarian, social-identity and value-expressive functions may reflect a similar underlying function because the resulting attitudes are changed via similar processes (Carpenter et al., 2013). In other words, the specific function that an attitude serves may be important for identifying what constitutes a strong argument, but the psychological processes that underlie the actual process of persuasion appear to operate similarly for all three of these functions. In contrast, however, attitudes that serve an ego-defensive function appear to be distinct and are associated with more defensive processing of persuasive messages (Lapinski & Boster, 2001). Similar to the work on ego-involvement within the social judgment perspective, this research suggests that attitudes that are closely associated with the self (in this instance, defending the self from threat) are more likely to be associated with biased message processing.

While interest in the attitude function perspective seems to be on-again, off-again, it has been demonstrated to be a fruitful way to think about persuasion (Rhodes et al., 2009). The basics of the theory have received support, though there are still disagreements as to exactly what are the functions that attitudes serve.

Process Theories of Persuasion

Theorizing about persuasion has a long history of focusing on how people process persuasive messages, based on the assumption that the types of processes that occur when a person is exposed to a persuasive message will influence the persuasiveness of that message (Hamilton, 2007). These models go back to the early research on persuasion, including Hovland et al.'s (1963) chain of responses model, which basically assumed that persuasion occurred to the extent that a message was attended to, comprehended, and accepted. If these stages did not occur, then persuasion would not occur. This model was followed by McGuire's initial six-step model of persuasion and then later his twelve-step model (McGuire, 1985). These early models often focused on a person's memory for a persuasive message, based on the assumption that if the earlier stages had occurred (e.g., the message was attended to, comprehended, and accepted), then the person should recall the message arguments. However, research generally was not consistent with this assumption (Eagly & Chaiken, 1993). A person's memory for a message is often not related to the persuasiveness of the message—particularly across time (Watts & McGuire, 1964).

The cognitive response model argued that these earlier models were wrong because they focused on what the message did to the person, which harkened back to the hypodermic needle model that characterized early thinking on the media (see Chapters 3 and 13). The cognitive response model argued that the critical issue in understanding persuasion was to understand how people cognitively respond to a message or elaborate on the message's content (Brock, 1967; Greenwald, 1968; Petty et al., 1981b). These elaborations—or cognitive responses—to the message determine the degree of persuasion that occurs (Petty et al., 1981b). Within this approach, people's elaborations on a message agree with the message (positive cognitive responses) or disagree with the message (negative cognitive responses). Positive cognitive responses should predict attitude change in the direction advocated by the message. Further, the more positive cognitive responses to a message that occur, the more attitude change should result. Conversely, negative cognitive responses will predict either no attitude change or a boomerang effect. A boomerang effect occurs when people's attitudes change in the opposite direction from that advocated by the message (Booth-Butterfield & Welbourne, 2002).[6] Finally, people may have a mix of positive and negative cognitive responses to a message. If the ratio of positive to negative is close to 1, then there should be no attitude change. However, as the ratio of positive to negative cognitive responses increases, there should be an increase in positive attitude change.

According to the cognitive response perspective, whether cognitive responses are predominately positive or negative is driven by the strength of the arguments within the message (Petty & Cacioppo, 1986; Petty et al., 1981a). If an argument within the message is strong, by definition the message recipient will have predominately positive cognitive responses. Conversely, if the message arguments are weak, by definition the message recipient will have predominately negative cognitive responses to that argument.

A number of different research domains supported the cognitive response perspective (Petty & Cacioppo, 1986; Petty et al., 1981b). However, research found that the basic assumption of the cognitive response approach, which is that message elaboration is necessary for persuasion to occur, did not always hold (Petty & Briñol, 2008; Petty & Cacioppo, 1986; Petty et al., 1981a). Indeed, extensive research suggested that persuasion can occur when people are not elaborating on the message at all. Thus, although the cognitive response perspective was supported in some aspects, it could not explain persuasion overall.

Dual Process Models of Persuasion

Later models attempted to account for the deficit in the cognitive response perspective. What distinguishes dual process models of persuasion such as the elaboration likelihood model from other models of persuasion such as the cognitive response approach is the basic assumption that people do not always process messages the same way across situations. When people are motivated and they have the ability to process a message, they will pay more attention to the arguments and content of the message. However, when people are not motivated and/or do not have the ability to process the message, they will focus on elements of the message other than the arguments that are advanced in the message. The basic distinction between two types of message processing in persuasion was first proposed in the early 1980s (Chaiken, 1980; Petty et al., 1981a). This line of research developed into several models of persuasion, but the elaboration likelihood model and the heuristic-systematic model are the most influential dual process models of persuasion.

The Elaboration Likelihood Model

The elaboration likelihood model (ELM) was formally proposed in 1986 (Petty & Cacioppo, 1986), although Petty and Cacioppo had been collaborating on research testing various assumptions of the model for over a decade before the model's formal appearance (Petty & Cacioppo, 1979, 1984; Petty et al., 1981a). The ELM has been a very influential model of persuasion across the social sciences (O'Keefe, 2013). As we will discuss, several competing theories have been proposed in response to the ELM. Of those competing models, we will discuss two prominent ones: the heuristic-systematic model or HSM (Chaiken et al., 1989) and the unimodel (Kruglanski et al., 2006; Kruglanski & Thompson, 1999). In addition, the ELM has undergone one major revision with its expansion to incorporate metacognitive elements into the model (Petty & Briñol, 2008; Petty et al., 2007).

The Basic Assumptions of the ELM

The initial assumption of the ELM is that people are motivated to hold correct attitudes (Petty & Cacioppo, 1986). This postulate does not mean that there is some idealized attitude that each individual strives to hold. Rather, an individual is motivated to have an attitude that fits within that person's psychological beliefs and values. The second assumption of the ELM gets to the heart of dual process models. Dual processing models of cognition assume that humans use two different processing styles. One is a quick and less effortful style that relies on well-learned information; the other is a qualitatively different style that is slower, more deliberative, generally requires more effortful processing, and relies on rules and symbolic logic. According to the ELM, what style a person uses, or, from a communication perspective, how much the person will cognitively elaborate on a persuasive message, will depend on individual and situational variables. Obviously, people do not process all persuasive messages in the same manner. In some instances, people will elaborate extensively on the issue-relevant arguments presented in the message. On other occasions, people focus more attention on elements of the message that are not germane to the content of the message, such as how other people respond to the message or the attractiveness of the source of the message. In any case, the premise is that messages and indeed all information can be processed in either this quick intuitive, or slow elaborative, manner.

The fundamental issue within the ELM is the extent to which people elaborate on the issue-relevant elements of a message. People who engage in a great deal of message elaboration are centrally processing a message. Central processing reflects the type of processing that was central to the cognitive response perspective that was discussed earlier. When a person is centrally processing a message, persuasion is driven by message elaborations or cognitive responses. When a message contains strong arguments and the cognitive responses are predominately positive, then attitude change should be in the direction advocated by the message. Conversely, if a message contains weak arguments and the cognitive responses are predominately negative, then either there will be no attitude change, or attitude change will go in the opposite direction from that advocated in the message. The ELM posits that the attitudes that result from central processing tend to be more resistant to change and more predictive of behavior (Petty et al., 1995).

Conversely, people who engage in very little or no message elaboration are peripherally processing a message. *Peripheral processing* involves the influence of non–issue-relevant aspects of the message and is the part of the ELM that was an expansion on the cognitive response perspective. Peripheral processing can include a number of different processes, such as the mere exposure effect or classical conditioning (Petty & Cacioppo, 1986). Within the persuasion context, attitude change that occurs as a result of persuasive messages tends to involve a focus on peripheral cues. Peripheral cues are elements of a message that people use to decide whether to agree with a message or not without actually elaborating on the message's arguments. Examples of common peripheral cues include character-istics of the message's source, the number of arguments contained in a message, the audience's reactions to a message, or social norms. Critically, none of these cues actually indicate whether the arguments within a message are strong or weak. Peripheral cues influence persuasion not through a process of elaboration, but rather operate as a simple rule-of-thumb that the message recipient uses to determine whether to agree with the message or not. Attitude change occurs in the direction advocated by the message when there are positive peripheral cues. Conversely, if a person is engaged in peripheral processing and the peripheral cues are negative, then either no attitude change will occur, or the attitude may move in the opposite direction to the position advocated in the message (e.g., a boomerang effect). The ELM assumes that attitude change that results from periph-eral processing is less resistant to counterattacks and less predictive of behavior than attitudes that are the result of central processing.

Of note, however, is the notion that the amount of cognitive elaboration of a message is not a simple yes-or-no process. Instead, the ELM introduced the notion of the elaboration continuum (Petty & Cacioppo, 1986; Petty et al., 1987; however, see O'Keefe, 2013; Stiff, 1986; Stiff & Boster, 1987). At one end of the continuum is peripheral processing of the message and at the other end is central processing of the message. The positions between these two extremes on the continuum represent a mix of both central and peripheral processing. As people move toward the peripheral-processing end of the continuum, they are engaging in relatively more peripheral processing and less central processing, and, conversely, as people move toward the central-processing end of the continuum, they engage in relatively more central processing and less peripheral processing. What factors influence where a person's processing of a particular message falls on the elaboration continuum? According to the ELM, there are two basic categories of factors that influence how a message is processed: motivation to process the message and the ability to process the message. As motivation and ability increase, the processing of the message should involve greater elaboration. However, when either motivation or ability is low, message processing should involve less elaboration. Examples of factors that influence people's *motivation* to elaborately process a message include the personal relevance of the message, diffusion of responsibility, mood, or the personal enjoyment of critically processing an argument (e.g., people high in need for cognition enjoy and are thus motivated to critically examine information; Cacioppo & Petty, 1982).

Examples of factors that influence people's *ability* to elaborately process a message include topic-relevant knowledge, distraction, message repetition, and the message's modality (e.g., print vs. video). Further, the factors that influence motivation and ability can be classified as either situational variables or individual differences variable. Obviously, distraction is a situational factor that influences the ability to process a message, while topic-relevant knowledge is an individual difference variable that influences people's ability to process a message.

There are several important things to note about central and peripheral processing. First, central processing can involve both objective and biased processing of persuasive message arguments. A common assumption is that because central processing typically requires more effort and people are motivated to hold correct attitudes (first assumption of the model), then central processing should be relatively objective. However, the assumption involving holding correct attitudes reflects a psychological judgment of correctness—are the attitudes consistent with the person's other attitudes and beliefs? If a message threatens a person's important values, beliefs, or behavior, then central processing will likely be biased (Johnson & Eagly, 1989; Petty & Cacioppo, 1990; Rhodes et al., 2008). Conversely, fear of invalidity can motivate people to process a message more objectively. Fear of invalidity refers to a person's motivation to make an objectively correct judgment. People who have a high fear of invalidity tend to show less biased processing of a message (Kruglanski, 1989; Schuette & Fazio, 1995).

Second, argument quality plays a critical role within the ELM. However, a number of scholars have noted that the model is silent as to what constitutes a strong argument (Hamilton et al., 1993; O'Keefe, 2002, 2013). From the perspective of the ELM, what constitutes a strong argument depends on the message recipient. For example, when an attitude serves different functions for an individual, what constitutes a strong argument will change (Petty & Cacioppo, 1986; Shavitt, 1990; Snyder & DeBono, 1985).

Finally, variables can influence the outcome of persuasion in one of four ways within the ELM: the variables can influence where message recipients fall on the elaboration continuum, influence whether processing is objective or biased,[7] operate as arguments, or operate as peripheral cues. It is important to note that the same variable can influence persuasion in multiple ways (Petty & Briñol, 2008). If a message is attributed to a liked source, the liked source can operate as a peripheral cue, can bias message processing if people are motivated to agree with the liked source, and can even motivate people to process the message more elaboratively because they want to know what this person thinks (Roskos-Ewoldsen et al., 2002).

Self-Validation Hypothesis

Recently, an extension of the ELM has been proposed by incorporating meta-cognition within the model (Petty & Briñol, 2008; Petty et al., 2007; Petty et al.,

2002). At a basic level, meta-cognitions refer to a person's thoughts about their thoughts. Within the ELM, meta-cognitions involve people's thoughts about their cognitive responses. Specifically, people may have a great deal of confidence in one of their cognitive responses to a message and much less confidence in another cognitive response. The judgment of confidence is a metacognitive thought. The self-validation hypothesis incorporates the idea that the greater the confidence in a cognitive response to a message, the more impact that cognitive response will have on the final attitude. The original ELM would predict that if there were equal numbers of positive and negative cognitive responses to a message, then there would not be any attitude change based on central processing.[8] However, the self-validation hypothesis would predict that attitude change would occur in the direction of the cognitive response that is held with more confidence.

The importance of the metacognitive model is that it highlights another set of variables that can influence attitude change and persuasion. To the extent that a variable increases the people's confidence in their cognitive responses, then the variable should result in greater persuasion. However, the metacognitive model is relatively new and has not been subject to extensive tests.

The Heuristic-Systematic Model (HSM)

The HSM was proposed independently of the ELM at approximately the same time (Chaiken, 1980; Chaiken et al., 1989; Eagly & Chaiken, 1993). While the models use different names for the processes—systematic processing instead of central processing and heuristic processing instead of peripheral processing—the models are very similar. First, the existence of both models indicates the importance of dual processing for theorizing about persuasion. Second, and perhaps more important, the competing models forced both models to be more specific in the predictions that each model made.

One of the ways in which the HSM extended the ELM concerned the motivations for attitude development in the first place. The ELM assumed that people were motivated to hold correct attitudes. While the HSM concurs with that assessment, the HSM also included motivations involving impression-formation and defensive motivation. That is, people are motivated to hold correct attitudes but also to hold attitudes that aid in their impression-formation and in maintaining their attitudes. Specifically, impression-formation reflects the normative pressures people feel to hold certain attitudes (Chaiken et al., 1989). Impression-formation motivation pushes people to form attitudes that are socially acceptable (Eagly & Chaiken, 1993). Defensive motivation occurs when a person is highly motivated to hold a certain attitude prior to acquiring information about the attitude object. In this situation, people will seek out and process information in a biased manner so that it is consistent with the attitude that they desire to form.

In addition to these differences, the HSM's treatment of heuristic processing is similar to but narrower than the ELM's notion of peripheral processing. Recall

that peripheral processing includes the mere exposure effect and classical conditioning. However, the HSM focuses only on the use of heuristic cues or mental
shortcuts when people are processing a message; it does not extend the notion
of heuristic processing to include theories of paired associations leading to liking,
for example (as discussed earlier in this chapter). The HSM also provides more
detail concerning which heuristics are likely to be used (Chaiken et al., 1989).
The HSM argues that heuristic cues would only influence persuasion to the extent
that the heuristic was available in memory. If a person does not have the heuristic,
then that heuristic cannot operate when processing a persuasive message. Second,
heuristic cues are more likely to influence persuasion if they are more accessible
from memory (Eagly & Chaiken, 1993; Roskos-Ewoldsen & Fazio, 1992).
Third, a heuristic is only likely to influence persuasion if the heuristic is judged
to be reliable. If people do not believe the heuristic is reliable, then they are less
likely to rely on that heuristic when making a decision.

The HSM also introduced the sufficiency principle to explain when people
were likely to process a message systematically or heuristically. The HSM assumes
that people generally will wait to form an attitude until they are sufficiently
confident in the information they are using to make the attitude judgment.
Further, people are more motivated to hold correct attitudes in some instances
than in others. The sufficiency threshold reflects the degree of confidence that
people want to have prior to forming an attitude. When there is a large gap
between people's actual confidence and the sufficiency threshold, they are more
likely to engage in systematic processing. When the gap is small, they are
more likely to rely on heuristic processing.

In addition, the HSM posits that systematic and heuristic processing can
operate additively in that both can simultaneously increase a person's confidence prior to making an attitude judgment. Finally, the HSM also hypothesizes
that systematic and heuristic processing can operate in an interactive manner.
For example, when an ambiguous argument comes from an expert, people may
use the heuristic of source expertise to judge the argument as stronger than
they would have done if the ambiguous argument had come from a low expert
source. In this way, heuristic processing (the source cue) influences the outcome
of systematic processing.

The Unimodel

The final process model we will address is the unimodel (Kruglanski et al.,
2006; Kruglanski & Thompson, 1999; O'Keefe, 2013). The unimodel opposes
the distinction between central (systematic) and peripheral (heuristic) processing.
According to the unimodel, there is only one type of processing that underlies
persuasion-based attitude change. Specifically, the unimodel maintains that the
ELM and HSM (and other dual process models) fundamentally conflate content
and process. Specifically, central processing focuses on the content of the message,

whereas heuristic processing focuses on information that is peripheral to the message. According to the unimodel, then, there are not two kinds of processing; rather, there are two different types of content. The unimodel maintains that there is no reason why a person could not elaborate on the source of a message or peripherally process a message argument. Indeed, the unimodel maintains that for both types of information, the underlying process is identical: what are the implications of evidence X for attitude Y. The evidence that is considered can include both message arguments and peripheral cues such as source expertise. These types of evidence can work together, interactively, or they may be weighted differently, but both are processed cognitively.

In addition, several variables relevant in the other models also occur in the unimodel. For example, motivation and ability continue to play important roles, but within the unimodel, motivation and ability influence how much energy a person is willing to expend engaging in the underlying reasoning process that is outlined in the model. When motivation and ability are high, people will engage in extensive reasoning and are willing to engage in processes that require more energy, such as processing the types of arguments that are typically employed in tests of the ELM or HSM. Conversely, when motivation and/or ability are low, people will not engage in as much processing of the message and will focus on that information that is easier to process—such as the types of peripheral cues that are used in tests of the ELM and HSM. Indeed, when research has made message arguments easy to process and peripheral cues difficult to process, people are more persuaded by message arguments when ability and/or motivation is low and more persuaded by peripheral cues when their ability and motivation are high (Kruglanski & Thompson, 1999). Thus, this evidence does seem to contradict the ELM, although it is not necessarily strong support for the unimodel.

Inoculation Theory

The theories that we have discussed thus far have focused exclusively on either attitude formation or persuasion (i.e., attitude change). However, there are situations where the goal is to *stop* people from changing their attitude, such as in a political campaign where a candidate who has the voters' support wants to make sure that the voters do not change their minds. Inoculation theory was developed by McGuire (1964) to explain how messages could decrease the likelihood that a person's attitude will be changed. The theory draws on an analogy to medicine involving vaccinations. One way in which a person is vaccinated or inoculated against a disease is by giving people a weakened form of the disease. In that way, the body learns to fight the disease because it is easy to defeat the weakened strain of the disease. Inoculation theory argues that creating resistance to attitude change should work the same way. A refutational pretreatment involves attacking people's attitudes with weak arguments that are easy to overcome, which should allow people to develop defenses for their attitude. For example, defending against a weak refutational pretreatment provides an opportunity for the person to practice counterarguing the opposing viewpoint. Extensive research has generally supported the logic on inoculation theory (Compton, 2013; Compton & Pfau, 2005; Pfau & Burgoon, 1988; Pfau et al., 2003).

However, research has demonstrated that several conditions have to exist for a refutational pretreatment to work. Specifically, people must perceive a threat to their attitude as part of the refutational pretreatment. The threat provides the necessary motivation to engage in counterarguing of the refutational pretreatment and to continue to develop counterarguments after the refutational pretreatment (Pfau et al., 2009; Pfau et al., 2010). Research has demonstrated that if a pretreatment does threaten the message recipient and motivates counterarguing, the recipient's attitude will be more resistant to change, and this resistance has even been found to last for months (Pfau & Van Bockern, 1994).

Conclusion

Research on persuasion and attitudes has dominated communication scholarship since the beginning of the discipline back in the middle part of the twentieth century. As this chapter hopefully makes clear, there are a multiplicity of approaches to theorizing about persuasion and attitudes. Likewise, attitudes and persuasion play an important role in many of the other domains covered within this book, such as health communication, political communication, and even media effects, but they are clearly central to persuasion.

Within these additional areas, it is important to keep Miller's distinctions between response-shaping (attitude formation), response-reinforcement, and response-changing (persuasion) in mind. We have reviewed prominent theories in two of these areas: attitude formation and persuasion. Attitude reinforcement has not been studied extensively to date, but there appears to be growing interest in this area. Likewise, there has been a recent resurgence of interest in reactance (Quick et al., 2013) as well as affect and emotion (Dillard & Nabi, 2006; Dillard & Seo, 2013). Lastly, there is a growing awareness that attitudes are more complex than simple evaluative responses to some object. Instead, attitudes can vary in their accessibility (see Chapter 11), and this has important implications for persuasion as well (Rhodes & Ewoldsen, 2013; Ewoldsen et al., 2015). So, while there is a solid foundation of research on persuasion and attitudes, there are still exciting vistas to be reached in the future.

Notes

1   Though often confused, the mere exposure effect is distinct from message repetition. The mere exposure effect involves repeated exposure only to the attitude object, independent of any information about that object or communication about that object. The repetition of a message tends to increase the effectiveness of a message, up to a

point, if the message contains strong arguments, because people are able to process the message more thoroughly with increased repetition. But at which point will increased repetitions tend to backfire and decrease the message's effectiveness (Cacioppo & Petty, 1979)?

2   While research has overwhelming demonstrated that the mere exposure effect results in more positive attitudes, some research suggests that if the initial attitude toward an object is negative, then a reverse mere exposure effect has been demonstrated, with people developing more negative attitudes toward the novel object (Brickman et al., 1972; Klinger & Greenwald, 1994).

3   Other examples of consistency theories include balance theory and congruity theory. While these theories were very popular when consistency theories were first developed in the 1950s and 1960s, they are rarely used today to explain attitude change and persuasion.

4   Throughout this section, we will discuss the discrepancy between a person's beliefs or attitudes and that person's beliefs. While the theory discusses discrepancies between two beliefs, the empirical research has almost exclusively involved discrepancies between beliefs or attitudes and a person's behavior. As Cooper (2007) notes, dissonance seems to begin with behavior.

5   The terms consonance and dissonance originate in music theory. A consonant chord is one where the notes fit together or sound good together (e.g., a 1, 3, 5 pattern). A dissonant chord in music is one that violates the standard structure of a chord (e.g., a 1, 2, 5 structure would be dissonant). The chord does not resonate and tends to sound aversive, causing arousal to the listener.

6   The occurrence of boomerang effects is somewhat controversial (Hamilton et al., 1993). While they are theoretically very interesting, they do not occur with as much frequency as one would expect based on the cognitive response model and the elaboration likelihood model (Hamilton et al., 1993; Park et al., 2007). Furthermore, there are serious methodological concerns regarding those studies that have reported boomerang effects.

7   Petty and Cacioppo (1986) treat these as three variables by combining variables that influence the extent of processing and variables that influence whether the message is processed in a biased manner. However, these two effects are clearly distinct. Petty and Cacioppo (1986) originally argued that there were three ways a variable could influence persuasion, because they had combined factors that influence where message processing falls on the elaboration continuum and variables that influenced whether processing was objective or biased. However, as will be discussed, different factors can influence how elaborately the message is processed and whether the message is processed in a biased manner. Consequently, we are treating them as two distinct ways in which persuasion can be influenced.

8   Of course, it is possible in this situation for a person to still be persuaded if there are peripheral cues that are presented and processed by the individual.

References

Allport, G. (1935). Attitudes. In C. Murchison (Ed.), *A handbook of social psychology* (pp. 789–844). Worcester, MA: Clark University Press.

Baeyens, F., Hermans, D., & Eelen, P. (1993). The role of CS–US contingency in human evaluative conditioning. *Behaviour Research and Therapy, 31*, 731–737.

Baker, W. E. (1999). When can affective conditioning and mere exposure directly influence brand choice? *Journal of Advertising, 28*, 31–46.

Beasley, R. K., & Joslyn, M. R. (2001). Cognitive dissonance and post-decision attitude change in six presidential elections. *Political Psychology, 22*, 521–540.

Bem, D. J. (1967). Self-perception: An alternative interpretation of cognitive dissonance phenomena. *Psychological Review, 74*, 183–200.

Bem, D. J. (1972). Self-perception theory. *Advances in Experimental Social Psychology, 6*, 1–62.

Booth-Butterfield, S., & Welbourne, J. (2002). The elaboration likelihood model. In J. P. Dillard & M. Pfau (Eds.), *Persuasion handbook: Developments in theory and practice* (pp. 155–175). Beverly Hills, CA: Sage.

Bornstein, R. F. (1989). Exposure and affect: Overview and meta-analysis of research, 1968–1987. *Psychological Bulletin, 106*, 265–289.

Bornstein, R. F., & D'Agostino, P. R. (1994). The attribution and discounting of perceptual fluency: Preliminary tests of a perceptual fluency/attributional model of the mere exposure effect. *Social Cognition, 12*, 103–128.

Breckler, S. J. (1984). Empirical validation of affect, behavior, and cognition as distinct components of attitude. *Journal of Personality and Social Psychology, 47*, 1191–1205.

Brehm, J. W. (1956). Postdecision changes in the desirability of alternatives. *Journal of Abnormal and Social Psychology, 52*, 384–389.

Brickman, P., Redfield, J., Harrison, A. A., & Crandall, R. (1972). Drive and predisposition as factors in the attitudinal effects of mere exposure. *Journal of Experimental Social Psychology, 8*, 31–44.

Brock, T. C. (1967). Communication discrepancy and intent to persuade as determinants of counterargument production. *Journal of Experimental Social Psychology, 3*, 296–309.

Burger, J. M., & Caldwell, D. F. (2003). The effects of monetary incentives and labeling on the foot-in-the-door effect: Evidence for a self-perception process. *Basic and Applied Social Psychology, 25*, 235–241.

Burgoon, J. K., Burgoon, M., Miller, G. R., & Sunnagrank, M. (1981). Learning theory approaches to persuasion. *Human Communication Research, 7*, 161–179.

Cacioppo, J. T., & Petty, R. E. (1979). Effects of message repetition and position on cognitive response, recall, and persuasion. *Journal of Personality and Social Psychology, 37*, 97–109.

Cacioppo, J. T., & Petty, R. E. (1982). The need for cognition. *Journal of Personality & Social Psychology, 42*, 116–131.

Carpenter, C., Boster, F. J., & Andrews, K. R. (2013). Functional attitude theory. In J. Dillard & L. Shen (Eds.), *Handbook of persuasion: Developments in theory and practice* (2nd ed., pp. 104–119). Los Angeles, CA: Sage.

Chaiken, S. (1980). Heuristic versus systematic information processing and the use of source versus message cues in persuasion. *Journal of Personality & Social Psychology, 39*, 752–756.

Chaiken, S., Liberman, A., & Eagly, A. H. (1989). Heuristic and systematic information processing within and beyond the persuasion context. In J. S. Uleman & J. A. Bargh (Eds.), *Unintended thought* (pp. 212–252). New York: Guilford Press.

Compton, J. (2013). Inoculation theory. In J. P. Dillard & L. Shen (Eds.), *The Sage handbook of persuasion: Developments in theory and practice* (pp. 220–236). Los Angeles, CA: Sage.

Compton, J. A., & Pfau, M. W. (2005). Inoculation theory of resistance to influence at maturity: Recent progress in theory development and application and suggestions for future research. In P. J. Kalbfleisch (Ed.), *Communication yearbook 29* (pp. 97–146). Mahwah, NJ: Lawrence Erlbaum Associates.

Cooper, J. (2007). *Cognitive dissonance: 50 years of a classic theory.* Los Angeles, CA: Sage.

Cooper, J. (2010). Vicarious cognitive dissonance: Changing attitudes by experiencing another's pain. In J. P. Forgas, J. Cooper, & W. D. Crano (Eds.), *The psychology of attitudes and attitude change* (pp. 125–140). New York: Psychology Press.

Cooper, J., & Fazio, R. H. (1984). A new look at dissonance. *Advances in Experimental Social Psychology, 17*, 229–268.

DeBono, K. G. (1987). Investigating the social-adjustive and value-expressive functions of attitudes: Implications for persuasion processes. *Journal of Personality and Social Psychology, 52*, 279–287.

DeBono, K. G. (2000). Attitude functions and consumer psychology: Understanding perceptions of product quality. In G. R. Maio & J. M. Olson (Eds.), *Why we evaluate: Functions of attitudes* (pp. 195–221). Mahwah, NJ: Lawrence Erlbaum Associates.

De Houwer, J., Thomas, S., & Baeyens, F. (2001). Association learning of likes and dislikes: A review of 25 years of research on human evaluative conditioning. *Psychological Bulletin, 127*, 853–869.

DeJong, W. (1979). An examination of self-perception mediation of the foot-in-the-door effect. *Journal of Personality and Social Psychology, 37*, 2221–2239.

Dickerson, C. A., Thibodeau, R., Aronson, E., & Miller, D. (1992). Using cognitive dissonance to encourage water conservation. *Journal of Applied Social Psychology, 22*, 841–854.

Dillard, J. P. (2010). Persuasion. In C. R. Berger, M. E. Roloff, & D. R. Roskos-Ewoldsen (Eds.), *The handbook of communication science* (pp. 203–218). Los Angeles: Sage.

Dillard, J. P., & Nabi, R. (2006). The persuasive influence of emotion in cancer prevention and detection messages. *Journal of Communication, 56*, S123–S139.

Dillard, J. P., & Seo, K. (2013). Affect and persuasion. In J. Dillard & L. Shen (Eds.), *Handbook of persuasion: Developments in theory and practice* (2nd ed., pp. 150–166). Los Angeles, CA: Sage.

Donsbach, W., & Mothes, C. (2012). The dissonant self: Contributions from dissonance theory to a new agenda for studying political communication. *Communication yearbook 36* (pp. 3–44). Beverly Hills, CA: Sage.

Eagly, A. H., & Chaiken, S. (1993). *The psychology of attitudes.* New York: Harcourt Brace Jovanovich.

Edwards, K. (1990). The interplay of affect and cognition in attitude formation and change. *Journal of Personality & Social Psychology, 59*, 202–216.

Ellithorpe, M. E., Ewoldsen, D. R., & Fazio, R. H. (2014). Socialization of dissonance processes: Reports of parenting style experienced during childhood moderate dissonance reactions. *Social Psychology & Personality Science, 5*, 84–91.

Ewoldsen, D. R., Rhodes, N., & Fazio, R. H. (2015). The MODE model and its implications for studying the media. *Media Psychology, 18*, 312–337.

Fabrigar, L. R., & Petty, R. E. (1999). The role of the affective and cognitive bases of attitudes in susceptibility to affectively and cognitively based persuasion. *Personality and Social Psychology Bulletin, 25*, 363–381.

Fazio, R. H. (1986). How do attitudes guide behavior? In R. H. Sorrentino & E. T. Higgins (Eds.), *The handbook of motivation and cognition: Foundations of social behavior* (pp. 204–243). New York: Guilford Press.

Fazio, R. H., & Roskos-Ewoldsen, D. R. (2005). Acting as we feel: When and how attitudes guide behavior. In T. C. Brock & M. C. Green (Eds.), *Persuasion: Psychological insights and perspectives* (2nd ed., pp. 41–62). Thousand Oaks, CA: Sage.

Fazio, R. H., Zanna, M. P., & Cooper, J. (1977). Dissonance and self-perception: An integrative view of each theory's proper domain of application. *Journal of Experimental Social Psychology, 13*, 464–479.

Festinger, L. (1957). *A theory of cognitive dissonance.* Stanford, CA: Stanford University Press.

Festinger, L., & Carlsmith, J. M. (1959). Cognitive consequences of forced compliance. *The Journal of Abnormal and Social Psychology, 58,* 203.

Fink, E. L., & Cai, D. A. (2013). Discrepancy models of belief change. In J. Dillard & L. Shen (Eds.), *Handbook of persuasion: Developments in theory and practice* (2nd ed., pp. 84–103). Los Angeles, CA: Sage.

Fink, E. L., Kaplowitz, S. A., & Bauer, C. L. (1983). Positional discrepancy, psychological discrepancy, and attitude change: Experimental tests of some mathematical models. *Communication Monographs, 50,* 413–430.

Greenwald, A. G. (1968). Cognitive learning, cognitive response to persuasion and attitude change. In A. G. Greenwald, T. C. Brock, & T. M. Ostrom (Eds.), *Psychological foundations of attitudes* (pp. 147–170). New York: Academic Press.

Groenland, E. A., & Schoormans, J. P. (1994). Comparing mood-induction and affective conditioning as mechanisms influencing product evaluation and product choice. *Psychology & Marketing, 11,* 183–197.

Grush, J. E., McKeough, K. L., & Ahlering, R. F. (1978). Extrapolating laboratory exposure research to actual political elections. *Journal of Personality and Social Psychology, 36,* 257–270.

Hamilton, J. C., Pinel, E. C., & Roskos-Ewoldsen, D. R. (2002). The effects of a racist act and public counter-demonstrations on race-related behavioral intentions: A natural experiment. *Journal of Applied Social Psychology, 32,* 2611–2620.

Hamilton, M. A. (2007). Motivation, social context, and cognitive processing as evolving concepts in persuasion theory. In D. R. Roskos-Ewoldsen & J. L. Monahan (Eds.), *Communication and social cognition: Theories and methods* (pp. 417–447). Mahwah, NJ: Lawrence Erlbaum Associates.

Hamilton, M. A., Hunter, J. E., & Boster, F. J. (1993). The elaboration likelihood model as a theory of attitude formation: A mathematical analysis. *Communication Theory, 3,* 50–65.

Hekkert, P., Thurgood, C., & Whitfield, T. W. (2013). The mere exposure effect for consumer products as a consequence of existing familiarity and controlled exposure. *Acta Psychologica, 144,* 411–417.

Herek, G. M. (1986). The instrumentality of attitudes: Toward a neofunctional theory. *Journal of Social Issues, 42,* 99–114.

Hovland, C. I., Harvey, O. J., & Sherif, M. (1957). Assimilation and contrast effects in reactions to communication and attitude change. *Journal of Abnormal and Social Psychology, 55,* 244–252.

Hovland, C. I., Janis, I. L., & Kelley, H. H. (1963). *Communication and persuasion: Psychological studies of opinion change.* New Haven, CT: Yale University Press.

Hullett, C. (2002). Charting the process underlying the change of value-expressive attitudes: The importance of value-relevance in predicting the matching effect. *Communication Monographs, 69,* 158–178.

Hullett, C. R. (2004). Using functional theory to promote sexually transmitted disease (STD): Testing the impact of value-expressive messages and guilt. *Communication Research, 31,* 363–396.

Hullett, C., & Boster, F. (2001). Matching messages to the values underlying value-expressive and social-adjustive attitudes: Reconciling an old theory with a contemporary measurement approach. *Communication Monographs, 68,* 133–153.

Im, H., & Ha, Y. (2011). The effect of perceptual fluency and enduring involvement on situational involvement in an online apparel shopping context. *Journal of Fashion Marketing and Management, 15,* 345–362.

Im, H., Lennon, S. J., & Stoel, L. (2010). The perceptual fluency effect on pleasurable online shopping experience. *Journal of Research in Interactive Marketing, 4,* 280–295.

Janiszewski, C. (1993). Preattentive mere exposure effects. *Journal of Consumer Research, 20,* 376–392.

Johnson, B. T., & Eagly, A. H. (1989). Effects of involvement on persuasion: A meta-analysis. *Psychological Bulletin, 106,* 290–314.

Jones, C. R., Olson, M. A., & Fazio, R. H. (2010). Evaluative conditioning: The "how" question. *Advances in Experimental Social Psychology, 43,* 205–255.

Katz, D. (1960). The functional approach to studying attitudes. *Public Opinion Quarterly, 24,* 163–204.

Kiesler, C. A., Collins, B. E., & Miller, N. (1969). *Attitude change.* Oxford: Wiley.

Klimmt, C., Hefner, B., & Vorderer, P. (2009). The video game experience as "true" identification: A theory of enjoyable alterations of players' self-perception. *Communication Theory, 19,* 351–373.

Klinger, M. R., & Greenwald, A. G. (1994). Preferences need no inferences? The cognitive basis of unconscious mere exposure effects. In P. M. Niedenthal & S. Kitayama (Eds.), *The heart's eye: Emotional influences in perception and attention* (pp. 67–85). San Diego, CA: Academic Press.

Knobloch-Westerwick, S. (2015). *Choice and preference in media use: Advances in selective exposure theory and research.* New York: Routledge.

Kruglanski, A. W. (1989). *Lay epistemics and human knowledge: Cognitive and motivational bases.* New York: Springer.

Kruglanski, A. W., & Stroebe, W. (2005). The influence of beliefs and goals on attitudes: Issues of structure, function, and dynamics. In D. Albarracin, B. T. Johnson, & M. P. Zanna (Eds.), *The handbook of attitudes* (pp 323–368). New York: Psychology Press.

Kruglanski, A. W., & Thompson, E. P. (1999). Persuasion by a single route: A view from the unimodel. *Psychological Inquiry, 10,* 83–109.

Kruglanski, A. W., Chen, X., Pierro, A., Mannetti, L., Erb, H. P., & Spiegel, S. (2006). Persuasion according to the unimodel: Implications for cancer communication. *Journal of Communication, 56*(s1), S105–S122.

Lapinski, M., & Boster, F. J. (2001). Modeling the ego-defensive function of attitudes. *Communication Monographs, 68,* 314–324.

McCarty, J. A. (2004). Product placement: The nature of the practice and potential avenues of inquiry. In L. J. Shrum (Ed.), *The psychology of entertainment media: Blurring the lines between entertainment and persuasion* (pp. 45–61). Mahwah, NJ: Lawrence Erlbaum Associates.

McGuire, W. J. (1964). Inducing resistance to persuasion: Some contemporary approaches. In L. Berkowitz (Ed.), *Advances in experimental social psychology* (vol. 1, pp. 192–229). New York: Academic Press.

McGuire, W. J. (1985). Attitudes and attitude change. In G. Lindzey & E. Aronson (Eds.), *Handbook of social psychology* (3rd ed., vol. 2, pp. 233–347). New York: Random House.

Maio, G. R., & Olson, J. M. (2000). What is a "value-expressive" attitude? In G. R. Maio & J. M. Olson (Eds.), *Why we evaluate: Functions of attitudes* (pp. 249–269). Mahwah, NJ: Lawrence Erlbaum Associates.

Matthes, J., Schemer, C., & Wirth, W. (2007). More than meets the eye. *International Journal of Advertising, 26,* 477–503.

Miller, G. R. (1980/2013). On being persuaded: Some basic distinctions. In J. P. Dillard & L. Shen (Eds.), *The Sage handbook of persuasion: Developments in theory and practice* (pp. 70–81). Los Angeles, CA: Sage. (Reprinted from M. Roloff & G. R. Miller (Eds.)

(1980), *Persuasion: New directions in theory and research* (pp. 11–28). Beverly Hills, CA: Sage.

Miller, G. R. (1987). Persuasion. In C. R. Berger & S. H. Chaffee (Eds.), *Handbook of communication science* (pp. 446–483). Newbury Park, CA: Sage.

Monahan, J. L., Murphy, S. T., & Zajonc, R. B. (2000). Subliminal mere exposure: Specific, general, and diffuse effects. *Psychological Science, 11*, 462–466.

Morgenstern, M., Isensee, B., & Hanewinkel, R. (2012). Seeing and liking cigarette advertisements: Is there a "mere exposure" effect? *European Addiction Research, 19*, 42–46.

O'Keefe, D. J. (2002). *Persuasion: Theory and research* (2nd ed.). Thousand Oaks, CA: Sage.

O'Keefe, D. J. (2013). The elaboration likelihood model. In J. Dillard & L. Shen (Eds.), *Handbook of persuasion: Developments in theory and practice* (2nd ed., pp. 137–149). Los Angeles, CA: Sage.

Park, H. S., Levine, T. R., Kingsley Westerman, C. Y., Orfgen, T., & Foregger, S. (2007). The effects of argument quality and involvement type on attitude formation and attitude change: A test of dual-process and social judgment predictions. *Human Communication Research, 33*, 81–102.

Petty, R. E., & Briñol, P. (2008). Persuasion: From single to multiple to metacognitive processes. *Perspectives on Psychological Science, 3*, 137–147.

Petty, R. E., & Cacioppo, J. T. (1979). Issue involvement can increase or decrease persuasion by enhancing message-relevant cognitive responses. *Journal of Personality and Social Psychology, 37*, 1915–1926.

Petty, R. E., & Cacioppo, J. T. (1984). The effects of involvement on responses to argument quantity and quality: Central and peripheral routes to persuasion. *Journal of Personality and Social Psychology, 46*, 69–81.

Petty, R. E., & Cacioppo, J. T. (1986). *Communication and persuasion: Central and peripheral routes to attitude change.* New York: Springer-Verlag.

Petty, R. E., & Cacioppo, J. T. (1990). Involvement and persuasion: Tradition versus integration. *Psychological Bulletin, 107*, 367–374.

Petty, R. E., Cacioppo, J. T., & Goldman, R. (1981a). Personal involvement as a determinant of argument-based persuasion. *Journal of Personality and Social Psychology, 41*, 847–855.

Petty, R. E., Ostrom, T. M., & Brock, T. C. (1981b). Historical foundations of the cognitive response approach to attitudes and persuasion. In R. E. Petty, T. M. Ostrom, & T. C. Brock (Eds.), *Cognitive responses in persuasion* (pp. 5–30). Hillsdale, NJ: Lawrence Erlbaum Associates.

Petty, R. E., Haugtvedt, C. P., & Smith, S. M. (1995). Elaboration as a determinant of attitude strength: Creating attitudes that are persistent, resistant, and predictive of behavior. In R. E. Petty & J. A. Krosnick (Eds.), *Attitude strength: Antecedents and consequences* (pp. 93–130). Mahwah, NJ: Lawrence Erlbaum Associates.

Petty, R. E., Briñol, P., & Tormala, Z. L. (2002). Thought confidence as a determinant of persuasion: The self-validation hypothesis. *Journal of Personality and Social Psychology, 82*, 722–741.

Petty, R. E., Briñol, P., & DeMarree, K. G. (2007). The meta-cognitive model (MCM) of attitudes: Implications for attitude measurement, change, and strength. *Social Cognition, 25*, 657–686.

Petty, R. E., Kasmer, J. A., Haugtvedt, C. P., & Cacioppo, J. T. (1987). Source and message factors in persuasion: A reply to Stiff's critique of the elaboration likelihood model. *Communication Monographs, 54*, 233–249.

Pfau, M., & Burgoon, M. (1988). Inoculation in political campaign communication. *Human Communication Research, 15*, 91–111.

Pfau, M., & Van Bockern, S. (1994). The persistence of inoculation in conferring resistance to smoking initiation among adolescents: The second year. *Human Communication Research, 20*, 413–430.

Pfau, M., Banas, J. A., Semmler, S. M., Deatrick, L., Lane, L., Mason, A., Nisbett, G., Craig, E., & Underhill, J. (2010). Role and impact of involvement and enhanced threat in resistance. *Communication Quarterly, 58*, 1–18.

Pfau, M., Roskos-Ewoldsen, D., Wood, M., Yin, S., Cho, J., Lu, K. H., & Shen, L. (2003). Attitude accessibility as an alternative explanation for how inoculation confers resistance. *Communication Monographs, 70*, 39–51.

Pfau, M., Semmler, S. M., Deatrick, L., Mason, A., Nisbett, G., Lane, L., Craig, E., Underhill, J., & Banas, J. (2009). Nuances about the role and impact of affect in inoculation. *Communication Monographs, 76*, 216–252.

Powers, T. L., & Jack, E. P. (2013). The influence of cognitive dissonance on retail product returns. *Psychology & Marketing, 30*, 724–735.

Quick, B. L., Shen, L., & Dillard, J. P. (2013). Reactance theory and persuasion. In J. P. Dillard & L. Shen (Eds.), *The Sage handbook of persuasion* (pp. 167–183). Thousand Oaks, CA: Sage.

Rescorla, R. A. (1988). Behavioral studies of Pavlovian conditioning. *Annual Review of Neuroscience, 11*, 329–352.

Rhodes, N., & Ewoldsen, D. R. (2013). Outcomes of persuasion: Cognitive, behavioral and social. In J. Dillard & L. Shen (Eds.), *Handbook of persuasion: Developments in theory and practice* (2nd ed., pp. 53–69). Los Angeles, CA: Sage.

Rhodes, N., Roskos-Ewoldsen, D. R., Edison, A., & Bradford, B. (2008). Attitude and norm accessibility affect processing of anti-smoking messages. *Health Psychology, 27*, S224–S232.

Rhodes, N., Roskos-Ewoldsen, D. R., Eno, C. A., & Monahan, J. L. (2009). The content of cigarette counter-advertising: Are perceived functions of smoking addressed? *Journal of Health Communication, 14*, 658–673.

Rogers, E. M. (1994). *A history of communication study: A biographical approach.* New York: Free Press.

Rosenberg, M. J., & Hovland, C. I. (1960). Cognitive, affective, and behavioral components of attitudes. In C. I. Hovland & M. J. Rosenberg (Eds.), *Attitude organization and change: An analysis of consistency among attitude components* (pp. 1–14). New Haven, CT: Yale University Press.

Roskos-Ewoldsen, D. R. (1997). Attitude accessibility and persuasion: Review and a transactive model. In B. Burleson (Ed.), *Communication yearbook 20* (pp. 185–225). Beverly Hills, CA: Sage.

Roskos-Ewoldsen, D. R., & Fazio, R. H. (1992). The accessibility of source likability as a determinant of persuasion. *Personality and Social Psychology Bulletin, 18*, 19–25.

Roskos-Ewoldsen, D. R., Bichsel, J., & Hoffman, K. (2002). The influence of accessibility of source likability on persuasion. *Journal of Experimental Social Psychology, 38*, 137–143.

Roskos-Ewoldsen, D., Yu, H. J., & Rhodes, N. (2004). Fear appeal messages effect accessibility of attitudes toward the threat and adaptive behaviors. *Communication Monographs, 71*, 49–69.

Schaffner, P. E., Wandersman, A., & Stang, D. (1981). Candidate name exposure and voting: Two field studies. *Basic and Applied Social Psychology, 2*, 195–203.

Schimmack, U., & Crites, S. L., Jr. (2005). The structure of affect. In D. Albarracin, B. T. Johnson, & M. P. Zanna (Eds.), *The handbook of attitudes* (pp. 397–435). New York: Psychology Press.

Schuette, R. A., & Fazio, R. H. (1995). Attitude accessibility and motivation as determinants of biased processing: A test of the MODE model. *Personality and Social Psychology Bulletin, 21*, 704–710.

Shavitt, S. (1990). The role of attitude objects in attitude functions. *Journal of Experimental Social Psychology, 26*, 124–148.

Sherif, C. W., Sherif, M., & Nebergall, G. (1965). *Attitude and attitude change: The social judgment-involvement approach.* Philadelphia, PA: Saunders.

Sherif, M., & Hovland, C. I. (1961). *Social judgment: Assimilation and contrast effects in communication and attitude change.* New Haven, CT: Yale University Press.

Sherman, S. J. (1980). On the self-erasing nature of errors of prediction. *Journal of Personality & Social Psychology, 39*, 211–221.

Sherman, S. J., & Gorkin, L. (1980). Attitude bolstering when behavior is inconsistent with central attitudes. *Journal of Experimental Social Psychology, 16*, 388–403.

Smith, M. B., Bruner, J. S., & White, R. W. (1956). *Opinions and personality.* New York: Wiley.

Snyder, M., & DeBono, K. G. (1985). Appeals to image and claims about quality: Understanding the psychology of advertising. *Journal of Personality and Social Psychology, 49*, 586–597.

Spangenberg, E. R., Sprott, D. E., Grohmann, B., & Smith, R. J. (2003). Mass-communicated prediction requests: Practical application and a cognitive dissonance explanation for self-prophecy. *Journal of Marketing, 67*, 47–62.

Staats, A. W., & Staats, C. K. (1958). Attitudes established by classical conditioning. *Journal of Abnormal and Social Psychology, 57*, 37–40.

Staats, A. W., Staats, C. K., & Crawford, H. L. (1962). First-order conditioning of meaning and the parallel conditioning of a GSR. *Journal of General Psychology, 67*, 159–167.

Stiff, J. B. (1986). Cognitive processing of persuasive message cues: A meta-analytic review of the effects of supporting information on attitudes. *Communication Monographs, 53*, 75–89.

Stiff, J. B., & Boster, F. J. (1987). Cognitive processing: Additional thoughts and a reply to Petty, Kasmer, Haugtvedt, and Cacioppo. *Communication Monographs, 54*, 250–256.

Stone, J., Aronson, E., Crain, A. L., Winslow, M. P., & Fried, C. B. (1994). Inducing hypocrisy as a means of encouraging young adults to use condoms. *Personality and Social Psychology Bulletin, 20*, 116–128.

Tesser, A. (1993). The importance of heritability in psychological research: The case of attitudes. *Psychological Review, 100*, 129–142.

Till, B. D., Stanley, S. M., & Priluck, R. (2008). Classical conditioning and celebrity endorsers: An examination of belongingness and resistance to extinction. *Psychology & Marketing, 25*, 179–196.

Walther, E., & Langer, T. I. N. A. (2010). For whom Pavlov's bell tolls: Processes underlying evaluative conditioning. In G. R. Maio & G. Haddock (Eds.), *The psychology of attitudes and attitude change* (pp. 59–74). London: Sage.

Wang, X. (2012). The role of attitude functions and self-monitoring in predicting intentions to register as organ donors and to discuss organ donation with family. *Communication Research, 39*, 26–47.

Watts, W. A., & McGuire, W. J. (1964). Persistence of induced opinion change and retention of the inducing message contents. *Journal of Abnormal and Social Psychology, 68*, 233–241.

Wilcox, K., & Laird, J. D. (2000). The impact of media images of super-slender women on women's self-esteem: Identification, social comparison, and self-perception. *Journal of Research in Personality, 34*, 278–286.

Winkielman, P., Schwarz, N., Fazendeiro, T., & Reber, R. (2003). The hedonic marking of processing fluency: Implications for evaluative judgment. In J. Musch & K. C. Klauer (Eds.), *The psychology of evaluation: Affective processes in cognition and emotion* (pp. 189–217). Mahwah, NJ: Lawrence Erlbaum Associates.

Yee, N., & Bailenson, J. (2007). The Proteus effect: The effect of transformed self-representation on behavior. *Human Communication Research, 33*, 271–290.

Yee, N., Bailenson, J., & Ducheneaut, N. (2009). The Proteus effect: Implications of transformed digital self-representation on online and offline behavior. *Communication Research, 36*, 285–312.

Zajonc, R. B. (1968). Attitudinal effects of mere exposure. *Journal of Personality and Social Psychology, 9*, 1–27.

Zajonc, R. B., & Rajecki, D. W. (1969). Exposure and affect: A field experiment. *Psychonomic Science, 17*, 216–217.

Zanna, M. P., Kiesler, C. A., & Pilkonis, P. A. (1970). Positive and negative attitudinal affect established by classical conditioning. *Journal of Personality & Social Psychology, 14*, 321–328.

13

POLITICAL COMMUNICATION

Much research about media that appeared after World War I has been interpreted as arguing for the "hypodermic needle" model of the media (see Chapter 3). This theory is often presented as maintaining that the media are an all-powerful entity that injects messages into people, and these messages then drive how people think and behave. Many of these writings were influenced by the propaganda efforts of both the U.S. government and the other governments that were involved in World War I. However, it is important to note that while the hypodermic needle model seems far-fetched to people today, the model did reflect the intellectual climate at the time. In the earlier part of the twentieth century, social scientific theories of human behavior reflected rather pessimistic images of people (Coleman & Ross, 2010). For example, Freud's writings promoted a view of people as being subject to the unconscious influences of the id. Likewise, behavioristic theories popular in the United States at that time argued that human behavior was strongly determined by the reward contingencies associated with stimuli external to the person. Finally, it is important to note that most of the writers who are credited with helping create the hypodermic needle model never explicitly argued for the model (Lubken, 2008).

As discussed in Chapter 3, there were examples from the early part of the twentieth century that could be interpreted as evidence that the media could have a strong influence on people's thoughts and behavior. The propaganda efforts of the U.S. government leading up to World War I were credited with playing an important role for the United States' involvement in that war (Glander, 2009; Rogers, 1994). Likewise, the Mercury Theatre's broadcast of *The War of the Worlds* provided evidence of a powerful media (Cantril et al., 1940). Perhaps more than one-fourth of the six million people who heard the broadcast believed that the

United States was being invaded either by Martians, Germans, or the Japanese (Cantril et al., 1940). However, research soon suggested a completely different version of the media, particularly of political communication.

Two-Step Flow Model and the Limited Effects Era

Against the backdrop of the "hypodermic needle" models of the media, Lazarsfeld et al. (1944) set out to study the influence of the media on presidential elections in an ambitious project during the 1940 presidential campaign between Franklin Delano Roosevelt and John Wilkee. The study was conducted in Erie County, Ohio, because its voting patterns had closely matched voting patterns for the country in previous presidential elections. The study was one of the early uses of a panel design, which meant that the same participants were interviewed seven times across the election cycle. The original study was expanded by Katz and Lazarsfeld (1955) in a study conducted in Decatur, Illinois. The Decatur study attempted to answer the questions raised by the original Erie County study as well as to expand beyond the domain of elections to more general political opinions and day-to-day choices.

Lazarsfeld et al. (1944) characterized their findings as demonstrating three general effects of the mass media on presidential campaigns. First, Lazarsfeld et al. (1944) interpreted their data as suggesting that many of the participants in their study had made up their minds once the candidates were officially nominated at each party's convention, and the media had no effect other than to motivate these voters to actually vote. Thus, the media *activated* those partisans to become committed voters. Second, the media *reinforced* the voting intentions of those partisans who were already committed to a candidate at the beginning of the campaign. Approximately half of people had made up their minds who they were going to vote for prior to the campaign really starting (campaigns starting more than 6 or 7 months prior to the election is a more recent phenomenon in the United States). This reinforcement function of the media on viewers' attitudes and behaviors remains understudied (Holbert, 2005). Finally, the media converted the voting preferences of less than 10 percent of voters (Lazarsfeld et al., 1944). These findings were surprising given the zeitgeist that the media had direct effects on people. Instead, people had made up their minds earlier than the start of the campaign, with the consequence that media campaigns only directly influenced a small subset of the electorate. Of course, these findings are in direct contradiction to the hypodermic needle model and suggest rather limited effects of the media.[1]

But perhaps most importantly, the study suggested that when people were undecided—those people who could be influenced by the media—they were indirectly influenced by the media via opinion leaders (Katz & Lazarsfeld, 1955; Lazarsfeld et al., 1944). When asked about their sources of political information, undecided voters reported that interpersonal conversations with other people were their most prevalent source of information about the two political candidates.

Likewise, these undecided voters also reported after the campaign that these political discussions were the most important influence on their final voting decisions. But who did these undecided voters talk to about the campaign? While the data from this original study were not conclusive, Lazarsfeld et al. (1944) discovered that there were people—whom they labeled as *opinion leaders*—who were highly interested in the campaign and were already firmly committed to one of the candidates—and who paid substantially more attention to the coverage of the campaign than the rest of the electorate. Lazarsfeld et al. (1944) hypothesized that it was these opinion leaders who were most likely to influence undecided voters. Katz and Lazarsfeld (1955) provided clear evidence of the role of opinion leaders as mediators of the media's influence in their follow-up study in Decatur, Illinois, where they studied women's everyday choices such as product purchases as well as their political opinions.

Thus, the two-step model of media influence hypothesizes that the media influences opinion leaders primarily by providing them information about the campaign, and these opinion leaders then influence other people through interpersonal channels of communication. Thus, the influence of the media is mediated by these opinion leaders and their political discussions with other people within their social network. Lazarsfeld et al. (1944) hypothesized that these interpersonal discussions had greater influence on undecided voters than the media, for several reasons. For example, people are often critical of media stories about political candidates, but they are less likely to be critical when talking with an opinion leader, particularly if they trust the opinion leader. Likewise, when opinion leaders talk with undecided voters, opinion leaders can immediately adapt what they are saying. In addition, Katz and Lazarsfeld (1955) argued that norms played a critical role in this process as well. Opinion leaders—as respected individuals within their social network—could exert normative pressure on people. Besides these explanations provided by Lazarsfeld et al. (1944), later research also suggested that opinion leaders influence how the media messages are interpreted by the people who look to that opinion leader for guidance (Hornik, 2006). These advantages of interpersonal communication as a source of social influence have been demonstrated in numerous studies (Rogers, 2003). More recent research has implicated the Internet in the two-step flow of information as well (Bennett & Manheim, 2006; Norris & Curtice, 2008). The argument can be advanced that the Internet should decrease the power of opinion leaders because people have more direct access to more personalized information. Targeting of political messages combined with the greater personalization of those messages could easily undermine opinion leaders and increase the fragmentation of the public when it comes to political issues (Bennett & Manheim, 2006). However, research suggests this is not a particularly prevalent behavior. Instead, initial research on British elections indicates that like newspapers and radio in the original Erie County study, opinion leaders do turn to the Internet for information and they do continue to influence others via interpersonal channels (Norris & Curtice, 2008).

The two-step flow model and the subsequent research on opinion leaders has had an important influence on both the study of political communication and the broader discipline. The study of opinion leaders played a major role in the development of the diffusion of innovations model, which will be discussed in the chapter on health communication (Chapter 15). Likewise, research on the interrelationship between the media and interpersonal communication supports the role of interpersonal communication in the transmission of media messages across the population (Southwell & Yzer, 2007). This research has also suggested new ways in which interpersonal communication can augment the influence of media campaigns, such as agenda setting (see later in this chapter) or by increasing people's resistance to counterattitudinal messages (Southwell & Yzer, 2009).

Not so Limited Effects Models

The limited effects models of the media were the consequence of the research emerging at the time of World War II and shortly thereafter, including research by Lazarsfeld et al. (1944) (Delia, 1987; Glander, 2009). Until the 1970s, political communication was felt to have little impact on how people voted or on their political opinions (Delia, 1987). However, a reaction to the limited effects model emerged in the 1970s. Specifically, three phenomena emerged from research on political communication suggesting that the media do have some, albeit limited, effects: agenda setting, political priming, and framing. These three areas have emerged as dominant research domains within political communication during the past three decades (Benoit & Holbert, 2010). The next section of this chapter will focus on these three phenomena and theoretical models that have emerged to explain them.

Agenda Setting

Lippmann (1922) argued that the media help shape the "pseudo-environment" that exists inside people's heads based on what stories are featured in the media. Lippmann argued that this was particularly true when the media covered events where readers had no personal experience of what was going on. His now-classic example involved people from Europe living on a fairly remote island in the south Atlantic who were not aware that World War I had started. Then, about 6 weeks after the outbreak of hostilities, a ship arrived with newspapers reporting the beginning of the war. The arrival of the ship changed the inhabitants' world, because with the arrival of the ship their world changed from one of peaceful coexistence to a situation where their home countries were at war with one another. So the arrival of the newspapers changed what these people thought were the important events that were going on around them. Consistent with Lippmann's idea, McCombs and Shaw (1972) demonstrated in a now-classic study of the 1968 presidential election that the media do influence what issues people judge to be most important. In other words, the media could influence the public's agenda. The idea that the media can shape what issues we think about, or what issues we think are important, is referred to as agenda setting (Iyengar & Kinder, 1987; McCombs, 2014; McCombs & Reynolds, 2009).

When the media set the agenda, they do not influence what people think; rather, the media coverage influences what people think about (Cohen, 1963). In what is now a classic demonstration of the media setting the public's agenda, the U.S. public's concern about the drug problem steadily increased during the late 1980s. In November of 1985, no respondents to a national political survey listed drugs as the number one problem facing the United States. However, four years later and after extensive coverage of the drug problem by the media, over 50 percent of the respondents listed drugs as the number one problem in the United States (Dearing & Rogers, 1996). Interestingly, objective measures of the drug problem suggested that, if anything, the drug problem was decreasing during this time period (Gozenbach, 1996). The media certainly played a role with this increased public concern about illegal drugs; in fact, several studies found evidence suggesting that the news media's extensive coverage on drugs in the mid to late 1980s raised public concerns about drug issues (Dearing & Rogers, 1996; Gozenbach, 1996). Several hundred studies conducted in countries around the world have demonstrated that the media can set the public's agenda (Dearing & Rogers, 1996; Iyengar & Kinder, 1987; McCombs, 2014; McCombs & Reynolds, 2009). Furthermore, media coverage of an issue can result in the public becoming more concerned about the issue even when real-world indicators of the problem may suggest that the problem is going away (Gozenbach, 1996). Indeed, a common finding is that the public's agenda is often divorced from real-world indicators of the seriousness of issues the public judges as important (McCombs, 2014). Critically, the same stories tend to be reinforced across diverse media outlets, making the agenda-setting outcome even stronger.

When discussing agenda setting, it is important to keep in mind that there are really three agendas that are important (Dearing & Rogers, 1996). The *public agenda* involves the issues that the public thinks are important. The *policy agenda* involves the issues that government officials and policy makers think are important. The *media agenda* involves the issues that the media are covering extensively. Research suggests that oftentimes the media set the public's agenda and the public then influences the policy agenda (Dearing & Rogers, 1996). In Dearing and Rogers' model, the media agenda sets the public agenda, but also directly influences the policy agenda. In addition, the public's agenda does influence the policy agenda, as policy makers respond to the electorates' concerns. Furthermore, what is actually occurring in the world influences all three agendas, as do people's personal experience, though research suggests that the influence of real-world events is often weak or nonexistent. Factors that influence the media's agenda will be discussed later in the chapter.

The primary theoretical mechanism that has been used to explain media's influence on the public's agenda is the finding that extensive coverage of an issue increases the psychological salience of the issue among audiences (Iyengar & Ottati, 1994; McCombs, 2014). This model draws from research in psychology suggesting that people are cognitive misers (Simon, 1957). The cognitive misers' perspective maintains that unless people are highly motivated when making a decision, they will rely on heuristics or simple rules-of-thumb. One heuristic that people use is the availability heuristic (Tversky & Kahneman, 1974, 1982). The availability heuristic suggests that people make judgments based on how easy it is to recall instances of something from memory. Of course, information that is more salient is also more memorable, so it is more likely to be recalled when people are trying to make a decision and to influence the decision they make. The availability heuristic is closely tied to work that has been discussed in other chapters on the accessibility of concepts or attitudes (see Chapters 8 and 12). As the accessibility of information increases, it will be more available in memory and more likely to influence the decisions that people make (Fazio, 1986).

The salience explanation of agenda setting rests on the assumption that media coverage of an issue makes it more available or accessible in memory (Iyengar & Ottati, 1994; McCombs, 2014). But how do the media make issues more salient? When people read the paper and the front-page headlines report a drought in a distant country, that will make the issue more salient (Dearing & Rogers, 1996; McCombs, 2014). If the media include graphic pictures of starving children, that will also increase the salience of the issue, because graphic images influence salience. Likewise, if all of the media are covering the same issue, thus increasing the likelihood that you will see multiple stories about the issue, this will also increase its salience. Also, if the media continue to cover the issue across weeks or even months, that will increase the salience of the issue. So there are a lot of different ways the media can increase the salience of an issue, including placement of the story, use of images, frequency and duration of coverage, and the number of media outlets covering the story. However, one of the difficulties with a salience explanation of agenda-setting effects is that "salience" is a tricky concept to define and more work is necessary to understand exactly what salience "is" (Weaver, 2014). Furthermore, research testing the role of salience and accessibility as predictors of agenda setting has provided mixed support for the role of salience (McCombs & Stroud, 2014).

While there are many impressive examples of how the media set the public's agenda, it is important to understand that the media do not always set the agenda. One factor that influences the media's role in setting agendas involves need for orientation (McCombs & Reynolds, 2009; McCombs & Stroud, 2014). People have a high need for orientation when an issue is personally important to them, but they want more information about the issue prior to making a decision. In this situation, the media are more likely to influence the public's agenda. While need for orientation can be conceptualized as an individual difference variable, because some people chronically have a higher need for orientation, situational factors can also influence need for orientation. As predicted by dependency theory (Ball-Rokeach & Jung, 2009), in crisis situations people's need for orientation will be higher because of the need for more information. In addition, research has demonstrated that the media are not likely to set the agenda for local issues because the issue likely impacts people directly (Behr & Iyengar, 1985).

A final issue to consider is how the Internet is influencing the agenda-setting function of the media, a topic that will be considered in greater depth in Chapter 14. Recall that much of the research supporting the agenda-setting function of the media was conducted in the latter half of the twentieth century when television and newspapers were the primary sources of information (McCombs, 2014). Today, however, surveys typically indicate that more and more people rely on the Internet for their political news (McCombs & Stroud, 2014). A critical question concerns whether people's greater ability to select what news to consume on the Internet undermines the ability of the media itself to set the agenda. In the case of many online sources, audience-clicking behavior, and not editorial decisions, determines the prominence of certain news stories. Indeed, what is given attention and what is not is determined by audiences, and not opinion leaders such as editors. Thus, contrary to traditional agenda-setting theory, where media set the agenda, at least in the case of online news sources, the public may set the agenda. However, traditional news sources may influence what audiences find click-worthy, because perhaps these are the stories they heard people talking about, heard mentioned on the radio, or simply saw in a newspaper headline while in line at the grocery store. In any case, it is likely that some combination of online behavior and traditional news outlets sets the agenda (see Chapter 14).

Political Priming

Political priming is the idea that the issues that the media are covering influence the information that people use to judge the president or other political issues (Iyengar & Kinder, 1987; Roskos-Ewoldsen & Roskos-Ewoldsen, 2009; Roskos-Ewoldsen et al., 2009). When judging how well the president is doing his or her job, people have a lot of different pieces of information they can use to make that judgment. For example, they could use the president's performance on the economy, civil rights, international affairs, the environment, or how well he or she dresses. The idea behind political priming is that the media influence what information people use to make these judgments. If the media are focusing primarily on environmental issues, environmental issues are made salient, and people will weigh their impressions of how well the president is doing overall based mostly on how well the president is doing with environmental issues. However, if the media are focusing on domestic economic issues, domestic economic issues are made salient and people will weigh their impressions of how well the president is doing overall based mostly on his or her performance on domestic economic issues more than other issues. During President George H. W. Bush's presidency (1988–1992), the media focused on the Gulf War and its success, and President Bush enjoyed very high approval ratings. But with the conclusion of the Gulf War, the media began covering the economy. Consequently, people started using their negative evaluations of President Bush's handling of the economy to judge his overall performance. Accordingly, President Bush's job performance ratings plummeted, despite the fact that people still thought he did a good job handling international affairs. But the ratings plummeted because they were using their salient evaluations of President Bush's poor handling of the economy when judging his overall performance (Iyengar & Simon, 1993).

The distinction between political priming and persuasion is important. In political priming, the emphasis is on how the media influence what information is *salient* when people make judgments. Conversely, persuasion involves changing people's evaluations of the information or of the candidate. Returning to the example of the first President Bush, persuasion would focus on changing people's evaluation of how well President Bush handled international affairs as a way to change their evaluation of his job performance. Conversely, as already discussed, political priming focuses on changing what information is *used or how that information is weighted* when making evaluations of the president's job performance. The existence of political priming has been well established (Roskos-Ewoldsen et al., 2007).

Early theorizing on political priming used the availability heuristic to explain the effects of media coverage on political priming (Iyengar & Simon, 1993). Initially, some scholars argued that priming is really just an extension of agenda setting (Iyengar & Kinder, 1987; McCombs, 2014). Consistent with the availability heuristic explanation of agenda setting, media coverage of an issue was hypothesized to influence which examples of current issues were accessed from memory when people made judgments of the president. Heavy coverage of an issue should result in more examples of that issue being stored in memory and those examples being more accessible from memory. Consequently, given the greater number of exemplars of an issue to recall from memory and the relative accessibility of those exemplars from memory, these exemplars should be brought to mind when evaluating the president. However, the availability explanation has not been well developed or subjected to empirical tests within the political priming domain (Roskos-Ewoldsen et al., 2009).

Price and Tewksbury's (1997) applicability model has been developed sufficiently to explain political priming (Scheufele & Tewksbury, 2007). Price and Tewksbury's (1997) model is based on network models of memory and the role that the media play in increasing the accessibility of information within these memory networks. Network models of memory assume that memory consists of a series of nodes and each node corresponds to a unique concept (e.g., President Obama or climate change). Associative pathways (or links) are formed between nodes that are related in some way (e.g., "President Obama" and "climate change"). Each node is hypothesized to have an activation threshold, and if the activation of the node exceeds the activation threshold, the node fires, which then spreads from that node along the associative pathways to other nodes. Priming operates within network models of memory by temporarily increasing the activation level (or accessibility) of a node. Chronic accessibility occurs when the activation threshold for a node is such that the threshold is reached very easily. Network models maintain that both chronic and temporary accessibility of concepts influence their likelihood of activation. In addition, Price and Tewksbury (1997) incorporate the notion of *applicability* of information into their model. Applicability refers to deliberate judgments of the relevance of information to the current situation. This component of the model will be discussed in greater detail in the section on framing effects. Within Price and Tewksbury's model, concepts that are activated by the media, either because they are chronically accessible or because they have been primed, influence how the message is perceived or interpreted.[2]

However, there is a problem for network models of memory as an explanation for political priming. Specifically, it is unclear what the time-course of political priming effects is. In other words, neither theorists nor empirical tests of the model have determined conclusively a time frame in which priming would or would not occur. Network models of memory generally maintain that priming effects are very short-lived. Yet, early research on political priming suggested that these priming effects could last weeks or even months (Roskos–Ewoldsen et al., 2007), which is much longer than predicted by network models of memory or that are found in the types of tasks that are used in research on media priming of violence or stereotypes (see Roskos–Ewoldsen et al., 2009). Consistent with the research from cognitive and social psychology, Carpentier et al. (2008) found that the effect of a news column about a political figure on judgments of that political figure faded within 30 minutes after exposure. Likewise, Althaus and Kim (2006) demonstrated that media coverage of the Gulf War impacted opinions for hours afterwards. However, these effects seemed to dissipate within 24 hours of the media exposure. On the other hand, contrary to the research in cognitive and social psychology and network models of memory, a meta-analysis of the political priming literature found effects of exposure that last for several weeks (Roskos–Ewoldsen et al., 2007).

Price and Tewksbury's (1997) network model can explain these long-term priming effects by assuming that continued media coverage makes the concepts chronically accessible as opposed to temporarily primed. When a concept is chronically accessible, the accessibility of the construct fades much more slowly (across weeks) and only if the concept is not reactivated. This makes sense, because frequent activation of a concept can make that concept chronically accessible, but the accessibility of the concept will diminish if it stops being activated, as would occur when the media stop covering an issue. This happened when the media stopped covering President Bush's performance related to the first Iraq

War (Roskos-Ewoldsen et al., 2009). However, whether long-term coverage creates chronically accessible concepts has not been demonstrated empirically, only suggested theoretically.

Despite the ambiguities involving the time-course of political priming, a rich outgrowth of research on political priming has recently occurred along several fronts, the first of which is whether different genres of media can produce political priming effects. For example, research has demonstrated that movies (Holbert & Hansen, 2006), crime dramas (Holbrook & Hill, 2005), and late-night talk shows (Moy et al., 2005) can operate as political primes for judgments of the president's performance. Further, simpler or familiar topics (such as general economic trends or issues of character) were more likely to prime evaluations of the president than more complex issues (such as domestic or international policies). There is also a growing focus on the types of information that are primed by news coverage (Kim, 2005; Kim et al., 2002; McCombs, 2014). Political priming has generally been presented as a "hydraulic model" where the media prime people to use certain information at the expense of competing information. In a study of political priming resulting from coverage of the first Gulf War, Kim (2005) found that news coverage did not narrow the types of information used in the judgment as predicted by the hydraulic model. Rather, Kim found that news coverage primed an increase in the variety of information that was used by people who pay careful attention to the media. While political priming is a well-established phenomenon, there is much research and theorizing that needs to be done in this area.

Framing

There are many different angles that a reporter can take for a story. *Framing* refers to how the story is presented or its angle (Entman, 2004; Iyengar, 1991). Another way to think about framing is what information is emphasized and made salient within a story and what information is de-emphasized or excluded from the story (Weaver et al., 2004). Unfortunately, there is no clear consensus on how to define framing (Kinder, 2007; Scheufele & Nisbet, 2008). However, there is consensus that how a story is framed is important, because the story's frame will make certain aspects of the story salient while other elements are de-emphasized, and consequently, this should influence how the story is understood. Furthermore, the story's frame can moderate or mitigate the effects of that story (Iyengar, 1991; Entman, 2004; Scheufele & Tewksbury, 2007). There has been extensive research on media framing, and this area of research has steadily grown over the past 25 years (Weaver, 2007). Unfortunately, the literature on framing is fractured, because framing research has foundations in both psychology and sociology, yet these two disciplines historically have taken distinct approaches to studying framing (Maher, 2001; Scheufele & Nisbet, 2008; Shah et al., 2009; Tewksbury & Scheufele, 2009). Because of this history, there are conceptual ambiguities as to exactly what constitutes framing and ultimately how frames influence audiences.

Despite these ambiguities, research has established that framing can have profound effects on people's interpretation of and memory for a story and very powerful effects on people's judgments regarding the issues covered in the story (Iyengar, 1991; Kahneman & Tversky, 1984; Shah et al., 2009). For example, research suggests that how political stories are framed contributes to the growing mistrust of the government (Cappella & Jamieson, 1997). An *issue frame* of a political story focuses on the background of the issues, what issues are important, and the pros and cons involved with the issue. Imagine a story about the role of U.S. combat advisors in a country that is currently at war. A story with an issue frame might include the history of similar situations where the United States had placed military advisors in a combat situation and the impact of this action on U.S. foreign policy.

On the other hand, a strategy frame focuses on politicians' motivations for the positions they are taking. For example, a story on the military advisors with a strategy frame might argue that a certain prominent politician opposes the U.S. placement of military advisors on the ground because it will take news coverage away from how poorly the other political party is doing. Because of this *strategy* frame's focus on the motivations of the politician's support for or opposition to a given policy, strategy frames tend to make the politician look self-interested and not particularly concerned about the greater good of the country. Consequently, strategy frames have been found to increase voter cynicism, whether the strategy frame focused on an issue or a political candidate (Cappella & Jamieson, 1997). Because most strategy frames often focus on the negative motivations of politicians, these frames reinforce the public's perceptions that politicians are only out for their own good.

While there are a number of theories of framing, there are three prominent theories of framing that we will discuss: prospect theory, Price and Tewksbury's applicability model, and second-level agenda-setting theory. Theories of how different frames emerge in the media will be discussed later in the chapter.

Kahneman and Tversky's prospect theory draws heavily from research on the psychology of choice under uncertainty (Kahneman & Tversky, 1979; Tversky & Kahneman, 1992; Wakker, 2010). Prospect theory starts with the assumption that when making a choice, people compare the choice to a reference point. Assume you are going to lose $100,000 in the next year. However, something happens so that this amount is cut in half. If your reference point is your current wealth, then you are still losing $50,000. However, if your reference point is your wealth after you had lost the $100,000, then you are gaining $50,000. If the reference point changes, people's choices will also change. At a very basic level, the reference point can influence whether a choice is perceived as involving gains (gaining $50,000) or losses (losing $50,000). Research on choice under uncertainty has consistently shown that people are risk-averse when dealing with gains, but risk seeking when focused on losses. Thus, if the decision is framed positively (gaining $50,000), people are more likely to be risk-averse and make a less risky choice. Conversely, if the same information is framed negatively (still losing $50,000), people are more likely to be risk seeking and make a riskier choice. This reversal in people's preferences has received widespread support. Scholars who study political framing argue that prospect theory is not relevant to political framing because research on political frames is not interested in people's choices, but rather how they evaluate what they are reading about. However, prospect theory has received support in research on the framing of health issues (Rothman et al., 2006; Rothman & Salovey, 1997; Salovey et al., 2002).

A second theory that has been proposed is Price and Tewksbury's (1997) applicability model (Scheufele & Tewksbury, 2007; Tewksbury & Scheufele, 2009). Applicability involves the degree to which the frame of a story maps onto that story. If a frame is applicable, then readers will accept the frame, the frame will tie together the information presented within the story, and this information will be stored with the issue in memory. For example, a history of racism frame should be judged as applicable for a story about a group of high school students hanging nooses from a tree after black students had gathered there, an incident that actually occurred in the fall of 2014 in California (www.ktla.com/2014/10/16/noose-found-hanging-from-tree-at-mayfair-high-school-in-lakwood). Consequently, this linkage will influence how people understand and remember the larger issue (hanging the nooses was meant as a racist act with the goal of intimidation). If people do not accept the applicability of the frame (a story about a racist act at a high school and a frame of adolescent pranks), then the frame will be rejected, the linkages between the information within the story (prank and hanging nooses) will not be formed, and the frame will not influence people's judgments of the issue. The critical issue for the applicability model is the fit between the frame and the issue (Price & Tewksbury, 1997; Scheufele & Tewksbury, 2007), with greater fit generally leading to greater acceptance of the frame and stronger framing effects.

Finally, some scholars have advanced the idea that agenda setting and framing are essentially the same phenomenon and that agenda setting can explain framing effects in what is referred to as second-level agenda setting (McCombs, 2014; c.f. Scheufele & Tewksbury, 2007; Weaver, 2007). Second-level agenda setting involves the role of the media in making certain attributes of issues or people more salient because those attributes are made more salient by the way the media cover the issue (see earlier section on agenda setting). Obviously, one way in which the media would make certain attributes more salient is through the particular framing of the story. Different frames will make different attributes of the issue more salient and hence those salient attributes are more likely to be considered when people are making judgments about that issue. In other works, second-level agenda setting goes beyond the original conception of agenda setting as simply influencing what people think is important to influencing how people *interpret* the issues or people that are covered, and it does this specifically by changing what attributes are considered when forming judgments

(McCombs, 2014; Scheufele, 1999).[3] According to this explanation, framing effects are a consequence of the frames that are presented most often in the media, making certain attributes of that issue (or person) more salient or accessible in memory, and these accessible attributes will influence people's evaluation of the issue.

The Content of Political News Coverage

Up to this point, this chapter has primarily focused on the impact of political news coverage on people's evaluation of political issues and candidates. However, an equally important question that has been alluded to several times in this chapter involves what factors influence what appears in the media. There are myriad stories that are not covered by the media (Shoemaker & Vos, 2009). So why do some stories get covered and others not? While these issues have not been studied as extensively as the impact of news coverage, numerous theories exist concerning what issues get covered by the media, including research on gatekeeping, agenda building, and framing. Gatekeeping focuses on whether a specific story is published or not. Agenda building focuses on the broader question of what topics are going to appear in print. Finally, the work on framing involves the slant that the story will take when published.

Gatekeeping

The oldest research tradition on the content of the news involves gatekeeping. The metaphor of a gatekeeper derives from Lewin's (1951) work on group dynamics. Lewin used the analogy of the meals that are served to a family. Obviously, there are myriad different types of foods available for the family, and the family likely has foods that it likes and foods that it dislikes. But the person(s) who does the gardening, shopping, and food preparation determines what food is served. Lewin used the metaphor of a gate through which this person brings the food to the family. If the food does not pass through the gate, it will not make it to the table. Likewise, Lewin's metaphor was used to represent the idea that there are people who make decisions as to what information makes it through the "gate" and actually appears in the media. The earliest research on gatekeeping involved a study of "Mr. Gate"—a newspaper editor for a newspaper in Iowa (White, 1950). White (1950) concluded that Mr. Gate served as the primary gatekeeper for the wire stories that were published in his newspaper, and his selection of stories reflected his judgment of the journalistic merits of a story and his implicit theories of what his readers would find interesting.

Since this original research—with its focus on the individual—numerous studies and theories of gatekeeping have been proposed. Most of these models have focused on the linear flow of the story, from the original event to the journalist through the various editors and ultimate publication or rejection of a story (Gieber, 1956; White, 1950). Much of the early research revolved around debates on who or what was most responsible for story selection. Some scholars argued that the individual editor(s) were most responsible, so that gatekeeping fell more within the domain of psychology (McNelly, 1959). Conversely, other scholars argued that the constraints of the journalistic system ultimately played a much larger role, so that gatekeeping fell more within the domain of sociology (Bass, 1969; Gieber, 1956).

However, the most complete and probably most influential model is Shoemaker and Vos's (2009) model, which draws heavily from Lewin's original field theory. This model is a descriptive typology of five primary levels of influence on what stories ultimately get published. So the model has moved from an active "agent" (e.g., the editor) to focus more on the multiple processes—both psychological and sociological—that influence the gatekeeping process. The five levels are the individual, communication routines, the organizational level, social institutional level, and the social system level. While a complete explication of the model is beyond the scope of this chapter, the basics of the five levels will be discussed.

The first level—the individual communication worker—focuses on the psychological aspects of people working within the media that influence the processes involved in news selection. Shoemaker and Vos (2009) move away from the earlier focus on whether bias influences content to focus more on the psychological processes that influence decision making and the type of decision-making criteria that are used. Some models argue that gatekeepers rely on their gut instincts when making a decision, which may reflect the role of time pressure and the use of heuristics in making newsworthiness judgments. Other models suggest a more reasoned approach, such as weighing the various risks involved with publishing a story (a risk-based model). Shoemaker and Vos's typological model also acknowledges the role of personality, individual values, and gatekeepers' understanding of their professional roles as important influences on the gatekeeping process at this level.

The second level involves communication routines (Shoemaker & Vos, 2009). Communication routines involve standard processes or patterns of behavior that have developed within a news organization for handling potential news stories (Cassidy, 2006; Shoemaker et al., 2001). In some ways, routines can operate as heuristics or rules-of-thumb that help ease decision making when people are under time pressure. Some of the standard routines that influence which stories get published within a news organization can include deadlines, judgments of newsworthiness, and news-gathering practices. Judgments of newsworthiness appear to be particularly important, because stories that are judged to be highly newsworthy get published despite the communication routines that are operating (Shoemaker et al., 2001).

The third level that influences gatekeeping within this model is the news organization. Characteristics of the organization, such as whether it is an independent or corporate-owned media outlet, influences the stories that are selected. When a newspaper is taken over by a chain, the extent of new coverage as well as the content of what is covered can change fairly substantially (McChesney, 1999). Gatekeeping is also influenced by the organization's culture, which can serve to chill the choice of stories that are selected or provide journalists with a great deal of latitude as to what stories to pursue. Likewise, whether the new organization's culture focuses on profits versus public interest can have a profound effect on the types of stories that appear in a media outlet (Mascaro, 2005).

Fourth is the social institutional level, which includes such things as advertisers, how the news outlet distributes its content (Donders & Evens, 2014), the audience (Lee et al., 2014), and the government and government regulations. For example, research has found that advertisers can have a substantial effect on the content that is ultimately published. One study found, for example, that women's magazines that took tobacco advertising dollars were less likely to cover the link between smoking and cancer (Kessler, 1989). Surveys of journalists for specialized magazines has found that over half of the journalists surveyed reported receiving pressure from advertisers to not publish unfavorable stories, and almost half of the journalists were aware of advertisers pulling advertisements in protest of stories that had been published in the magazines (Hays & Reisner, 1990, 1991).

Finally, the fifth level is the social system, which outlines how the larger culture and the ideologies of that culture can influence gatekeeping (Shoemaker & Vos, 2009). While there has not been extensive research on gatekeeping across different countries, certainly the legal structures within countries (Herman & Chomsky, 1988; Starr, 2004) and the implicit models of the media that have emerged in those countries influence what stories are likely to be published within a particular country (Akhavan-Majid & Wolf, 1991; Siebert et al., 1956; Yin, 2008). Likewise, ideological differences between countries can help explain what stories are likely to be featured in the news outlets in various countries (Shoemaker & Vos, 2009).

Of course, an important question that has emerged is whether the nature of gatekeeping is changing with the Internet (see Chapter 14). With people having more access to more and different news sources, does gatekeeping diminish in its importance? Some research suggests that gatekeeping diminishes in importance with new media, though gatekeepers have discovered subtler ways to influence what stories reach the public (Coddington & Holton, 2014). Research certainly indicates that gatekeepers are relying on different sources of information, but the basic information that is considered remains the same. For example, the fourth level of Shoemaker and Vos's (2009) model includes the media outlet's audience. Research indicates that news organizations use information from the web to learn more about their audience (Lee et al., 2014; Tandoc, 2014). This research submits that the Internet simply provides new avenues for obtaining information concerning the traditional influences on gatekeeping.

Models of Agenda Building

As discussed earlier in this chapter, research on agenda setting focuses on the influence of the media's agenda on what issues people think are important. Given the extensive research showing the impact of media agenda setting, an interesting question is what influences the media's agenda, or how is the media agenda built? Historically, this has been an understudied area of research that emerged much later than the original work on agenda setting (Dearing & Rogers, 1996).

One of the earliest models of agenda building was developed by Dearing and Rogers (1996). As they note in their model, obviously real-world events play a critical role in determining what the media's agenda is, but real-world indicators are hardly a sufficient explanation of what topics the media cover, as a number of case studies that were discussed earlier have demonstrated (Dearing & Rogers, 1996; Gozenbach, 1996). Within their model, Dearing and Rogers argue that the policy agenda influences the media agenda, as the media cover the issues that local, state, and national politicians address. In addition, intermedia agenda setting is another important source of agenda building. Research has consistently demonstrated that if particular highly respected media outlets such as the *New York Times* or the *Washington Post* cover an issue, then other media outlets will also publish stories on that issue (Bennett et al., 2006; Dearing & Rogers, 1996; Denham, 2014; Lim, 2011; McCombs, 2014).

Finally, professional journalistic values concerning what constitutes an important story influence agenda building, and research suggests that there is a consensus as to what constitutes important stories (McCombs, 2014). However, it is important to note that while there is a fairly strong relationship between various media outlets in what stories they cover, the particular wire story that is published about an event varies widely across media outlets, which suggests that agenda building and gatekeeping are two distinct, though related, processes (Stempel, 1985).

Framing

A highly related question to the one concerning what content gets covered by the media is the basic question of how that content is framed. As discussed earlier, how a story is framed can have important impacts on the public's understanding of and knowledge about an issue. So why are certain frames used by journalists and other frames not used? There are currently two dominant models that attempt to explain why journalists use the frames that they do: the indexing model and the cascading model.

The indexing model maintains that the media frame stories by reflecting the frames that government officials provide for an issue (Bennett, 1990). Bennett (1990) hypothesizes that this process of allowing government officials to dictate the frame for an issue has developed as a journalistic norm that emerged out of a history of granting government officials the benefit of the doubt as to how an issue should be framed by the news media. Consequently, journalists typically reflect the current administration's framing of an event and offer little or no counterframes to the administration's frame (c.f. Althaus, 2003).

There are several caveats to the theory. First, the theory only applies to the mainstream media. Obviously, alternative media are created, in part, out of a need to challenge the mainstream, so the indexing model applies primarily to the mainstream media and certainly does not apply consistently to various Internet sources such as blogs. However, the indexing model does predict that journalists will provide oppositional or counterframes when there is not a clear consensus on an issue among the political elite (Bennett, 1990; Bennett et al., 2006). For example, consistent with the indexing model, when pictures were leaked of torture by U.S. soldiers at the Abu Ghraib prison, the mainstream media followed President Bush's framing of the issue as a relatively isolated incident of "abuse" as opposed to presenting the oppositional frame of "torture" (Bennett et al., 2006). However, the media provided multiple frames of the civil wars in Central America during the Reagan administration when Congress challenged the administration's position on these wars. When Congress stopped challenging President Reagan's frame, the media likewise stopped featuring oppositional frames (Bennett, 1990). Similarly, there are some issues where alternative voices—and hence frames—will be acknowledged by the mainstream media, but these tend to be issues involving social protest. However, often these voices are covered, but the coverage will tend to discredit these alternative frames.

The second model concerning why certain frames are featured in the media is Entman's (2004) cascading model. The cascading model extends the indexing model in several ways. First, the cascading model uses the metaphor of spreading activation within a network to explain how frames spread (recall our discussion of spreading activation and network models earlier in this chapter and in Chapter 7). The cascading of a frame occurs because the frame will spread through a network across multiple levels. Frames start with the current administration, which can include important secretaries within the executive branch, such as the Secretary of Defense or State. The next level includes other elites, such as current and former members of Congress, experts, and foreign leaders (in the case of foreign affairs). Below the elites is the media, but as Entman (2004) argues, the distinction between top media personalities and the elites is blurry. In any case, the media include both news organizations and journalists. Of course, at the lowest level of the cascade is the public. There are two important considerations to remember with the cascading model. First, activation spreads across a network within levels as well as across levels. Intramedia influences are one example of how a frame can spread within a level as one media outlet influences how other media outlets are likely to frame a story. Likewise, the frames can spread within a level via interpersonal channels—though this is an understudied phenomenon. In addition, a frame can move from a lower level to a higher level within the cascade.

Critically, the cascading model also deals with how frames spread and with factors that influence the likelihood that counterframes will develop. Central to the model is the idea of cultural congruence. Each culture has beliefs, ideologies, myths, and schemas that dominate that culture (Shore, 1996; Strauss & Quinn, 1997). A frame has high cultural congruence the greater the overlap between the frame and the culture's beliefs or schema. If the White House develops a frame with high cultural congruence, there is a greater likelihood that the frame will dominate discussion of the issue (Rowling et al., 2011). However, as the degree of cultural congruence becomes lower, the more likely counterframes will emerge and challenge this frame. For example, the "torture" frame for Abu Ghraib would have difficulty gaining traction in the United States because it is incongruent with U.S. cultural beliefs concerning its soldiers, namely that the United States does not use torture. Other factors that influence how frames spread and the likelihood that counterframes will emerge include a variety of motivations. For example, as dual process models such as the elaboration likelihood model note, people do not expend a lot of cognitive energy processing messages unless highly motivated. Consequently, the default is for the administration's frame to dominate, because people will not be highly motivated to challenge it. Conversely, frames that are dissonant with people's beliefs will likely motivate people to develop counter-frames (Entman, 2004). Thus, within Entman's model, the frames that are adopted in the media reflect structural forces as well as cultural and psychological processes.

Conclusion

Political communication stretches back to almost a century ago with the early work on the use of propaganda in World War I. But perhaps the classic work in political communication was Lazarsfeld et al.'s (1944) study of the 1940 presidential election, which laid the foundation for the two-step flow model and the era of minimal effects, which dominated this area of research for a number of years. This chapter has covered a number of theories related to political communication that have arisen since that early work. Much of this work has reestablished that the media can and do have important influences on the political processes, and this research also helped to end the era of minimal effects. During the past 30 years, agenda setting, priming, and framing have dominated the research on political communication and helped reestablish the importance of studying the media in order to understand the political process (Benoit & Holbert, 2010). As our understanding of these areas has grown, new areas of research are starting to develop. Likewise, research has helped to address issues concerning why certain political topics are covered in the media. All of this research points to a complex dynamic relationship between the media, the political system, and the public.

Notes

1   In another demonstration of the limited impact of the media on political campaigns, Schramm and Carter (1959) studied the effectiveness of Republican Senator William Knowland's 20-hour telethon that attempted to salvage his campaign for governor of California (the telethon was held on October 31 and November 1, 1958). Schramm and Carter (1959) reported that the telethon was competently run. Consistent with Lazarsfeld et al.'s (1944) findings, their phone survey of 564 people living in San Francisco found that the majority of people who watched the telethon were already committed supporters of Knowland, so, at best, the campaign could only reinforce these viewers' attitudes and intentions to vote. Of the 563 people surveyed, only two reported that the telethon influenced who they intended to vote for in the upcoming election—one was convinced to vote for Knowland and one reported being convinced to vote against Knowland.

2   In an experimental test of the accessibility component of political priming, Miller and Krosnick (2000) manipulated media exposure to current issues (e.g., drugs and immigration). They gathered measures of participants' beliefs about the most important problems in the nation and approval of the current president's performance, and they found the basic priming effect. Participants who were exposed to the media coverage weighed those issues more heavily when judging the president's performance than those not exposed to the media coverage. To test whether the accessibility of these issues mediated this relationship, accessibility toward the issues was measured via a reaction-time procedure. Contrary to an accessibility explanation, those participants who were quicker at the reaction-time task did not weigh the accessible information more heavily than those who were slower. Thus, the researchers concluded that network models of spreading activation, which rely on the accessibility of concepts, could not be the direct cause of political priming. Rather, the researchers argued that when the concepts that are highly accessible are activated, the activation causes a second, deliberative process. However, Miller and Krosnick (2000) incorrectly interpret the role of deliberative processing as meaning that accessibility is not an important component of the political priming effect. Recent research on automaticity has demonstrated that automatic processing can lead to deliberative processing (Rhodes et al., 2008; Roskos-Ewoldsen et al., 2002; Roskos-Ewoldsen et al., 2004). Thus, the deliberative processing for which they found evidence may well be a consequence of increases in the accessibility of the constructs primed by the manipulated media coverage.

3   Research has demonstrated that attitudes can be changed by changing the accessibility of the attributes of the attitude object (Roskos-Ewoldsen & Fazio, 1997). This is particularly likely to be the case when people are forming attitudes or when they are motivated to reconsider their attitude. Because first-level agenda setting influences the perceived importance of an issue, this may serve as a catalyst for people to reconsider their attitudes toward the issue that is being covered. Consequently, changing the accessibility of various attributes of an issue may change people's attitudes toward the issue. However, Roskos-Ewoldsen and Fazio (1997) argue that this should only occur when people are forming an evaluation of a topic or are highly motivated to reconsider their evaluation. If people already have an evaluation of the topic, then accessible attributes are less likely to influence people's attitude because they will simply recall their already formed attitude (see Chapter 15).

References

Akhavan-Majid, R., & Wolf, G. (1991). American mass media and the myth of libertarianism: Toward an "elite power group" theory. *Critical Studies in Mass Communication, 8,* 139–151.

Althaus, S. L. (2003). When news norms collide, follow the lead: New evidence for press independence. *Political Communication, 20*, 381–414.

Althaus, S. L., & Kim, Y. M. (2006). Priming effects in complex information environments: Reassessing the impact of news discourse on presidential approval. *Journal of Politics, 68*, 960–976.

Ball-Rokeach, S. J., & Jung, J.-Y. (2009). The evolution of media system dependence theory. In R. L. Nabi & M. B. Oliver (Eds.), *The Sage handbook of media processes and effects* (pp. 531–544). Los Angeles: Sage.

Bass, A. Z. (1969). Refining the "gatekeeper" concept; A UN radio case study. *Journalism Quarterly, 46*, 69–72.

Behr, R. L., & Iyengar, S. (1985). Television news, real-world cues, and changes in the public agenda. *Public Opinion Quarterly, 49*, 38–57.

Bennett, W. L. (1990). Toward a theory of press–state relations in the United States. *Journal of Communication, 40*, 103–125.

Bennett, W. L., & Manheim, J. B. (2006). The one-step flow of communication. *The Annals of the American Academy of Political and Social Science, 608*, 213–232.

Bennett, W. L., Lawrence, R. G., & Livingston, S. (2006). None dare call it torture: Indexing and the limits of press independence in the Abu Ghraib scandal. *Journal of Communication, 56*, 467–485.

Benoit, W. L., & Holbert, R. L. (2010). Political communication. In C. R. Berger, M. E. Roloff, & D. R. Roskos-Ewoldsen (Eds.), *The handbook of communication science* (2nd ed., pp. 437–451). Los Angeles: Sage.

Cantril, H., Herzog, H., Gaudet, H., & Koch, H. (1940). *The invasion from Mars: A study in the psychology of panic.* Princeton, NJ: Princeton University Press.

Cappella, J. N., & Jamieson, K. H. (1997). *Spiral of cynicism: The press and the public good.* Oxford: Oxford University Press.

Carpentier, F. D., Roskos-Ewoldsen, D. R., & Roskos-Ewoldsen, B. (2008). A test of network models of political priming. *Media Psychology, 11*, 186–206.

Cassidy, W. P. (2006). Gatekeeping similar for online, print journalists. *Newspaper Research Journal, 27*, 6–23.

Coddington, M., & Holton, A. E. (2014). When the gates swing open: Examining network gatekeeping in a social media setting. *Mass Communication and Society, 17*, 236–257.

Cohen, B. C. (1963). *The press and foreign policy.* Princeton, NJ: Princeton University Press.

Coleman, S., & Ross, K. (2010). *The media and the public: "Them" and "us" in media discourse.* Oxford: Wiley Blackwell.

Dearing, J., & Rogers, E. (1996). *Agenda setting.* Thousand Oaks, CA: Sage.

Delia, J. G. (1987). Communication research: A history. In C. R. Berger & S. H. Chaffee (Eds.), *Handbook of communication science* (pp. 20–98). Thousand Oaks, CA: Sage.

Denham, B. E. (2014). Intermedia attribute agenda setting in the *New York Times*: The case of animal abuse in US horse racing. *Journalism & Mass Communication Quarterly, 91*, 17–37.

Donders, K., & Evens, T. (2014). Government intervention in marriages of convenience between TV broadcasters and distributors. *Javnost—The Public, 21*, 93–110.

Entman, R. M. (2004). *Projections of power: Framing news, public opinion, and U.S. foreign policy.* Chicago: University of Chicago Press.

Fazio, R. H. (1986). How do attitudes guide behavior? In R. H. Sorrentino & E. T. Higgins (Eds.), *The handbook of motivation and cognition: Foundations of social behavior* (pp. 204–243). New York: Guilford Press.

Gieber, W. (1956). Across the desk: A study of 16 telegraph editors. *Journalism Quarterly*, *33*, 423–432.

Glander, T. (2009). *Origins of mass communications research during the American cold war*. New York: Routledge.

Gozenbach, W. (1996). *The media, the president, and public opinion. A longitudinal analysis of the drug issue, 1984–1991*. Mahwah, NJ: Lawrence Erlbaum Associates.

Hays, R. G., & Reisner, A. E. (1990). Feeling the heat from advertisers: Farm magazine writers and ethical pressures. *Journalism Quarterly*, *67*, 936–942.

Hays, R. G., & Reisner, A. E. (1991). Farm journalists and advertiser influence: Pressures on ethical standards. *Journalism & Mass Communication Quarterly*, *68*, 172–178.

Herman, E. S., & Chomsky, N. (1988). *Manufacturing consent: The political economy of the mass media*. New York: Pantheon.

Holbert, R. L. (2005). Debate viewing as mediator and partisan reinforcement in the relationship between news use and vote choice. *Journal of Communication*, *55*(1), 85–102.

Holbert, R. L., & Hansen, G. J. (2006). Fahrenheit 9–11, need for closure and the priming of affective ambivalence. *Human Communication Research*, *32*, 109–129.

Holbrook, R. A., & Hill, T. G. (2005). Agenda-setting and priming in prime time television: Crime dramas as political cues. *Political Communication*, *22*, 277–295.

Hornik, R. (2006). Personal influence and the effects of the national youth anti-drug media campaign. *The Annals of the American Academy of Political and Social Science*, *608*, 282–300.

Iyengar, S. (1991). *Is anyone responsible? How television frames political issues*. Chicago: University of Chicago Press.

Iyengar, S., & Kinder, D. R. (1987). *News that matters: Television and American opinion*. Chicago: University of Chicago Press.

Iyengar, S., & Simon, A. (1993). News coverage of the Gulf Crisis and public opinion: A study of agenda-setting, priming, and framing. *Communication Research*, *20*, 365–383.

Iyengar, S., & Ottati, V. (1994). Cognitive perspective in political psychology. In R. S. Wyer, Jr. & T. K. Srull (Eds.), *Handbook of social cognition, Vol. 2, Applications* (pp. 143–187). Hillsdale, NJ: Lawrence Erlbaum Associates.

Kahneman, D., & Tversky, A. (1979). Prospect theory: An analysis of decisions under risk. *Econometrica*, *47*, 263–291.

Kahneman, D., & Tversky, A. (1984). Choices, values, and frames. *American Psychologist*, *39*, 341–350.

Katz, E., & Lazarsfeld, P. F. (1955). *Personal influence: The part played by people in the flow of mass communication*. New York: Free Press.

Kessler, L. (1989). Women's magazines' coverage of smoking related health hazards. *Journalism Quarterly*, *66*, 316–322, 445.

Kim, S., Scheufele, D. A., & Shanahan, J. (2002). Think about it this way: Attribute agenda-setting function of the press and the public's evaluation of a local issue. *Journalism & Mass Communication Quarterly*, *79*, 7–25.

Kim, Y. M. (2005). Use and disuse of contextual primes in dynamic news environments. *Journal of Communication*, *55*, 737–755.

Kinder, D. R. (2007). Curmudgeonly advice. *Journal of Communication*, *57*, 155–162.

Lazarsfeld, P. F., Berelson, B., & Gaudet, H. (1944). *The people's choice: How the voter makes up his mind in a presidential election*. New York: Duell, Sloan and Pearce.

Lee, A. M., Lewis, S. C., & Powers, M. (2014). Audience clicks and news placement: A study of time-lagged influence in online journalism. *Communication Research, 41,* 505–530.

Lewin, K. (1951). *Field theory in social science: Selected theoretical papers* (D. Courtwright, Ed.). Oxford: Harpers.

Lim, J. (2011). Intermedia agenda setting and news discourse: A strategic responses model for a competitor's breaking stories. *Journalism Practice, 5,* 227–244.

Lippmann, W. (1922). *Public opinion.* New York: Free Press.

Lubken, D. (2008). Remembering the straw man: The travels and adventures of hypodermic. In D. W. Park & J. Pooley (Eds.), *The history of media and communication research: Contested memories* (pp. 19–42). New York: Peter Lang.

McChesney, R. W. (1999). *Rich media, poor democracy: Communication politics in dubious times.* New York: The New Press.

McCombs, M. (2014). *Setting the agenda* (2nd ed.). Malden, MA: Polity Press.

McCombs, M., & Reynolds, A. (2009). How the news shapes our civic agenda. In J. Bryant & M. B. Oliver (Eds.), *Media effects: Advances in theory and research* (3rd ed., pp. 1–16). New York: Routledge.

McCombs, M. E., & Shaw, D. L. (1972). The agenda-setting function of mass media. *Public Opinion Quarterly, 36,* 176–187.

McCombs, M., & Stroud, N. J. (2014). Psychology of agenda-setting effects. Mapping the paths of information processing. *Review of Communication Research, 2*(1), 68–93.

McNelly, J. T. (1959). Intermediary communicators in the international flow of news. *Journalism Quarterly, 36,* 23–26.

Maher, T. M. (2001). Framing: An emerging paradigm or a phase of agenda setting? In S. D. Reese, O. H. Gandy, Jr., & A. E. Grant (Eds.), *Framing and public life: Perspectives on media and our understanding of the social world* (pp. 83–94). Mahwah, NJ: Lawrence Erlbaum Associates.

Mascaro, T. A. (2005). The chilling effect of politics: CBS news and documentaries during the Fin-Syn debate in the Reagan years. *American Journalism, 22,* 69–97.

Miller, J. M., & Krosnick, J. A. (2000). News media impact on the ingredients of presidential evaluations: Politically knowledgeable citizens are guided by a trusted source. *American Journal of Political Science, 44,* 295–309.

Moy, P., Xenos, M. A., & Hess, V. K. (2005). Priming effects of late-night comedy. *International Journal of Public Opinion, 18,* 198–210.

Norris, P., & Curtice, J. (2008). Getting the message out: A two-step model of the role of the internet in campaign communication flows during the 2005 British general election. *Journal of Information Technology & Politics, 4,* 3–13.

Price, V., & Tewksbury, D. (1997). New values and public opinion: A theoretical account of media priming and framing. In G. A. Barnett & F. J. Boster (Eds.), *Progress in communication sciences: Advances in persuasion* (vol. 13, pp. 173–212). Greenwich, CT: Ablex.

Rhodes, N., Roskos-Ewoldsen, D. R., Edison, A., & Bradford, B. (2008). Attitude and norm accessibility affect processing of anti-smoking messages. *Health Psychology, 27,* S224–S232.

Robinson, J. P. (1976). Interpersonal influence in election campaigns: Two step-flow hypotheses. *Public Opinion Quarterly, 40*(3), 304–319.

Rogers, E. M. (1994). *A history of communication study: A biographical approach.* New York: Free Press.

Rogers, E. M. (2003). *Diffusion of innovations* (5th ed.). New York: Free Press.

Roskos-Ewoldsen, D. R., & Fazio, R. H. (1997). The role of belief accessibility in attitude formation. *Southern Communication Journal, 62,* 107–116.

Roskos-Ewoldsen, D. R., & Roskos-Ewoldsen, B. (2009). Media priming. In R. Nabi & M. B. Oliver (Eds.), *Handbook of media effects and processes* (pp. 177–192). Thousand Oaks, CA: Sage.

Roskos-Ewoldsen, D. R., Bichsel, J., & Hoffman, K. (2002). The influence of accessibility of source likability on persuasion. *Journal of Experimental Social Psychology, 38,* 137–143.

Roskos-Ewoldsen, D. R., Yu, H. J., & Rhodes, N. (2004). Fear appeal messages effect accessibility of attitudes toward the threat and adaptive behaviors. *Communication Monographs, 71,* 49–69.

Roskos-Ewoldsen, D. R., Klinger, M., & Roskos-Ewoldsen, B. (2007). Media priming. In R. W. Preiss, B. M. Gayle, N. Burrell, M. Allen, & J. Bryant (Eds.), *Mass media theories and processes: Advances through meta-analysis* (pp. 53–80). Mahwah, NJ: Lawrence Erlbaum Associates.

Roskos-Ewoldsen, D. R., Roskos-Ewoldsen, B., & Carpentier, F. D. (2009). Media priming: An updated synthesis. In J. Bryant & M. B. Oliver (Eds.), *Media effects: Advances in theory and research* (3rd ed., pp. 74–93). New York: Routledge.

Rothman, A. J., & Salovey, P. (1997). Shaping perceptions to motivate healthy behavior: The role of message framing. *Psychological Bulletin, 121,* 3–19.

Rothman, A. J., Bartels, R. D., Wlaschin, J., & Salovey, P. (2006). The strategic use of gain- and loss-framed messages to promote healthy behavior: How theory can inform practice. *Journal of Communication, 56,* 202–220.

Rowling, C. M., Jones, T. M., & Sheets, P. (2011). Some dare call it torture: Cultural resonance, Abu Ghraib, and a selectively echoing press. *Journal of Communication, 61,* 1043–1061.

Salovey, P., Schneider, T. R., & Apanovitch, A. M. (2002). Message framing in the prevention and early detection of illness. In J. P. Dillard and M. W. Pfau (Eds.), *The persuasion handbook: Developments in theory and practice* (pp. 391–406). Thousand Oaks, CA: Sage.

Scheufele, D. A. (1999). Framing as a theory of media effects. *Journal of Communication, 49,* 103–122.

Scheufele, D. A., & Nisbet, M. C. (2008). Framing. In L. L. Kaid & C. Holtz-Bacha (Eds.), *Encyclopedia of Political Communication* (vol. 1, pp. 254–257). Thousand Oaks, CA: Sage.

Scheufele, D. A., & Tewksbury, D. (2007). Framing, agenda setting, and priming: The evolution of three media effects models. *Journal of Communication, 57,* 9–20.

Schramm, W., & Carter, R. F. (1959). Effectiveness of a political telethon. *Public Opinion Quarterly, 23,* 121–127.

Shah, D. V., McLeod, D. M., Gotlieb, M. R., and Lee, N.-J. (2009). Framing and agenda setting. In R. L. Nabi & M. B. Oliver (Eds.), *The Sage handbook of media processes and effects* (pp. 83–98). Thousand Oaks, CA: Sage.

Shoemaker, P. J., & Vos, T. P. (2009). *Gatekeeping theory.* New York: Routledge.

Shoemaker, P. J., Eichholz, M., Kim, E., & Wrigley, B. (2001). Individual and routine forces in gatekeeping. *Journalism & Mass Communication Quarterly, 75,* 233–246.

Shore, B. (1996). *Culture in mind: Cognition, culture, and the problem of meaning.* Oxford: Oxford University Press.

Siebert, F. S., Peterson, T., & Schramm, W. (1956). *Four theories of the press.* Urbana, IL: University of Illinois Press.

Simon, H. (1957). *Models of man: Social and rational.* New York: Wiley.

Southwell, B. G., & Yzer, M. C. (2007). The roles of interpersonal communication in mass media campaigns. *Communication yearbook 31* (pp. 419–462). New York: Lawrence Erlbaum Associates.

Southwell, B. G., & Yzer, M. C. (2009). When (and why) interpersonal talk matters for campaigns. *Communication Theory, 19,* 1–8.

Starr, P. (2004). *The creation of the media: Political origins of modern communication.* New York: Basic Books.

Stempel, G. H., III (1985). Gatekeeping: The mix of topics and the selection of stories. *Journalism Quarter, 62,* 791–796.

Strauss, C., & Quinn, N. (1997). *A cognitive theory of cultural meaning.* Cambridge: Cambridge University Press.

Tandoc, E. C. (2014). Journalism is twerking? How web analytics is changing the process of gatekeeping. *New Media & Society, 16,* 559–575.

Tewksbury, D., & Scheufele, D. A. (2009). News framing theory and research. In J. Bryant & M. B. Oliver (Eds.), *Media effects: Advances in theory and research* (pp. 17–33). New York: Routledge.

Tran, H. (2014). Online agenda setting: A new frontier for theory development. In T. J. Johnson (Ed.), *Agenda setting in a 2.0 world: New agendas in communication* (pp. 205–229). New York: Routledge.

Tversky, A., & Kahneman, D. (1974). Judgment under uncertainty: Heuristics and biases. *Science, 185,* 1124–1131.

Tversky, A., & Kahneman, D. (1981). The framing of decisions and the psychology of choice. *Science, 211,* 453–458.

Tversky, A., & Kahneman, D. (1982). Availability: A heuristic for judging frequency and probability. In D. Kahneman, P. Slovic, & A Tversky (Eds.), *Judgment under uncertainty: Heuristics and biases* (pp. 163–178). Cambridge: Cambridge University Press.

Tversky, A., & Kahneman, D. (1992). Advances in prospect theory: Cumulative representation of uncertainty. *Journal of Risk & Uncertainty, 5,* 297–323.

Wakker, P. P. (2010). *Prospect theory for risk and ambiguity.* Cambridge: Cambridge University Press.

Weaver, D. (2007). Thoughts on agenda setting, framing, and priming. *Journal of Communication, 57,* 142–147.

Weaver, D. (2014). Foreward. In T. J. Johnson (Ed.), *Agenda setting in a 2.0 world: New agendas in communication* (pp. ix–xiv). New York: Routledge.

Weaver, D., McCombs, M., & Shaw, D. L. (2004). Agenda-setting research: Issues, attributes and influences. In L. L. Kaid (Ed.), *Handbook of political communication research* (pp. 257–282). Mahwah, NJ: Lawrence Erlbaum Associates.

White, D. M. (1950). The "gate keeper": A case study in the selection of news. *Journalism Quarterly, 27,* 383–390.

Yin, J. (2008). Beyond the four theories of the press: A new model for the Asian & the world press. *Journalism & Communication Monographs, 10,* 3–62.

14

SOCIAL MEDIA

With the advent of Web 2.0, social networking sites such as Facebook, Instagram, LinkedIn, and Twitter, as well as social media sites such as YouTube and Wikipedia, have become ubiquitous in the lives of many people in developed nations, offering new opportunities for social connection, entertainment, and business opportunities (Levinson, 2013); in other words, a new technology often, if not invariably, introduces new affordances. Typically, these Internet sites and the communications they enable are referred to as "social media." However, media have arguably always been social, with audiences discussing the older media such as books, television, and films. Thus, to distinguish these new media forms (e.g., Twitter) from older media forms (e.g., television), many in both the academy and industry have referred to newer forms as "social" media. Although some have argued that this distinction is technically imprecise (e.g., Levinson, 2013), the term "new" media is similarly imprecise, because new is always a relative term. Thus, we utilize here the term social media, because social media are distinct from older media in that every consumer is a potential producer, social media are free, social media are adapted by users, and social media are outside the permanent control of either the users or the initial producers.

The use of social media has also been broad and varied, making it a powerful tool whose applications were most likely not foreseen at its initial inception. In developing nations, social media are often partly credited with such movements as the political protests in Tunisia in 2010 (Levinson, 2013), the Egyptian revolution that began in 2011 (Evangelista, 2011), and the revolution in Libya (Levinson, 2013). In addition, eleven million businesses have reported that they have a company profile page on Facebook (McGee, 2012). Indeed, the recent growth in the number and use of social networking sites has created new opportunities for online advertising (Zeng et al., 2009). Furthermore, social outcomes for adolescents have been studied as well, typically with more emphasis on problematic effects than on affordances. In the United States, more than 90 percent of all 12–17-year-olds use the Internet (Lenhart et al., 2010), spending an average of 6½ hours per day online (Donald Roberts, 2010). In any case, the rise of this form of media has stimulated a growing body of research on the effects of these social media technologies across a variety of populations (Whitlock et al., 2006).

Although social media itself is in its infancy (that is, compared to older technologies such as film), communication research on social media has already begun to coalesce around several pivotal topics. Like much research in communication, research on social media has focused on who is using it, what is being done with it, and the effects of using social media. In the following sections we will consider the research that attempts to examine these issues, reviewing, first, evidence concerning who is using it; then, with uses and gratifications as an overt or sometimes implicit framework, we will consider how social media are used. In both cases, research has considered social media use by both individuals and business entities. Lastly, we will look at its effects, focusing on two areas that have received considerable research attention: the effect of social media on human social connectedness and the effect of social media on large-scale political changes.

Who Is Using Social Media?

With the seeming ubiquity of social media, it may seem more appropriate to ask who is *not* using social media than to ask who is using it. For example, in 2011, Sally Deneen of *Success* magazine quipped that "if Facebook were a nation, it would be its third largest behind only China and India" (Deneen, 2011), with some 800 million users. In fact, in the United States alone, 90 percent of adolescents have Facebook accounts (Lenhart et al., 2010). Twitter is the second most popular site with 700 million users as of July 2014 (www.statisticbrain.com/ Twitter-statistics/ [retrieved September 2014]). Thus, it is clear that social media are indeed new, but have been quickly adopted. In fact, adoption appears so ubiquitous that it has prompted some to ask who doesn't use them. Turan et al. asked precisely this question when they studied adolescents and college students who do not use Facebook (Turan et al., 2013). Utilizing in-depth interviews with a sample of students in Turkey, the researchers found several main reasons for social media rejection. Participants stated that Facebook could waste time, was an unnecessary tool, and could lead to Facebook addiction. Although these reasons might parallel those offered by students in the United States who do not use social media, other reasons ran counter to evidence from U.S. samples. Specifically, Christofides et al. (2012) note that American adolescents tend to disclose more personal information, and use privacy settings less than adults. Common across cultures, however, is the sense among users that Facebook could waste time.

For those who do use social networking sites, however, it appears that a clear pattern of use has emerged. Whereas early use of online communication seemed to occur between individuals with no offline connection, such as past acquaintances with whom individuals had lost touch (Kraut et al., 1998), current research suggests that social network sites (SNS) are primarily used for connecting with existing friends and extending these relationships from an offline into an online environment (Ellison, 2007). In fact, contacts that people maintain online tend to mirror the contacts they have offline both in content and frequency. That is, individuals connect via Facebook, Twitter, and Instagram with their real-life friends. While individuals may have extensive online networks, the networks with whom they actually maintain online relationships are approximately as large and as dispersed as those they maintain offline.

In addition to individual use, however, companies and organizations have been quick to adopt social media as a means for connecting with clients and customers. For example, Naylor et al. (2012) found that by 2011, approximately 83 percent of Fortune 500 companies were using some form of social media to connect with consumers (Walker et al., 2012). Furthermore, McGee (2012) reported that eleven million businesses have a company profile page on Facebook. Celebrities also use social media in order to maintain a strong fan base, which likely leads to a strong capital base, as well. For example, Twitter Counter reports that of the top ten most followed sites, seven are celebrities (www.Twittercounter.com/pages/100). Thus, social media are used by individuals within their own social networks, but are also used by corporations and celebrities, as well. From a uses and gratifications perspective, then, we might next ask why social media are used, what functions they serve, and what needs they satisfy.

Uses and Functions of Social Media

The uses and gratifications perspective argues that media use, like many other behaviors, is functional and motivated by individuals' needs (see Chapter 8). Specifically, one of the earliest theses on uses and gratifications suggested that media use is motivated by social and psychological needs. In turn, we expect media to fulfill some of these needs and seek them out in somewhat patterned and predictable ways (Katz et al., 1974). Although early uses and gratifications research focused on radio and television use at a time when the term "mass media"' was more easily defined, its basic assumptions and tenets hold true even in an era of Web 2.0. We use Twitter, Facebook, and Instagram for many of the same reasons we reported using television four decades ago; however, advances in technology have provided new affordances, perhaps expanding the needs that media can serve.

Consider the fact that in its earliest days, the uses and gratifications approach suggested that there are nine motivations for television use (Rubin, 1983). Later, Lin (1999) whittled this down to three primary factors for television use: companionship and escape, information and surveillance, and personal identity.

Given that one of Lin's top three motives was companionship, it is perhaps unsurprising that college students report using Facebook first and foremost for connecting with existing friends. In fact, one of the main reasons offered for Facebook use is to maintain social ties. That is, similar to the earliest identified uses of television, Facebook offers us another means for fulfilling an existing need, a finding well in line with the tenets of uses and gratifications.

Although surprisingly little published research has been conducted from a uses and gratifications perspective on the uses of social media, *per se*, the research that does exist suggests that motives for social media use are similar to those of earlier media, although the functional affordances of social media are certainly greater. Unlike television, for example, social media allow us to contact friends, upload photos, and stream video both directly to particular individuals or to larger groups all at once; thus, using media for "social" reasons offers many more affordances in a social media universe than it did in a more traditional one. Nevertheless, when the uses of television are considered, social media do share many in common with television. In 1983, Rubin listed nine motives for television use: relaxation, companionship, habit, passing time, entertainment, social interaction, information, arousal, and escape. Taken in total, these seem to address many of the uses of social media: to interact, surely, but also out of habit, to pass time, and to get information.

For example, Christofides et al. (2012) noted that adolescents use social media to share and connect with others, two uses that might be identified as social interaction and companionship. Similarly, Ancu (2012) studied older adults ($N=218$) and found that establishing and maintaining relationships were among the top reasons this age group used social media as well. Therefore, from adolescents to older adults, social interaction and companionship, to use the language of uses and gratifications, are among the top social media use motives. Interestingly, Ancu (2012) also found that older adults used Facebook to play games, thus illustrating a second use of social media: entertainment. Similarly, social media such as YouTube might be used to build social connections; its value as an entertainment medium is undeniable. Introduced in 2005 with the logo "Broadcast Yourself," all of the ten most viewed YouTube videos are entertainment videos, and nine of those are music videos, with most of the performers already well-known stars such as Jennifer Lopez and Justin Bieber. The single exception is the well-known home video: "Charlie bit my finger—again" (www.en.videotrine.com/all/ YouTube/all-time [retrieved September 2014]).

Third, research has shown that individuals use social media to share and learn information (Lenhart et al., 2010). On Facebook, for example, they can post status updates, pictures, write information, or ask questions on friends' walls. Although these strategies may be referred to as social interaction, they may also serve the functions of information sharing and surveillance, two of the original nine dimensions of uses and gratifications. Pempek et al. (2009) found that college students use social networking sites to express personal ideas about topics such as religion and politics. Furthermore, information sharing and surveillance were certainly functions of Facebook use in 2009, when Facebook was used effectively in the "Boycott Whole Foods" Campaign (Kang, 2012) and ultimately affected the business practices of the retailer. Twitter was used effectively to sidestep the Iranian government's decision to shut down more traditional media in an effort to control the 2009 political uprising. Whereas traditional journalists and news outlets were easier for the Iranian government to spot and shut down, anyone with a cell phone could share information about the uprising via Twitter. In this case, social media were certainly used to share and learn crucial political information. Increasingly large numbers of individuals are also using social media to share and learn information about unfamiliar brands (Naylor et al., 2012). Thus, simple information sharing, whether in the face of obstruction of other sources of information or not, has allowed social media a sometimes lofty place.

Overall, then, and consistent with early research on uses and gratifications (e.g., Rubin, 1983), research shows that social media can be used for many of the same reasons that older media have been used. Social media such as Facebook and Twitter are used in an attempt to fulfill social needs such as companionship and social interaction, to fulfill information sharing and surveillance needs, and, of course, for entertainment.

Despite similarities between older media use motives and newer ones, at least one novel use of media has emerged through the affordances of social media: identity construction. As noted by Valkenburg and Peter (2008), and similar to an argument made earlier by Walther (1996), social media provide opportunities for identity expression. Posting pictures, selectively, sending out information or quips via Twitter, even editing information and visuals for the consumption of others, all of these actions can contribute to the construction of an online social identity. On one hand, this identity may merely reflect the one presented offline; however, as Walther (1996) has argued, experimentation due to a reduction in auditory and visual cues allows individuals to emphasize positive attributes while hiding negative attributes. In a related line of work, Pempek et al. (2009) found that college students use social networking sites to express personal ideas about topics such as religion and politics, topics which also help individuals construct and maintain social identities. Thus, one main function of social media that is not met by older media is identity construction, and the affordances of social media make identity construction a convenient and flexible process.

Effects of Social Media

Whereas social media were initially designed as a tool for social interaction, research on the effects of social media can be grouped as having to do with social interaction and social connection; having to do with marketing and purchase outcomes; and having to do with political movements and political outcomes. It makes sense, given the original nature of social media, to begin the discussion of effects by talking about them as a means for connecting people socially. And to do so, we first turn to the hyperpersonal model of communication (Walther, 1996). Although, at its inception, the hyperpersonal model was not intended to apply to social media, because social media had not yet arrived on the technological landscape, it is relevant in ways that will become apparent.

Introduced nearly two decades ago, the hyperpersonal model of communication followed earlier research and fears about the Internet, in some cases claiming, or in other cases finding, that with the lack of cues present in online communication during its infancy, communication had become more impersonal (Walther, 1996). However, critics of the impersonal model suggested that online communication or computer-mediated communication (CMC) could in fact be *more* personal, or hyperpersonal. By affording communicators the opportunity to develop and edit their self-presentations, communicators could optimize messages about themselves and spend time thinking about and crafting feedback. Consequently, CMC could offer affordances and opportunities not often present in face-to-face communication. Of course, this has been found to be the case only under certain circumstances, and research on CMC has focused on when mediated interaction is impersonal, when CMC is interpersonal, and when CMC is hyperpersonal. In any case, the hyperpersonal model suggests that in some cases, mediated interpersonal communication can be more, rather than less personal and therefore may be optimal for creating relationships in some situations.

A model that is somewhat in conflict with the more utopian perspective of the hyperpersonal model, however, is the social-identity/deindividuation model, or SIDE model. Again, like the hyperpersonal model, the SIDE model was intended to apply to computer-mediated communication, and not social media *per se*. However, in terms of the uses of social media, the SIDE model is certainly applicable to social media specifically. In any case, the SIDE model grew out of classic deindividuation theory, which examines how individuals behave in crowds, finding that individuals often behave in more antisocial ways in crowd situations. Festinger and colleagues (1952) were the first to propose that anonymity was a key element in the effects of deindividuation. Emerging from these basic ideas, the SIDE model was first named by Lea and Spears (1991), and applied and extended the premise of deindividuation to computer-mediated communication. Early research in this area suggested that, similar to deindividuation theory, users of online computing were inclined to communicate in less socially appropriate ways because, first, they did not have access to the verbal and non-verbal cues of the other communicators involved in the interaction, and second, because of feelings of anonymity (Postmes et al., 2001). More specifically, the SIDE model predicts that in CMC, the sense of self diminishes while the sense of group increases, and people feel less responsible for their own behaviors. This phenomenon would help explain behaviors such as cyberbullying.

In addition to theorizing about how individuals might use the Internet to engage in communication, early theorizing concerning the possible effects of online communication argued that online activity might reduce individuals' social connectedness, that is, might harm their relationships with friends and family. For example, Kraut et al. (1998) followed people in their first two years of having access to the Internet and found that greater Internet use was associated with declines in family communication, declines in (in vivo) social network size, and increases in loneliness and depression. However, as Internet access increased, the way in which people interacted online changed as well. Valkenburg and Peter (2008) argued that instead of connecting with strangers, people started using the Internet primarily for maintaining already existing relationships. This change itself led to *increases* in their feelings of social connectedness instead of the decreases that had been reported in earlier research (Valkenburg & Peter, 2008), an argument that is supported by Ellison's (2007) finding that shows that SNS connect people online, albeit more frequently, with existing friends (Ellison, 2007). Thus, one of the main effects of social media seems to be increases in social connectedness. And the relationship between SNS use and social connectedness does not appear to be merely correlational.

An experiment among undergraduates showed that increased Facebook activity reduced loneliness, and that this decline in loneliness was due to students feeling more socially connected to their friends on a daily basis (Deters & Mehl, 2012). Shen et al. (2013) found a similar association between perceived online need satisfaction and increased joy and satisfaction among Chinese children. And in a recent large-scale study, questionnaires about Facebook use were administered to 530 undergraduate students (Aubrey & Rill, 2013). The authors found that using Facebook habitually was associated with gains in social outcomes. Specifically, those who used Facebook habitually had stronger connections within their Facebook group, a phenomenon referred to as bonding. However, habitual use also resulted in online bridging between individuals outside of their group, which in turn resulted in greater offline network capital. The authors also found that using Facebook for social reasons as opposed to status-seeking motives mediated the relationship between habitual Facebook use and bonding outcomes. In other words, mere use of Facebook does not necessarily increase social bonds, only using Facebook for social reasons does so.

Köbler et al. (2010) further explored the formation of social connectedness on Facebook and found significant associations between active Facebook use and feeling socially connected. People felt more connected to their friends when they used Facebook's status update function more often, when they shared more information through Facebook, when they actively followed others' status updates, and when they posted reactions to others' posts or comments. Similarly, Grieve et al. (2013) found that although Facebook social connectedness clearly differed from offline social connectedness, higher levels of Facebook social connectedness were associated with higher psychological well-being including lower levels of depression and anxiety, and higher levels of subjective well-being. Thus, the use of SNS seems to facilitate feelings of social connectedness with psychological benefits being similar to those accrued from offline social connections.

Thus, it appears that use of SNS can improve psychological and social well-being; however, it is reasonable to ask how and why this is possible? After all, some would argue that online interactions differ in specific ways from offline interactions. To address this issue we can consider the concept of social presence. Although there are many definitions of presence, one of the earliest and most classic definitions simply states that presence is the illusion that a mediated experience is not mediated (Lombard & Ditton, 1997). One aspect of presence is a feeling of social presence, or the notion that a mediated interaction is nonmediated. Recently, Cheung et al. (2011) found that social presence was the most important factor in determining students' Facebook use, and that features of social presence encouraged students to collaborate and work together on Facebook. Thus, the effect of SNS use on feelings of social connectedness and well-being may be due to the fact that SNS work when we feel as if they are just like nonmediated interactions. They make us feel as if the other person is actually there and thus increase feelings of social awareness.

In fact, Wagner and Strohmaier (2010) appropriately identified the SNS activity streams like the Facebook home page (i.e. the web page that shows others' messages and activities) as a new form of communication and called them "social awareness streams." Seeing other people using the medium increases a user's awareness of those other users' presence. This social awareness of other users being present makes it possible to feel connected to them. Recently, Riedl et al. (2013) developed a model explaining the formation of online social connectedness through social awareness and social presence. They explain that the level of social connectedness derived from one's social network is partly determined by the extent to which someone perceives his social network as sufficient. The extent to which an SNS user perceives his social network as sufficient, and thus as providing beneficial outcomes like emotional support and trust, is dependent on the experience of social presence and social awareness. Both social presence and social awareness thus allow the SNS user to experience feelings of social connectedness within his online social network.

Overall, then, concerns about social media, especially regarding potential impact on social and emotional well-being, were initially supported by the data. Early on, spending time in chat-rooms and engaging in social interaction online was associated with less interaction with offline others. However, current research on social media indicates that this form of communication acts as an extension of our offline lives. We interact with people we already know and in doing so, we feel more connected and less lonely. This process is particularly effective through the joint mechanisms of social presence and social awareness. Thus, social media appear to offer a generally positive effect on social interaction.

Despite these findings, no chapter on social media and social well-being would be complete without a discussion of the negative social aspects of social media such as cyberbullying and cyber-gossip. Both bullying and gossip existed long before the introduction of the Internet or indeed before any advances in communication technology beyond speech. What makes these potentially more destructive is the lethal combination of immediate and widespread dissemination on one hand, combined with potential anonymity of the sender on the other. It is precisely this kind of phenomenon that is applicable to the SIDE, for example. Krcmar (2012) discusses how a third characteristic, adolescent egocentrism, creates a perfect storm for cyberbullying. With an easy-to-reach audience, possible anonymity and a need to feel socially valued by peers, adolescence may be a time in which developmental characteristics and technological affordances combine to make cyberbullying even more likely. Cases such as Phoebe Prince, a 15-year-old girl who committed suicide after relentless cyberbullying, and Tyler Clementi, an 18-year-old Rutgers student who committed suicide after his sexual encounter was secretly videotaped and streamed online, suggest that while bullying is certainly an old problem, cyberbullying in its broad reach is even more problematic. Although a large audience can be witness to bullying, a near-limitless audience can be audience to it online. In addition, online intimidation can more easily mask the perpetrator, thus making the bully less accountable and therefore more empowered.

Although cyberbullying is undeniably harmful, cyberstalking can have negative repercussions as well. Whereas cyberbullying may be committed by a group of individuals, cyberstalking is typically a solitary individual making online connections with a single user. The essence of cyberstalking is persistent, unwanted online monitoring or contacting of the target, again, made simpler through online communication (Beech & Bishop, 2015). One-quarter of the more than 3 million stalking victims reported that at least some of the stalking was conducted online. In fact, technological advances such as Google Earth and websites such as Foursquare allow others to know and track your whereabouts at any time (Kincaid, 2009), although Foursquare has since tightened their security settings, thus allowing only those in your social network to access the information. To demonstrate the dangers of location sharing, a site called Please Rob Me was launched in 2010. It scraped public tweets that allowed users to know who was not at home (McCarthy, 2010). Although the stated purpose of the site was to make users aware of possible property theft, the site could also be said to provide information on stalking victims, as well.

Marketing

One area of SNS use that is of particular interest economically, is the use and effectiveness of social media as a marketing tool. Several studies have examined how SNS are used to advertise to users and what effects messages received through SNS have. However, the rapid growth of social media in the last few years calls into question findings from even 5 years ago. For example, in 2013 Twitter use nearly doubled from the previous year; however, Facebook use still far exceeds that of Twitter. With 1,189 million monthly active users on Facebook, compared to only 232 million monthly active users on Twitter, it appears that Facebook would still be advertisers' social media platform of choice (Bennett, 2013).

It is perhaps unsurprising, therefore, that Agozzino (2010) found that among over 1,000 millennials (those born between 1980 and 2000), respondents engaged with email and Facebook more than other social media tools. Agozzino also investigated links between company/brand relationships and Millennial students' active social media behavior. Utilizing information about their relationships with the top 10 most social companies/brands as named by Ad Age, as well as their engagement with social media tools in general, she found no significant correlations to indicate they were interested in continuing their relationship with that particular company/brand, despite the fact that many reported being familiar with brands through Facebook and email.

Despite these findings, Naylor et al. (2012) found that by 2011, approximately 83% of Fortune 500 companies were using some form of social media to connect with consumers. Furthermore, surveys suggest that consumers are increasingly relying on social media to learn about unfamiliar brands. Thus, it may be that self-report data from users of SNS about products and product advertising may not be the most effective way to discern effects. Instead, Naylor et al. (2012) found that the mere virtual presence of some brands on SNS influenced target consumers brand evaluations and purchase intentions. In addition, Cingel and colleagues (2014) utilized an experimental design to test the effect on adolescents of seeing a "liked" unhealthy or healthy food on a friends' Facebook page (Cingel et al., 2014). The researchers investigated participants' product liking and purchase intention. They found that adolescents reported more positive attitudes toward the advertised brand when the brand was an unhealthy food product that was liked by a Facebook friend. Additionally, adolescents' intentions to also "like" the company page on Facebook partially mediated the relationship between attitudes toward the brand and intentions to buy. Thus, additional evidence suggests that product advertising on SNS such as Facebook is an effective marketing strategy.

News

Social Media Editor is one of the newest newsroom positions, often held by editors who are younger and more technologically savvy than their traditional news counterparts (Wasike, 2013). The role of the social media editor is to monitor the social media sphere for the latest trends, to obtain the relevant material for the editor, to maintain an online presence for the organization and to interact with the readers and post articles online (Wasike, 2013). The mere emergence of a job title called a social media editor indicates that news outlets are also aware of the impact of social media, willing to invest in social media and perhaps hopeful that social media editors may allow them a means to slow their decline in readership. Indeed news delivered via social media differs from news that appears in more traditional news formats.

But is social media in the newsroom just another media to deliver traditional stories? One content analysis comparing the editor's news frames in social media, to the traditional media (TV and print) they represent, Wasike (2013) found that TV social media editors were more personal with their Twitter followers, using a more familiar tone and more informal language than the television outlet itself. The social media editors also posted more articles that had a technology frame. Print social media editors, or those who worked for traditionally print outlets such as newspapers, used a human interest frame more often than the print outlet itself. Conflict and economic frames were also common among print social media editors compared to their physical newspaper counterparts. Overall, then, social media emphasized human interest and economic frames in contrast with print and television editors who utilized conflict, and economic frames. The authors attributed this to differences in audiences for traditional and social media outlets with audiences for social media outlets being younger and obviously more technologically savvy than audiences for traditional media. In fact, it is social media, and not the more traditional news media outlets that have been linked with several recent cases of social change and upheaval. Whereas traditional news media have long been considered (or considered themselves) the watchdog of our political and economic engines, social media have been identified as a possible effective tool for reporting on events and mobilizing citizens.

Another possible effect of social media, although one that has not been given much attention in the academic research literature, is that of agenda setting (see Chapter 7). For example, news of the Trayvon Martin case, in which an unarmed black teenager who was on his way home from the corner store, was shot and killed by a community watch volunteer, initially received limited attention by traditional news outlets. Outside of his home town of Miami, the case received little attention. Through petitions circulated on social media, the case eventually reached national attention and that of more traditional news organizations, thus setting not only the public agenda, but the agenda of news outlets from the *New York Times* to CNN. Thus, consistent with agenda-setting theory, which proposes and has found that one of the main effects of news media is that it determines what news stories are deemed important by the general public, social media can influence what stories traditional media pays attention to and ultimately the general public's opinions of issue importance.

In fact, surveys today indicate that a growing number of people rely on the Internet for their political news (McCombs & Stroud, 2014). A critical question concerns whether people's greater ability to select what news to consume on the Internet undermines the ability of the media to set the agenda. Likewise, stories that are more prominent (e.g., the lead story on the nightly news or the top-of-the-fold story on the first page of the newspaper) are more likely to influence the public's agenda. But many Internet news outlets let the public determine the prominence of stories by how frequently a story is clicked on. Indeed, the prominence that traditional media give to stories may be influenced by how frequently the story is clicked on that media outlet's website. Stories that have the highest traffic (e.g., greatest number of clicks) are moved to more prominent locations on the website. Thus, the argument can be made that the public are helping to set the media's agenda through their clicking behavior and this could undermine the media's influence to set the public's agenda. Conversely, the argument can be made that this has always been the case. Successful news outlets have always tailored their coverage of issues based on what the public is interested in. In addition, given the Internet news outlets' reliance on traditional media for the content of the stories, the traditional media should still play an important role in setting the agenda through the selection of stories that are covered. A new research tradition is emerging on agenda-melding which focuses on the dynamic relationship between traditional media and nontraditional media such as the Internet (McCombs & Stroud, 2014). Research does suggest that traditional media still has a stronger influence on agenda setting than do nontraditional media (Martin, 2013; McCombs et al., 2014; Shehata & Strömbäck, 2013).

In addition to Internet and social media sources influencing agenda setting, another important question is whether the nature of gatekeeping is changing as a result. Because people have more access to news sources through the Internet, it is possible that traditional news outlets no longer determine what news makes it and what does not make it to the public, a process known as gatekeeping. Recent research has suggested that gatekeeping diminishes in importance with the advent of new media, though gatekeepers have discovered other and often less overt ways to influence what stories reach audiences (Coddington & Holton, 2014). Research indicates that although the basic information that is considered remains the same, gatekeepers may be relying on different sources of information. For example, several studies have found that news organizations use information from the web to learn more about their audience (Tandoc, 2014). This research may suggest that the Internet simply provides new options for obtaining information concerning the traditional influences on gatekeeping.

Social and Political Change

Of course social media are not the first media to effect political change. In 1942 and 1943, a group of students and one professor from the University of Munich, started a nonviolent group to protest against Nazi Germany. They used leaflets and graffiti to spread their messages. In 1979, audio cassettes of the Ayatollah Khomeini made their way around Iran and fomented a revolution against the dictatorial shah. As individuals gained access to social media, with its ever-greater reach, they harnessed its power to encourage social change. The social media campaign created on Facebook to boycott Whole Foods (Kang, 2012) eventually helped change the retailers' practices; and the Occupy Wall Street movement, which began in 2011 to "fight back against the richest 1% of people that are writing the rules of an unfair global economy" is an ongoing social movement.

These movements were started on, enabled by, and furthered through social media, in part due to the broad reach that social media offers cheaply, a broad reach that cannot be achieved without tremendous financial resources through more traditional media means. The hope for social media was that it would offer a utopia of free speech and an opportunity for political change both in the U.S. and Europe as well as in countries with more repressive governments.

Recently, researchers investigated how digital and social media use for informational purposes could contribute to fostering democratic processes and the creation of social capital (Gil de Zúñiga et al., 2012). Based on a U.S. national data set, researchers considered if mere access to social media and frequency of social media use could be linked to social capital. The argument suggested that through the use of social media, individuals might not only increase their social connectedness as pointed out earlier in the chapter, but they might also be encouraged to engage in civic and political activities. Utilizing an early framework that saw the Internet itself as a possible political utopia, the authors considered if openness and free speech, which might be stifled in other environments, might flourish on social media. Results indicated that after controlling for demographic variables, traditional media use offline and online, political knowledge and political efficacy, seeking information via SNS was a positive and significant predictor of people's social capital and civic and political participatory behaviors, online. Furthermore, information seeking through SNS was also a significant predictor of offline civic and political engagement. Thus, it appears that SNS can be used to enhance engagement.

Perhaps one of the best known examples of the effect of social media on political and social change is that of the Arab uprisings, collectively known as the Arab Spring. Beginning in Tunisia in 2010, protestors against the repressive regime used Facebook and Twitter to coordinate actions on the ground and getting the word out to the rest of the world (Ingram, 2011). In less than one month, the protestors and their supporters were able to overthrow the regime and the police, electing a constituent assembly within one year. Although social media certainly did not cause this regime change, it did help with much-needed coordination, again, due to its quick and broad reach. When the Egyptian revolution began a mere month later in Egypt, an anti-Mubarak (the repressive political leader) Facebook page was seen as a trigger-point in the movement (Evangelista, 2011). Although social media were once again credited with coordination efforts in the uprising, they were certainly not a sufficient condition, and were, arguably, not a necessary one either. The main consensus seems to be that social media helped, and communication, regardless of its means, is always an important part of any social movement.

To further clarify the issue, Soengas-Pérez (2013) analyzed the use of the Internet and social networks to understand the contribution of communication technology in societies whose traditional media are either repressed, state controlled, or both. Specifically, Soengas-Pérez (2013) interviewed young people who had been at the site of the conflict and involved in the protests and those abroad who were supportive of it. Individuals from Tunisia, Egypt, and Libya were involved in the interviews. Findings suggested that virtual support for uprisings was not based on coordinated actions, rather a confluence of similar acts coinciding in time and on the same platforms took place. Thus, the often-held belief that coordinated online actions led to the uprisings was not supported. Instead, the author argued that the Internet and social networks served as elements for supporting the process and offered an opportunity to counterbalance the government-supportive media and any censorship that may have occurred. The author therefore credited social media with aiding in the revolutions, while downplaying the media-induced overstatements that social media caused the revolutions.

In a similarly more nuanced approach, Skoric and Poor (2013) conducted a qualitative analysis of a student protest, followed by a national survey of young people in Singapore, in order to understand the role of social media in political movement and social change. Results suggested that social media use was positively related to traditional political participation; however, traditional media were still an indicator of and provided impetus for political engagement. Specifically, the study found that, compared to generic Facebook use, participants' attention to news in traditional media was a better predictor of both traditional and online participation than the generic use of Facebook, again calling into question the notion that social media may offer a cure for political apathy and a conduit for political action. In fact, Red (2013) considered precisely these questions in an assessment of the use of information and communication technologies and social networking sites by social organizations in the lead-up to Mexico's July 2012 presidential election. This election was particularly crucial because the party that had ruled the country for seven decades through a semi-authoritarian regime was poised to regain power. In part through the use of social media, supposedly apolitical youth were reached and encouraged to participate in the process. However, Red argued that social media may have been used to reach out to the apolitical and disaffected; however, it was unclear if these actions ultimately had any significant effect on election outcomes.

In sum, while social media helped overcome the isolation of some Arab societies by making conflicts clear, first-hand, and visible to those abroad, it also showed that social media were sometimes faced with similar constraints as traditional media due to propaganda in each country. In other political and social change movements, social media could help the movement, but like the traditional media that preceded it, the content of the media and the characteristics of the user made a difference in terms of the outcomes. Thus, although some research shows an increase in political engagement and social capital through the use of SNS, other scholars argue that like older media, social media may not offer the political utopia initially hoped for. Instead, social media seem to be best at coordination and organization, largely due to the technological affordances of speed and reach.

Conclusions

Marvin (1990) argued that the introduction of each new technology brings with it both concerns for the effects and prophesies for the ways in which it will meet society's needs and cure its ills, and concerns over the consequences, coupled with hopes for its affordances. While there remains little doubt that social media have had an effect on our social interactions, the way we behave as consumers and targets of advertisers, and the way we engage in the political process, Marvin's comments ring somehow true. For example, traditional media theory, such as uses and gratifications (Rubin, 1983), is an excellent framework for understanding how social media are used and to investigate what motivates social media use. Research that has investigated social movements has found that social media can be used to coordinate large groups of people, but that traditional media, as well as simply a confluence of similarly timed events, may often offer alternative compelling explanations for social media's seeming effects.

Thus, like media that have come before it, social media *offer* the possibility of change, potential effects, and means of connections, but outcomes are often dependent on the actions of human users. We use social media to make connections, but often those connections are made with those we know offline (Ellison, 2007). While this is an important outcome, especially because evidence suggests that we can strengthen those ties through social media, it is not a paradigm-changing outcome. Instead, we would argue that social media may ultimately create a paradigm shift which then must be matched in the arena of research. However, that shift will only occur when human beings use social media in paradigm-shifting ways.

References

Agozzino, A. L. (2010). *Millennial students' relationship with 2008 top 10 social media brands via social media tools.* Doctoral dissertation, Bowling Green State University.

Ancu, M. (2012). Older adults on Facebook: A survey examination of motives and use of social networking by people 50 and older. *Florida Communication Journal, 40,* 1–12.

Aubrey, J. S., & Rill, L. (2013). Investigating relations between Facebook use and social capital among college undergraduates. *Communication Quarterly, 61,* 479–496.

Beech, M., & Bishop, J. (2015). Cyber-stalking or just plain talking? Linguistic properties of rape-threat messages reflect underlying compulsive behaviours. In J. Bishop (Ed.), *Psychological and social issues surrounding internet and gaming addiction* (pp. 111–137). Hershey, PA: IGI Global.

Bennett, S. (2013, November 5). *Facebook vs Twitter: Revenue, users, average time spent, key mobile data.* Retrieved from www.mediabistro.com/alltwitter/facebook-vs-twitter-data-stats_b51335

Cheung, C. M., Chiu, P. Y., & Lee, M. K. (2011). Online social networks: Why do students use Facebook? *Computers in Human Behavior, 27,* 1337–1343.

Christofides, E., Muise, A., & Desmarais, S. (2012). Risky disclosures on Facebook: The effect of having a bad experience on online behavior. *Journal of Adolescent Research, 27,* 714–731.

Cingel, D., Lauricella, A., Wartella, E., Caspel, D. V., & Krcmar, M. (2014). *Investigating the role of online social influence on adolescents' attitudes toward food companies and purchase intentions: An experimental study.* Paper presented at the 100th annual conference of the National Communication Association, Chicago, IL.

Coddington, M. & Holton, A. (2014). When the Gates Swing Open: Examining Network Gatekeeping in a Social Media Setting. *Mass Communication & Society, 17,* 236–257.

Cyberstalking (n.d.). In *Netlingo Online Dictionary.* Retrieved September 30, 2014, from www.netlingo.com/word/cyberstalker.php

Deneen, S. (2011, March 31). *The Facebook Age: Mark Zuckerberg.* Retrieved from www.success.com/article/the-facebook-age-mark-zuckerberg

Deters, F., & Mehl, M. R. (2012). Does posting Facebook status updates increase or decrease loneliness? An online social networking experiment. *Social Psychological and Personality Science.* doi: 10.1177/1948550612469233.

Donald Roberts, U. F. (2010). *Generation M2: Media in the lives of 8- to 18-year-olds.* Menlo Park: Kaiser Family Foundation.

Ellison, N. (2007). Social network sites: Definition, history, and scholarship. *Journal of Computer-Mediated Communication, 13,* 210–230.

Evangelista, B. (2011, February 13). *Facebook, Twitter, and Egypt's upheaval.* Retrieved from www.sfgate.com/business/article/Facebook-Twitter-and-Egypt-s-upheaval-2475263.php.

Festinger, L., Pepitone, A., & Newcomb, T. (1952). Some consequences of de-individuation in a group. *Journal of Abnormal and Social Psychology, 47,* 382–389.

Gil de Zúñiga, H., Jung, N., & Valenzuela, S. (2012). Social media use for news and individuals' social capital, civic engagement and political participation. *Journal of Computer-Mediated Communication, 17,* 319–336.

Grieve, R., Indian, M., Witteveen, K., Tolan, G. A., & Marrington, J. (2013). Face-to-face or Facebook: Can social connectedness be derived online? *Computers in Human Behavior, 29,* 604–609.

Ingram, M. (2011, April 25). *The future of media: Storify and the curatorial instinct.* Retrieved from www.gigaom.com/2011/04/25/the-future-of-media-storify-and-the-curatorial-instinct/

Kang, J. (2012). A volatile public: The 2009 Whole Foods boycott on Facebook. *Journal of Broadcasting & Electronic Media, 56,* 562–577.

Katz, E., Blumler, J., & Gurevitch, M. (1974). Utilization of mass communication by the individual. In J. G. Blumler & E. Katz (Eds.), *The uses of mass communications: Current perspectives on gratifications research* (pp. 19–32). Beverly Hills, CA: Sage.

Kincaid, J, (2009, March 18). SXSW: *Foursquare scores despite its flaws.* Retrieved March 16, 2011, from www.en.wikipedia.org/wiki/The_Washington_Post

Köbler, F., Riedl, C., Vetter, C., Leimeister, J. M., & Krcmar, H. (2010). Social connectedness on Facebook—An explorative study on status message usage. *AMCIS 2010 Proceedings.* Paper 247. Retrieved from www.aisel.aisnet.org/amcis2010/247

Kraut, R., Patterson, M., Lundmark, V., Kiesler, S., Mukophadhyay, T., & Scherlis, W. (1998). Internet paradox: A social technology that reduces social involvement and psychological well-being? *American Psychologist, 53*(9), 1017–1031.

Krcmar, M. (2012). The effect of media on children's moral reasoning. In R. Tamborinin (Ed.), *Media and the moral mind* (pp. 198–217). New York: Routledge.

Lea, M., & Spears, R. (1991). Computer-mediated communication, de-individuation and group decision-making. *International Journal of Man–Machine Studies, 34,* 283–301.

Lenhart, A., Purcell, K., Smith, A., & Zickurh, K. (2010). Social media & mobile internet use among teens and young adults. *Pew Internet & American Life Project*. Retrieved from www.pewinternet.org/2010/02/03/social-media-and-young-adults/

Levinson, P. (2013). *New new media* (2nd ed.). Boston, MA: Pearson.

Lin, C. (1999). Online-service adoption likelihood. *Journal of Advertising Research, 3,* 79–89.

Lombard, M., & Ditton, T. (1997). At the heart of it all: The concept of presence. *Journal of Computer-Mediated Communication, 3.*

McCarthy, C. (2010, February 17). The dark side of geo: PleaseRobMe.com. Retrieved from www.cnet.com/news/the-dark-side-of-geo-pleaserobme-com/

McCombs, M., & Stroud, N. J. (2014). Psychology of agenda setting effects: Mapping the paths of information processing. *Review of Communication Research, 2,* 68–93.

McCombs, M. E., Shaw, D. L., & Weaver, D. H. (2014). New directions in agenda-setting theory and research. *Mass Communication & Society, 17,* 781–802.

McGee, M. (2012, July 26). *More businesses have Facebook pages (11m) than claimed Google+ local listings (8m).* Retrieved from www.smallbusinesssem.com/more-facebook-pages-than-claimed-google-local-listings/6159/

Martin, H. J. (2013). The economics of word of mouth: Designing effective social media marketing for magazines. *Journal of Magazine & New Media Research, 14,* 1–12.

Marvin, C. (1990). *When old technologies were new.* New York: Oxford University Press.

Naylor, R., Lamberton, C., & West, P. (2012). Beyond the "like" button: The impact of mere virtual presence on brand evaluations and purchase intentions in social media settings. *Journal of Marketing, 76,* 105–120.

Pempek, T., Yermolayeva, Y., & Calvert, S. (2009). College students' social networking experiences on Facebook. *Journal of Applied Developmental Psychology, 30,* 227–238.

Postmes, T., Spears, R., Sakhel, K., & De Groot, D. (2001). Social influence in computer-mediated communication: The effects of anonymity on group behavior. *Personality and Social Psychology Bulletin, 27,* 1242–1254.

Red, M. (2013). Rocking the vote in Mexico's 2012 Presidential Election: Mexico's popular music scene's use of social media in a post-Arab Spring context. *International Journal of Communication, 7,* 1205–1219.

Riedl, C., Köbler, F., Goswami, S., & Krcmar, H. (2013). Tweeting to feel connected: A model for social connectedness in online social networks. *International Journal of Human–Computer Interaction, 29,* 670–687.

Rubin, A. (1983). Television uses and gratifications: The interactions of viewing patterns and motivations. *Journal of Broadcasting & Electronic Media, 27,* 37–51.

Shehata, A. & Strömbäck, J. (2013). Not (yet) a new era of minimal effects: A study of agenda setting at the aggregate and individual levels. *International Journal of Press/Politics, 18*(2), 234–255.

Shen, C. X., Liu, R., & Wang, D. (2013). Why are children attracted to the internet? The role of need satisfaction perceived on-line and perceived in daily real life. *Computers in Human Behavior, 29,* 185–192.

Skoric, M. M., & Poor, N. (2013). Youth engagement in Singapore: The interplay of social and traditional media. *Journal of Broadcasting & Electronic Media, 57,* 187–204.

Soengas-Pérez, X. (2013). The role of the internet and social networks in the Arab uprisings: An alternative to official press censorship. *Comunicar, 21,* 147–155.

Tandoc, E. C. (2014). Journalism is twerking? How web analytics is changing the process of gatekeeping. *New Media and Society, 16,* 559–575.

Turan, Z., Tinmaz, H., & Goktas, Y. (2013). The reasons for non-use of social networking websites by university students. *Comunicar, 21*, 137–145.

Valkenburg, P. M., & Peter, J. (2008). Adolescents' identity experiments on the internet: Consequences for social competence and self-concept unity. *Communication Research, 35*, 208–231.

Wagner, C., & Strohmaier, M. (2010). *The wisdom in tweetonomies: Acquiring latent conceptual structures from social awareness streams*. Proceedings of the 3rd International Semantic Search Workshop, New York.

Walther, J. B. (1996). Computer-mediated communication: Impersonal, interpersonal, and hyperpersonal interaction. *Communication Research, 23*, 3–43. Retrieved from www.en. wikipedia.org/wiki/Interpersonal_communication

Wasike, B. (2013). Framing news in 140 characters: How social media editors frame the news and interact with audiences via Twitter. *Global Media Journal (Canadian Edition), 6*(1), 5–23.

Whitlock, J., Powers, J., & Eckenrode, J. (2006). The virtual cutting edge: The internet and adolescent self-injury. *Developmental Psychology, 42*, 407–417.

Zeng, F., Huang, L., & Dou, W. (2009). Social factors in user perceptions and responses to advertising in online social networking communities. *Journal of Interactive Advertising, 10*(1), 1–13.

15

HEALTH COMMUNICATION

The study of health communication really emerged in the late 1950s and early 1960s with a focus on health promotion. In other words, the prominent question to emerge was: how can we use the media to encourage people to engage in positive health behaviors? There were two distinct theoretical developments that occurred during this time period: diffusion of innovations and the health belief model. The health belief model set the stage for research on fear appeals, such as the extended parallel process model. Research on health communication has also focused on models of the attitude–behavior relationship, such as the theory of reasoned action and its derivatives. This makes sense, because many health campaigns specifically focus on changing people's attitudes as a way to decrease unhealthy behaviors or to increase healthy behaviors.

Research on interpersonal communication in the health care context is a newer area of research. Much of the work in this area is still fairly atheoretical; however, models of doctor–patient interaction are beginning to evolve. There is also a growing literature on the negative effects of the media on health behaviors. Because much of the research in this area relies on media effects theories (see Chapter 7), those models will not be discussed in this chapter. Instead, this chapter will focus on theories whose main area of application is that of health communication. We will cover theories such as the diffusion of innovations, the health belief model, the theory of reasoned action and its derivatives, stages of change, as well as topics such as fear appeals and patient–provider communication.

Diffusion of Innovations

The research on diffusion of innovations draws on the two-step flow model of communication that was presented in Chapter 13 (Dearing & Meyer, 2006;

Rogers, 2003; Srivastava & Moreland, 2015). The diffusion of innovations model focuses on the more general question of how information or innovations spread, and it has been used by communication scholars across a number of content domains. The model is discussed here, however, because it has been used quite frequently to study the diffusion of health-related information (Bandura, 2006; Haider & Kreps, 2004; Rogers, 2003; Singhal et al., 2006), and the tradition of medial sociology has influenced the development of the theory itself (Srivastava & Moreland, 2015). Research has found across a number of different domains that innovations spread in a fairly uniform manner. It is important to note that the term "innovation" is used very broadly to refer to essentially anything that is judged to be "new," including technological developments such as new medical procedures or new drugs, health care interventions, and breaking news (Rogers, 2003).

The diffusion model assumes that people go through five stages when making the decision to act on a diffusion (Rogers, 2003). For example, if the director of a medical clinic is deciding whether to adopt medical robots, the director would go through these five stages. The first stage is the *knowledge* stage, and this involves becoming aware of and learning about the medical robots. In the second stage —*persuasion*—the director of the clinic (the adopter) would actively seek out information about the medical robots to learn more about, and to begin to evaluate the utility of, the robots for the clinic. As Haider and Kreps (2004) note, an important function of this stage is the reduction of uncertainty about the innovation. For people with a higher need to reduce uncertainty, this stage can take longer than for people with a higher tolerance for uncertainty. The third stage is the *decision* stage, and in this stage the clinic director actively makes the choice of whether to accept or reject the medical robots. Psychological theories of decision making can help explain the processes that occur in this stage (Bandura, 2006). The fourth stage is the *implementation* stage. In this stage, the clinic director might bring medical robots into the clinic for a trial period to either confirm or disconfirm the earlier decision to adopt the innovation. The final stage is the *confirmation* stage, where the individual (or group) confirms that the right decision was made.

Of course, if any of these stages are negative then the innovation will not be adopted. For example, if the adopter is not aware of the innovation (knowledge phase), or if the innovator begins the initial use of the innovation (the implementation stage) but decides not to use the innovation any more, the innovation process will be stopped—at least at this time. Several things separate people who adopt a diffusion early on versus later, including their communication network, personality factors, and their threshold for moving through the five stages (Dearing & Meyer, 2006; Hornik, 2004). People who have a higher threshold before going to the next stage will take longer to adopt an innovation than will people with lower thresholds.

Across all of the domains where the diffusion process has been studied, research had consistently demonstrated that innovations take time to diffuse and that when mapped across time, there are five general categories of people: innovators, early adopters, early majority, late majority, and laggards (see Figure 15.1; Rogers, 2003; Srivastava & Moreland, 2015). As the name implies, innovators are the first people to try an innovation, such as a new medical intervention, and they tend to be highly adventurous as well as more educated (Dearing & Meyer, 2006). Interestingly, innovators are not likely to be tied into the local networks, so they generally are not opinion leaders. Instead, innovators are part of a network that bypasses the local community and is connected to a larger group of innovators. For example, doctors that are involved in national or international medical conferences will learn about new medical procedures earlier and consequently are more likely to be innovators. Because innovators are not part of the local network, they are also less influenced by norms (Dearing & Meyer, 2006; Rogers, 2003). It is through this network that extends beyond their local communities that innovators learn about an innovation earlier than most people are aware of the innovation's existence. This also tends to be the smallest category of people.

The second category, early adopters, are the most likely to be opinion leaders, because they are tied into the local network. Like innovators, they tend to be more adventuresome and to take risks, which means they will adopt innovations sooner than others within their social network. But because they are typically not cosmopolitan, they learn about innovations somewhat slower than innovators. So instead of learning about the innovation at a medical conference, a doctor who is an early adopter may read about the innovation in trade publications or learn about the new procedure from innovators who have already adopted it. As opinion leaders, the early adopters play a critical role in the diffusion process through a mix of interpersonal communication and social norms (Kincaid, 2004).

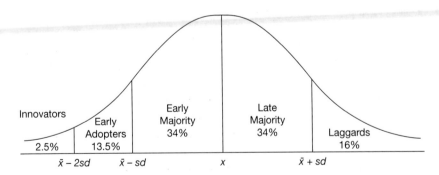

FIGURE 15.1 The five types of adopters that emerge across time according to the diffusion of innovation theory.

Source: Rogers (2003).

The early majority (third category) are the most adventuresome of the general population, because they have lower thresholds for moving from one stage in the decision process to the next (Dearing & Meyer, 2006). In addition, opinion leaders play an important role in the early majority adopting an innovation through interpersonal communication and normative pressure exerted by the opinion leaders to adopt the innovation (Valente, 2006). A doctor in the early majority is likely to learn about new medical procedures from a mix of trade publications and opinion leaders, and the opinion leaders may apply normative pressure on the doctor to adopt the new procedures. The late majority (fourth category) are slow to adopt an innovation and often do so more because of normative pressures from their local networks (e.g., the majority of doctors in the local community now use the new procedure) than from a real desire to use the innovation. As the name suggests, laggards (fifth category) are the last to adopt an innovation. Research suggests that laggards tend to be socially isolated and resistant to change.

Diffusion theory is one of the few theories of communication that actively theorizes about time (Rogers, 2003), which is important because time should be a central concern of communication scholars (Lang & Ewoldsen, 2010). Specifically, diffusion theory is concerned with the amount of time that it takes for a diffusion to saturate a population. Obviously, the time that it takes a diffusion to spread among a population can vary widely and depends on the nature of the linkages within the network (Bandura, 2006; Valente, 2006). The diffusion curve tracks the percentage of a population that has adopted the diffusion across time, and it typically is an S-shaped curve (see Figure 15.2; Rogers, 2003). Initially, very few people adopt an innovation (e.g., only the innovators), so the curve starts off very slow. The rate of adoption picks up as early adopters begin using the innovation. The rate of adoption further increases as the influence of these opinion leaders spreads to the early majority. Typically, this involves the fastest rate of adoption of the innovation. Then the rate of adoption slows down as the adoption process transitions to the late adopters and slows down even more as it transitions to the laggards.

Diffusion of innovations has been an important theory for communication scholars for half of a century, and the theory has been used broadly to implement health campaigns (Haider & Kreps, 2004). The theory has generated over 5,000 published reports across the social sciences. But like any good theory, it is still generating questions that need to be addressed to further our understanding of how health campaigns—particularly in developing countries—can be better understood and improved (Hornik, 2004). Likewise, as with all theories, the theory has limitations. For example, the theory does have an innovation bias and assumes that innovations are generally always good (Rogers, 2003). Likewise, the theory is broad in that it attempts to explain a lot of behavior across time, but this breadth means that there are large sections of the theory that are still in need of development and fine-tuning. For example, only recently has research begun to explicate the role of social norms in the diffusion process (Kincaid, 2004).

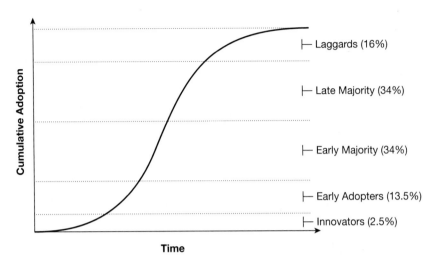

FIGURE 15.2 The five types of adopters shown as the cumulative percentage of the population that adopts an innovation.

Source: Rogers (2003).

The Health Belief Model

The health belief model emerged in the late 1950s and early 1960s as an outgrowth of applied studies focusing on public health issues (Rosenstock, 1974). The health belief model draws from Lewin's (1997) field theory with the idea that there are multiple positive and negative forces or motivations that push people toward or away from certain behaviors (Rosenstock, 1974; Maiman & Becker, 1974). But following trends in social psychology in the 1950s and 1960s, one of the major influences on the theory was models of subjective expected utility (Maiman & Becker, 1974). Subjective expected utility models maintain that people decide whether to engage in a behavior such as exercising based on the perceived outcome or value of exercising. These outcomes are a function of the subjective value that a person places on an outcome (v) and their perceived likelihood or expectation that the outcome will occur (e). At a very basic level, the subjective expected utility of a choice is typically hypothesized to be a multiplicative function of value and the likelihood that the outcome will occur, such that the subjective expected utility (SEU) = $v \star e$ (Luce, 2003). If the subjective expected utility of exercising is positive, then people should be predisposed to exercise.[1]

In the context of health behaviors, the health belief model defined the value of the outcome as the perceived severity or seriousness of a health outcome (e.g., how bad or severe would it be to come down with the flu) and perceived likelihood was defined as people's perceived susceptibility to obtaining or getting the negative outcome (e.g., how likely are you to come down with the flu).

Importantly, both severity and susceptibility are perceptual variables within the model, so that one person may judge coming down with the flu to be extremely severe and another person would judge it as not at all severe, and the same is true for people's perceived susceptibility (Rosenstock, 1974). The model predicts that when perceived severity and perceived vulnerability are high, people should be motivated to engage in behaviors to avoid the outcome. But the perceived benefits and costs of engaging in the preventative behavior in this instance are also important. If the costs of engaging in the preventative behavior are judged to be high, then people will be less likely to engage in the preventative behavior. Conversely, if the benefits of the outcome are judged to be high, then people are more likely to engage in that behavior. More recently, the emphasis has switched to focusing on the efficacy of the response. *Response efficacy* deals with the perception of how likely it is that the outcome behavior will achieve the goal (e.g., will a flu shot help people avoid getting the flu). If response efficacy is low, people are not likely to engage in the behavior, but as efficacy increases, the likelihood that people will engage in the behavior also goes up. Finally, a relatively unexplored component of the early model involved cues to action. These are prompts or reminders in the environment that hopefully will increase the likelihood that people will engage in the target behavior. Cues to action include such things as media campaigns (posters promoting flu shots), observing the threatening behavior (e.g., seeing people with the flu), or interpersonal communication with family members (Janz & Becker, 1984). Clearly, the model captures Lewin's (1997) idea of competing forces pushing and pulling a person in different directions in terms of behavioral engagement.

Overall, research has supported the health belief model (Janz & Becker, 1984; Kirscht, 1974). However, there are limitations to the model. For example, McGuire (2001) argues that the model basically takes a learning theoretic approach to persuasion somewhat like the hypodermic needle model of the early twentieth century, because the model does not address how people respond to messages about health threats. Likewise, many of the tests of the health belief model involved fear appeal messages (Janz & Becker, 1984), but the model does not explain how fear appeals work. That is, criticisms of the model tend to point out its somewhat analytical approach, which simultaneously does not address the mechanisms of behavior change.

The Extended Parallel Process Model of Fear Appeals

The study of fear appeals has a long history within the social sciences and much of this work has been tied to health communication (Boster & Mongeau, 1984). Based on models like the health belief model and the subjective expected utility model, it was assumed that fear appeal messages should be highly persuasive, because focusing on the severity of an illness should increase perceptions of the costs associated with the health outcome. Likewise, a message that focuses on how vulnerable people are to the health outcome should increase perceptions of how likely it is that they will experience the aversive health outcome. In other words, there should be a linear increase in the effectiveness of a message as the level of fear aroused by the message increases.

However, extensive research has demonstrated that fear appeal messages do not operate in a simple linear fashion (Boster & Mongeau, 1984; Floyd et al., 2000). Probably the classic study in this area was Janis and Feshbach's (1953) study of fear appeals and dental hygiene. This study demonstrated the complexities involved in studying fear appeal messages. Participants who were exposed to the high fear appeal message showed more ambivalent attitudinal responses to the message than did the participants who were exposed to either the low or moderate fear appeal messages. However, on the critical behavioral measures, participants in the high fear appeal message condition had not changed their behaviors, and the most behavioral change was found for participants in the low fear condition, suggesting that the high fear appeal message undermined the effectiveness of the message. Therefore, a linear and simple relationship between fear and behavior change appeared to be an inaccurate model for the issue.

A typical reaction to counterintuitive findings such as those by Janis and Feshbach's (1953) data is an upsurge in research and theorizing about that domain, and that was certainly the case for fear appeals. One important line of research involved Leventhal's (1970) dual process model. Leventhal hypothesized that people respond to fear appeal messages in two fairly independent ways: fear control or danger control. Fear control occurs when people judge the threat presented in a fear appeal message to be real, but do not feel that there are any effective ways to avoid the aversive outcome presented in the message. For example, some people justify smoking because they believe they will die of some type of cancer anyway. Consequently, people who believe there is nothing they can do to avoid getting cancer will defensively process the message because there is nothing they think they can do about the threat. In this instance, a fear appeal message will likely backfire. Conversely, danger control occurs when people judge that they are susceptible to a severe outcome, but they can effectively avoid that outcome. Consequently, people are motivated to engage in the behavior that decreases their susceptibility to a severe threat, and the fear appeal message will be successful. If a person is convinced that she is at risk for heart disease and that exercise will help manage that risk, she is more likely to exercise because she has engaged in danger control processing. The dual process model was important because it could explain when fear appeal messages would work (e.g., people engage in danger control) and when fear appeal messages would fail (e.g., people engage in fear control). Research has generally supported Leventhal's formulation (Leventhal et al., 1983; Witte, 1994). However, the dual process model has been criticized because it does not adequately predict when danger control versus fear control processes will occur.

A second line of research was Rogers' (1975) work on protection motivation theory (PMT). PMT involved an elaborate extension of the health belief model, but the PMT focused on both the elements of a fear appeal message and the cognitive processes that mediated the effectiveness of those elements of the message. In the original model, Rogers (1975) hypothesized that an effective fear appeal message included, first, information on the magnitude of the noxious outcome associated with the health threat, with *appraised severity* operating as the associated cognitive process. Second, a fear appeal message could include the probability that the threat would occur, and the *expectancy of exposure* was the associated cognitive process. Finally, a message could include information about the efficacy of a coping response, with *belief in the efficacy* of the coping response operating as the associated cognitive process. When a message contains these three elements and the associated cognitive processes occurred, then there would be an increase in protection motivation.[2] Protection motivation is the desire to act in a way to avoid the health threat. It is important to note that fear is not an important variable in protection motivation theory, and that behavior change could occur from a fear appeal message without fear being aroused.

Protection motivation theory was later expanded to include self-efficacy (Maddux & Rogers, 1983), because it became clear that even when people knew of a way to avoid a threat, they might not engage in the protective behavior because they did not think *they* could engage in the behavior. For example, most smokers know that stopping smoking will decrease the dangers of smoking (high response efficacy), but many smokers do not feel they can stop smoking because cigarettes are addictive (low self-efficacy). Even if a person believes there is an effective way to avoid the health risk, if they do not believe they can engage in that behavior, then they are less likely to experience protection motivation (Maddux & Rogers, 1983). The theory was further modified to focus on threat appraisal (a combination of severity of the outcome and the likelihood of the outcome occurring) and coping appraisal (a combination of response and self-efficacy) (Floyd et al., 2000; Rogers & Prentice-Dunn, 1997). Threat appraisal and coping appraisal closely mirror Leventhal's fear control and danger control processes.

While research has generally supported PMT (Floyd et al., 2000), the theory has been criticized because it is not really a theory of fear appeals. The PMT relies more on cognitive appraisal processes than emotional processes to explain the effects of fear appeal messages. More recently, the extended parallel process model, or EPPM, was proposed to reincorporate fear into the study of fear appeal messages (Witte, 1994, 1995; Witte et al., 1993), but the theory draws heavily from PMT and Leventhal's dual process model. The model contained eleven propositions when it was originally proposed (Witte, 1994). A summary of the model follows.

Extending the health belief model and the PMT, the EPPM maintains that there are four crucial elements to an effective fear appeal message: severity, susceptibility, response efficacy, and self-efficacy (Witte, 1994, 1995). If suscept-ibility and vulnerability are low, then people will not perceive a threat and they will stop processing the message. However, if severity and susceptibility are high, then people should perceive a threat that can lead to fear. When fear is activated, people are motivated to further process the message to see if something can be done to avoid the threat.[3] However, if response and/or self-efficacy are low, then *fear control processes* should occur and people will be motivated to undertake defensive processes such as avoiding future information on the topic or derogating the source of the information (Witte, 1994; Roskos-Ewoldsen et al., 2004). The theory goes further and proposes that when fear control processes occur, the people exposed to the fear message may actually experience a boomerang effect and move in the opposite direction of that advocated in the message (Witte, 1994).

However, if fear is elicited and self- and response efficacy are high, then perceived efficacy should be high and people will engage in *danger control processes*. Danger control processes involve an increase in protection motivation, which leads to people changing their attitudes, behavioral intentions, and behavior to avoid the aversive threat. So within the EPPM, fear is related to danger control processing, which was not the case for PMT. If the danger control process results in an at-risk judgment, and the efficacy judgment suggests that the individual can respond to the threat, then the fear that motivated the processing of the message should decrease. Critically, attitude and behavior change are driven by perceptions of response efficacy according to the EPPM, but people will not be motivated to process the efficacy component of a message unless they have already experienced fear because vulnerability and severity are high.

The EPPM has been extensively tested since its introduction a little over 20 years ago (Roberto, 2013; Witte & Allen, 2000; Witte et al., 2002). The model had a substantial influence on the study of fear appeals and health campaigns, but may also provide a fruitful way to study emotional appeals in general (Lewis et al., 2013). However, all evidence is not entirely consistent with the model (Popova, 2012; Witte & Allen, 2000), and research suggests that the model may be too simplistic an approach to the study of fear appeals (Carrera et al., 2010; Napper et al., 2014; Roskos-Ewoldsen et al., 2004). Indeed, only a few of the original propositions in the theory have received unequivocal support, and several of the foundational propositions have received very mixed support (Popova, 2012).

Education and Entertainment

Entertainment-education (or edutainment) is the deliberate use of entertainment media to disseminate health-related messages (Greenberg et al., 2004; Singhal & Rogers, 2004). Initially, edutainment involved long-term health campaigns aimed at a variety of issues such as HIV and AIDS or domestic violence, but edutainment can also take the form of a single episode of a TV program or a single comic book. The goals of edutainment can range from increasing awareness of an issue, disseminating health-related information, changing attitudes and social norms, and ultimately changing behaviors (Piotrow & de Fossard, 2004).

Edutainment has been used to promote healthy behaviors since the late 1950s (Poindexter, 2004; Sabido, 2004), though some people argue that the practice can be traced back to the ancient Greeks. Edutainment has been utilized because it can provide a wider reach and avoid some of the resistance that traditional campaigns face (Moyer-Guse, 2008). Early campaigns were used primarily in developing countries (Poindexter, 2004); however, edutainment has been used around the globe. It has been used successfully to address a number of different health-related issues, ranging from HIV and safe sex to domestic violence, breast cancer, organ donation, and family planning (Beck, 2004; Bouman, 2004; Khalil & Rintamaki, 2014; Moyer-Guse & Nabi, 2010; Usdin et al., 2004).

Edutainment is not a theory of health promotion. Rather it is a strategy that is used to promote healthy behaviors (Singhal & Rogers, 2004). However, a number of theories have been used to design edutainment campaigns (Sood et al., 2004), including several theories that have been discussed in this volume, such as social cognition theory (Bandura, 2004; Singhal & Rogers, 2004), diffusion of innovations (Rogers, 2003), and the elaboration likelihood model. But theories specific to edutainment have also been developed, including the extended elaboration likelihood model (E-ELM; Slater & Rouner, 2002) and the entertainment overcoming resistance model (EORM; Moyer-Guse, 2008).

As discussed in Chapter 12, the elaboration likelihood model (ELM) is one of the dominant models of persuasion. Consequently, the ELM is a good starting point for studying edutainment. The initial assumption for the ELM is that people process a message because they are motivated to hold a correct attitude (Petty & Cacioppo, 1986). However, people are rarely motivated to form correct attitudes about various topics when they are watching entertainment media (Slater, 2002; Slater & Rouner, 2002). Instead, a fundamental motive for engaging in narrative is entertainment. Consequently, people who are watching edutainment likely have very different motivations for processing the message than do people who are listening to a persuasive appeal on the same topic (Slater & Rouner, 2002).

Based on these differences in how people process expository versus narrative texts, Slater and Rouner (2002) proposed the Extended-ELM (E-ELM). Within the ELM, the distinction is made between central and peripheral processing; however, this distinction makes little sense when discussing edutainment. Unlike motivations for consuming persuasive media, people process narratives in order to be absorbed (or transported) by the *story*. Slater and Rouner (2002) argue that persuasion based on edutainment will be a function of engagement with that story and absorption with the characters. One of the consequences of engagement and absorption is that people are much less likely to counterargue a message that they disagree with, because they are focused on following the story and the characters (Kreuter et al., 2007; Moyer-Guse, 2008; Slater & Rouner, 1996). In order to retain enjoyment, people typically avoid counterarguing because it would have the potential to undermine story engagement, and thus decrease story enjoyment. Recall that for counterattitudinal messages, counterarguing undermines the persuasiveness of the message (Petty & Cacioppo, 1986). By decreasing people's counterarguing of the counterattitudinal message, the relative number of positive responses to the message increases, which should result in more attitude change.

A further reason that edutainment may be more persuasive is that people suspend their disbelief while watching fictional narratives (Slater & Rouner, 2002). Research has demonstrated that once people accept something as true—such as they might do while watching a fictional narrative—they have to effortfully undo that belief (Gilbert, 1991). Consequently, things that are viewed in a narrative are not counterargued and may have a tendency to be more believable (Slater & Rouner, 2002). Research has generally been consistent with the model (Khalil & Rintamaki, 2014; Moyer-Guse & Nabi, 2010).

Like the E-ELM, the EORM focuses on entertainment messages that are primarily counterattitudinal (Moyer-Guse, 2008). But the EORM has a broader focus than the Extended-ELM. The EORM has a series of seven propositions focusing on why edutainment will be more effective than standard persuasive appeals. For example, the EORM hypothesizes that parasocial interactions with the main characters will decrease reactance to counterattitudinal behaviors. Reactance occurs when people feel that their freedom to engage in certain behaviors is restricted. For example, ordinances that restrict smoking can create reactance in smokers. Reactance can often create a situation where people become more strongly committed to a threatened behavior such as smoking. The EORM maintains that when viewers have a parasocial interaction with a character, and that character advocates something that would restrict the viewers' behavior (e.g., the character advocates to another character to quit smoking), that character's behavior will not create reactance because it is not perceived as persuasive or in some way restricting the viewers' freedom (Moyer-Guse, 2008; Moyer-Guse & Nabi, 2010). The EORM also hypothesizes that edutainment should overcome people's selective avoidance of topics they find fearful, because they are unlikely to shut off a program that they are enjoying if the show brings up a threatening topic. However, it is important to note that research testing the E-ELM and the EORM has found that people's prior attitudes and behavior moderate the effectiveness of edutainment (Igartua & Barrios, 2012; Moyer-Guse & Nabi, 2011).

Attitude–Behavior Relationship

Clearly, communication research into the effectiveness of health or political campaigns has to consider the relationship between attitudes and behavior because, arguably, behavior is often the only true variable of interest, with attitude being relevant only insofar as its ability to predict behavior is concerned. Indeed, research on health campaigns has drawn heavily on several of the theories that will be discussed concerning the attitude–behavior relationship. However, the early evidence on the ability of attitudes to predict behavior was spotty. The classic early study of the attitude–behavior relationship was LaPiere's (1934) study of racial attitudes and behavior. Despite serious methodological shortcomings, the study was cited as evidence that racist attitudes toward Asians did not predict discriminatory behaviors toward Asians. Indeed, the Supreme Court cited this study in *Brown vs. Board of Education*—the Supreme Court decision that abolished segregation in public schools—to justify that people's racist attitudes would not result in racist behavior when integration occurred (Jackson, 2005). Making a similar point about the inability of attitudes to predict behavior, Corey (1937) found that people's attitudes toward cheating, as measured on a survey of social attitudes taken on the first day of class, did not predict the students' cheating behavior on weekly quizzes across the semester ($r = .03$).

The early research on the attitude–behavior relationship was so dismal that Wicker (1969) argued that the correlation never exceeded .30 (a small to moderate relationship) and that the study of attitudes should be abandoned. Obviously, the attitude concept was not abandoned and attitude scholars responded by developing models of the attitude–behavior relationship. In the next section of this chapter we will discuss the theory of reasoned action (TRA) and its derivatives, including the theory of planned behavior (TPB) and the integrated model (Fishbein & Ajzen, 1975; Fishbein & Ajzen, 2010). Then we will discuss Fazio's (1986) process model of the attitude–behavior relationship. We will close the discussion of models of the attitude–behavior relationship with the motivation and opportunity as determinants (MODE) model, which integrates the proceeding models into an overarching framework (Ewoldsen et al., 2015; Fazio, 1990).

The Theory of Reasoned Action and Its Progenies

The most influential model of the attitude–behavior relationship for health communication scholars has been the theory of reasoned action (TRA) and its derivatives (Fishbein & Ajzen, 1975; Fishbein & Ajzen, 2010). There have been hundreds of studies testing the TRA across a large number of different behavioral domains such as exercising, condom use and safe sex, and family planning (Albarracin et al., 2001; Fishbein & Ajzen, 2010; Sheppard et al., 1988). The TRA maintains that behavior is a function of attitudes toward the behavior, subjective norms, how the attitudes toward the behavior and subjective norms are weighted by the individual, and behavioral intentions (see Figure 15.3). The most proximal determinant of behavior is behavioral intention (BI), which reflects a person's decision to engage in a behavior. Behavioral intention would reflect the plan or goal of beginning to exercise. Clearly, people who intend to engage in exercise behavior are more likely to engage in exercise behavior than people who do not intend to exercise. Furthermore, the TRA incorporates BI, because while a person may have the intention to engage in a behavior, there are other factors that influence whether a person can engage in the behavior (e.g.,

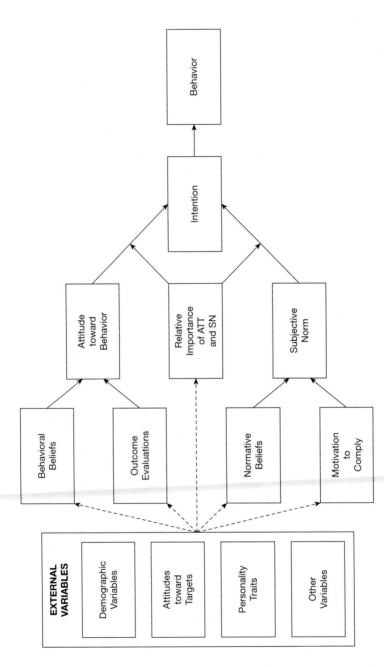

FIGURE 15.3 A schematic of the theory of reasoned action. At the left side of the figure are distal factors that predict behavior by influencing subjective norms, attitude toward the behavior, or how these two factors are weighted to predict behavioral intention.

Source: Fishbein & Ajzen (1975).

whether the person has the requisite skills, resources, or ability to engage in the behavior). For example, a person may intend to exercise but not have any place where she can exercise.

Within the TRA, behavioral intention is predicted by two things: attitude toward the behavior (A_B) and subjective norms (SN). The TRA focuses on a person's attitude toward the target behavior because the attitude toward the object and the attitude toward the behavior may not always converge. A person may like the exercise bike, but not like riding the exercise bike. The attitude toward the behavior is a function of the salient beliefs about performing the behavior. There are two components of these beliefs that are important for predicting the A_B: the evaluation of how good or bad the outcome is (abbreviated as e) and the likelihood that the outcome will occur (abbreviated as b). So a person may like losing weight from exercising but perceive the likelihood that he would lose weight as low. The following formula captures how these two components of the beliefs are combined to predict A_B: $A_B = \sum b_i e_i$ In this model, b and e are multiplied by each other for each salient belief and then summed across the salient beliefs (Fishbein & Ajzen, 1975). According to the theory, the number of salient beliefs typically ranges from five to nine, due to limitations in short-term memory.

The other component of the original TRA that predicts behavioral intention is subjective norms. Norms have long been identified as important predictors of people's behaviors (Cialdini et al., 1991; Rhodes & Ewoldsen, 2013; Rimal & Real, 2003). Subjective norms involve a person's perception of what other people expect him or her to do. If a person perceives that her family wants her to exercise, then she should experience normative pressure to exercise if she is motivated to do what her family wants her to do. As with A_B, there are two components of subjective norms. There is the belief that important other people do or do not want the individual to engage in the behavior (abbreviated as b in the model), and then there is the motivation of the person to comply with what these important others want her or him to do (abbreviated as m in the model). The formula for subject norms is as follows: SN= $\sum b_i m_i$. As with beliefs, these two components of the norms are multiplied for each important other person (or group of people) and then summed to determine the subjective norm.

Research has consistently found that subjective norms play an important role in predicting behavior (e.g., health behavior, health adherence), but meta-analysis generally find that A_B is a stronger predictor of behavioral intention than subjective norms (Albarracin et al., 2001; Sheppard et al., 1988). However, it is important to note that people may weight subjective norms and attitudes differently when forming behavioral intentions. One personality variable that moderates the attitude–behavior relationship is self-monitoring (Snyder, 1987). Research has demonstrated that people can differ in how much they monitor the situation or their own attitudes when deciding how to act. People who are high self-monitors are more responsive to the larger situation, whereas low self-monitors are guided more by their own attitudes. Low self-monitors' behavior is consistently predicted by their attitudes. So low self-monitors' attitudes toward exercising will be more predictive of their behavioral intentions than their subjective norms. Conversely, high self-monitors' attitudes tend to be less predictive of their behavior unless the situation is one that promotes acting consistently with their attitude (Snyder & Kendzierski, 1982). The TRA captures this difference between high and low self-monitors through this weighting function. High self-monitors will tend to weigh the link between subjective norms and behavioral intentions more than low self-monitors. Conversely, low self-monitors will tend to weigh the link between attitude toward the behavior and behavioral intentions more than high self-monitors. For example, high self-monitors, more so than low self-monitors, may utilize their subjective norms toward exercise, for example, in their intentions to engage in exercise behavior.

According to the original TRA, the only proximal predictors of behavior are behavioral intentions, attitude toward the behavior, subjective norms, and the weights on the paths leading to behavioral intention. Any other variable that influences behavior is considered a distal variable and can only influence behavior through one of these four components of the model. We have already seen how this works for self-monitoring through its influence on how people weight subjective norms and attitudes toward the behavior when predicting behavioral intentions. As another example, people's attitude toward the object (the exercise bike) may influence their attitude toward the behavior (riding the exercise bike), and through this process, the attitude towards the object would influence behavior.

One of the criticisms of the original TRA was that it was limited to volitional behaviors (Yzer, 2013). The theory of planned behavior (TPB) was proposed as a modification of the original TRA, with the goal to expand the original model to nonvolitional behaviors (Ajzen, 1991; Ajzen & Madden, 1986). Specifically, the TPB incorporated self-efficacy (see Chapter 15) into the model under the rubric of perceived behavioral control.[4] Perceived behavioral control involves the perception of how easy a behavior is to carry out. If perceived behavioral control is high, then the TPB and the TRA are identical. However, if perceived behavioral control is low, then perceived behavioral control predicts behavior directly as well as being mediated by behavioral intention (see Figure 15.4).

The final modification to the original TRA and the TPB is the integrative model of behavioral prediction (Fishbein & Yzer, 2003). The integrative model incorporates components of the health belief model into the model. Specifically, the integrated model adds skills and environmental constraints to the TRA/TPB. Both skills and environmental constraints are predicted to operate directly on behavior. Clearly, if people do not have the requisite skills to engage in a behavior, they will be less likely to engage in the behavior. Likewise, if there are strong environmental constraints that make it difficult for people to engage in the behavior, such as the lack of resources or legal constraints on performing the behavior, then people are less likely to perform that behavior.

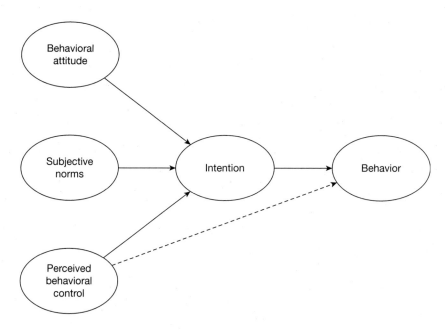

FIGURE 15.4 The theory of planned behavior expands the theory of reasoned action by incorporating perceived behavioral control as a predictor of behavioral intention and directly predicting behavior.

Source: Ajzen (1991).

As noted earlier, the empirical research supporting the TRA and the TPB is extensive (Albarracin et al., 2001). There has been less research testing the integrative model because of its relative newness. However, there have been a number of criticisms of the TRA, and by extension, the TPB and the integrated model. Perhaps the most telling criticism of these models is not that the models are inaccurate, but that the scope of these models is limited because they focus more on deliberative behaviors or behaviors that are tied to forethought (Fazio, 1986), which does not necessarily include all, or even most human behaviors.

The Process Model of the Attitude–Behavior Relationship

Attitudes can vary in their strength (Petty & Krosnick, 1995). One important characteristic of attitudes that is tied to the strength of the attitude is how accessible an attitude is in memory (Arpan et al., 2007; Dillard, 1993; Fazio, 1986). Attitude accessibility refers to the ease by which an attitude is activated from memory. Attitudes that are highly accessible from memory are easily activated from memory and may even be so accessible that the mere presence of the attitude object in the environment may result in the attitude coming to mind without the person trying to activate the attitude (Fazio et al., 1986; Roskos-Ewoldsen & Fazio, 1992). For example, people with highly accessible pro-smoking attitudes will likely have that attitude activated from memory whenever they see a cigarette. Extensive research has demonstrated that as the accessibility of an attitude increases, it becomes more likely that the attitude will predict behavior (Fazio, 1986; Fazio & Roskos-Ewoldsen, 2005). Attitudes that are accessible in memory are also more functional, because they are more likely to influence how information is processed, how social stimuli will be categorized, how decision making occurs, and even what people orient their attention to in the environment (Fazio & Roskos-Ewoldsen, 2005; Fazio et al., 1994; Rhodes et al., 2008).

Drawing on the research on attitude accessibility, the process model of the attitude–behavior relationship was developed (Fazio, 1986). The process model maintains that once an attitude is activated from memory, it will influence what we attend to in the environment (Roskos-Ewoldsen & Fazio, 1992) and how the object of our attention is categorized or understood (Fazio et al., 1994; Young et al., 2014). For example, people with highly accessible positive or negative attitudes toward smoking are more likely to notice smoking behavior in their environment. Based on these processes, the accessible attitude influences how the object is perceived, particularly when the object is ambiguous (Fazio & Williams, 1986; Fazio et al., 1994). The perception of the attitude object then influences how the current event is defined. Social situations tend to be characterized by ambiguity (Fazio, 1990; Latane & Darley, 1970). This ambiguity provides the opportunity for attitudes to bias how the situation is perceived. For example, if a negative attitude toward smoking is activated in memory, that attitude will influence how a cigarette is interpreted (as a harmful object) so that the object is seen as negative, and consequently the current event will likely be defined as undesirable or even noxious (Fazio, 1986).

At the same time, norms operate to influence how people define a situation and decide on appropriate behaviors for that situation. Norms can vary in their accessibility from memory, and norms that are more accessible from memory are more likely to influence behavior than norms that are less accessible from memory (Rhodes & Ewoldsen, 2009; Rhodes et al., 2014). If the situation is defined as formal, then a different set of norms will operate to influence how the person interprets the situation and determines what behaviors are appropriate given the formality of the situation. Other behaviors would likely be seen as appropriate if the situation is informal. Likewise, an adolescent with a highly accessible anti-smoking norm is less likely to begin smoking than an adolescent with a highly accessible pro-smoking norm (Rhodes et al., 2014). These two processes— attitudes influencing how an event is interpreted, and norms influencing how the situation is defined—are the mechanisms by which accessible attitudes and norms influence behavior, according to the process model (Fazio, 1986). Extensive research has supported the process model (Fazio & Roskos-Ewoldsen, 2005; Rhodes & Ewoldsen, 2013).

Motivation and Opportunity as Determinants: The MODE Model

At this point, we have two models of the attitude–behavior relationship: the TRA/TPB/integrative model and the process model of the attitude–behavior relationship. The motivation and opportunity as determinants (or MODE) model integrates these two approaches by specifying when each model predicts behavior (Ewoldsen et al., 2015; Fazio, 1990). The MODE model starts with the distinction between deliberative and spontaneous behaviors. When people engage in deliberative behaviors, such as beginning to exercise or whether to have a medical procedure done, they tend to carefully consider as much of the available information as they can and thoughtfully consider the various options prior to making a decision. Conversely, spontaneous behaviors such as smoking or drinking alcohol do not involve the effortful consideration of the available information and tend to be more spur of the moment. Spontaneous behaviors tend to rely on information that is highly accessible when making a decision. Based on this description of deliberative and spontaneous behaviors, it should be clear that the MODE model hypothesizes that deliberative behaviors are better predicted by the TRA/TPB/integrative model. Conversely, spontaneous behaviors are better predicted by the process model of the attitude–behavior relationship with its reliance on accessibility as an explanatory mechanism (Fazio, 1990; Rhodes & Ewoldsen, 2013).

But when are people more likely to engage in deliberative as opposed to spontaneous behaviors, especially regarding health behaviors? As the name of the MODE model suggests, motivation and opportunity play key roles. When motivation is low, people likely make decisions based on what information comes to mind most quickly, because they do not want to expend the energy to engage in an exhaustive search of memory. In this situation, information that is more accessible from memory is more likely to influence people's behavior. Conversely, when people are highly motivated, they will devote more resources to the decision process, and thus are more likely to engage in active memory search (or environment search) for information such as beliefs, attitudes, and norms that are relevant to the decision, and to ultimately use more of that information when making that decision. In this situation, accessible information can play a role in decision making, but the relative influence of the accessible information is likely diminished because additional information is brought to bear in making the decision in a more deliberative fashion.

In addition to motivational concerns, the opportunity for careful consideration of the available information is also an important determinant of processing. When people are provided with less opportunity to consider the available information, they are more likely to rely on information that is accessible and quickly comes to mind (Fazio, 1990). For example, when an adolescent is offered a cigarette at a party, she doesn't have time to consider all of her beliefs about smoking, and accessible attitudes and norms will predict whether she accepts the cigarette or not. The opportunity to consider the available information—as opposed to accessible information—is necessary if people are going to control for the effects of automatically activated information when making a decision. Factors such as time and available cognitive resources can influence a person's opportunity to make deliberative judgments (Fazio, 1990). Thus, according to the MODE model, if an adolescent is motivated and has the opportunity to consider whether she should accept a cigarette, then the processes laid out by the TRA and its related theories should predict her behavior. Conversely, if she does not have the motivation and/or the opportunity to consider what she should do, then her accessible attitudes and norms will likely predict her behavior as predicted by the process model (Fazio, 1990; Rhodes & Ewoldsen, 2013).

Stages of Change

A number of different theories have been presented in this chapter, sometimes leaving readers questioning which theory is correct, or at least best supported by the evidence. As discussed in the section on the MODE model, the answers are typically not that straightforward. Indeed, McGuire (1983) made the seemingly extreme argument that most theories are correct—the important issue for scholars is to determine *when* the theory is correct. In other words, good theorizing involves identifying the limiting conditions of a theory, or when and where that theory will operate. The stages of change approach provides such a framework for possibly identifying when different theories of health behavior will or will not be successful (Slater, 1999).

When people are engaged in a negative health behavior (e.g., smoking) or want to start a positive health behavior (e.g., exercising), they do not simply wake up one day and decide to quit the negative behavior or start the positive behavior. Behavior change occurs across time, and the stages of change framework attempts to capture this process. The model maintains that there are five stages that people progress through when changing health-related behaviors (Prochaska & DiClemente, 1983; Prochaska et al., 1992). People in the *precontemplation* stage do not acknowledge that there is a problem. In terms of the health belief model, they judge themselves to be low in severity or low in vulnerability (or both) to a health threat. For example, they may believe that even though they smoke, they are really not at risk for getting cancer. People in the *contemplation* stage are becoming aware that there may be an issue, but they have not yet committed to making a change. People in this stage may experience a lot of vacillation. The *preparation* stage occurs when people form a clear intention to change their behavior, but typically only small changes occur in this stage. People who are getting ready to quit smoking are in this stage. As the name implies, in the *action* stage people make major changes in their behavior, such as quitting smoking. Finally, in the *maintenance* stage, people actively avoid backsliding and work on maintaining the changed behavior. For example, former smokers may avoid places where they used to smoke, so they don't have cravings to begin smoking again. Over 1,500 studies have tested the stages of change model (Norcross et al., 2011). Research suggests that the model is applicable to both positive and negative behaviors (Prochaska et al., 1994). But it is also important to note that people do not move directly through the stages. Instead, for many behaviors, people will relapse, so that the model really operates as a spiral, with people making it to a given stage and then moving back to an earlier stage before beginning to move through the stages again.

The framework has proved useful for health communication scholars. Research on the stages of change model has found that certain processes operate to move people between different stages (Prochaska et al., 1992). For example, people in the precontemplation stage often go through a process that is referred to as consciousness raising, which involves becoming more aware of the problem and seeking out more information. This process is often a precursor to moving to the contemplation stage. If there is similarity in the types of processes that people go through as they move from one stage to another, this suggests that health communication scholars should tailor their strategies to the stage that people are likely to be going through (Cho & Salmon, 2006; Slater, 1999; c.f. Fishbein & Ajzen, 2010). For example, the preparation stage involves people forming the intention to change their behavior. Because the theory of reasoned action/planned behavior focuses on behavioral intention, interventions based on these theories may be particularly effective for people at this stage of change. Conversely, the process model of the attitude–behavior relationship may be more suited to the action and maintenance stages (e.g., maintaining an exercise routine), because accessible attitudes are more predictive of spontaneous behavior (Ewoldsen et al., 2015; Fazio, 1990) and accessible attitudes play an important role in the maintenance of behavior change (Rhodes & Ewoldsen, 2013; Rhodes et al., 2008).

Interpersonal Health Communication

Interpersonal health communication refers to any communication about health concerns that occurs between individuals. Although traditionally this area has focused on the study of doctors and patients in medical consultations (e.g., Bain, 1979; Bertakis, 1977), the scope has expanded to include communication behaviors involving patients with a range of staff members of health care organizations (Street, 2003; Thompson, 2003), and with family members (Scott & Caughlin, 2015). Health communication includes conversations about medical diagnoses and treatments, as well as conversations about such topics as healthy eating (Dailey et al., 2014), infertility (Bute, 2009), and other health-related behaviors such as cigarette smoking (Bandi et al., 2008). However, the main thrust of this work has been devoted to characterizing the nature of the doctor–patient relationship.

The study of doctor–patient communication began as a result of a shift in thinking about medicine and medical treatments from a biomedical model to a biopsychosocial model (Katz, 1995). Specifically, the biomedical model, which characterized the practice of medicine through the middle of the twentieth century, assumed simply that infectious agents were responsible for disease, and that biological treatments (such as antibiotics) would cure the disease. In contrast, the biopsychosocial model, which began to gain traction in the latter half of the twentieth century, posits that there are biological, psychological, and social contributors to disease, ill health, and indeed wellness itself. From this perspective, one needs to understand not just the biology of the disease, but the social and psychological conditions surrounding the person who is experiencing ill health. Because of this broader conceptualization of health and illness, more emphasis was placed on the nature of the communication between patients and doctors in the medical consultation (Roter et al., 1997).

Institutions overseeing medical training have begun to be concerned about the nature of communication with patients, and physician training in many medical schools includes formal training in clinical communication skills (Benbassat & Baumal, 2002). This focus on communication in medical training has fed interest in research in this area. However, because the impetus arose out of practical concerns, there has been scant theorizing in this area of health communication. Although some researchers have developed models of communication in the medical encounter, models which have served to draw attention to variables of interest, there have been no real theories that have emerged to help organize or drive the research in this area (Babrow & Mattson, 2011; Cegala & Street, 2010).

Doctor–Patient Communication

Ideally, research on doctor–patient communication would examine the dynamic nature of the communication between doctor and patient in a medical encounter, tracking how the doctor's behavior influences the patient and vice versa. Because of the complexity of conducting that type or work, it is rarely done. The main shortcoming in this area of work has primarily focused on communicative behaviors enacted by the doctor in the medical encounter (Cegala & Street, 2010).

Making use of observational techniques, including video and audio recordings of medical consultations, two general styles of interaction have been identified in the communication patterns exhibited by medical professionals. The first is a doctor-centered style. This style of communication, which has been associated with adherence to a biomedical model of health and illness, is characterized by asking closed-ended questions and talking primarily about symptoms and treatment. In the typical doctor-centered interview, the doctor often stands, and the patient is seated on the examining table. It conveys a sense of the doctor as the expert and the patient as a passive recipient of the doctor's treatment. In contrast, a patient-centered communication style, which comes from a biopsychosocial model of health, is characterized by a sense that the doctor and patient are partners in the patient's health, with the doctor assuming a consultative role. Communicative behaviors include more open-ended questions, allowing the patient time to talk about the broad impacts of the illness on the patient's work and family life, and allowing the patient the opportunity to express concerns, fears, and hopes about the illness and the treatment (Murad et al., 2014; Roter, 1977; Street, 2003).

Research evaluating these different styles of communication in the medical encounter has determined that a patient-centered style tends to convey important benefits compared with a doctor-centered style: patients are more satisfied with their visit, are more likely to comply with treatment, and are less likely to bring suit against the physician (Brown et al., 2003). Although to some extent these findings are dependent on characteristics of the patient (Cegala & Post, 2009), the findings suggest the importance of training physicians to use a more patient-centered style. Training doctors to develop the communication skills necessary to engage in patient-centered communication has generally been successful (Helitzer et al., 2011; Mjaaland & Finset, 2009), although such interventions have not always been successfully linked to patient health outcomes (Manze et al., 2015). Finding significant effects of physician training programs on measurable health outcomes is difficult, because health outcomes are often affected by many variables, and communication typically operates through mechanisms such as trust and commitment to treatment (Street, 2013).

The other side of the doctor–patient dyad is, of course, the patient. Research has been conducted to identify the skills patients have that yield a more successful outcome in the clinical encounter, with promising results (Cegala & Post, 2009). Patient behavior that appears to be essential to good outcomes for health care decision making, compliance with prescribed treatments, and patient satisfaction generally focus on patients' active participation in the medical interview, in particular asking questions and verifying information (Cegala et al., 2000). Even more promising, communication skills intervention programs with patients appear to yield dramatic improvements in measureable outcomes (Cegala et al., 2013).

The main shortcoming in this area of work in health communication, as mentioned earlier, is the lack of an overarching theory to organize the emerging knowledge in doctor–patient communication (Cegala & Street, 2010). Another limitation in the work is the lack of focus on the dyad, and how the communication styles of doctors and patients mutually influence one another. Finally, the outcomes measured in this work tend to be short-term indicators such as compliance with treatments and patient satisfaction. The effects of communication style within the medical encounter on longer-range health outcomes are as yet unknown. In part, this is because the effect size is likely to be small—many variables certainly affect long-term health outcomes, and the communication between the doctor and patient may explain only a small portion of the variance. However, it is important that work in this area begin to address these broader outcomes.

Patient Narratives

Somewhat related to doctor–patient communication is the idea of patient narratives. It has been demonstrated that giving patients 3 minutes at the beginning of a medical encounter to speak without interruption, and perhaps with neutral prompts from the physician to encourage elaboration, conveys enormous benefits in terms of the richness of the information gleaned about the patient's illness and its impact on the patient and the patient's functioning in work and family life (Cegala, 2005). This is because of the importance of narrative, particularly illness narratives. As humans, we have a need to tell our story. Being able to tell the story of one's illness can be a transforming process for someone facing a serious illness (Sharf & Vanderford, 2003). An important consideration is that often in a medical encounter the physician and the patient are speaking in different voices: the physician speaks in the voice of medicine, while the patient speaks in the voice of the lifeworld (Mishler, 1984). Given that doctors and patients have such different ways of communicating, it is clear that misunderstandings are common. Research in narrative approaches to health communication has found benefits to patients who are able to construct a story of their illness. Narratives help patients to make sense of their illness experiences, to construct a sense of control over their illness, to build new identities that incorporate the changes brought about by illness, and to aid in decision making (Sharf & Vanderford, 2003). This area of research is growing, and has the potential to inform not just patient–provider communication, but also the understanding of the impact of illness on all facets of an individual's life.

Conclusion

This chapter focused on several of the major programs of research in health communication. The early research on health communication focused on media interventions aimed at improving health outcomes. While this research had a health focus, much of this research translates into other domains besides health communication. Diffusion of innovations has been applied across a broad array of topics. Likewise, research on fear appeals has had a strong health focus; however, this research has broader implications for our understanding of both persuasion and how emotion is processed. The research on interpersonal communication is in its infancy, but great advances have been made in our understanding of interpersonal communication in a health care context.

Notes

1   Of course, the choice is typically more complex than this, because people may have some threshold that has to be overcome before engaging in an action, so that the SEU may need to be substantially higher than zero before a person will choose that option. By far the most developed theory of expected utility is Tversky and Kahneman's prospect theory (Kahneman & Tversky, 1979; Tversky & Kahneman, 1992; Wakker, 2010).

2   Rogers (1975) was careful to note that the effect of these three components of the message were not simply additive (a statistical main effect), but interaction, so that including all three elements made the message substantially more effective.

3   However, Nabi et al. (2008) demonstrated that if people are already knowledgeable about a health-related threat (e.g., that they are susceptible to the threat and it is severe), then messages need only focus on response and self-efficacy to be effective. If people are already fearful, it is not necessary for a message to increase that fear to be effective.

4   There has been fairly extensive debate as to whether perceived behavioral control as originally developed by Ajzen (1991) is the same as self-efficacy. While there may be methodological differences in how the two are measured, theoretically, it is clear that Ajzen (1991) incorporated self-efficacy within perceived behavioral control (Yzer, 2013).

References

Ajzen, I. (1991). The theory of planned behavior. *Organizational Behavior and Human Decision Processes, 50*, 179–211.

Ajzen, I., & Madden, T. J. (1986). Prediction of goal-directed behavior: Attitudes, intentions, and perceived behavioral control. *Journal of Experimental Social Psychology, 22*, 453–474.

Albarracin, D., Johnson, B. T., Fishbein, M., & Muellerleile, P. A. (2001). Theories of reasoned action and planned behavior as models of condom use: A meta-analysis. *Psychological Bulletin, 127*, 142–161.

Arpan, L., Rhodes, N., & Roskos-Ewoldsen, D. R. (2007). Accessibility, persuasion, and behavior. In D. R. Roskos-Ewoldsen & J. Monahan (Eds.), *Communication and social cognition: Theories and methods* (pp. 351–376). Mahwah, NJ: Lawrence Erlbaum Associates.

Babrow, A. S., & Mattson, M. (2011). Building health communication theories in the 21st century. In T. L. Thompson, R. Parrott, & J. F. Nussbaum (Eds.), *The Routledge handbook of health communication* (2nd ed., pp. 18–35). New York: Routledge.

Bain, D. J. (1979). The content of physician/patient communication in family practice. *Journal of Family Practice, 8*, 745–753.

Bandi, P., Cokkinides, V. E., Westmaas, J. L., & Ward, E. (2008). Parental communication not to smoke and adolescent cigarette smokers' readiness to quit: Differences by age. *Journal of Adolescent Health, 43*, 612–615. doi:10.1016/j.jadohealth.2008.04.019.

Bandura, A. (2004). Social cognitive theory for personal and social change by enabling media. In A. Singhal, M. J. Cody, E. M. Rogers, & M. Sabido (Eds.), *Entertainment-education and social change: History, research, and practice* (pp. 75–96). Mahwah, NJ: Lawrence Erlbaum Associates.

Bandura, A. (2006). On integrating social cognitive and social diffusion theories. In A. Singhal & J. W. Dearing (Eds.), *Communication of innovations: A journey with Ev Rogers* (pp. 111–135). New Delhi: Sage.

Beck, V. (2004). Working with daytime and prime-time television shows in the United States to promote health. In A. Singhal, M. J. Cody, E. M. Rogers, & M. Sabido (Eds.), *Entertainment-education and social change: History, research, and practice* (pp. 207–224). Mahwah, NJ: Lawrence Erlbaum Associates.

Benbassat, J., & Baumal, R. (2002). A step-wise role playing approach for teaching patient counseling skills to medical students. *Patient Education and Counseling, 46*, 147–152.

Bertakis, K. D. (1977). The communication of information from physician to patient: A method of increasing patient retention and satisfaction. *Journal of Family Practice, 5*, 217–222.

Boster, F. J., & Mongeau, P. (1984). Fear-arousing persuasive messages. In R. N. Bostrom & B. H. Westley (Eds.), *Communication yearbook 8* (pp. 330–375). Newbury Park, CA: Sage.

Bouman, M. (2004). Entertainment-education television drama. In A. Singhal, M. J. Cody, E. M. Rogers, & M. Sabido (Eds.), *Entertainment-education and social change: History, research, and practice* (pp. 225–242). Mahwah, NJ: Lawrence Erlbaum Associates.

Brown, J. B., Stewart, M., & Ryan, B. L. (2003). Outcomes of patient–provider interaction. In T. L. Thompson, A. M. Dorsey, K. I. Miller, & R. Parrott (Eds.), *Handbook of health communication* (pp. 141–162). Mahwah, NJ: Lawrence Erlbaum Associates.

Bute, J. J. (2009). "Nobody thinks twice about asking": Women with a fertility problem and requests for information. *Health Communication, 24*, 752–763. doi:10.1080/10410 230903265920.

Carrera, P., Munoz, D., & Caballero, A. (2010). Mixed emotional appeals in emotional and danger control processes. *Health Communication, 25*, 726–736.

Cegala, D. J. (2005). The first three minutes. In E. B. Ray (Ed.), *Health communication in practice: A case study approach* (pp. 3–10). Mahwah, NJ: Lawrence Erlbaum Associates.

Cegala, D. J., & Post, D. M. (2009). The impact of patients' participation on physicians' patient-centered communication. *Patient Education and Counseling, 77*, 202–208. doi:10.1016/j.pec.2009.03.025.

Cegala, D. J., & Street, R. L. (2010). Interpersonal dimensions of health communication. In C. R. Berger, M. E. Roloff, & D. R. Roskos-Ewoldsen (Eds.), *The handbook of communication science* (2nd ed., pp. 401–417). Los Angeles, CA: Sage.

Cegala, D. J., Chisolm, D. J., & Nwomeh, B. C. (2013). A communication skills intervention for parents of pediatric surgery patients. *Patient Education and Counseling, 93*(1), 34–39. doi:10.1016/j.pec.2013.03.015.

Cegala, D. J., McClure, L., Marinelli, T. M., & Post, D. M. (2000). The effects of communication skills training on patients' participation during medical interviews. *Patient Education and Counseling, 41*, 209–222.

Cho, H., & Salmon, C. T. (2006). Fear appeals for individuals in different stages of change: Intended and unintended effects and implications on public health campaigns. *Health Communication, 20*, 91–99.

Cialdini, R. B., Kallgren, C. A., & Reno, R. R. (1991). A focus theory of normative conduct: A theoretical refinement and reevaluation of the role of norms in human behavior. *Advances in Experimental Social Psychology, 24*, 201–243.

Corey, S. M. (1937). Professed attitudes and actual behavior. *Journal of Educational Psychology, 28*, 271–280.

Dailey, R. M., Thompson, C. M., & Romo, L. K. (2014). Mother–teen communication about weight management. *Health Communication, 29*, 384–397. doi:10.1080/1041 0236.2012.759052.

Dearing, J. W., & Meyer, A. (2006). Revisiting diffusion theory. In A. Singhal & J. W. Dearing (Eds.), *Communication of innovations: A journey with Ev Rogers* (pp. 29–60). New Delhi: Sage.

Dillard, J. P. (1993). Persuasion past and present: Attitudes aren't what they used to be. *Communication Monographs, 60*, 90–97.

Ewoldsen, D. R., Rhodes, N., & Fazio, R. H. (2015). The MODE model and its implications for studying the media. *Media Psychology, 18*, 312–337.

Fazio, R. H. (1986). How do attitudes guide behavior? In R. M. Sorrentino & E. T. Higgins (Eds.), *The handbook of motivation and cognition: Foundations of social behavior* (pp. 204–243). New York: Guilford Press.

Fazio, R. H. (1990). Multiple processes by which attitudes guide behavior: The MODE model as an integrative framework. In M. Zanna (Ed.), *Advances in experimental social psychology* (vol. 23, pp. 75–109). Orlando, FL: Academic Press.

Fazio, R. H., & Williams, C. J. (1986). Attitude accessibility as a moderator of the attitude–perception and attitude–behavior relations: An investigation of the 1984 presidential election. *Journal of Personality and Social Psychology, 51*, 505–514.

Fazio, R. H., & Roskos-Ewoldsen, D. R. (2005). Acting as we feel: When and how attitudes guide behavior. In T. C. Brock and M. C. Green (Eds.), *The psychology of persuasion* (2nd ed., pp. 41–62). New York: Allyn & Bacon.

Fazio, R. H., Roskos-Ewoldsen, D. R., & Powell, M. C. (1994). Attitudes as determinants of attention and perception. In S. Kitayama & P. M. Niedenthal (Eds.), *The heart's eye: Emotional influences on perception and attention* (pp. 197–216). Orlando, FL: Academic Press.

Fazio, R. H., Sanbonmatsu, D. M., Powell, M. C., & Kardes, F. R. (1986). On the automatic activation of attitudes. *Journal of Personality and Social Psychology, 50*, 229–238.

Fishbein, M., & Ajzen, I. (1975). *Belief, attitude, intention and behavior: An introduction to theory and research*. Reading, MA: Addison-Wesley.

Fishbein, M., & Ajzen, I. (2010). *Predicting and changing behavior: The reasoned action approach*. New York: Psychology Press.

Fishbein, M., & Yzer, M. C. (2003). Using theory to design effective health behavior interventions. *Communication Theory, 13*, 164–183.

Floyd, D. L., Prentice-Dunn, S., & Rogers, R. W. (2000). A meta-analysis of research on protection motivation theory. *Journal of Applied Social Psychology, 30*, 407–429.

Gilbert, D. T. (1991). How mental systems believe. *American Psychologist, 46*, 107–119.

Greenberg, B. S., Salmon, C. T., Patel, D., Beck, V., & Cole, G. (2004). Evolution of an E-E research agenda. In A. Singhal, M. J. Cody, E. M. Rogers, & M. Sabido (Eds.), *Entertainment-education and social change: History, research, and practice* (pp. 191–206). Mahwah, NJ: Lawrence Erlbaum Associates.

Haider, M., & Kreps, G. L. (2004). Forty years of diffusion of innovations: Utility and value in public health. *Journal of Health Communication, 9*(s1), 3–11.

Helitzer, D. L., LaNoue, M., Wilson, B., de Hernandez, B. U., Warner, T., & Roter, D. (2011). A randomized controlled trial of communication training with primary care providers to improve patient-centeredness and health risk communication. *Patient Education and Counseling, 82*, 21–29. doi:10.1016/j.pec.2010.01.021.

Hornik, R. (2004). Some reflections on diffusion theory and the role of Everett Rogers. *Journal of Health Communication, 9*(s1), 143–148.

Igartua, J.-J., & Barrios, I. (2012). Changing real-world beliefs with controversial movies: Processes and mechanisms of narrative persuasion. *Journal of Communication, 62*, 514–531.

Jackson, J. P., Jr. (2005). *Science for segregation: Race, law and the case against Brown v. Board of Education*. New York: New York University Press.

Janis, I. L., & Feshbach, S. (1953). Effects of fear-arousing communications. *Journal of Abnormal & Social Psychology, 48*, 78–92.

Janz, N. K., & Becker, M. H. (1984). The health belief model: A decade later. *Health Education Quarterly, 11*, 1–47.

Kahneman, D., & Tversky, A. (1979). Prospect theory: An analysis of decisions under risk. *Econometrica, 47*, 263–291.

Katz, J. (1995). Informed consent: Ethical and legal issues. In J. D. Arras & B. Steinbock (Eds.), *Ethical issues in modern medicine* (4th ed., pp. 87–97). Mountain View, CA: Mayfield.

Khalil, G. E., & Rintamaki, L. S. (2014). A televised entertainment-education drama to promote positive discussion about organ donation. *Health Education Research, 29,* 284–296.

Kincaid, D. L. (2004). From innovation to social norm: Bounded normative influence. *Journal of Health Communication, 9*(s1), 37–57.

Kirscht, J. P. (1974). Research related to the modification of health beliefs. *Health Education Monographs, 2,* 455–469.

Kreuter, M. W., Green, M. C., Cappella, J. N., Slater, M. D., Wise, M. E., Storey, D., Clark, E. M., O'Keefe, D. J., Erwin, D. O., Holmes, K., Hinyard, L. J., Houston, T., & Woolley, S. (2007). Narrative communication in cancer prevention and control: A framework to guide research and application. *Annals of Behavioral Medicine, 33,* 221–235.

Lang, A., & Ewoldsen, D. (2010). Beyond effects: Conceptualizing communication as dynamic, complex, nonlinear, and fundamental. In S. Allan (Ed.), *Rethinking communication* (pp. 109–120). Cresskill, NJ: Hampton Press.

LaPiere, R. T. (1934). Attitudes vs. actions. *Social Forces, 13*(2), 230–237.

Latane, B., & Darley, J. M. (1970). *The unresponsive bystander: Why doesn't he help?* New York: Prentice-Hall.

Leventhal, H. (1970). Findings and theory in the study of fear communications. In L. Berkowitz (Ed.), *Advances in experimental social psychology* (vol. 5, pp. 119–186). New York: Academic Press.

Leventhal, H., Safer, M. A., & Panagis, D. M. (1983). The impact of communications on the self-regulation of health beliefs, decisions, and behavior. *Health Education Quarterly, 10,* 3–29.

Lewin, K. (1997). *Resolving social conflicts: Field theory in social science.* Washington, DC: APA. (Original work published 1948).

Lewis, I., Watson, B., & White, K. M. (2013). Extending the explanatory utility of the EPPM beyond fear-based persuasion. *Health Communication, 28,* 84–98.

Luce, R. D., (2003). Rationality and choice under certainty and uncertainty. In S. L. Schneider & J. Shanteau (Eds.), *Emerging perspectives on judgment and decision research* (pp. 64–83). Cambridge: Cambridge University Press.

Maddux, J. E., & Rogers, R. W. (1983). Protection motivation and self-efficacy: A revised theory of fear appeals and attitude change. *Journal of Experimental Social Psychology, 19,* 469–479.

Maiman, L. A., & Becker, M. H. (1974). The health belief model: Origins and correlates in psychological theory. *Health Education Monographs, 2,* 336–352.

Manze, M. G., Orner, M. B., Glickman, M., Pbert, L., Berlowitz, D., & Kressin, N. R. (2015). Brief provider communication skills training fails to impact patient hypertension outcomes. *Patient Education and Counseling, 98,* 191–198. doi:10.1016/j.pec.2014.10.014.

McGuire, W. J. (1983). A contextualist theory of knowledge: Its implications for innovation and reform in psychological research. *Advances in Experimental Social Psychology, 16,* 1–47.

McGuire, W. J. (2001). Input and output variables currently promising for constructing persuasive communications. In R. E. Rice & C. K. Atkin (Eds.), *Public communication campaigns* (3rd ed., pp. 22–48). Thousand Oaks, CA: Sage.

Mishler, E. G. (1984). *The discourse of medicine: Dialectics of medical interviews.* Norwood, NJ: Ablex.

Mjaaland, T. A., & Finset, A. (2009). Communication skills training for general practitioners to promote patient coping: The GRIP approach. *Patient Education and Counseling, 76*, 84–90. doi:10.1016/j.pec.2008.11.014.

Moyer-Guse, E. (2008). Toward a theory of entertainment persuasion: Explaining the persuasive effects of entertainment-education messages. *Communication Theory, 18*, 407–425.

Moyer-Guse, E., & Nabi, R. L. (2010). Explaining the effects of narrative in an entertainment television program: Overcoming resistance to persuasion. *Human Communication Research, 36*, 26–52.

Moyer-Guse, E., & Nabi, R. L. (2011). Comparing the effects of entertainment and educational television programming on risky sexual behavior. *Health Communication, 26*, 416–426.

Murad, M. S., Chatterley, T., & Guirguis, L. M. (2014). A meta-narrative review of recorded patient–pharmacist interactions: Exploring biomedical or patient-centered communication? *Research in Social & Administrative Pharmacy, 10*, 1–20. doi:10.1016/j.sapharm.2013.03.002.

Nabi, R. L., Roskos-Ewoldsen, D., & Dillman Carpentier, F. (2008). Subjective knowledge and fear appeal effectiveness: Implications for message design. *Health Communication, 23*, 191–201.

Napper, L. E., Harris, P. R., & Klein, W. M. P. (2014). Combining self-affirmation with the extended parallel process model: The consequences for motivation to eat more fruit and vegetables. *Health Communication, 29*, 610–618.

Norcross, J. C., Krebs, P. M., & Prochaska, J. O. (2011). Stages of change. *Journal of Clinical Psychology, 67*, 143–154.

Petty, R. E., & Cacioppo, J. T. (1986). The elaboration likelihood model of persuasion. *Advances in Experimental Social Psychology, 19*, 123–205.

Petty, R. E., & Krosnick, J. A. (1995). *Attitude strength: Antecedents and consequences.* Mahwah, NJ: Lawrence Erlbaum Associates.

Piotrow, P. T., & de Fossard, E. (2004). Entertainment-education as a public health intervention. In A. Singhal, M. J. Cody, E. M. Rogers, & M. Sabido (Eds.), *Entertainment-education and social change: History, research, and practice* (pp. 39–60). Mahwah, NJ: Lawrence Erlbaum Associates.

Poindexter, D. O. (2004). A history of entertainment-education, 1958–2000. In A. Singhal, M. J. Cody, E. M. Rogers, & M. Sabido (Eds.), *Entertainment-education and social change: History, research, and practice* (pp. 21–38). Mahwah, NJ: Lawrence Erlbaum Associates.

Popova, L. (2012). The extended parallel process model illuminating the gaps in research. *Health Education & Behavior, 39*, 455–473.

Prochaska, J. O., & DiClemente, C. C. (1983). Stages and processes of self-change of smoking: Toward an integrative model of change. *Journal of Counseling and Clinical Psychology, 51*, 390–395.

Prochaska, J. O., DiClemente, C. C., & Norcross, J. C. (1992). In search of how people change: Applications to addictive behaviors. *American Psychologist, 47*, 1102–1114.

Prochaska, J. O., Velicer, W. F., Rossi, J. S., Goldstein, M. G., Marcus, B. H., Rakowski, W., Fiore, C., Harlow, L. L., Redding, C. A., Rosenbloom, D., & Rossi, S. R. (1994). Stages of change and decisional balance for 12 problem behaviors. *Health Psychology, 13*, 39–46.

Rhodes, N., & Ewoldsen, D. R. (2009). Attitude and norm accessibility and cigarette smoking. *Journal of Applied Social Psychology, 39*, 2355–2372.

Rhodes, N., & Ewoldsen, D. R. (2013). Outcomes of persuasion: Cognitive, behavioral and social. In J. Dillard & L. Shen (Eds.), *Handbook of persuasion: Developments in theory and practice* (2nd ed., pp. 35–65). Los Angeles: Sage.

Rhodes, N., Roskos-Ewoldsen, D. R., Edison, A., & Bradford, B. (2008). Attitude and norm accessibility affect processing of anti-smoking messages. *Health Psychology, 27*, S224–S232.

Rhodes, N., Ewoldsen, D. R., Shen, L., Monahan, J. L., & Eno, C. (2014). The accessibility of family and peer norms as predictors of young adolescent risk behavior. *Communication Research, 41*, 3–26.

Rimal, R. N., & Real, K. (2003). Understanding the influence of perceived norms on behaviors. *Communication Theory, 13*, 184–203.

Rippetoe, P. A., & Rogers, R. W. (1987). Effects of components of protection-motivation theory on adaptive and maladaptive coping with a health threat. *Journal of Personality & Social Psychology, 52*, 596–604.

Roberto, A. J., (2013). Editor's note for the extended parallel process model: Two decades later. *Health Communication, 28*, 1–2.

Rogers, E. M. (2003). *Diffusion of innovations* (5th ed.). New York: Free Press.

Rogers, R. W. (1975). A protection motivation theory of fear appeals and attitude change. *Journal of Psychology, 91*, 93–114.

Rogers, R. W., & Prentice-Dunn, S. (1997). Protection motivation theory. In D. Gochman (Ed.), *Handbook of health behavior research: Vol. 1, Determinants of health behavior: Personal and social* (pp. 113–132). New York: Plenum.

Rosenstock, I. M. (1974). Historical origins of the health belief model. *Health Education Monographs, 2*, 328–335.

Roskos-Ewoldsen, D. R., & Fazio, R. H. (1992). On the orienting value of attitudes: Attitude accessibility as a determinant of an object's attraction of visual attention. *Journal of Personality and Social Psychology, 63*, 198–211.

Roskos-Ewoldsen, D., Yu, H. J., & Rhodes, N. (2004). Fear appeal messages affect accessibility of attitudes toward the threat and adaptive behaviors. *Communication Monographs, 71*, 49–69.

Roter, D. L. (1977). Patient participation in the patient–provider interaction: The effects of patient question asking on the quality of the interaction, satisfaction, and compliance. *Health Education Monographs, 5*, 281–315.

Roter, D. L., Stewart, M., Putnam, S. M., Lipkin, M., Jr., Stiles, W., & Inui, T. S. (1997). Communication patterns of primary care physicians. *Journal of the American Medical Association, 277*, 350–357.

Sabido, M. (2004) The origins of entertainment-education. In A. Singhal, M. J. Cody, E. M. Rogers, & M. Sabido (Eds.), *Entertainment-education and social change: History, research, and practice* (pp. 61–74). Mahwah, NJ: Lawrence Erlbaum Associates.

Scott, A. M., & Caughlin, J. P. (2015). Communication nonaccommodation in family conversations about end-of-life health decisions. *Health Communication, 30*, 144–153. doi:10.1080/10410236.2014.974128

Sharf, B. F., & Vanderford, M. L. (2003). Illness narratives and the social construction of health. In T. L. Thompson, A. M. Dorsey, K. I. Miller, & R. Parrott (Eds.), *Handbook of health communication* (pp. 63–89). Mahwah, NJ: Lawrence Erlbaum Associates.

Sheppard, B. H., Hartwick, J., & Warshaw, P. R. (1988). The theory of reasoned action: A meta-analysis of past research with recommendations for modifications and future research. *Journal of Consumer Research, 15,* 325–343.

Singhal, A., & Rogers, E. M. (2004). The status of entertainment-education worldwide. In A. Singhal, M. J. Cody, E. M. Rogers, & M. Sabido (Eds.), *Entertainment-education and social change: History, research, and practice* (pp. 3–20). Mahwah, NJ: Lawrence Erlbaum Associates.

Singhal, A., Njogu, K., Bouman, M., & Elias, E. (2006). Entertainment-education and health promotion: A cross-continental journey. In A. Singhal & J. W. Dearing (Eds.), *Communication of innovations: A journey with Ev Rogers* (pp. 199–229). New Delhi: Sage.

Slater, M. D. (1999). Integrating application of media effects, persuasion, and behavior change theories to communication campaigns: A stages-of-change framework. *Health Communication, 11,* 335–354.

Slater, M. D. (2002). Involvement as goal-directed strategic processing: Expanding the elaboration likelihood model. In J. P. Dillard & M. Pfau (Eds.), *The persuasion handbook: Developments in theory and practice* (pp. 175–194). Thousand Oaks, CA: Sage.

Slater, M. D., & Rouner, D. (1996). Value affirmative and value protective processing of alcohol education messages that include statistics or anecdotes. *Communication Research, 23,* 210–235.

Slater, M. D., & Rouner, D. (2002). Entertainment-education and elaboration likelihood: Understanding the processing of narrative persuasion. *Communication Theory, 12,* 173–191.

Snyder, M. (1987). *Public appearances/private realities: The psychology of self-monitoring.* New York: Freeman.

Snyder, M., & Kendzierski, D. (1982). Acting on one's attitude: Procedures for linking attitude and behavior. *Journal of Experimental Social Psychology, 18,* 165–183.

Sood, S., Menard, T., & Witte, K. (2004). The theory behind entertainment-education. In A. Singhal, M. J. Cody, E. M. Rogers, & M. Sabido (Eds.), *Entertainment-education and social change: History, research, and practice* (pp. 117–152). Mahwah, NJ: Lawrence Erlbaum Associates.

Srivastava, J., & Moreland, J. J. (2015). Diffusion of innovations: Communication evolution and influences. *Communication Review, 15,* 294–312.

Street, R. L., Jr. (2003). Communication in medical encounters: An ecological perspective. In T. L. Thompson, A. M. Dorsey, K. I. Miller, & R. Parrott (Eds.), *Handbook of health communication* (pp. 63–89). Mahwah, NJ: Lawrence Erlbaum Associates.

Street R. L. (2013). How clinician–patient communication contributes to health improvement: modeling pathways from talk to outcome. *Patient Education and Counseling, 92,* 286–291.

Thompson, T. L. (2003). Provider–patient interaction issues. In T. L. Thompson, A. M. Dorsey, K. I. Miller, & R. Parrott (Eds.), *Handbook of health communication* (pp. 91–93). Mahwah, NJ: Lawrence Erlbaum Associates.

Tversky, A., & Kahneman, D. (1992). Advances in prospect theory: Cumulative representation of uncertainty. *Journal of Risk & Uncertainty, 5,* 297–323.

Usdin, S., Singhal, A., Shongwe, T., Goldstein, S., & Shabalala, A. (2004). No short cuts in entertainment-education: Designing Soul City step-by-step. In A. Singhal, M. J. Cody, E. M. Rogers, & M. Sabido (Eds.), *Entertainment-education and social change: History, research, and practice* (pp. 153–176). Mahwah, NJ: Lawrence Erlbaum Associates.

Valente, T. W. (2006). Communication network analysis and the diffusion of innovations. In A. Singhal & J. W. Dearing (Eds.), *Communication of innovations: A journey with Ev Rogers* (pp. 61–82). New Delhi: Sage.

Wakker, P. P. (2010). *Prospect theory for risk and ambiguity.* Cambridge: Cambridge University Press.

Wicker, A. W. (1969). Attitudes versus actions: The relationship of verbal and overt behavioral responses to attitude objects. *Journal of Social Issues, 25,* 41–78.

Witte, K. (1994). Fear control and danger control: A test of the extended parallel process model (EPPM). *Communication Monographs, 61,* 113–134.

Witte, K. (1995). Generating effective risk messages: How scary should your risk communication be? In B. R. Burleson (Ed.), *Communication yearbook 18* (pp. 229–254). Thousand Oaks, CA: Sage.

Witte, K., & Allen, M. (2000). A meta-analysis of fear appeals: Implications for effective public health campaigns. *Health Education & Behavior, 27,* 591–615.

Witte, K., Girma, B., & Girgre, A. (2002). Addressing underlying mechanisms to HIV/AIDS preventive behaviors in Ethiopia. *International Quarterly of Community Health Education, 21,* 163–176.

Witte, K., Stokols, D., Ituarte, P., & Schneider, M. (1993). Testing the health belief model in a field study to promote bicycle safety helmets. *Communication Research, 20,* 564–586.

Young, A. I., Ratner, K. G., & Fazio, R. H. (2014). Political attitudes bias the mental representation of a presidential candidate's face. *Psychological Science, 25,* 503–510.

Yzer, M. (2013). Reasoned action theory: Persuasion as belief-based behavior change. In J. Dillard & L. Shen (Eds.), *The Sage handbook of persuasion: Developments in theory and practice* (2nd ed., pp. 120–136). Los Angeles: Sage.

16

RELATIONSHIPS, MARRIAGE, AND FAMILY COMMUNICATION

As Chapter 10 has shown, the scientific study of interpersonal communication and interpersonal relationships has a long and intertwined history (see Chapter 10). Arguably, the main focus of interpersonal communication theorizing and research at its inception has been on the development of close personal relationships. Theories such as social penetration theory (Altman & Taylor, 1973), uncertainty reduction theory (Berger & Calabrese, 1975), and the stage model of relationship development (Knapp, 1984) explicated the types of communication that take place when persons get to know each other and move toward ever-greater intimacy in their relationships. Some of these early theories proposed novel explanatory mechanisms, whereas others employed already established theories from psychology and related fields. An example of the former is uncertainty reduction theory, which proposed that individuals are intrinsically motivated to reduce uncertainty in interpersonal relationships. An example of the latter is social penetration theory, which used social exchange theory to explain why people self-disclose.

While the early theories were typically perceived as general relationship theories and assumed to apply to most, if not all, interpersonal relationships, by now it is generally accepted that interpersonal communication depends significantly on relationship context. Communication manifests and functions differently in different types of interpersonal relationships. Thus, communication in romantic relationships is different from communication in sibling relationships, and communication between Facebook friends different from communication between new roommates.

Partly in response to this realization, but also because of longstanding interest in certain types of relationships that originated from disciplines outside of communication, there are now several areas of communication devoted to specific relationship types. Two of the largest areas encompass communication in marriages and family communication, and are the focus of this chapter.

Historical Background

At least since the beginning of the twentieth century, marriages and families have been investigated by social scientists of various academic disciplines, for obvious reasons. From a macro or sociological perspective, marriages and families are considered to be basic forms of social organization. Marriages and families constitute the social building blocks of societies, and how marriages and families function affects and reflects societal functioning more generally. Furthermore, the family is also thought of as the primary socialization agent of children and adolescents. Thus, understanding marriages and families is part and parcel of understanding society and societal processes.

From a micro or psychological perspective, marriages and families are equally important. For most persons, these relationships are their most intimate, most important, and most enduring relationships, and greatly affect their mental and physical health. In addition, relationships with parents and other family members also affect the acquisition and development of a number of psychological processes relevant to children and grown adults alike, including attachment, core beliefs and values, motivation, as well as the psychological processes underlying interpersonal relationships.

The longstanding interest in marriages and families by social sciences does not necessarily translate to a correspondingly rich corpus of research on marital and family *communication*, however. Although interaction and communication are core variables in either area, their conceptualizations are often quite simplistic, especially in family research (Koerner, 2009). Here, communication is often broadly categorized as, for example, warm or cold, or operationalized in terms of relationship satisfaction or stability. Marital research fares better in this regard, with communication being conceptualized often at the level of specific verbal or nonverbal behaviors. What is lacking here, however, is often the recognition that the meaning of behaviors is not fixed, but varies with a number of personal, relationship, and contextual factors.

Another reason for the relative lack of high-quality social science research of marital and family communication is that within the discipline of communication itself, the use of social science to study communication and relationships is controversial. A significant proportion of marital and family communication scholars eschew the social scientific approach in favor of more qualitative or even critical approaches, limiting the amount of research conducted and the number of researchers trained in the scientific investigation of marital and family communication.

Despite these limitations, it is still impossible to summarize it or even to provide a comprehensive overview of all scientific research on marital and family communication in a single chapter. Thus, below we will briefly review a few of the theories in the areas of marital and family communication that we believe illustrate different types of approaches and foci. Particular attention will be paid to theories that emerged from within the communication discipline or that had significant impact on it. The chapter concludes with an outlook on future developments in these areas.

Marital Communication

Generally speaking, research in marital communication has reached significant theoretical and methodological sophistication, with a large proportion of System 2 theories. Because much of the research aimed to explain and predict marital satisfaction and (in)stability, these outcomes are among the best understood. For example, satisfaction and stability have been explained by variables representing specific cognition and affect relevant to how persons communicate in marriages, such as anxiety and depression (Whisman et al., 2007), attributions (Bradbury & Fincham, 1992), empathic accuracy (Thomas et al., 1997), expectations (Vanzetti et al., 1992) and their accessibility (Fincham et al., 1995). Research that explicitly focused on the effects of marital communication on satisfaction and stability includes research on the expression of positive affect, the provisions of social support, demand/withdrawal patterns, and marital conflict.

Expressing Positive Affect

One approach to studying marital satisfaction and stability is to focus on those communication behaviors that affect those outcomes positively. The expression of positive affect is one such aspect of marital communication that has received a lot of attention recently, and it is generally associated with increased intimacy and relationship satisfaction (Caughlin & Huston, 2002), especially when communicated nonverbally. The notion that positive affect is central to inter-personal relationships and that it is communicated mainly nonverbally was already articulated by Watzlawick et al. (1967). In the context of marriage communication, expressing positive affect has been related to increased intimacy (Gottman et al., 1977).

The effects of nonverbal communication of both positive and negative affect have been researched by Noller (1980, 1982; Noller & Gallois, 1986), who found that effective nonverbal communication is associated with increased marital satisfaction, and also that women are better encoders and decoders of nonverbal affect than men. Reasoning that affect that is perceived as referring to either the partner or the relationship should have different effects than affect perceived to be related to neither. Koerner and Fitzpatrick (2002a) distinguished between relationship-relevant and relationship-irrelevant nonverbal affect and found that only relationship-relevant affect was associated with marital satisfaction. Whether this association also holds for the verbal communication of positive affect is as yet undetermined.

Social Support

Another communication behavior frequently associated with marital satisfaction and stability is the provision of social support, which also has significant positive associations with mental and physical health (Gardner & Cutrona, 2004). Some researchers define social support as fulfilling basic interpersonal needs (Kaplan et al., 1977), or communication that functions to comfort, encourage, reassure, and problem solve (Gardner & Cutrona, 2004). Other researchers, such as Burleson (1994, 2003), defined social support more narrowly as communication intended to help another to cope effectively with emotional distress, mainly through cognitive reappraisal. Communication behaviors that function as support include validating the emotional experience of the distressed person, expressing sympathy for, and affiliation with, the distressed person, and providing assistance in addressing the underlying causes for distress.

Theoretical accounts of the effects of social support on marriages vary, mainly because of different assumptions about the underlying causes for distress. Thus, Cutrona's (1990, 1996; Gardner & Cutrona, 2004) optimal matching theory is based on the assumption that a number of unmet needs cause psychological distress, and that communication that addresses that need is supportive. For example, targets that experienced a need for information find communication that provides information supportive, targets that experience a lack of affiliation find affiliative communication supportive, and so forth.

In interpersonal communication, most research on social support has been conducted by Burleson and his associates (Burleson, 2003; Burleson & Mortenson, 2003; Burleson et al., 2005; Jones & Burleson, 2003). This research is based on a theoretical model grounded in Lazarus's (1991) theory of emotion, which makes emotional support through cognitive reappraisal central to the support process. It de-emphasizes other forms of support, such as informational or instrumental support. According to this model, supportive communication is a linear process. In the first step, spouses acknowledge and legitimize the emotional distress of the other. Then, they help the distressed partner to reduce their distress by reappraising the situation (Burleson & Goldsmith, 1998). This step involves talking about the partner's situation and feelings in ways that validates them and also allows them to reinterpret their situation in ways that are less emotionally distressful.

Demand–Withdrawal

An alternate way of investigating satisfaction and stability in marriage is to focus on the communication behaviors that are associated with dissatisfaction and instability. Among the most researched of such negative behaviors in marriage is demand–withdrawal. Demand–withdrawal is defined as one partner demanding, criticizing, or otherwise calling for change in the other, and the partner responding with avoidance or refusal to change. Although sometimes conceptualized in the context of marital conflict, it is more typically investigated in the context of marital problem solving or during relationship talk. Early investigations of demand–withdrawal (Christensen, 1987, 1988; Christensen & Heavey, 1990) generally identified it as a gendered pattern of wife demand–husband withdrawal. More recent investigations, however, suggest that this genderization might have been the result of demand characteristics of earlier studies (relationship talk often being perceived as the wife's topic, and patterns of husband demand–wife withdrawal have also been observed, particularly in discussions of topics chosen by the husband (Klinetob & Smith, 1996).

Demand–withdrawal patterns are negatively associated with marital satisfaction (Christensen, 1987, 1988), although the explanatory mechanism for this association has not yet been fully explicated. One possibility is that the demands of one partner lead to negative affect by the withdrawing partner, who feels pressured or coerced and experiences reactance or the loss of autonomy. Another possibility is that the demanding partner experiences frustration because of the uncooperativeness of their spouse, or because they are unable to achieve their goals in the face of partner resistance and avoidance. A third possibility is that the negative affect introduced by demand–withdrawal escalates, and it is this escalation that has the negative effects on the relationship's satisfaction and stability.

The communication scholar most frequently associated with investigating the causal processes linking demand–withdrawal to marital satisfaction and stability is Caughlin (2002; Caughlin & Huston, 2002; Caughlin & Vangelisti, 2000). In a longitudinal study, Caughlin (2002) assessed forty-six married couples at two times about a year apart. Results indicated that demand–withdrawal has a stable association with dissatisfaction, but also that, at least for wives, demand–withdrawal also was associated with an increase in marital satisfaction. Caughlin interpreted these results as providing support for both the enduring dynamics model, which suggests that relationship processes develop early in marriage and remain relatively stable, and the accommodation model, which suggests that spouses make adjustments in their behaviors and their responses to behaviors as marriages mature. Not supported was the disillusionment model, which suggests that spouses get more dissatisfied in marriages because they lose some of the positive illusions they had about each other during courtship.

Marital Conflict

Another area of communication behaviors associated with dissatisfaction and divorce is marital conflict. The most extensive research on marital conflict is probably that of Gottman and his associates (Gottman, 1993, 1994; Gottman & Krokoff, 1989; Gottman & Leverson, 1986). Investigating the communication behaviors in newlyweds that are most predictive of relationship dissatisfaction and instability, Gottman found that conflict behaviors were particularly powerful predictors of dissatisfaction and divorce (Gottman et al., 1998). In particular, behaviors associated with negative affect for the partner, such as criticism, defensiveness, contempt, and withdrawal, were predictive of dissatisfaction and divorce (Gottman, 1994). Surprisingly, expressing anger, which has been suggested by others to be a particularly corrosive behavior in marriages (e.g., Hendrix, 1988), was not only not associated with divorce, but predicted greater marital satisfaction over time (Gottman & Krokoff, 1989).

Over time, Gottman has developed an explanatory mechanism for the effects of the negative behaviors that identified physiological responses to conflict as the variable that mediates the relationship between conflict behaviors and dissatisfaction. Using various measures of physiological arousal (e.g., blood pressure, heart rate, and skin conductance), his research showed that spouses that are getting physiologically aroused by the negative affect expressed by their partners often reciprocate or escalate the negative behaviors, whereas spouses that are able to soothe themselves or are soothed by their partners engage in more positive behaviors, or at least avoid reciprocation and escalation of them. For men, the arousal also often leads them to emotionally withdraw from the relationship, which has long-term negative effects on relationship satisfaction and stability (Gottman & Levenson, 1992).

The role of physiological arousal, however, is not necessarily the same for all couples. For example, in the case of violently abusive husbands, Coan et al. (1997) found two different types of batterers: one type that is more violent outside marriage and whose heart rate slows down during marital conflict, and another type whose violence is largely confined to marriages and whose heart rate increases during marital conflict. This suggests not only that whether a spouse gets physiologically aroused during conflict affects the outcomes that conflict has for the relationship, but also that there are individual differences in arousal patterns that have profound effects on behaviors.

The effects of expressing affect during conflict, however, are not limited only to negative emotions. In at least one study, Gottman et al. (1998) found that only the expression of positive affect for the partner predicted marital satisfaction and stability over time. Uncharacteristically, the expression of negative affect had no predictive power in this study.

While explicating the role that expressing affect plays during marital conflict, Gottman (1993) also observed that conflict seems to affect different couples differently. Based on these observations, he proposed a marital typology that includes three functional and two dysfunctional types. The first of the functional types is the *validating* couple. In this type, both partners openly communicate their needs and desires and are receptive of those of the other person. They are supportive, engage in collaborative problem solving, and maintain largely positive affect throughout the conflict. They are also able to repair any damage caused to the relationship as a result of the conflict by apologizing, soothing the other, and expressing positive affect for one another. The second functional type is the *volatile* couple. In these couples, both partners are relatively more competitive with one another and freely express negative affect toward the other. These couples, however, manage to compensate for their open expression of negative affect by also expressing a surplus of positive affect, which ultimately enables them to maintain their relationship. The third functional type is the *avoidant* couple. Both partners avoid open conflict and often even fail to acknowledge their divergent interests. As a result, they do not engage in any form of problem solving, nor do they express their negative affect. Although these couples consequently fail to resolve their differences, they individually accommodate the other, and because they do not create a lot of hurt feelings, they are able to maintain their relationships even in the absence of expressions of positive affect for one another.

The hostile and the hostile-detached couple constitute Gottman's (1993) two dysfunctional couple types. Conflict in these couples is characterized by the open expression of negative affect, often with the intent to hurt or denigrate the other, without any or only minimal positive affect. Couples with these conflict styles are unlikely to stay together for very long and, if married, usually divorce.

Marriage Typologies

The marital theories discussed thus far each focus on a particular type of communication, essentially presuming that the effects that communication behaviors have are similar across individuals and couples. This presumption, however, is fundamentally at odds with the insight that communication behavior is context dependent (Watzlawick et al., 1967). Similar behaviors affect different couples differently, and different couples communicate differently in similar situations. These variations, however, are not just the noise of extraneous variables and influences that can safely be ignored when theorizing about the associations between the variable of interest. To the contrary, these variations are at least partially systematic and contribute to, or moderate, the associations between variables of interest and therefore cannot simply be treated as error variances.

Essentially, these variations are the result of an important attribute of marriages, indeed of all relationships, namely that marriages create their own, unique contexts that affect how couples communicate. We have already mentioned Gottman's (1994) conflict typology which is based mainly on empirical observation without being fully explained by a theoretical model. Fortunately, this typology converges with another important marital typology, Fitzpatrick's (1988) marital types.

Fitzpatrick's typology is one of the most sophisticated and influential marriage typologies (Fincham, 2004). It is broad in scope because it aims to explain all communication in marriage, rather than only one or two interpersonal processes. Furthermore, it is based both on theory and on empirical observation. It categorizes marriages based on how spouses represent their marriages cognitively in terms of marital beliefs and values and on how these beliefs are expressed through behavior. Specifically, categorization is based on spouses' reports of their *ideology* (i.e., beliefs and values relevant to marriage), behavioral *interdependence* (i.e., coordination of schedules and the sharing of space), and *communication* (i.e., whether couples engage in or avoid conflict).

Based on these three dimensions, individuals are categorized into one of three marital types: traditional, independent, and separate. *Traditionals* have a conventional ideology, are very interdependent, and have a moderately expressive communication style with their spouses during conflict. *Independents* have an unconventional ideology, are moderately interdependent, and report a very expressive communication style during conflict. *Separates* have a conventional ideology, are not very interdependent, and report little expressivity in their conflict communication. In about two-thirds of marriages, both spouses have the same marital type; the remaining marriages fall into a mixed type (most often traditional wife/separate husband) (Fitzpatrick, 1988).

In addition to its broad scope, this typology has two additional strengths. First, it is based equally on theory (the three underlying dimensions were identified based on prevailing marital theories) and empirical observation (the three types represent naturally occurring clusters in the conceptual space defined by the three dimensions). Second, it also explains how different marriages achieve similar outcomes in different ways based on the relational context that they define for themselves. That is, spouses in different types of marriages confronting the same set of challenges might communicate differently but achieve similar outcomes, or they communicate similarly but achieve different outcomes. During conflict, for example, Fitzpatrick's traditionals behave like Gottman's validators, interdependents behave like volatiles, and separates behave like avoiders.

Another recent marital typology that also seems to converge with Fitzpatrick's typology is Caughlin and Huston's (2006) typology. Based on their own and others' research on how affect is expressed in marriage, they concluded that positive affect and antagonism (i.e., conflict) are not mutually exclusive endpoints of a single continuum, as often assumed. Rather, these two dimensions are orthogonal to one another and define a conceptual space defining different types of emotional climate in marriages (Caughlin & Huston, 2006). *Tempestuous* marriages are high on both antagonism and affection and correspond to Fitzpatrick's independent and Gottman's volatile type. *Warm* marriages are high on affection and low on antagonism and correspond to Fitzpatrick's traditional and Gottman's validating type. *Bland* marriages are low on both dimensions and correspond to Fitzpatrick's separate and Gottman's avoiding type. Caughlin and Huston's fourth type, *hostile* marriages, are low on affection and high on antagonism and do not correspond to any of Fitzpatrick's stable types, but correspond to Gottman's hostile/hostile-detached type. As Caughlin and Huston surmise, this is not a stable type of marriage and these couples usually head for divorce.

The fact that Fitzpatrick's typology, which is based on general cognitive representations of marriages and actual communication behaviors in multiple contexts, converges with typologies of marriages that emerge from research focusing on specific aspects of marriages (i.e., conflict and expression of affect) suggests the broader validity of the typology. In addition, it also suggests that there is convergence in the various research projects on marital communication, and that the field could benefit from theorizing that, rather than focusing on individual communication phenomena, tries to provide a comprehensive account of marital relationships.

Family Communication

As already mentioned, there is less social scientific research on family communication than on marital communication. Thus, even though the overall number of phenomena and variables relevant to family communication probably exceed those of marital communication, the number of empirically established relationships between variables and thus the sum total of established empirical knowledge about family communication is smaller than the knowledge about marital communication. Nonetheless, this knowledge is not insignificant, and at least in scope, theories of family communication are at least as impressive as those of marital communication. As is the case for research on marital communication, much research and theorizing is directed at more narrowly defined family communication phenomena and processes.

Family Secrets

One good example of communication research devoted to exploring a specific aspect of family communication is Vangelisti's work on family secrets (1994, 1997; Vangelisti et al., 2001). According to Vangelisti (1994), family secrets can be differentiated by *form* (who keeps information from whom), *topic* (what is kept secret), and *function* (what are the effects of keeping the secret for the family). Forms vary from *individual* secrets (only one family member knows, but other family members and outsiders do not), to *intra-family* secrets (some family members know, but others and outsiders do not), to *whole family* secrets (all family members know but outsiders do not). Topics vary from the *conventional* (e.g., children's grades, illness of a parent) to *rule violations* (e.g., alcohol use, out of wedlock pregnancy) to *taboos* (e.g., marital infidelity, physical and sexual abuse). The functions of secrets identified by Vangelisti (1994) were essentially positive for family relationships and included *bonding, evaluation, maintenance, privacy, defense,* and *communication.*

Vangelisti (1994) found interesting associations between the form, topic, and function of secrets and their associations with satisfaction. For example, taboo secrets were most likely to be whole family secrets and least likely to be individual secrets, whereas rule violations were most likely to be individual secrets and least likely to be whole family secrets. There was no association between form and topic for conventional secrets. As far as the association between form and function was concerned, Vangelisti found that whole family secrets mainly served the evaluative, defense, and privacy functions, intra-family secrets mainly served the maintenance function, and individual secrets mainly served the evaluative and privacy functions.

As far as revealing family secrets to outsiders was concerned, Vangelisti (1997; Vangelisti et al., 2001) found that a member's satisfaction with their family relationships was negatively associated with revealing secrets to outsiders, whereas closeness and similarity with the outsider was positively associated with revealing family secrets. This suggests that revealing or sharing family secrets is used to manage one's interpersonal relationships, both with family members and with outsiders. Revealing secrets reduces the importance and intimacy of family relationships, and family members can use such revelations to assert greater autonomy and independence from their families. At the same time, revealing family secrets also increases the intimacy and interdependence of the family member's relationship with the outsider, and family members can use revealing secrets to increase the closeness of these relationships. How family members balance such contradictory demands in cases where they desire closeness with both family members and outsiders is an interesting question yet to be explored.

As is often the case with emerging research areas, there is not yet a theoretical account that explains why secret topics and forms interact the way they do, and why they bring about the functions that have been identified. In other words, this research is still in the observation stage rather than the theory stage.

Affective Communication in Families

Another example of a sophisticated research program of a narrow phenomenon in family communication is Floyd's investigation of the expression of affection in families and development of his affective exchange theory (AET; Floyd, 2001; Floyd & Morman, 2003). Floyd's research has a couple of interesting attributes that make it unique compared to more conventional research programs. First, unlike most other theories of human communication, which attempt to explain a phenomenon but take the phenomenon itself as given, Floyd provided a theoretical explanation for why affect is exchanged in family relationships by explicitly grounding AET on the theory of evolution. He argues that humans' ability to experience and express affection has evolved because it created significant benefits in terms of survival and reproduction. Thus, rather than standing on its own, AET is tied to a larger, extremely powerful explanatory framework of human behavior. Also, whereas most other scholars have studied affection in the context of romantic relationships, Floyd's investigations of AET were done almost exclusively in the context of father–son relationships.

Tying AET to the theory of evolution not only placed the theory into a larger, powerful explanatory framework that is relevant to all behavioral sciences, it also led to the formulations of very specific and unique hypotheses. For example, because parental affection is motivated by enabling one's offspring to survive and propagate, fathers should be more affectionate with biological as opposed to step-children, a prediction supported by Floyd and Morman (2001). Similarly, fathers should also be more affectionate with heterosexual sons than with bisexual or homosexual sons, a prediction supported by reports from hetero- and homosexual adult men on their relationships with their fathers (Floyd, 2001). This finding was replicated by Floyd et al. (2004), who also found that fathers' knowledge of their sons' sexuality mediated these relationships, such that fathers who knew that their sons were bisexual or homosexual were less affectionate with them than fathers of such sons who did not know their sons' sexual orientations.

By investigating AET in the context of father–son relationships, Floyd and his associates not only demonstrated the importance of affection for non-romantic relationships, but also described in great detail a family relationship that is otherwise often neglected by family communication scholars. For example, Floyd et al. (2004) found that affection in father–son relationships is expressed more through supportive behavior than through direct verbal or nonverbal expression of affection. Also, by comparing current fathers' reports on their relationships with their own fathers to their and their sons' reports on their current father–son relationships, Morman and Floyd (2002, 2006) were also able to demonstrate the impact that changing cultural norms have on this family dyad. Specifically, the researchers found that both fathers and sons in contemporary relationships report much more affectionate communication than current fathers had with their own fathers. This suggests that while evolved psychological processes do play a role in father–son relationships, so do cultural forces as well.

Olson's Circumplex Model

As is the case with marital communication, there are also research programs and theoretical models that aim to explain how families communicate in general, rather than focusing on specific types of communication. One such theory that emerged not from communication but from an allied discipline is Olson's circumplex model of family functioning (1981, 1993; Olson et al., 1979; Olson et al., 1983). Not only does this model make communication a central variable of family functioning, it also conceptualizes family communication in relatively sophisticated terms.

Olsen (1981, 1993) argues that family systems are best described and their functioning is best understood by considering two fundamental attributes of families: cohesion and adaptability. Specifically, according to the circumplex model, moderate levels on either dimension are associated with best functioning, whereas extremes on the dimensions are associated with less than optimal functioning. For cohesion, that means that families that are *separated* or *engaged* function better than families that are either *disengaged* or *enmeshed*, and for adaptation this means that families that are *flexible* or *structured* function better than families that are *rigid* or *chaotic.* Families that are moderate on both dimensions function best, followed by families that are moderate on one dimension but extreme on the other dimension, and families that are extreme on both dimensions are the least functional.

In the model, communication is identified as a third, facilitating dimension (Olson, 1981, 1993), meaning that a family's communication determines where the family falls along the two dimensions of cohesion and adaptability. Communication also allows families to change their location along the dimensions, which is particularly important for the application of the circumplex model to family therapy. In such applications, once a counselor has measured where along the two dimensions a family falls, the counselor can suggest specific communication behaviors that move a family more toward more moderate levels on the dimensions, thereby increasing or restoring family functioning. Specific communication skills identified by Olson that facilitate such movements include speaking skills, such as speaking for self and avoiding speaking for others, listening skills, such as active listening and empathy, as well as general communication skills, such as self-disclosure, clarity, continuity and tracking, and showing respect and regard for other.

Family Communication Patterns Theory

A theory that emerged from within the communication discipline and that, like Olson's model, links specific communication behaviors in families to a wide range of family and child outcomes is family communication patterns theory (FCPT; Fitzpatrick & Ritchie, 1994; Koerner & Fitzpatrick, 2002b, 2002c, 2004, 2006; Ritchie & Fitzpatrick, 1990). FCPT is based on the assumption that creating a shared social reality is a basic process that is necessary for families to function and that defines family relationships. Families create a shared reality through two communication behaviors: *conversation* orientation and *conformity* orientation, which also determine families' communication patterns. Conversation orientation refers to open and frequent communication between parents and children, with the purpose of co-discovering the meaning of symbols and objects that constitute social reality. It is associated with warm and supportive relationships characterized by mutual respect and concern for one another. Conformity orientation, in contrast, refers to more restricted communication between parents and children, with the purpose for persons of authority, typically the parents, to define social reality for the family. It is associated with more authoritarian parenting and less concern for the children's thoughts and feelings.

Theoretically orthogonal, these two orientations define a conceptual space with four family types. Consensual families are high on both conversation orientation and conformity orientation. Their communication is characterized by a tension between pressure to agree and to preserve the existing hierarchy of the family, on the one hand, and an interest in open communication and in exploring new ideas, on the other. Parents resolve this tension by listening to their children and explaining their values and beliefs to their children in the hope that the children will adopt the parents' belief system. Children in these families are usually well adapted and satisfied.

Pluralistic families stress conversation orientation over conformity orientation. Their communication is characterized by open, unconstrained discussions that involve all family members and a wide range of topics. Parents in these families do not attempt to control their children and are accepting of different opinions, although they also explain their own values and beliefs to their children. Children of these families learn to be independent and autonomous and to communicate persuasively, and they are generally satisfied with their family relationships and well adjusted.

Protective families stress conformity over conversation orientation. Their communication is characterized by an emphasis on obedience to parental authority and by little concern for conceptual matters. Parents in these families decide for their children and see little value in explaining their reasoning to them, although they state their beliefs and values and expect their children to follow their rules. Children in protective families learn that there is little value in family conversations and to distrust their own decision-making ability. These children are not as satisfied as, and often also less well adjusted than, children of the two earlier discussed family types.

Laissez-faire families stress neither conformity nor conversation orientation. Their communication is characterized by few, usually uninvolving interactions. Members of laissez-faire families are emotionally distant from one another, and family members have little interest in the thoughts and feelings of other family members. Children of these families learn that there is little value in family conversation and that they have to make their own decisions. Because they do not receive much support from their parents, however, they come to question their decision-making ability and are especially susceptible to peer influence. They also are below average in satisfaction and the least well adjusted of all family types.

Family communication patterns have been associated with a number of family processes, such as conflict resolution (Koerner & Fitzpatrick, 1997), confirmation and affection (Schrodt et al., 2007), family rituals (Baxter & Clark, 1996), and understanding (Sillars et al., 2005), as well as with child outcomes, such as communication apprehension (Elwood & Schrader, 1998), conflict with romantic partners (Koerner & Fitzpatrick, 2002c), resiliency (Fitzpatrick & Koerner, 2005), and children's mental and physical health (Schrodt & Ledbetter, 2007).

Conclusion and Future Directions

While it is difficult to predict the future, there are two common threads in the research reviewed here that allow us to at least guess where the future of the social scientific investigation of marital and family communication might be heading. The first common thread is that the models and theories are expanding, and necessarily becoming more complex to account for the complexity of communication behaviors and the outcomes that are associated with them. The second common thread is that research findings that seem to be isolated and specific to a particular context, behavior, or process converge into broader, more comprehensive models. More often than not, such comprehensive models are relationship typologies.

Sometimes the increased complexity of theoretical models results from the inclusion into the models of additional variables to increase the precisions of the models' explanations. One example of this process is the research on marital satisfaction and stability, which in addition to conflict behaviors started to consider expressions of positive and negative affect as a causal factor in satisfaction and stability, and also redefined affection and antagonism as orthogonal, rather than opposing ends of the same continuum.

Other times, the increase of complexity is not just due to the number of variables included in the models, but also because the models include variables of very different types that belong to very different explanatory systems. For example, Gottman's (1993) model of marital conflict not only includes the expression of different types of affect as variables, but also individuals' cognitive and physiological processes. Similarly, Floyd's (2001; Floyd & Morman, 2000, 2001, 2003, 2005) work on affective exchange integrates interpersonal behaviors expressing affection, heritable psychological dispositions, evolved behaviors, and social influences associated with historical, cultural, or larger societal changes.

The tendency for convergence of empirical observations and narrowly defined theoretical models into larger, more comprehensive and complex theories of human behavior is equally apparent and an indication of greater maturity of the field. We have already described the example of how research on marital conflict and the emotional climate of marriages converges with and fleshes out Fitzpatrick's (1988) marital typology. We expect that a similar process will also take place in the field of family communication. Because it is based on fundamental and necessary cognitive processes, family communication patterns theory is a likely candidate for a theory that will be able to integrate a number of what currently appear to be unrelated or even divergent theoretical models, such as models of parenting (Baumrind, 1967), family secrets (Vangelisti, 1994, 1997), and fathering (Floyd & Morman, 2000).

In the near future, based on the currently established knowledge of basic empirical facts about marital and family communication in marriages and also due to increased technological and statistical sophistication, communication scholars will be able to construct and test empirically ever more complex theoretical models of communication. These models will not only be integrated horizontally, that is, in the number of similar variables they include, but also vertically. That is, they will integrate basic physiological and cognitive processes with processes dependent on the specific relational context created by the relationship itself, and with processes dependent on culture and society at large.

If the past can be described as the painstaking assembly of empirical knowledge about the associations of variables relevant to communication and the development of theoretical explanations and models of narrowly defined processes and phenomena, the future lies in the integration of these models into theoretical explanations that do justice to the complexity of human behavior. In other words, marital and family communication scholars are poised to leave the era of mere observation behind and enter the era of creative, thoughtful, and scientific theorizing.

References

Altman, I., & Taylor, D. (1973). *Social penetration: The development of interpersonal relationships.* New York: Holt.

Baumrind, D. (1967). Child care practices anteceding three patterns of preschool behavior. *Genetic Psychology Monographs, 75,* 43–88.

Baxter, L. A., & Clark, C. L. (1996). Perceptions of family communication patterns and the enactment of family rituals. *Western Journal of Communication, 60,* 254–268.

Berger, C. R., & Calabrese, R. J. (1975). Some exploration in initial interaction and beyond: Toward a developmental theory of communication. *Human Communication Research, 1,* 99–112.

Bradbury, T. N., & Fincham, F. D. (1992). Attributions and behavior in marital interaction. *Journal of Personality and Social Psychology, 63,* 613–628.

Burleson, B. R. (1994). Comforting messages: Features, functions, and outcomes. In J. A. Daly & J. M. Wiemann (Eds.), *Strategic interpersonal communication* (pp. 135–161). Hillsdale, NJ: Lawrence Erlbaum Associates.

Burleson, B. R. (2003). Emotional support skills. In J. O. Greene & B. R. Burleson (Eds.), *Handbook of communication and social interaction skills* (pp. 551–594). Mahwah, NJ: Lawrence Erlbaum Associates.

Burleson, B. R., & Goldsmith, D. J. (1998). How the comforting process works: Alleviating emotional distress through conversationally induced reappraisals. In P. A. Anderson & L. K. Guerrero (Eds.), *Handbook of communication and emotion: Theory, research, application and contexts* (pp. 245–280). San Diego, CA: Academic Press.

Burleson, B. R., & Mortenson, S. R. (2003). Explaining cultural differences in evaluations of emotional support behaviors: Exploring the mediating influences of value systems and interaction goals. *Communication Research, 30,* 113–146.

Burleson, B. R., Samter, W., Jones, S. M., Kunkel, A. W., Holmstrom, A. J., Mortenson, S. T., & MacGeorge, E. L. (2005). Which comforting messages really work best? A different perspective on Lemieux and Tighe's "receiver perspective." *Communication Research Reports, 22,* 87–100.

Caughlin, J. P. (2002). The demand/withdraw pattern of communication as a predictor of marital satisfaction over time. *Human Communication Research, 28,* 49–85.

Caughlin, J. P., & Vangelisti, A. L. (2000). An individual difference explanation of why married couples engage in the demand/withdraw pattern of conflict. *Journal of Social and Personal Relationships, 17,* 523–551.

Caughlin, J. P., & Huston, T. L. (2002). A contextual analysis of the association between demand/withdraw and marital satisfaction. *Personal Relationships, 9,* 95–119.

Caughlin, J. P., & Huston, T. L. (2006). The affective structure of marriage. In A. Vangelisti & D. Perlmann (Eds.), *The Cambridge handbook of personal relationships* (pp. 131–155). Cambridge: Cambridge University Press.

Christensen, A. (1987). Detection of conflict patterns in couples. In K. Hahlweg & M. J. Goldstein (Eds.), *Understanding major mental disorder: The contribution of family interaction research* (pp. 250–265). New York: Family Process Press.

Christensen, A. (1988). Dysfunctional interaction patterns in couples. In P. Noller & M. A. Fitzpatrick (Eds.), *Perspectives on marital interaction* (pp. 31–52). Avon, UK: Multilingual Matters.

Christensen, A., & Heavey, C. L. (1990). Gender and social structure in the demand/withdraw pattern of marital conflict. *Journal of Personality and Social Psychology, 59*, 73–82.

Coan, J., Gottman, J., Babcock, J., & Jacobson, N. (1997). Battering and the male rejection of influence from women. *Aggressive Behavior, 23*, 375–388.

Cutrona, C. E. (1990). Stress and social support: In search of optimal matching. *Journal of Social and Clinical Psychology, 9*, 3–14.

Cutrona, C. E. (1996). *Social support in couples*. Thousand Oaks: CA: Sage.

Elwood, T. D., & Schrader, D. C. (1998). Family communication patterns and communication apprehension. *Journal of Social Behavior and Personality, 13*, 493–502.

Fincham, F. D. (2004). Communication in marriage. In A. Vangelisti (Eds.), *Handbook of family communication* (pp. 83–103). Mahwah, NJ: Lawrence Erlbaum Associations.

Fincham, F. D., Garnier, P. C., Gano-Phillips, S., & Osborn, L. N. (1995). Preintraction expectations, marital satisfaction, and accessibility: A new look at sentiment override. *Journal of Family Psychology, 9*, 3–14.

Fitzpatrick, M. A. (1988). *Between husbands and wives: Communication in marriage*. Newbury Park, CA: Sage.

Fitzpatrick, M. A., & Ritchie, L. D. (1994). Communication schemata within the family: Multiple perspectives on family interaction. *Human Communication Research, 20*, 275–301.

Fitzpatrick, M. A., & Koerner, A. F. (2005). Family communication schemata: Effects on children's resiliency. In S. Dunwoody, L. B. Becker, D. McLeod, & G. Kosicki (Eds.), *The evolution of key mass communication concepts: Honoring Jack M. McLeod* (pp. 115–139). Cresskill, NJ: Hampton Press.

Floyd, K. (2001). Human affection exchange I: Reproductive probability as a predictor of men's affection with their sons. *Journal of Men's Studies, 10*, 39–50.

Floyd, K., & Morman, M. T. (2000). Affection received from fathers as a predictor of men's affection with their own sons: Testing the modeling and compensation hypotheses. *Communication Monographs, 67*, 347–361.

Floyd, K., & Morman, M. T. (2001). Human affection III: Discriminative parental solicitude in men's affectionate communication with their biological and nonbiological sons. *Communication Quarterly, 49*, 310–327.

Floyd, K., & Morman, M. T. (2003). Human affection exchange II: Affectionate communication in father–son relationships. *Journal of Social Psychology, 143*, 599–612.

Floyd, K. & Morman, M. T. (2005). Fathers' and sons' reports of fathers' affectionate communication: Implications of a naive theory of affection. *Journal of Social and Personal Relationships, 22*, 99–109.

Floyd, K., Sargent, J. E., & Di Corcia, M. (2004). Human affection exchange VI: Further tests of reproductive probability as a predictor of men's affection with their adult sons. *Journal of Social Psychology, 144*, 191–206.

Gardner, K. A., & Cutrona, C. E. (2004). Social support communication in families. In A. Vangelisti (Eds.), *Handbook of family communication* (pp. 495–512). Mahwah, NJ: Lawrence Erlbaum Associates.

Gottman, J. M. (1993). The roles of conflict engagement, escalation or avoidance in marital interaction: A longitudinal view of five types of couples. *Journal of Consulting and Clinical Psychology, 61*, 6–15.

Gottman, J. M. (1994). *What predicts divorce?* Hillsdale, NJ: Lawrence Erlbaum Associates.

Gottman, J. M., & Levenson, R. W. (1986). Assessing the role of emotion in marriage. *Behavioral Assessment, 8*, 31–48.

Gottman, J. M., & Krokoff, L. J. (1989). The relationship between marital interaction and marital satisfaction: A longitudinal view. *Journal of Consulting and Clinical Psychology, 57*, 47–52.

Gottman, J. M., & Levenson, R. W. (1992). Marital processes predictive of later dissolution: Behavior, physiology, and health. *Journal of Personality and Social Psychology, 63*, 221–233.

Gottman, J. M., Markman, H., & Notarius, C. (1977). The topography of marital conflict: A sequential analysis of verbal and nonverbal behavior. *Journal of Marriage and the Family, 39*, 461–477.

Gottman, J. M., Coan, J., Carrere, S., & Swanson, C. (1998). Predicting marital happiness and stability from newlywed interactions. *Journal of Marriage and the Family, 60*, 5–22.

Hendrix, H. (1988). *Getting the love you want: A guide for couples.* New York: Henry Holt.

Jones, S. M., & Burleson, B. R. (2003). Effects of helper and recipient sex on the experience and outcomes of comforting messages: An experimental investigation. *Sex Roles, 48*, 1–19.

Kaplan, B. H., Cassel, J. C., & Gore, S. (1977). Social support and health. *Medical Care, 15*, 47–58.

Klinetob, N. A., & Smith, D. A. (1996). Demand–withdraw communication in marital interaction: Tests of interpersonal contingency and gender role hypotheses. *Journal of Marriage and the Family, 58*, 945–957.

Knapp, M. L. (1984). *Interpersonal communication and human relationships* (1st ed.). Boston, MA: Allyn & Bacon.

Koerner, A. F. (2009). The scientific investigation of family communication. In C. Berger, M. Roloff, & D. Roskos-Ewoldsen (Eds.), *The handbook of communication science* (pp. 471–488). Thousand Oaks, CA: Sage.

Koerner, A. F., & Fitzpatrick, M. A. (1997). Family type and conflict: The impact of conversation orientation and conformity orientation on conflict in the family. *Communication Studies, 48*, 59–75.

Koerner, A. F., & Fitzpatrick, M. A. (2002a). Nonverbal communication and marital adjustment and satisfaction: The role of decoding relationship relevant and relationship irrelevant affect. *Communication Monographs, 69*, 33–51.

Koerner, A. F., & Fitzpatrick, M. A. (2002b). Toward a theory of family communication. *Communication Theory, 12*, 70–91.

Koerner, A. F., & Fitzpatrick, M. A. (2002c). Understanding family communication patterns and family functioning: The roles of conversation orientation and conformity orientation. *Communication yearbook 26* (pp. 37–69). New York: Routledge.

Koerner, A. F., & Fitzpatrick, M. A. (2004). Communication in intact families. In A. Vangelisti (Ed.), *Handbook of family communication* (pp. 177–195). Mahwah, NJ: Lawrence Erlbaum Associations.

Koerner, A. F., & Fitzpatrick, M. A. (2006). Family communication patterns theory: A social cognitive approach. In D. O. Braithwaite & L. A. Baxter (Eds.), *Engaging theories in family communication: Multiple perspectives* (pp. 50–65). Thousand Oaks, CA: Sage.

Lazarus, R. S. (1991). *Emotion and adaptation*. New York: Oxford University Press.

Morman, M. T., & Floyd, K. (2002). A "changing culture of fatherhood": Effects on affectionate communication, closeness, and satisfaction in men's relationships with their fathers and their sons. *Western Journal of Communication, 66,* 395–411.

Morman, M. T., & Floyd, K. (2006). Good fathering: Father and son perceptions of what it means to be a good father. *Fathering: A Journal of Theory, Research and Practice about Men as Fathers, 4,* 113–136.

Noller, P. (1980). Gender and marital adjustment level differences in decoding messages from spouses and strangers. *Journal of Personality and Social Psychology, 41,* 272–278.

Noller, P. (1982). Channel consistency and inconsistency in the communication of married couples. *Journal of Personality and Social Psychology, 43,* 732–741.

Noller, P., & Gallois, C. (1986). Sending emotional messages in marriages. *British Journal of Social Psychology, 25,* 287–297.

Olson, D. H. (1981). Family typologies: Bridging family research and family therapy. In E. E. Filsinger & R. A. Lewis (Eds.), *Assessing marriage: New behavioral approaches* (pp. 74–89). Beverly Hills, CA: Sage.

Olson, D. H. (1993). Circumplex model of marital and family systems. In F. Walsh (Ed.), *Normal family processes* (2nd ed., pp. 104–137). New York: Guilford Press.

Olson, D. H., Sprenkle, D. H., & Russell, C. S. (1979). Circumplex model of marital and family systems: Cohesion and adaptability dimensions, family types, and clinical applications. *Family Process, 18,* 3–28.

Olson, D. H., Russell, C. S., & Sprenkle, D. H. (1983). Circumplex model of marital and family systems, VI: Theoretical update. *Family Process, 22,* 69–83.

Ritchie, L. D., & Fitzpatrick, M. A. (1990). Family communication patterns: Measuring interpersonal perceptions of interpersonal relationships. *Communication Research, 17,* 523–544.

Schrodt, P., & Ledbetter, A. M. (2007). Communication processes that mediate family communication patterns and mental well-being: A mean and covariance structures analysis of young adults from divorced and non-divorced families. *Human Communication Research, 33,* 330–356.

Schrodt, P., Ledbetter, A. M., & Ohrt, J. K. (2007). Parental confirmation and affection as mediators of family communication patterns and children's mental well-being. *Journal of Family Communication, 7,* 23–46.

Sillars, A., Koerner, A. F., & Fitzpatrick, M. A. (2005). Communication and understanding in parent–adolescent relationships. *Human Communication Research, 31,* 103–128.

Thomas, G., Fletcher, G. J. O., & Lange, C. (1997). On-line empathic accuracy in marital interaction. *Journal of Personality and Social Psychology, 72,* 838–850.

Vangelisti, A. L. (1994). Family secrets: Forms, functions and correlates. *Journal of Social and Personal Relationships, 11,* 113–135.

Vangelisti, A. L. (1997). Revealing family secrets: The influence of topic, function, and relationships. *Journal of Social and Personal Relationships, 14,* 679–705.

Vangelisti, A. L., Caughlin, J. P., & Timmerman, L. (2001). Criteria for Revealing Family Secrets. *Communication Monographs, 68,* 1–27.

Vanzetti, N. A., Notarius, C. I., & NeeSmith, D. (1992). Specific and generalized expectancies in marital interaction. *Journal of Family Psychology, 6,* 171–183.

Watzlawick, P., Bavelas, J. B., & Jackson, D. D. (1967). *Pragmatics of human communication.* New York: W. W. Norton.

Whisman, M. A., Uebelacker, L. A., & Weinstock, L. M. (2007). Psychopathology and marital satisfaction: The importance of evaluating both partners. *Journal of Consulting and Clinical Psychology, 72,* 830–838.

17

THE FUTURE OF COMMUNICATION

Since its academic introduction in the form of propaganda studies after World War I, social scientific approaches to communication have struggled but been able to maintain scholastic and practical relevance, all the while suffering from identity crises (e.g., Gonzalez, 1988; Peters, 1986, 1988), concerns over our legitimacy (Frey, 2009; Seeger, 2009), and occasional hand-wringing about the very interdisciplinary nature of our work (Herbst, 2008; Scott, 2009). In considering the future of communication as social science, it is perhaps wise to first consider some of these historical and ongoing concerns as a means of providing a direction for the future. After all, an understanding of these historical concerns would aid the discipline to move forward in self-aware and productive ways. Thus, in this chapter we will discuss communication's interdisciplinary nature, consider the debate over communication's credibility, consider its external impact, and reflect on how theory and technological adaptation may coalesce as distinct but interdependent ideas. We will then conclude with considerations for the future direction of communication scholarship.

Interdisciplinarity, Post-Disciplinarity, and Circling the Wagons

Like many fields in the social sciences, communication emerged from several disciplines (see Chapter 3), whose researchers found themselves studying similar and related phenomena. Thus, the very emergence of the field of communication was interdisciplinary, if by "interdisciplinary" we mean "a sense of a unified field, produced through the historical convergence of subcultures, social structures, and training practices" (Herbst, pp. 603–614). The current definition of interdisciplinary, however, has evolved to include the notion of a field that grows through, and is strengthened by, interdisciplinarity. This is defined simply as scholars who collaborate but identity with different academic disciplines. Indeed, several scholars have argued for sustained or even increased emphasis on an interdisciplinary approach to communication (Berger, 2005; Herbst, 2008; Scott, 2009; Sherry, 2004). By drawing on research evidence from psychology, sociology, political science, and other disciplines, we can strengthen the basis for our own scholarship, craft well-formulated hypotheses based on the extant evidence, and not just that which emerges from communication departments, and ultimately build theory that is important, relevant, meaningful, and *valid*. In this way, an interdisciplinary approach is not only useful to us as scholars but it makes for good science.

Specifically, Scott (2009) has argued for interdisciplinary work because, broadly speaking, it stands to improve the quality of the extant literature. He defends the idea that "calls for interdisciplinarity . . . [still] seem especially relevant to scholars examining communication technology," mainly because research has indicated that relying on evidence from various fields can strengthen the scholarship conducted in one (pp. 753–757). Similarly, Sherry (2004) has argued that interdisciplinary work strengthens our scientific insights into communication; however, his definition of interdisciplinarity is somewhat narrower: he operationalizes it as research conducted by scholars from various disciplines working cooperatively on one study. Lastly, Hummert (2009) argues for interdisciplinarity based on the value of such work to the academy and to society, but defines it more broadly than Sherry (2004), with an emphasis on theory, method, and application. Hummert (2009, p. 222) claims "programs that are most successful are interdisciplinary in their approach to theory, methods, and publication venues. Clearly, if we want to ensure that our research makes a difference, we cannot afford to be insular." Hummert advocates for communication to have "translational" applications that can speak to situations outside of the academy (2009).

Despite the seemingly obvious benefit of, say, being familiar with research on one's topic that comes out of other disciplines, there are those who are not completely in favor of interdisciplinary scholarship or at least try to reframe the issue. For example, Herbst (2008) concedes that "communication studies . . . was [clearly and] stunningly interdisciplinary from the start" and argues that the field was started and legitimized by scholars from various disciplines (e.g., sociology, political science, economics, psychology, literary criticism, and marketing) during the mid-twentieth century with a "wonderful disrespect (or disinterest?) in disciplinary constraints" (pp. 603, 614). However, Herbst (2008) goes on to argue that communication is now post-disciplinary in nature. By post-disciplinary he means that a field has reached a time period in which interdisciplinarity is taken for granted; a time period in which "antidisciplinarity," "characterized by fields like Women's Studies, which was unable to convince traditional departments to heed gender as lens for social analysis" (Herbst, 2008, p. 603), has become unproductive as a theoretical approach; and what remains is a "a determined eclecticism about methods and subject matter" (Menand, 2001, p. 12).

In fact, Herbst (2008) provides at least four reasons why post-disciplinarity is preferable to the more passé interdisciplinarity. First, "if you argue that your field is important, unique, and adds particular value to the academy, it cannot simply be 'interdisciplinary' or synthetic." Second, "administrators . . . need to see that a field really does stand on its own and therefore deserves its own protected resources and space." Third, talk of interdisciplinarity feels stale and even a bit comical, given how overused and abused the term is at this point, and fourth, interdisciplinary approaches are accepted and taken for granted (Herbst, 2008, pp. 603–614).

Whereas all of these arguments of interdisciplinarity and post-disciplinarity seem somewhat ineffectual, a point Herbst (2008) also makes when she claims the arguments to be "pretentious, mind-numbingly boring, and not particularly useful," the debates seem to continue. Thus, we honor their history here, but suggest that communication research simply continue with a healthy and necessary respect for evidence from all fields as we seek to answer theoretically interesting and practically relevant questions. This is not to say that discussions of theory and method are not important. In fact, these theoretical and methodological questions are crucial to progress in the knowledge base. However, circling the wagons to protect an academic space, as evidenced by discussions about whether or not we should attend to research outside of our field, or work with scholars from other disciplines, seems unimportant and even counterproductive. In sum, we should just get on with our work.

Credibility in Communication

Communication, as an area of study, has often been criticized for being *practical*, a term that in some academic circles almost amounts to a slur. For example, Herbst (2008) states that at its inception and even today, communication can be seen as "an industrial effort, training students in the practical arts of public relations and journalism" (p. 603). As the struggle for scholarly credibility continued, communication accomplished, slowly and painstakingly, three major goals. First, communication itself, through the rise of mass media, became an increasingly important, and yes, practical, pursuit. This led administrators to acknowledge that communication as a field could stand on its own and therefore deserved its own protected resources and space. However, with this admittedly practical role in the academy, scholars worked to retain their place in the academy, while simultaneously attempting to establish communication journals, boldly intent on publishing communication scholarship. During the early and middle parts of the previous century, communication scholars also began to form their own organizations (e.g., the NCA and ICA) (Herbst, 2008, pp. 603–614). These early steps toward legitimacy were a necessary condition to gain the even more valuable prize: scholarly recognition and validity. Communication has sought "to prove to other fields that we matter" (Herbst, 2008, p. 606).

This continued concern is noted by Harwood (2010) when he claims that the fact that there are scholarly publications devoted to determining whether an academic field has had an impact (see, for example, Scott, 2009) is demonstrable proof that the field struggles with issues of legitimacy. After all, it is unlikely that such introspection would occur in a medical journal, or even one in psychology. Thus, scholarship that asks: "has communication made a difference?" (see Hummert, 2009; Seeger, 2009) indicates that we struggle with the question of our own being.

For example, Sherry (2004, p. 101) has stated that communication lacks any real "milestone" research and that we have "reached the limits of the scientific paradigm of the initial milestone studies." Whereas this statement was written over a decade ago, more recent theorists (Condit, 2009) have claimed that the few communication theories that have been developed were created by scholars outside the discipline. Regardless of the merit of these claims, any field should work to maintain its legitimacy, not simply to improve its standing or in order to exist in a self-important academy, but simply to *be* legitimate. As Peters argued decades ago (1986), communication's legitimacy should lie in its power, not in its academic worth. Thus, what might aid in legitimacy?

Condit (2009) argues that the nature of the field of communication itself requires a new set of academic practices for evaluation of communication, because it is both complex and emergent. She argues that the Enlightenment brought with it a focus on science, objectivity, rationality, and epistemic certainty. As a result, several social sciences have grafted their own research onto this logic, despite the fact that a human, social process such as communication makes these modernist academic practices inadequate to studying such a dynamic phenomenon. What might this new set of academic practices look like? Although no clear answer is apparent, at least a few changes which could encourage validity, and the natural legitimacy that would accompany it, have been suggested.

For example, Sherry (2004) argues for an entirely new paradigm. Because media effects in communication took off when theories of biological determinism in other fields were waning, communication theories centered heavily on environmental influences on individuals. Theories in psychology and media effects were based on social learning theories and those rooted in social psychology. With the environment as the presumed starting place for the individual and his/her social interactions, little room remained for the biological variables that may hold sway. Sherry (2004) states that as neuroscience began to balance out the nature/nurture debate, giving significantly more credence to biological explanations for behavior, both previous and future communication research was greatly implicated, as many did not build in room for biology to explain much of communicative interactions. Without emphasis on biology, the very nature of the social process of communication could not, and cannot, be understood. Sherry calls for a greater emphasis on evolution, biology, and neuroscience in our understanding of human interaction. As such, the nature of our methods, our theories, indeed our ontology must shift to keep up.

Legitimacy can also be improved through the increased validity that would result from improved methods and more precise measures. Communication science scholars have used a number of research methodologies, such as surveys, content analyses, and experiments. However, Condit (2009, p. 6) notes that one topic that communication scholars need to focus on more in the future is "develop[ing] methods of rigorous observation that [will] allow them to see anew the phenomena that common sense had already labeled and theorized," a goal Condit claims that biology and psychology scholars have achieved. Similarly, Harwood (2010) emphasizes the need for the development of standardized, valid, and shared methods for analyzing message content. Specifically, he claims that message content analyzed through content analysis continues to "rely on pain-staking and one-off manual coding systems developed for specific research projects" (Harwood, 2010, p. 297). Although these scholars make a call for new methods, it is worth noting that in the era of big data, means to electronically comb through literally millions of messages, and ever more precise measurement tools for both physiology and self-report (see Chapter 6), the call seems a bit dated. Indeed, new methods are emerging through big data and new data-analytic methods.

Lastly, and as implied above, legitimacy in communication must be sought out through appropriate means. An assessment of discussion in the field of communication indicates that legitimacy has been sought and encouraged through the garnering of physical space and resources within universities (Herbst, 2008), through recognition of our journals by those outside of the field of communication (Scott, 2009), and through publication of our findings in the popular press so that communication research is publicly available (Condit, 2009). Whereas these are all laudable goals and important in certain obvious and practical ways, they are not, in our view, legitimacy as it should be defined. To be legitimate is to be justifiable and rightful. To be justifiable and rightful our work must matter; and to matter, our work must be valid. In this line of argument, well-designed work about important questions is valid, valid work can be justified on its own account because the answers matter, and when the answers matter, the work is legitimate. Thus, although seeking *recognition* for our work may be necessary and practical to keep us going as a field, it is not sufficient. In fact, only valid research *should* be recognized and thus validity should be our ultimate litmus test—not recognition. So, in order to consider our legitimacy, we must consider our validity, and ultimately, our relevance. Thus, we will also consider our impact.

The Impact of Communication Research

In order to consider the legitimacy of communication, it is important to ask what communication has *done* to improve the lives of others, materially. In addressing this issue, Seeger (2009) has taken the unequivocal stance that communication research has an ethical obligation to make a positive difference in the lives of others. He argues that despite the fact that "scholars in a variety of fields"—

communication included—"do not believe they have any responsibility for facilitating the application of their work" (p. 13), communication scholars, precisely because of the obvious and immediate application of their work, are obligated, ethically, to consider application as a hallmark of sound scholarship.

The divide between research that has immediate practical application and research designed to answer theoretical or even broad empirically driven questions is evidenced by a historic split between basic research and applied research. Basic research includes more observational, theory-based questions, whereas applied research implies more direct interventions into communicative processes. Sherry (2010) suggests a similarity between this divide and that of the natural sciences, where basic research on chemical compounds, for example, can yield a beneficial medical innovation, but applied research is necessary to more broadly construct, package, and disseminate the vaccine or pill that has been created. In communication research this might exist as the difference between research on the effects of specific source variables on individuals' likelihood of engaging in behavior change and a study that applies those source variables to a specific behavior change campaign and then tests for its effectiveness in a particular population.

Whereas this artificial distinction may have some, if limited value, such as keeping basic research value and bias-free, it seems obvious, and inevitable, that the two forms of research must build on each other. According to Hummert (2009), the relationship between basic and applied research should be transactional. Basic research should clearly be used in the development of applied research projects, but findings of applied research may help basic research consider additional contextual variables that may matter. For example, if a given model of social influence has been tested and supported in the lab, but has not adequately predicted behavior change in a given campaign situation, it is worth considering what aspects of the campaign, or the particular real-world sample, may account for differences between the basic and applied research situations. These considerations allow for the further development of theory. In this way, theory development can and should be iterative, and work hand in hand with applied research. However, currently, applied and basic research are still conducted, most frequently, as separate and unrelated research processes.

There are several reasons for this. For example, Harwood (2010) has argued that a strong emphasis on theory forces researchers to focus on message forms, rather than message content. A clean manipulation of a message, one that may perform well as a lab-based study, may not be connected to messages as they actually occur in, say, a social marketing campaign. Seeger (2009) suggests that the reason for this is that basic researchers tend to have a fairly narrow agenda that emphasizes publication and tenure. As a result, the complexities of real-world messages are streamlined and made into messages that can be easily manipulated in the lab, written up as results, and published in a journal. Seeger argues that whereas this may assist in theory building, or more cynically, in achieving tenure for the scholar, it does little to forward the practical use of research to improve health campaigns, for example. In sum, real messages are complex and not suited for a laboratory study; however, clean messages are necessary for a soundly designed experiment. The publication process may well encourage scholars to focus on clean, if externally less valid, messages. Seeger also suggests that jargon-laden research articles are generally inaccessible to the practitioners who might benefit from them.

Both scholars make excellent points, and the publication process does favor research that is theoretically derived and consists of clean manipulations. Furthermore, the distinction made between basic and applied research shares something in common with the methodological distinction between internally valid research, where we can confidently conclude that the manipulation was the thing that caused the effect, and externally valid research, where the effect can be generalized to situations outside of the lab. Often, these two, internal and external validity, are presented as a trade-off, a methodological balancing act. Analogically, we assume applied research is externally valid but lacks internal validity; whereas we assume basic research is internally valid but lacks external validity. However, an alternative way of thinking about this balancing act is that the two, internal and external validity, are actually symbiotically related, and not in opposition at all. Quite simply, the more valid our lab findings are, the more likely we can confidently use them in applied situations. If they do not apply outside of the lab, we need to ask careful questions about what has changed outside of the lab so that lab findings can be generalizable. This may, or may not, take us back into the lab. But there is little reason to think that improving the lab would harm generalizability, or vice versa. This would be one way of de-emphasizing the distinction between basic and applied research. Indeed, a better way to think about it may be to shift from a focus on the generalizability of the research to a focus on understanding the generalizability of our theories.

Other scholars have also offered several proposed solutions and directions for research that avoid the basic/applied binary and help encourage communication to be a more synthesized field of study. Kahl (2010) has suggested that, first, undergraduate programs should fully utilize service learning. In doing so, students are encouraged and taught to apply theory and see it in action as a main component of communication classes. Given the increasing enrollment to the communication major at most universities, service learning may help students and the broader community benefit from and ultimately see the benefit of communication research.

Second, at the graduate level, Kahl (2010) has suggested that students be encouraged to engage in more applied research, or, at the very least, seek out application of their work in practical and meaningful ways. Thus, from the onset, scholars would be trained to think about the practical application of their work, and would consider *if* their scholarship had practical merit and how that practical merit might be enacted. Frey (2009) and Herbst (2008) have made suggestions that would be similar in outcome, if not in form. Specifically, both have stated that communication as a field should undertake more translational scholarship (Frey, 2009) that minimizes the use of jargon and makes communication research accessible to practitioners.

Third, Seeger (2009) has emphasized the importance of public policy and designing research that ultimately may have policy implications. This would require an emphasis on contemporary problems that are already high on policy makers' priority lists. Of course, given the rapidity of change in the focus of policy makers, this suggestion may take a certain amount of foresight. Furthermore, Frey (2009) has noted that the current environment is "evidence-aversive" and characterized by a "growing ambivalence of public and private bodies to academic involvement in policy" (p. 209). Despite these constraints, the need to simply recognize the intersection of research and public policy would be one way of encouraging the practical application of communication scholarship. Further, when research does have public policy implications, it is crucial for scholars to make this research accessible to the press. Since this requires time and effort to achieve, it may even require a change in the academic reward system. Whereas granting tenure based solely on research that has policy implications would surely narrow the focus of many scholars and limit the vital breadth of scholarly work, simply offering some reward for this kind of scholarship may be beneficial to keep it going in the long run. In any case, the arguments forwarded above offer some small suggestions on how to ensure that communication remains important, relevant, and, above all, non-self-indulgent.

Perhaps the most sound piece of advice, as we consider the future of communication vis-à-vis its impact, is to simply end the rigid distinctions between, and nationalistic attachments to, basic and applied research. The two are clearly and necessarily linked. A holistic approach would allow for stronger applied scholarship that benefits from theory, and theoretically driven research that has benefitted from considering its application outside of the lab. This iterative process would ultimately result in stronger applied and stronger basic scholarship. Or more succinctly: this iterative process would result in stronger scholarship.

Theory, New Technology, and a Move Forward

Despite the fact that journal editors, scholars, and students in the field of communication "are rather hung up on theory" (Harwood, 2010, p. 297), scholars have argued that theory has not been enough of a focus of communication research. In fact, Condit (2009) has argued that the few communication theories that do exist were created by scholars outside of the discipline, a statement that, while not entirely correct, does have some value. Perhaps it is more accurate to say that communication scholars continue to utilize theory from psychology, sociology, and other relevant disciplines, a practice that leads us right back to the interdisciplinary debate! In any case, theory remains something that is vital to any discipline and indeed is vital to understanding human behavior regardless of the discipline. Thus, like anyone pursuing an understanding of the world, communication scholars must continue to use, refine, and build theory about communication. In short, if we want to talk about the future of communication, we need to think about theory.

During the 1980s and 1990s, much ink was spilled about the mass communication and interpersonal communication divide (e.g., Reardon & Rogers, 1988). Although Reardon and Rogers (1988) challenged the intellectual and theoretical distinction between the two areas, they also provided evidence for the fact that communication scholars in each of the two subfields did not cross-cite to any great extent. They argued, as many did at the time, that there was little justification for the distinction and that the fact of distinct theories in each area was due more to historical convenience and university politics than to any meaningful differences in the processes. Still, the debate continued, because scholars in these two major areas, with exceptions, still did not work together or cite each other all that much until more recently. However, the rise of the Internet and the subsequent introduction of social media have done much to eliminate the apparent distinction between mass and interpersonal communication practically speaking, if not theoretically. Because the Internet is clearly a channel that allows for a type of interpersonal communication that is often made available to mass audiences, the historical struggle and divide between mass and interpersonal communication appears a bit outdated, even quaint. Instead, current theorizing must emphasize what many have argued all along: communication is a process of messages sent across channels between individuals, one or both of whom are intent on creating meaning in the mind of the other. Indeed, many additional variables, such as noise, feedback, context, and attention, become crucial to the process. But the *channel* (face to face, for example, or via the Internet) is and should be considered a variable, no more or less important than any other. Change the variable of channel and the process of communication may indeed change, but it remains communication, with repetitive, recognizable patterns that ultimately allow us, as researchers, to generate and test theory.

As communication scholars look to the future, several scholars have made their cases for what areas should receive our focus, both empirically and theoretically. Scott (2009) has focused his attention on the intersection of technological innovations, social media, and the obvious communications that are therein enabled. In his eyes, a big research area for communication to tackle now is presence/virtuality studies that better articulate conditions under which wireless/mobile communication create the feeling of "being there" with people. Therefore, the field of presence, which is very much alive and thriving, even establishing its own journal (i.e., *Presence*, established 1994), should continue to be a focus moving forward. After all, presence, which is often considered an important variable in areas of video gaming and virtual reality, will become increasingly important as online activities become ever more diverse and important to our daily functioning.

A second area that is important in terms of communication and technology, but that also gets at the heart of more traditional communication theories and practices, is that of privacy and surveillance as well as the areas of anonymity and identity. All are crucial when we consider our online lives, but privacy, surveillance, anonymity, and identity took place as part of the communication process long before the Internet arrived on the scene to radically insinuate itself into our communicative lives. Issues of self-disclosure, social connectedness, relationship development, privacy, intrusion, secrets, deception, identity development, and information sharing, among many others, have surely predated the Internet. Yet there is little doubt that technology has made many of these issues at once simpler and more complex. We can *do* many of these things more quickly and easily; however, with this ease come ethical questions, social changes, and new ways of seeing communication itself. All of this requires new research, often investigating "old" topics because we sense, rightly, that the very playing field on which we are doing all of these things has changed, and the process has likely changed with it. So we must continue to refine and develop theory. However, as argued above, technological adaptation has erased many older boundaries, such as the one between mass and interpersonal communication, and has offered us the opportunity to think about *communication* as a process influenced by, but not bounded by, its channel.

Despite the opportunities that technological adaptation has offered us theoretically, Scott (2009) points out that, as scholars, we will have a hard time developing theories as quickly as the innovations that may precede them. To that end, Scott suggests that communication scholars should focus on generating models that can help explain and predict the development of these new innovations so that the field can stay ahead of the curve. However, that leaves us with theory that is technology dependent. Instead, it seems that what technology offers us is a chance to consider communication across various channels, looking, as always, for patterns in these processes, and ultimately developing communication theory where technology (and its many operationalizations and measures that are connected to it) is a *variable* in the larger process (Okdie et al., 2014). Then, we really will be ahead of the curve, or free from it.

Future of Communication Research

Based on the discussion in this chapter, the future of communication lies in several areas: in making our research relevant and useful (Frey, 2009), in maintaining legitimacy in the academy (Condit, 2009), in keeping our discipline strong (Seeger, 2009). However, it is quite possible that all of these goals could be achieved through strong theory, realized through valid research. In simply practicing theory, whether through the unification of theory with data (Berger, 2005) or the unification of findings and application (Frey, 2009), we may achieve the goals we set out to achieve: to explain, predict, and ultimately improve the communication process.

Nearly three decades ago, Peters (1986), in his analogy of communication as a nation state, asserted that communication's legitimacy rests in its power rather than its academic worth. In his view, communication suffered from intellectual poverty insofar as it has a wealth of subdisciplines, scholars, methodologies, and subject matter, but no coherence. Coherence can be achieved, and one main way may be through harnessing technology, understanding how communication continues to work both with and without it, and in so doing, create a coherent communication theory. In doing so, we move closer to a holistic view of communication processes and legitimize our academic pursuits.

References

Berger, C. R. (2005). Interpersonal communication: Theoretical perspectives, future prospects. *Journal of Communication, 55*, 415–447. doi:10.1111/j.1460-2466.2005. tb02680.x

Condit, C. M. (2009). You can't study and improve communication with a telescope. *Communication Monographs, 76*, 3–11.

Frey, L. R. (2009). What a difference more difference-making communication scholarship might make: Making a difference from and through communication research. *Journal of Applied Communication Research, 37*, 205–214. doi:10.1080/00909880902792321.

Gonzalez, H. (1988). The evolution of communication as a field. *Communication Research, 15*, 302–308.

Harwood, J. (2010). A difference we can call our own. *Journal of Applied Communication Research, 38*, 295–298. doi:10.1080/00909882.2010.490843.

Herbst, S. (2008). Disciplines, intersections, and the future of communication research. *Journal of Communication, 58*, 603–614. doi:10.1111/j.1460-2466.2008.00402.x.

Hummert, M. L. (2009). Not just preaching to the choir: Communication scholarship does make a difference. *Journal of Applied Communication Research, 37*, 215–224. doi:10. 1080/00909880902792313.

Kahl, D. H. (2010). Making a difference: (Re)Connecting communication scholarship with pedagogy. *Journal of Applied Communication Research, 38*, 298–302. doi:10.1080/ 00909882.2010.490845.

Okdie, B. M., Ewoldsen, D. R., Muscanell, N. L., Guadagno, R. E., Eno, C. A., Valez, J. A., Dunn, R. A., O'Mally, J., & Reichert Smith, L. (2014). Missed programs (you can't TiVo this one): Why psychologists should study media. *Perspectives on Psychological Science, 9*, 180–195.

Peters, J. D. (1986). Institutional sources of intellectual poverty in communication research. *Communication Research, 13*, 527–559. doi:10.1177/009365086013004002.

Peters, J. D. (1988). The need for theoretical foundations: Reply to Gonzalez. *Communication Research, 15*, 309–17.

Reardon, K. K., & Rogers, E. M. (1988). Interpersonal versus mass media communication: A false dichotomy. *Human Communication Research, 15*, 284–303.

Scott, C. R. (2009). A whole-hearted effort to get it half right: Predicting the future of communication technology scholarship. *Journal of Computer-Mediated Communication, 14*, 753–757. doi:10.1111/j.1083-6101.2009.01467.x.

Seeger, M. (2009). Does communication research make a difference: Reconsidering the impact of our work. *Communication Monographs, 76*, 12–19.

Sherry, J. L. (2004). Media effects theory and the nature/nurture debate: A historical overview and directions for future research. *Media Psychology*, *6*, 83–109. doi:10.1207/s1532785xmep0601-4.

Sherry, J. L. (2010). The value of communication science. *Journal of Applied Communication Research*, *38*, 302–306. doi:10.1080/00909882.2010.490847.

AUTHOR INDEX

Abelman, R. 140
Abraham, L. 125
Adorno, T. 41, 45, 47
Agozzino, A. L. 277
Ajzen, A. 10, 297–301, 303–305
Allport, G. W. 44
Althaus, S. L. 252
Altman, I. 182, 317
Alwitt, L. F. 155–156
Ancu, M. 271
Anderson, C. A. 129–130
Anderson, D. R. 155
Anderson, J. A. 22–24
Appiah, O. 125
Aristotle 32
Arnett, J. 146
Asch, S. E. 208
Atkin, D. 140

Ball-Rokeach, S. J. 250
Bandura, A. 8–9, 13, 44, 113, 116, 118, 148–150
Barnlund, D. 25
Baxter, L. A. 185–187
Baym, G. 22–24, 58
Belch, G. 104
Belch, M. 104
Bem, D. J. 221–222
Benjamin, W. 41
Bennett, S. 269

Berelson, B. 25
Berger, C. R. 5–6, 12, 28, 182, 317
Bergstrom, C. T. 20
Bickham, D. S. 157
Bilandzic, H. 169–170
Blumler, J. G. 184
Bolls, P. 115
Bonini, C. P. 177–178
Boyd, D. 108
Brosius, H. B. 119
Brown, P. 190
Bryant, J. 139, 143
Burgoon, J. K. 189
Burleson, B. R. 320
Bush, G. H. W. 251–252
Busselle, R. W. 169–170

Cacioppo, J. T. 227–231, 233, 261, 295
Calabrese, R. J. 182, 317
Caldini, R. 208
Campbell, D. T. 94, 97
Canary, D. J. 183
Cantril, H. 44, 46
Capra, F. 48
Caughlin, J. P. 183, 321, 324
Chaffee, S. H. 6, 37
Chaiken, S. 231–233
Charters, W. W. 43
Cheung, C. M. 275
Christofides, E. 269, 271

Cicero 32
Cingel, D. P. 277
Comstock, G. 118
Comte, A. 64, 76
Condit, C. M. 30, 165, 339–340, 343
Conway, J. C. 146
Cooley, C. H. 187
Corey, S. M. 297
Crawford, K. 108
Curtis, S. 128
Cutrona, C. E. 320

Dallinger, J. M. 190
Daly, K. 9
Dearing, J. 248, 259
Delia, J. G. 38
Deneen, S. 269
Dewey, J. 39, 43
Domke, D. 125
Durkheim, E. 76
Dworkin, A. 51

Elder, G. H. 103
Ellison, N. 274
Engel, D. 119
Entman, R. M. 260–261
Ericsson, K. 91
Ewoldsen, D. R. 117, 234, 289, 297, 299, 302–305

Fazio, R. H. 297
Feshbach, S. 292
Festinger, L. 77, 217–220, 273
Field, D. E. 155
Fink, E. J. 58–60
Finn, S. 145
Fisch, S. M. 159
Fishbein, M. 10, 297–301, 303–305
Fiske, S. T. 86, 165, 187, 191
Fitzpatrick, M. A. 319, 323–324, 328–330
Floyd, K. 326–327, 330
Floyd, L. 330
Forman, H. J. 43
Frank, E. 106
French, J. 207
Frenkel-Brunswik, E. 45
Freud, S. 41, 244
Frey, L. R. 29, 342–343
Fromm, E. 41

Gantz, W. 58–60
Gerbner, G. 116–118,
Goffman, E. 122
Goktas, Y. 269
Goldhoorn, C. 121
Gonzalez, H. 19
Gottman, J. M. 183, 321–324, 330
Graesser, A. C. 168–169
Gramsci, A. 52
Greene, K. 145
Grieve, R. 274

Habermas, J. 41
Haider, M. 287
Hall, M. A. 106
Hall, S. 51–53, 163–166
Hample, D. 190
Hartmann, T. 121
Harwood, J. 339–341
Hecht, M. L. 188
Hegel, G. W. F. 185
Herbst, S. 337–338, 342
Hodge, R. 165
Hoffner, C. A. 121
Hoggart, R. 52
Horkheimer, M. 41
Horton, D. 120
Hovland, C. 43, 48–51, 222–223, 226
Hume, D. 64
Hummert, M. L. 337, 341
Huston, A. C. 158
Huston, T. L. 324

James, W. 187
Jamieson, K. H. 30
Janis, I. L. 292
Jerit, J. 122
Jones, C. R. 216
Josephson, W. L. 124
Jung, E. 188
Jung, S.-Y. 250

Kahl, D. H. 342
Kahneman, D. 254–255
Katz, D. 195–196
Katz, E. 40, 50, 139, 245–246, 306–307
Kendall, K. 30
Khan, R. L. 195–196

Kim, K. S. 128
Kim, Y. K. 121, 252–253
Knapp, M. L. 180, 182, 317
Knobloch, L. K. 144
Köbler, F. 274
Koerner, A. F. 189, 318–319, 328–329
Kraut, R. 184, 274
Krcmar, M. 27, 91, 99, 123, 127–128,
  130, 138–139, 141–142, 145, 148–150,
  166, 276
Krebs, P. M. 304–305
Kreps, G. L. 287
Kruglanski, A. W. 232–233
Kuhn, T. 50

Lang, A. 130–132, 160–163
Lang, P. J. 33
Langston, M. C. 168–169
LaPiere, R. T. 297
Larsson, A. O. 108
Lasswell, H. 39–40, 47, 49–51, 113
Lazarsfeld, P. 44–45, 47, 50, 245–246,
  261
Lazarus, R. S. 320
Lea, M. 273, 276
Leventhal, H. 292–293
Levinson, D. J. 45
Levinson, S. 190
Lewin, K. 30, 43, 256–258, 290
Lewis, S. C. 107
Lim, C. M. 121
Lin, C. A. 140, 270–271
Lippmann, W. 40, 122, 247
Locke, J. 64
Luce, R. D. 290–291

McCombs, M. 122, 247
McGee, M. 270
McGuire, W. J. 226, 233–234, 291,
  304
McLeod, J. M. 68–69
McLuhan, M. 29
Mahrt, M. 107
Marcuse, H. 41
Marvin, C. 282
Marwell, G. 189
Marx, K. 41, 51–53
Mashey, J. 106
Maslow, A. H. 181, 202

Masterson, J. 25
Mead, G. H. 43, 184
Miller, G. R. 213, 233
Moe, H. 108
Monahan, J. L. 214
Morley, D. 164–165
Morman, M. T. 326–327, 330
Morris, P. 104
Moyer-Guse, E. 295–296
Munsterberg, H. 42
Myers, K. K. 197–199

Nabi, R. L. 115, 141–142, 146
Naylor, R. 270, 277
Nichols, K. 104
Noller, P. 319
Northouse, P. 203
Norcross, J. C. 304–305

O'Keefe, D. J. 220
O'Neal, E. C. 145
Oliver, M. B. 115
Olson, D. H. 327–328

Padilla-Walker, L. M. 104
Park, R. 43
Parkin, F. 164
Pavitt, C. 3, 72, 75
Pempek, T. 271–272
Perloff, R. M. 120
Perse, E. M. 121, 141
Peter, J. 272, 274
Peters, J. D. 19–20, 24, 339, 346
Petty, R. E. 227–231, 233, 261, 295
Plato 32, 73–75
Poor, N. 281
Popper, K. 64, 78, 80
Potter, R. F. 115
Price, V. 119, 251–252, 254–255
Prochaska, J. O. 304–305

Raney, A. A. 143
Raven, B. 207
Razio, R. H. 303–304
Reagan, R. 260
Reardon, K. K. 344
Red, M. 281
Riedl, C. 275
Rhodes, N. 303–304

Rice, M. L. 158
Ritchie, L. D. 328–329
Rogers, E. M. 37, 43, 47–48, 248, 257, 259, 286–290, 344
Rogers, R. W. 293–294
Roloff, M. E. 317
Rosvall, M. 20
Roskos-Ewoldsen, B. 52, 154, 250–253, 294
Roskos-Ewoldsen, D. R. 52, 123–124, 127, 154, 156, 164, 166–167, 212–213, 224, 230, 232
Rouner, D. 295–296
Rubin, A. M. 121, 140–141, 146

Sanford, R. N. 45
Scharkow, M. 107
Schmitt, D. R. 189
Schramm, W. 48–50, 114
Schutz, W. C. 202
Scott, C. R. 337, 344–345
Scott, R. L. 62
Seeger, M. 30–31, 340–343
Shannon, C. E. 183
Shaw, D. L. 122, 247
Shen, C. X. 274
Sherif, M. 208, 222–223, 341
Sherry, J. L. 337, 339
Shoemaker, P. J. 257–258
Sillars, A. 183
Simon, A. F. 122
Simon, H. 91
Skoric, M. M. 281
Slater, M. D. 146, 295–296
Soengas-Pérez, X. 280
Spears, R. 273, 276
Stanley, J. C. 94, 97
Steiner, G. 25
Strizhakova, Y. 142
Strohmaier, M. 275

Taylor, D. 182, 317
Taylor, S. L. 145
Tewksbury, D. 119, 251–252, 254–255
Tian, Q. 121
Timmerman, C. E. 29
Tinmaz, H. 269
Trenholm, S. 25
Tripp, D. 165
Tuckman, B. 205
Turan, Z. 269
Tversky, A. 254–255

Valkenburg, P. M. 272, 274
van den Broek, P. 167–8
Van den Bulck, J. 117
van Dijk, T. A. 167
Vangelisti, A. L. 325–326
Vos, T. P. 257–258

Wagner, C. 275
Walters, R. H. 116, 118
Walther, J. B. 272–273
Wasike, B. 278
Watzlawick, P. 323
Weaver, J. B. III 145
Weaver, W. 183
White, D. M. 256
Wicker, A. W. 297
Williams, R. 52
Witte, K. 293–294
Witten, I. H. 106
Wohl, R. R. 120
Wright, J. C. 158

Yzer, M. C. 300, 303

Zajonc, R. B. 214
Zanna, M. P. 215
Zillmann, D. 128, 139, 144
Zwaan, R. A. 168–169

SUBJECT INDEX

absolutism 90
Abu Ghraib 260–261
academic world 31–33
accessibility 249, 251–252, 319
accommodation model 321
acculturation 197, 199, 206
active processing 155, 157
Ad Age 277
adolescents 271
advertising 45, 114, 258, 276; online 268
affective exchange theory (AET) 326–327, 330
affective factors 139, 142–145, 149–150, 214
age 147
agendas: agenda-melding 279; building 259; setting 121–123, 247–250, 254–255, 278–279
aggression 41, 65–66, 82, 102–103, 145; conducting research 92–93, 97, 99, 102–103; generalized aggression model (GAM) 129–130; mass media effects models 124, 126, 128; theory 4, 6–8, 10–11
alienation 41, 53, 146
analysis 69
analytic approach 16
anger 144–145, 322
anxiety 97, 224, 274, 319

applicability model 252, 254–255
Arab Spring 280
arousal 139, 141, 143–144, 146, 149–150, 217–219, 322
Asia 33
assimilation effects 223
atomism 61
attention 155–160, 162; attentional inertia 156, 158; attentional sampling 158
attitudes: accessibility 213, 301–302, 304–305; attitude-behavior relationship 212, 296–304; bolstering 219; change 49, 213, 218, 223, 226–228, 296; formation 213–217, 220, 234; functions 224–226; tripartite model 213–214
attributions 183, 221, 319
attrition see mortality
auditory features 155, 157–158
Austria 44, 78
axiology 22–24, 59–61, 63, 70

backward inferences 169
behavioral intention (BI) 297, 300
behavior change 121, 189, 291–294, 304–305, 341
behaviorism 77, 244
beliefs 217
best practice studies 89
bias 5, 53, 96, 101–102, 179, 206, 257, 302; interparticipant 95; media 120;

philosophical underpinning 61–62, 65;
  positivism/causality/explanation 82–84,
  86; selection 94
bibliographical approach 38
biology 339–340
biomedical model 306
biopsychosocial model 306–307
blogs 260
boomerang effect 226
bottom-up approach 195, 197

Canada 29
capacity models 159–163
cascading model 260–261
causality 4, 7–8, 15, 61, 64–67, 76, 81,
  91, 103–104
cell phones 142
central processing 228–232
Centre for Contemporary Cultural Studies
  (CCCS) 51–53
chain of responses model 226
Chicago School of Sociology 43, 53
children 39, 42, 113, 126, 138, 155–159,
  219
China 274
choice shift 208
CIA 51
circumplex model 327–328
coding schemes 104–105
coercion 189, 207, 321
cognition 159, 214, 319; cognitive misers
  161, 249; cognitive processing 5,
  160–162, 293; cognitive reappraisal
  320; cognitive resources 155, 160–161;
  cognitive structures 188; meta-
  cognition 230–231
cognitive dissonance theory 77–78,
  220
cognitive-level theories 123–128
cognitive psychology 16, 252
cognitive response model 226–227
Cold War 50–51
Committee on Public Information (CPI)
  39, 46
communication 18; interdisciplinarity
  19–20; phenomena view 25–26;
  philosophical roots 20–24; study
  characteristics 26–29; see also history
  of communication

Communication and Mass Media
  Complete 34
communism 51
companionship 270–272
compliance 120; compliance-gaining
  189–190, 221
comprehension 44, 66, 96, 156–161,
  163–171
computer-mediated communication
  (CMC) 273
conceptual clarity 65, 141
conceptual models 6, 9–10
conditioning 215–217, 232
conflict strategies 183
conflict typology 323
consistency theories 217
consonant beliefs 218–219
content analysis 40, 59, 61, 104–105, 109,
  114, 116
contrast effects 223
control 92, 94, 97
control groups 92–93, 97–98
controlled environments 97
convenience samples 86–87, 102
cooperation 189, 202, 337
Coronation Street 166
correlation analysis 66–67
cost-benefit analysis 181
covering law model 67
crime 117
critical scholarship 28, 39, 41, 45, 52,
  58–63, 65, 318
critical/cultural studies 58–61
Cronbach's alpha 82
cross-sectional design 102–103
cultivation theory 116–118
cultural congruence 261
cultural studies 51–53, 58–59, 61–63,
  163
culture 41, 199, 205–206, 327
cyber-gossip 275
cyberbullying 273, 275–276
cyberstalking 276

Dallas 165–166
danger control 292, 294
data 32, 61, 67, 119, 292, 345; analysis
  5, 12, 65, 105–107, 340; big data 89,
  105–109, 340; collection 3–5, 12,

102, 105, 108–109, 114, 190; mining
106–107
deception detection 24
decision-making 91, 129, 205–206, 208,
257, 329
deduction 61
defiance 120
deindividuation theory 273
deliberative behaviors 228, 301,
303–304
demand-withdrawal 320–321
democracy 39–40, 280
demographics 116, 119, 146–147,
280
dependency theory 250
depression 274, 319; Beck Depression
Inventory 96
determinism: biological 339; economic
41, 164; reciprocal 148
dialectical theory 185–186
diffusion of innovations model 247,
286
diffusion theory 286–289
discrimination 212
disillusionment model 321
disposition theories 139, 143
dissonance theory 217–220
doctor-patient communication
306–307
dominant reading 164–165
dual code landscape model 168
dual process models 5, 227–233, 261,
292–293
dyadic communication 184

education 42, 44, 47, 113, 125;
educational content 157, 159–160;
edutainment 294–296; sex education
24
ego-involvement 119, 223
Egypt 268, 280–281
elaboration likelihood model (ELM)
227–231, 233, 261, 295
elderly people 121, 271
elitism 52
email 277
empathic accuracy 319
encoding/decoding model 53,
163–166

enduring dynamics model 321
Enlightenment 41, 76, 339
entertainment overcoming resistance
model (EORM) 295–296
environmental factors 69, 96, 98,
117–118, 129–130, 148–150, 161
epistemology 22, 24–25, 29, 58–61,
63–64, 70, 72–81, 87, 90
escapism 146
ethics 209, 341
ethnicity 188
ethnography 62, 114
Europe 33, 38, 44, 46, 280
event-indexing model 168–169
evolution 131, 326–327, 339
excitation 139, 142–145; excitation
transfer (ET) 128–129
experimental design 4, 24, 63, 92, 94,
97–109
experimental manipulations see
manipulations
explananda/explanantia 67–68
extended elaboration likelihood model
(E-ELM) 295–296
extended parallel process model (EPPM)
293–294
external validity 97–98, 101

Facebook 268–272, 274–277, 280,
317
factorial design 99, 271
falsifiability 13, 15, 186
falsification 78–80
family communication 318, 325–329;
family communication patterns theory
(FCPT) 328–329; secrets 325–326
fascism 39, 44, 46, 53
fear 117
fear appeals 291–294
feedback 114–115, 184
feminism 27
field theory 43, 257, 290
foundationalism 23
Foursquare 276
framing 259–261; framing effects 252,
255–256; framing theory 121–123
Frankfurt School 38, 41–42, 45, 64
free will 76
functional approach 179–190

gatekeeping 256–258, 279
gender 8, 52, 76, 124–125, 206, 246, 321,
    337; interpersonal communication
    (IPC) 188; media use models 146–147;
    roles 118, 166; studies 52
generalizability 86, 342
generalized aggression model (GAM)
    129–130
Germany 38–39, 42, 45–46
Google Earth 276
Greece 37, 62, 295
groupthink 207

habituation 158
Hawthorne effect 94
health communication 30–32, 255,
    341–342; attitude/behavior relationship
    296–302; diffusion of innovations
    286–289; education/entertainment
    294–296; fear appeals 291–294;
    health belief model 290–291;
    interpersonal 305–308; stages of
    change 304–305
hegemony 52–53
heuristic-systematic model (HSM)
    231–233
heuristics 249, 251, 257
hierarchies 194–197, 205, 328; hierarchy
    of needs 202
history of communication 37–38;
    between world wars 38–47; post war
    49–53; World War II 47–49
holism 6, 343
human needs 181, 202–203
humanism 76–77
hydraulic model 253
hyperpersonal model 273
hypodermic needle model 40, 43, 226,
    244–245, 291
hypotheses 91, 107, 327, 337; null 75,
    79–80

idealism 72
identity 140, 188, 203, 225, 270,
    272–273, 345
ideology 52–53, 147, 165, 258, 261
impersonal model 273
indexing model 259-260, 269
individual difference variables 119

informal networks 204
information exchange 183–184
information processing 5, 130
information sharing 271–272, 345
informational influence 208
innovation 199, 201, 344–345; diffusion
    of 286–289, 295
inoculation theory 233–234
Instagram 268, 270
Institute for Social Research see Frankfurt
    School
instrumental media use 141
instrumentation 96, 98, 102
integrative approach 129
integrative model of behavioral prediction
    300, 303
intellectual development 45
interclass correlation 82
interdependence 182, 189, 324
interdisciplinarity 19–20, 22, 41, 43, 68,
    336–337, 343
interlocutors 27–28
internal validity 94–95, 97–98, 342
internet 141, 215, 246, 268–270, 274,
    278–279, 345
interpersonal communication (IPC)
    33, 43, 59, 154, 191, 317, 344;
    definition 177–179; health 286, 288,
    305–308; individual experiences
    184–185; influencing others 188–190;
    information exchange 183–184;
    relationship development/maintenance
    180–183; social reality 187–188;
    see also family communication; marital
    communication
interpersonal goals 203–204, 207,
    209
interpersonal power 186–187, 207
interpersonal relationships 177, 180–183,
    186, 188, 194–195, 260, 317–318,
    326
interpretive research 58, 60
interpretive theory 58
intertextuality 186
intimacy 181–182, 319
intramedia influences 260
Iran 272
Italy 39, 46
iteration 5–6

Journal for Social Research 41
journalism 38, 259, 269, 338
journals 34, 38, 40, 53, 343

knowledge claims 73–75, 78–80

landscape model 167–168
language 9, 52, 179, 185
leadership 203
learning 181, 271
learning theory 48, 291
legitimacy 338–340, 345–346
Library of Congress 47–48
Libya 268, 281
limited-capacity model of motivated
    mediated message processing (LC4MP)
    130–132, 160–163
limited effects paradigm 50, 245–247
LinkedIn 268
local networks 288–289
loneliness 121, 141, 274
longitudinal designs 103

macro processes 195
macro theory 69–80, 122, 187, 318
magic bullet model *see* hypodermic
    needle model
manipulations 84–85, 92, 99, 341–342;
    manipulation checks 92–93
marital communication 319–325
marital conflict 321–323, 330
marital types 323–325, 330
marketing *see* advertising
marriages 318
mass communication 13, 33, 46–47, 50,
    104, 113–115, 344
mass culture 52
mass media 4, 38, 63, 104, 140, 270,
    338
mass media effects 113–115, 129–132;
    arousal-based models 128–129;
    cognitive-level theories 123–128;
    sociological-level theories 116–123;
    see also media effects
materialism 177
maturation 95, 98
meaning 25, 184–187
mechanisms 66–67

media 45, 49, 91, 245; alternative 260;
    framing 253–256; influence 246,
    248–251; mainstream 260; mass 4, 38,
    63, 104, 140, 270, 338; outlets 29;
    processes 115–116; selection 45, 144
media choice 138–139, 142–145, 148–149
media effects 40, 46, 108, 114–115,
    121–128, 286, 339; use models 138,
    140, 148; *see also* mass media effects
media studies 50
media use models 120–121, 138;
    excitation/affect-based approaches
    142–145; personality factors 145–146;
    selective exposure 139; socio cognitive
    theory 148–150; sociological factors
    146–148; uses/gratifications 139–142
media violence 4, 6–8, 11, 27, 138
membership negotiation theory 197–199
memory 5, 78, 123–127, 130–131,
    159–162, 167–168, 187, 251–252,
    301
mental health 118, 320
mental models 127–128, 166–167, 170
mental representation approach 165
mere exposure effect 214–215, 232
message characteristics 119, 184, 190
message discrepancy 222–223
message processing 18, 154, 170,
    228–232; capacity model 159–163;
    children 155–159; comprehension
    163–170
message production 18
message sources 217
message system analysis *see* content analysis
meta-analyses 4, 214
meta-communication 185
meta-theoretical approach 148–150, 191;
    frameworks 190, 195
methodology 72, 89–98, 108, 338, 340,
    342; history of communication 40, 45;
    philosophical underpinnings 58–60,
    62–63, 65–66
Mexico 281
micro theory 70, 318
minimal effects era 50, 261
modernism 41
mood adjustment/management 139,
    144–145, 149
mortality 95–96

motivation 159, 162, 181, 229, 231, 299, 303

motivation and opportunity as determinants (MODE) model 297, 303-304

movies 39, 42, 44, 145, 163, 165, 167, 169

music 45, 146

narrative comprehension and engagement model 169–170

narrative theory 24

narratives 159–160, 169–170, 295–296; patient 308

National Communication Association 33

natural sciences 59, 61, 63, 67, 75–76, 89, 341

naturalism 63–68, 72

Nazism 42, 45, 47

negative affect 319, 321–323, 330

negotiated reading 164–165

neo-Marxism 41, 53

network capital 274

network models 125–127, 251–252

New Left 51–52

New Left Review 51

news media 114, 121, 124, 144, 277–279; political 256–261

newspapers 39–40, 114, 256, 278

non-summativity 196

nonverbal communication 177, 184–185, 318–319, 327

normative influence 208

norms 139, 196–199, 205–207, 288, 302; cultural 139, 179, 199, 206, 327; social 10, 119–121, 229, 288–289, 295; subjective norms (SN) 299

null hypotheses 75, 79–80

observation 4–5, 8, 14, 81–82, 326, 330–331, 340–341

observational modeling 118

Office of Facts and Figures (OFF) 48

one-group pretest–posttest design 98

ontology 22, 24, 29, 58–61, 68, 70, 90, 339

openness 196

operational linkages 6, 9–11

operationalization 10–11, 81–87

opinion leaders 246, 288–289

oppositional reading 164–165

optimal matching theory 320

organizational communication 154, 194–204, 206–207, 209

organizational culture 197–200, 258

organizational goals 203–204

organizations 257; as machines 200–201; as networks of relationships 202–204

orientation 249–250

Our Movie Made Children 42–43

parasocial interaction 120–121

parents 42, 85

parsimony 14, 16

participant observation 62

participatory decision making 203

passive processing 155, 157

Payne Fund 42–43, 138

pedagogy 31

perceived behavioral control 300

perceived norms 119

perceptual fluency 214

performance studies 18, 33

performing arts 72

peripheral processing 228–230, 232

personality factors 139, 145–146, 149

personological factors 129–130, 148–149

persuasion 3, 44, 48–49, 63, 189–190, 212, 291, 295–296; attitude 213–217; discrepancy-based models 222–224; dissonance theory 217–222; dual process models 227–232; inoculation theory 233–234; motivational approaches 224–226; process theories 226–227; unimodel 232–233

Pew Foundation 147

phenomenology 72

philosophical underpinnings 58–62, 72, 89; distinctions/categorizations 68–70; epistemology 73–75; naturalism/post-positivism 63–67, 78–80; operationalizations 81–87; positivism 75–78

The Photoplay: A Psychological Study 42

planned behavior 10

politeness theory 190

political change 269, 279–281

political communication 244, 278; agenda
    setting 247–250; campaigns 109, 214,
    233, 296; framing 253–256; limited
    effects era 245–247; news media
    256–261; political priming 250–253
political science 113, 337
polysemic approach 53, 62, 164–165
polyvalence 165
pornography 96, 129
positive affect 143, 215, 319, 322–324
positivism 63–64, 65, 75–79, 90; logical
    positivism 64
post-disciplinarity 337–338
post-positivism 63–68, 77–80, 83, 87
postmodernism 41
pragmatism 18, 24–25, 31, 33–34, 61, 69,
    180
praxeology 22–23
praxis 41
predictive power 14
presence 344
priming 46, 123–125; political 250–253
The Prisoner 165
privacy 103, 269, 326, 345
propaganda 39–40, 46–48, 51, 113–114,
    244, 261, 336
Propaganda Technique in the World War 39
proposition statements see theoretical
    linkages
prospect theory 254–255
protection motivation theory (PMT)
    293–294
Proteus effect 221
proximal explanations 196
psychological needs 139, 181
psychology 67, 86, 212, 249, 257, 318,
    337, 339–340, 343; history of
    communication 43, 48; interpersonal
    communication (IPC) 179, 191; mass
    media effects 113, 123–125; small
    group/organizational communication
    195, 201, 205
public address 72
Public Opinion 40
public policy 343; policy agenda 248, 259
public relations 31, 338

qualitative methods 24, 58, 179, 186, 281,
    318

quantitative methods 42, 45, 65, 92, 179
quantitative studies 18, 24, 66
questionnaires 81–85, 91, 102, 140, 274

race 52, 124–125, 128, 147, 206, 220,
    255, 297
radio 39, 44–47, 114
Radio Research Project 44–45
random assignment 92–93, 97
random sampling 100–101
rationality 74
reactance 234, 296, 321
realism 72, 169
reality programming 146
recruitment 101
relational model theory 191
relational turbulence 182–183
relational uncertainty 182
relationship development 181, 345
relationship networks 202, 207
relationship testing 66
relationship types 188
relativism 90
reliability 82–83
reliability statistics 105
Renaissance 76
repeated measures design 95–96
representative sampling 100–101, 107
research 19, 22, 30, 269, 279, 337,
    340–343, 345; experimental design
    98–109; health communication 301,
    305, 307; history of communication
    37, 44, 49–51, 53; methodology
    89–98; philosophical underpinnings 58,
    62, 65; social media 269, 279; theory 4,
    15; validity 98–109
research institutions 50
resource allocation 130–131
response-changing 213, 234
response efficacy 291
response-reinforcement 213, 234
response-shaping 213, 234
rhetoric 27–28, 30, 32–33, 37, 59–60,
    62–63
Rhetoric Society of America 33
risky shift 208
ritualized media use 140–141
Rockefeller Foundation 44, 46–47, 49,
    53

salience 249–251; beliefs 299
sampling frames 105
schemas 125–127, 167, 187, 261
scientific method 75–78
scientific realism 72, 75, 81, 87
selective attention 154
selective exposure 139, 144, 148–150, 220
self-actualization 181, 188
self-completion 188
self-concept 218–219
self-disclosure 181–182, 345
self-efficacy 293–294, 300
self-monitoring 299–300
self-perception theory 221–222
self-prophesy 220
self-regulation 196
self-validation hypothesis 230–231
semiotics 63
sender–message–receiver model 184
sensation seeking 145–146
sexuality 327
signal learning 215
Singapore 281
situation models 167
situational factors 190
small group communication 194–195, 205–209
soap operas 165–166
social capital 280
social change 279–281
social class 52, 164
social cognitive theory 126–127
social connectedness 269, 273–275, 280, 345
social constructionism 23
social engineering 64–65
social exchange approach 181–182
social influence 154
social integration 182
social judgment theory 222–223
social learning theory 116, 118
social media 147, 199, 268–269, 282, 344; effects 272–276; marketing 276–277; news 277–279; social/political change 279–281; uses/functions 270–272
social network sites (SNS) 270, 274–277, 280–281
social penetration theory 182, 317

social psychology 44–45, 148, 212, 252, 290
social reality 187–188
social roles 205
social sciences 19–20, 26, 30, 89, 191, 212, 337; history of communication 37, 42–43, 45, 47, 49; philosophical underpinnings 22, 24, 58–61, 64–66; positivism/causality/explanation 72–74, 82, 86; relationships/family communication 318, 325; theory 4, 6–7, 12, 16
social structures 187
social support 320
social-identity/deindividuation (SIDE) model 273, 276
socialism 41
socialization 118, 197
socio-cultural approach 179
socio cognitive theory 8–9, 13, 44, 113, 118, 148–150
sociology 67, 116–123, 212, 257, 287, 318, 337, 343; history of communication 43, 52; interpersonal communication (IPC) 179, 187; media use models 139, 146–148
solipsism 90
Solomon four-group design 98–99
Soviet Union 50
speech communication 37, 60
spontaneous behaviors 189, 197, 303, 305
stage model of relationship development 182, 317
stages of change model 304–305
static group comparison 98
statistics 11, 68
stereotypes 40, 117, 123–125, 128, 252
stimuli 129–131, 139, 146, 161, 166, 168, 214, 244; conditioned stimuli (CS) 215–216; unconditioned stimuli (UCS) 215–216
strategic communication 194–195
stratified random sampling 101–102
structural equation models (SEM) 12
studies 4, 42–43, 97, 122
subjective expected utility (SEU) models 290–291
sufficiency principle 232
supervisors 198

surveillance 140, 270–272, 345
surveys 45, 61, 90, 92, 99–104, 114;
    General Social Survey (GSS) 100
symbolic information 9, 52
symbolic interactionism 43, 185
symbols 25–26, 212–213
System 1 theories 5–6
System 2 theories 5–6, 319
system jumping 69–70
system theory 195–196

technology 18, 268, 282, 337, 344
technology gap 178
television 6–8, 11, 270–271, 278; mass
    media effects 116–118, 121, 124, 126;
    media use models 140, 142, 146–147;
    message processing 155–159, 161–162,
    165–166; theory 6–8, 11
testability 13, 15
texts 62
theoretical linkages 7–9, 25, 28, 130, 142,
    330, 341, 343
theory of emotion 320
theory of planned behavior (TPB) 10,
    297, 300–301, 303, 305
theory of reasoned action (TRA)
    297–301, 303–305
think-aloud protocol 91
third-person effect 118–120
top-down approach 91, 195, 197, 201
translational scholarship 337, 343
traveling lens model 158
Tunisia 268, 280–281
Turkey 269
Twitter 108–109, 268, 270, 272, 276,
    278, 280
two-step flow model 245–247, 286
Type I error 3
typologies 23–24, 142

UK 38, 51–53, 163, 246
uncertainty reduction theory (URT) 182,
    317

unimodel 232–233
unintended consequences 140
universality 85–87
USA 33, 86, 101, 147, 212, 269, 280;
    history of communication 37, 39, 42,
    44–48, 50–51; political communication
    244–245, 248, 254, 260–261
uses and gratifications approach 45, 120,
    138–142, 148–149, 270–272, 282
utilitarianism 209

validity 82–86, 94, 98–109, 340
value-neutrality 64–65
variable analysis 65
variables 6–13, 67
video games 6, 11, 27, 65–66, 147, 221,
    344; massive multiplayer online games
    (MMOs) 108; research 91–93, 97, 99,
    102–103, 108
viewing motives 142
violent media 4, 6–8, 11, 27, 65–66, 252;
    mass media effects 117, 124, 126,
    128–130; media use models 138–139,
    145–147; research 92–93, 97, 102–103;
    theory 4, 6–8, 11
virtual reality 344
Virtual Worlds Exploratorium Project
    108
visual stimulus 156–157
voyeurism 146

The War of the Worlds 39, 45–46, 244
web 2.0 268, 270
well-being 204, 274–275
wholeness 196
Why We Fight 48
Wikipedia 268
World War I 38–39, 46–47, 51, 244, 247,
    261, 336
World War II 25, 32, 37–38, 40, 42,
    47–49, 51, 53, 212

YouTube 268, 271